ISAIAH
A Logion Press Commentary

Stanley M. Horton
Foreword By **Roger D. Cotton**

Springfield, Missouri
02-3016

All Scripture quotations, unless otherwise indicated, are taken from the HOLY BIBLE: NEW INTERNATIONAL VERSION®; NIV®. Copyright ©1973, 1978, 1984 by International Bible Society. Used by permission of Zondervan Publishing House. All rights reserved.

©2000 by Gospel Publishing House, Springfield, Missouri 65802-1894. All rights reserved. No part of this book may be reproduced, stored in a retrieval system, or transmitted in any form or by any means—electronic, mechanical, photocopy, recording, or otherwise—without prior written permission of the copyright owner, except brief quotations used in connection with reviews in magazines or newspapers.

Logion Press books are published by Gospel Publishing House.

Library of Congress Cataloging-in-Publication Data
  Horton, Stanley M.
  Isaiah: a Logion Press commentary / Stanley M. Horton.
  p. cm
  Includes bibliographical references and index.
  ISBN 0-88243-301-6 (hard cover)
  1. Bible. O.T. Isaiah—Commentaries. I. Title.
  BS1515.3 .H67 2000
  224'.1077—dc21   00-039065

Printed in the United States of America

CONTENTS

Foreword 5
Preface 7
Isaiah Synopsis 9
Introduction to Isaiah 11
   Background 11
      The end of northern Israel 13
      Judah in Isaiah's day 14
      The Assyrian invasions 16
      Chronology of the time of the prophet Isaiah 22
   Critical views of the Book of Isaiah 22
Overview of Isaiah's Message 29
   Introduction 29
   Isaiah: the prophet and his message 29
   Early prophecies 30
   Isaiah's vision and call 30
   God's angry hand and His saving hand 31
   Judgment on foreign nations 32
   Judgment and restoration for Judah 33
   Hezekiah and Sennacherib's invasions 33
   Comfort and deliverance 35
   Glory for God's people; judgment for others 37
Isaiah Outline 39
Isaiah NIV Translation, Notes, and Comments 49
Appendix A: Great Themes in the Book of Isaiah 473
    1. God, the Holy One of Israel 473
    2. God, the Mighty One of Israel 475
    3. God, the Omniscient One 475
    4. God, the Creator of all 476
    5. God, the Redeemer and Savior 477
    6. God, the Restorer of Israel and Jerusalem 478

    7. God, the Savior of the Gentiles 479
    8. The Servant of God 480
    9. The Holy Spirit of God 481
    10. God Deserves Pure Worship 484
Appendix B: Map of the Assyrian Empire 486
Selected Bibliography 489
Scripture Index 491
Subject Index 503

FOREWORD

Isaiah is one of the richest and most beautiful books in the Bible—both theologically and literarily. Among the Old Testament books there is no greater use of the Hebrew language, no greater expression of the gospel message and the nature of God. Isaiah the prophet is the premier Old Testament theologian. It is fitting that Logion should publish a commentary on Isaiah by the premier Pentecostal Old Testament theologian.

Stanley Horton is a wonderful example of a Spirit-led scholar. He knows the original Hebrew and the views of the scholars *and* the voice of the Holy Spirit. He has spent a lifetime studying and teaching the Bible, especially the Old Testament. Isaiah has been one of his most intense studies since he made it the focus of his doctoral dissertation. In it he showed that the perspective of the whole book fits the traditional authorship of the eighth century B.C. prophet in Israel. That is in contrast to many modern scholars who theorize one or more later authors in Babylon for chapters 40 to 66.

Stanley Horton is a great example of Christian humility and demonstrates this in his writing, gently presenting what he believes to be the truth. At the same time, he considers different interpretations, allowing the reader to choose among them.

Because Stanley Horton has been immersed in the book of Isaiah for years, he has a wonderful grasp of its contents. His careful and reverent reading of the text brings out the message God intended. Horton has a gift for getting down to what really matters, bringing the insights of the scholars simply and clearly to the student of the Bible. This book will be helpful to lay people as well, who need this great book of Isaiah put into language they can understand. Dr. Horton's work demonstrates a solid biblical theology that allows the inspired Bible writer to speak what he meant in his day: The reader is able to hear Isaiah preach his own messages in his own ancient context.

Yet, Horton shows the relevance of the divine principles behind the ancient texts. He continually relates the prophecies to Christ. The book concludes with an appendix of great theological themes in Isaiah. This brings together in a compact but insightful way many of the wonderful truths brought out in the book.

It is an honor for me to recommend this work. Stanley Horton has been the greatest influence on my love for, understanding of, and work in the Old Testament. I believe students of the Bible will be blessed by the spirituality and clarity of the message as Horton brings it out. I am grateful that his insights into this very important book of the Old Testament are finally in print to bless the church both inside and outside the classroom.

Roger D. Cotton, Th.D.
Professor of Old Testament
Assemblies of God Theological Seminary

PREFACE

The Book of Isaiah has always been one of my favorites. I gave it special attention in my doctoral studies. My dissertation, accepted by the Central Baptist Theological Seminary, was entitled "A Defense on Historical Grounds of the Isaian Authorship of the Passages in Isaiah Referring to Babylon."

The Book of Isaiah was important to Jews in the time before Christ. Fifteen Hebrew manuscripts of Isaiah have been found among the Dead Sea Scrolls. Jesus and the New Testament writers also considered it important for they quoted from Isaiah 411 times. Isaiah's prophecies had a profound effect on Jerusalem and Judah in his day. They continue to bless all who study them today.

In line with the usage of both the KJV and the NIV, Lord is used in capitals and small capitals where the Hebrew of the Old Testament has the personal name of God, Yahweh. The Hebrew wrote only the consonants YHWH. Later traditions followed the New Latin JHVH and added vowels from the Hebrew for "lord" to remind them to read *Lord* instead of the divine name. But this was never intended to be read "Jehovah."

In quoted Scripture, words I wish to emphasize are highlighted with italics.

For easier reading, Hebrew, Aramaic, and Greek words are all transliterated with English letters.

A few abbreviations have been used:

Gk.: Greek
Heb.: Hebrew
ASV: American Standard Version
KJV: King James Version
NIV: New International Version

My special thanks go to Glen Ellard, Paul Zinter, and Leta Sapp at Gospel Publishing House and to all who assisted in preparing this book. Thanks also to my wife, Evelyn, for her encouragement.

This is a revised version of a commentary originally accompanied by the Hebrew text and published 1995 by The World Library Press Inc., Springfield, Mo., Gregory Lint, executive editor.

ISAIAH SYNOPSIS

Date: Isaiah was the greatest of the prophets of the last half of the eighth century B.C. Uzziah, Jotham, Ahaz, Hezekiah, and probably Manasseh felt the impact of his prophetic preaching.

Background: A false, government-aided prosperity encouraged a corrupt luxury accompanied by oppression of the poor and a sensual, immoral, heathenish religion (2 Chron. 26:16–18,20; 27:2; 28:1–27; 29:6–9).

Isaiah's Call: A vision of God led to a vision of self and sin. Confession led to cleansing and consecration. The work was to be difficult, but it laid the foundation for a remnant to return and prepared the way for the Messiah (chap. 6).

Brief Outline:

Chaps.1–5 Judgment and Hope	Chaps. 6–12 The Holy One Exalted	Chaps. 13–23 Foreign Prophecies
Chaps. 24–35 General Judgment	Chaps. 36–39 Hezekiah	Chaps. 40–48 Comfort
Chaps. 49–55 Redemption	Chaps. 56–66 Glory	

The Great Arraignment: A broken-hearted Father invites His children to return (chap. 1).

10 / Isaiah Synopsis

The Enlarging Picture of the Messiah:

7:10–17	Born of a virgin.
8:8	Immanuel—The *with-us* God.
9:1–7	Wonderful, Counselor, Mighty God, Father of Eternity, Prince of Peace.
11:1–10	Descendant of David, Spirit-anointed. (Read here Rom. 8:18–25.)
16:5	The throne of justice and love.
28:16	The chief Cornerstone.
32:1–5,15–18	The Messiah is King.
42:1–12	The divinely-chosen and -sustained Servant who gently and mercifully restores the Jews and brings light to the Gentiles.
49:1–13	The Servant is God's weapon to rouse and extricate and regather the people.
50:4–11	The Servant, taught by God, teaches and strengthens others.
52:13 to 53:12	"The Mount Everest of Messianic Prophecy." The Servant by His vicarious, substitutionary suffering and death pleases God and makes possible His matchless salvation.
54	Israel's growth as the result of the Servant's redemptive work.
55	The wide-open door to "whoever wills."
61:1–11	The Messiah's saving, healing, liberating ministry brings joy. (Read Luke 4:16–21.)

Great expository sermons are almost ready-made in chapters 1; 6; 40; 49; 50; 53; 55.

Key Verses: 6:3; 45:22; 55:6–7; 59:2.

The Certainty of the Fulfillment of God's Word: 40:8; compare with Matthew 24:35.

No one is a failure who lives according to the will of God!

INTRODUCTION TO ISAIAH

Background

God could have put His people, Israel, in a distant, sheltered oasis where no one would bother them. Instead He put them at the crossroads of the ancient world. This "promised land" would be a vital center for the spread of the gospel when Jesus came. But in Isaiah's day, it was a place where the armies of the known world came into conflict. To the northeast, Assyria was the dominant power, with its cities of Nineveh and Asshur on the Tigris River (see map, Appendix B). However, Babylon, on the Euphrates River, was the cultural, commercial, and religious center for all Mesopotamia. To the south, Egypt, along the Nile River, was a great and wealthy nation.

Assyria's goal was to dominate Babylon and conquer Egypt. To this end, its kings habitually sent their armies every year to conquer, pillage, and destroy cities and nations that stood in the way. The Assyrians were noted for their cruelty and kept inventing new ways to torture their captives.

Archaeologists have found at Nineveh the bas-relief of the conquest of Lachish; it shows captive Jews being led before King Sennacherib of Assyria by ropes attached to giant fish hooks put through their jaws, something Amos had already prophesied for northern Israel (Amos 4:2).[1] Jews are also depicted as impaled before the city walls, a prototype of the form of capital punishment called crucifixion.[2]

---

[1] The relief from his palace is in the British Museum. A full-size replica is in the Oriental Institute of the University of Chicago.

[2] For further study on the archaeological background see Keith N. Schoville, *Biblical Archaeology in Focus* (Grand Rapids: Baker Book House, 1982); James B. Pritchard, ed., *Ancient Near Eastern Texts Relating to the Old Testament,* 2d. ed. (Princeton: Princeton University Press, 1955).

Isaiah, however, began to prophesy in what seemed to be good times. Not since the days of Solomon had Israel and Judah enjoyed such prosperity. In the days of Elisha, Damascus caused trouble for the northern kingdom of Israel, capturing part of their territory (e.g. 2 Kings 8:12). But the days of Syrian domination were over.

In 805 B.C. Adad-Nirari III of Assyria knocked out Damascus. Though Israel and Judah paid tribute to Assyria for a few years, Adad-Nirari died in 783 B.C., and his successors were weak. They had trouble from Armenia (Urartu) on their northern border, and an Assyrian defeat followed an eclipse of the sun in 763 B.C. Then successive occurrences of the bubonic plague decimated their people. As a result, the Assyrian kingdom fell apart into a group of city states (the case when Jonah went to Nineveh). Egypt was also weakened by internal disputes. Thus, for about fifty years Israel and Judah had no problems from foreign invasions.

Jehoash of Israel (798–781 B.C.) regained territory captured by Hazael of Damascus (2 Kings 13:25). Amaziah of Judah (796–767 B.C.) took control of Edom (2 Kings 14:7) and dared Jehoash to fight him (2 Kings 14:8). Jehoash then defeated Amaziah at Beth Shemesh, broke down a six-hundred-foot section of Jerusalem's wall, stripped the temple and palace of gold and silver, and took hostages. This made Amaziah unpopular and conspirators assassinated him at Lachish (2 Kings 14:19). The people then put his son Uzziah (also called Azariah) on the throne. He had already been coregent with his father since 790 B.C.

Prosperity had already begun to return to northern Israel when Jeroboam II took the throne in 791 B.C. Encouraged by the prophet Jonah (2 Kings 14:25), he won victories and extended political control from the entrance to Hamath on the north to the Dead Sea on the southeast.

Jeroboam's long and prosperous reign lasted to 753 B.C. and was paralleled by prosperity in Judah under Uzziah (790–739). Both enjoyed peace, regained most of the territory of Solomon's empire between Egypt and the Euphrates River (2 Kings 14:22, 25; 2 Chron. 26:9, 11–15), and were enriched by control of major trade routes. Merchants brought in luxuries from trade with Tyre and Sidon, as well as from the Red Sea trade by way

Introduction to Isaiah / 13

of Ezion Geber (modern Elath on the Gulf of Aqaba).

The wealthy enjoyed luxury, built large homes of squared stones, decorated walls and furniture with beautiful ivory carvings (cf. Amos 3:15; 6:4), and enjoyed rich food and wine. At the same time moral corruption and economic injustice toward the poor increased. Amos, Hosea, Isaiah, and Micah all pronounced God's judgment on the rich who were getting richer at the expense of the downtrodden poor. Greedy merchants cheated them, demanded high interest, and sold some of them into slavery. Corrupt priests made the situation worse by demanding multiplied sacrifices and by allowing idolatry and immorality to be mixed with the worship of the LORD.

THE END OF NORTHERN ISRAEL

The era of prosperity was soon to end. After the death of Jeroboam II, the northern kingdom of Israel, though warned by Amos and Hosea, was full of debauchery. Under the judgment of God it rapidly degenerated.

Jeroboam's son, Zechariah, reigned only six months and was assassinated by Shallum. Shallum reigned one month and was assassinated by Menahem. Menahem reigned ten years. However, in the first year of his reign, Pekah took over the territory in Gilead on the east side of the Jordan and claimed the kingdom. In 742 B.C., Menahem died and his son Pekahiah reigned for two years. He was then murdered by his two bodyguards and fifty Gileadites.

Then Pekah took the throne in Samaria and reigned eight more years. During that time he made an alliance with Rezin of Damascus, king of Syria, and invaded Judah twice. The first invasion was successful (2 Chron. 28:5–8). When Pekah and Rezin threatened a second invasion, King Ahaz of Judah—against the God-given advice of Isaiah—appealed to Tiglath-Pileser III of Assyria for help. The Assyrian king then defeated Syria and killed Rezin. He also took captive people from the northernmost part of Israel. Hoshea, the last king of northern Israel, assassinated Pekah in 732 B.C. Then Tiglath-Pileser III of Assyria placed him on Israel's throne.

Tiglath-Pileser's son, Shalmaneser V, reigned only five years. As one of his first acts, he came west against the Philistines. At that time King Hoshea of Israel gave assurance of his loyalty as a vassal of Assyria. But as soon as Shalmaneser was back in Assyria, Hoshea quit paying tribute to Assyria and made an alliance with So (Sibe) of Egypt. But it was a mistake to put trust in Egypt for it was weak and was of no help. Shalmaneser came and conquered Israel. In 724 B.C. he took Hoshea prisoner, though the steep sides of Samaria's hill and its great fortifications enabled it to endure a siege for nearly three years. Samaria fell in 722 just before Shalmaneser died. Then northern Israel became an Assyrian province (which they called Samaria), fulfilling prophecies of its final end by Amos, Hosea, Isaiah, and Micah.

The next Assyrian king, Sargon II (721–705 B.C.), then made a campaign to the west and retook Samaria in 720 B.C. In his annals he says he took 27,290 Israelites into exile, replacing them with people from other countries he had conquered.[3] (Cf. 2 Kings 17:3–6.)

JUDAH IN ISAIAH'S DAY

Since Isaiah's call came in the year that King Uzziah died (739 B.C.), he was old enough to be aware of Uzziah's pride that led to his downfall. In 750 B.C., God afflicted Uzziah with leprosy when he presumed to offer incense on the golden altar which belonged to the Holy of Holies in the temple. He did it even though Azariah and eighty other priests tried courageously to stop him (2 Chron. 26:10–20). He spent the remaining eleven years of his life under quarantine in a special house built for him (2 Kings 15:5).

Jotham, his son, took the throne and reigned until 731 B.C. He was a good but weak king. He "rebuilt the Upper Gate of the temple of the LORD" (2 Chron. 27:3), did other rebuilding, and conquered the Ammonites (vv. 3–5). However, in view of the renewed Assyrian threat when Tiglath-Pileser III usurped the throne of Assyria in 745 B.C., Jotham brought his son Ahaz to the throne in 744 to reign as coruler with him.

---

[3]Herbert M. Wolf, *Interpreting Isaiah* (Grand Rapids: Zondervan Publishing House, Academie Books, 1985), 20; Samuel J. Schultz, *The Old Testament Speaks,* 4th ed. (San Francisco: Harper, 1990), 199 n. 10.

Ahaz reigned until 715 B.C. Like the kings of Israel he mixed the worship of the Baals with the worship of the Lord, sacrificed his sons in fire, worshiped in the high places on the hilltops, "and under every spreading tree" (2 Chron 28:4; see also vv. 2–3). He faced threats not only from Assyria, but from Israel and Damascus as well, so he brought his son Hezekiah to the throne to reign as co-king with him in 728 B.C.

Twice Pekah of Israel and Rezin of Damascus joined to invade Judah. The first time they took many prisoners and killed 120,000 soldiers (2 Chron. 28:5–8). When they threatened a second invasion, saying they would put a puppet king on the throne to force Judah to join them against Assyria, Ahaz sent to Tiglath-Pileser of Assyria for help and paid tribute to him (2 Chron. 28:16,21).

When Tiglath-Pileser took Damascus in 732 B.C. he demanded that Ahaz and others come there to pay homage to him. While there Ahaz saw an altar and had a replica of it made and put in the temple court (2 Kings 16:10–16). Ahaz also turned against the LORD, closed up the temple, and worshiped other gods (2 Chron. 28:22–25). They did not help. Edomites threw off Judah's yoke and invaded Judah from the south. Philistines invaded from the west (2 Chron. 28:17–18). Ahaz remained a weak vassal of Assyria until he died in 715 B.C.

Soon after Ahaz died, because of a great spiritual revival and celebration of the Passover, Hezekiah began counting the years of his reign over again, so that the twenty-nine years of his reign lasted to 686 B.C.[4] A few years later, in spite of Isaiah's warnings of Egypt's inability to help, Hezekiah broke the alliance Ahaz had made with Assyria and sent to Egypt for help. Like Hoshea, Hezekiah miscalculated the power of Egypt and Assyria. Egypt was defeated, and in 701 Sennacherib destroyed all the walled cities of Judah except Jerusalem (2 Kings 18:13).

God judged Hezekiah with a sickness that was to be fatal. God was gracious, however, and answered Hezekiah's prayer,

---

[4]B. H. Carroll, *The Prophets of the Assyrian Period*, vol. 7 of *An Interpretation of the English Bible*, ed. J. W. Crowder (Nashville: Broadman Press, 1948), 175; William F. Albright, "New Light from Egypt on the Chronology and History of Israel and Judah," *Bulletin of the American Schools of Oriental Research* 130 (April 1953): 9; Rudolph Kittel, *A History of the Hebrews*, trans. Hope W. Hogg and E. B. Speirs (London: Wills & Norgate, 1909), 2:355.

healing him and granting him fifteen years of life. Five years later, in 696 B.C., he brought his son, Manasseh, to the throne to reign with him.[5] Then, in 688 B.C., the Assyrians again threatened Jerusalem,[6] but their army was destroyed by the angel of the LORD.

After Hezekiah died, in 686, Manasseh soon turned away from God and massacred those who resisted his restoration of idolatry. Jewish tradition says he tied Isaiah to a log and sawed him in half (cf. Heb. 11:37).

THE ASSYRIAN INVASIONS

The renewed Assyrian threat came with the accession of Tiglath-Pileser III to the throne of Assyria in 745 B.C. He was determined to reestablish the Assyrian Empire and restore its glory and power. With startling suddenness, a new era of brutal Assyrian conquests began. He put together a massive army and a corps of engineers who, for the first time in history, used great siege machines to break down the walls of cities they attacked. He also skinned captives alive, piled up decapitated heads, and impaled people (over sharpened stakes), in order to terrify the people of the next city and cause them to surrender.

At first he followed the custom of previous conquerors. After a city surrendered, he would take an oath of loyalty from the people who were left, tell them how much taxes or tribute to pay each year, and let them go back to rebuild their homes. However, when he returned to Assyria, many of the conquered cities would rebel, and he would have to go back and reconquer them. So he instituted a new tactic. He took the political and religious leaders, teachers, and skilled workers captive and resettled them in another conquered country. Then he replaced them with others from still other conquered cities or countries. The native people would be without their leaders and thus would not be likely to rebel. The leaders who were taken captive would not be with people they knew, and would not have a base for fomenting rebellion either. This policy was intended

---

[5]Edwin R. Thiele, *The Mysterious Numbers of the Hebrew Kings* (Grand Rapids: Zondervan Publishing House, 1983), 64, 176; Schultz, Old Testament Speaks, 210, 214.
[6]See comments on 37:9.

Introduction to Isaiah / 17

to make it possible for the Assyrians to make new conquests each year, rather than having to station or reinforce garrisons. His successors and the Babylonians followed the same policy of taking captured people into exile. This helped to fulfill the prophecies of the scattering of the people of Israel (cf. Deut. 28:64). It also helped to spread the Aramaic language so that the Jews who returned after the Babylonian exile spoke Aramaic instead of Hebrew in their homes. Thus, Jesus and His disciples spoke and preached in Aramaic.

After defeating the Armenians to the north and Babylonians to the southeast, in 738 B.C. King Tiglath-Pileser III took his armies west as far as Hamath on the Orontes River. In 737 B.C., according to Assyrian records, Menahem of Israel paid heavy tribute to save Samaria and protect his throne (see 2 Kings 15:19–20 where Tiglath-Pileser is called by his Babylonian name Pul). Tiglath-Pileser then pressed on through Galilee and down the coast as far as Joppa by 734. Tyre paid an enormous tribute of 150 talents. In 733 he came back through Galilee and took over the territory of Zebulun and Naphtali. In 732 he took Damascus and destroyed it.

During this time both Israel and Judah were torn between pro-Assyrian factions who wanted to surrender and anti-Assyrian factions who wanted to resist. Though Menahem paid tribute to Assyria to prevent the capture of the southern part of northern Israel, Judah paid no tribute at this time, but did so later under Ahaz.

Two years before he died, Tiglath-Pileser III was crowned king of Babylon and took the name Pulu (called Pul; 2 Kings 15:19). His son, Shalmaneser V (726–722 B.C.), conquered Samaria in 722, and was succeeded by Sargon II (721–705). Sargon, according to his records, deported over twenty-seven thousand Israelites to places in Assyria and Media, replacing them with people from Syria and Babylonia who intermarried with remaining Israelites and became Samaritans (2 Kings 17:24). Later Assyrian kings, including Ashurbanipal, continued this process (Ezra 4:9–10).

While Sargon was preoccupied with revolts in the north, Azuri of Ashdod, encouraged by Egypt, revolted. Again, Egypt was no help. In 711 B.C., Sargon invaded Philistia, besieged

Ashdod, and crushed the revolt. This time Judah listened to Isaiah and wisely did not join Ashdod (Isa. 20:1–5).

Merodach-Baladan,[7] the Chaldean from the Sealand near the Persian Gulf,[8] took Babylon after Shalmaneser died. He reigned as king there for twelve years. Then, with the west settled down, Sargon drove him out in 609 B.C.[9]

When Sargon was killed in a border skirmish in 705 B.C., Merodach-Baladan again took Babylon.[10] Sargon's son Sennacherib (705–681) retook Babylon in only six months. In 703, he deported over 208,000 people from Babylonia.[11] Then he moved west. Phoenicia, Philistia, Moab, and Ammon paid tribute, but Hezekiah and the armies of Judah withstood him. Sennacherib considered Hezekiah the ringleader of rebellion in that part of the world and captured "all the fortified cities of Judah" (2 Kings 18:13)—according to his records, 46 of them—and took 200,150 Judeans captive,[12] leaving Hezekiah in Jerusalem shut up "like a bird in a cage,"[13] but unconquered. In the process, Sennacherib at Eltekeh defeated an Egyptian army sent to help and scattered mercenaries Hezekiah had hired from Arabia.

Then Merodach-Baladan took advantage of Sennacherib's absence in the west and took over in Babylon again. Because Babylon was so important to Sennacherib, he left Jerusalem in 701 and defeated Merodach-Baladan. But from 700 to 689 B.C., Sennacherib continued to have trouble with Babylon. In 691 a combined army of Chaldeans, Elamites, and Arameans (hired by the native Babylonians) defeated him. When the Elamite king became ill in 689, Sennacherib headed for Babylon, seeking revenge. After a nine-month siege Babylon capitulated. He then leveled the city to the ground and dug

---

[7] *Marduk-apla-iddina,* "Marduk has given a son." See 39:1.

[8] Raymond Philip Dougherty, *The Sealand of Ancient Arabia* (New Haven: Yale University Press, 1932), 48.

[9] Daniel David Luckenbill, *Ancient Records of Assyria and Babylonia,* 2 vols. (Chicago: University of Chicago Press, 1926–27), 2:14.

[10] Ibid., 2:133.

[11] Daniel David Luckenbill, *The Annals of Sennacherib* (Chicago: University of Chicago Press, 1924), 5, 25, 54–55.

[12] Ibid., 33; idem, *Ancient Records,* 2:120.

[13] Luckenbill, *Ancient Records,* 2:120, 143.

trenches from the river to make its site a swamp. Because the priests of Babylon had used gold from their temples to hire the Elamites, Sennacherib smashed temples and idols, saving only the statues of their chief gods, Bel and Nebo. These he carried off to Nineveh (see Isa. 46:1–2).[14]

With Babylon destroyed, Sennacherib's chief goal was now Egypt. In 688 B.C. he started in that direction by way of Arabia. After conquering the king and queen of Arabia,[15] he proclaimed himself king of Arabia and continued toward Egypt. His records do not mention any other military campaigns after that (though he lived seven more years). Esarhaddon (681–669), his son and successor, suggests Sennacherib continued west in 688, heading across southern Palestine toward Egypt.[16] He intended to capture Jerusalem on the way. However, an Egyptian army headed by the Ethiopian Tirhakah[17] started in his direction. So, Sennacherib sent a letter to Hezekiah, letting him know of his intention (2 Kings 19:9–14). He never met the Egyptians. This indicates that it was at this time that the angel of the LORD brought sudden death to 185,000 of his soldiers (2 Kings 19:35). Then Sennacherib returned to Nineveh and stayed there (v. 36).

Herodotus, the fifth-century B.C. Greek tourist who wrote down what the guides told him, called Sennacherib the king of Arabia, which was his latest title, and told a story of mice eating the bowstrings of the Assyrians. At least he corroborates the fact that the Assyrians and Egyptians did not do battle at this time. Apparently, later Egyptians attributed the sudden death of the 185,000 to bubonic plague, which was carried by rodents.

Babylon was too important to be left as ruins in a swamp, so Esarhaddon rebuilt it and made it one of his capitals. According to his records, Manasseh paid tribute to him (cf. 2 Chron. 33:11).

---

[14]Benjamin R. Downer, "The Added Years of Hezekiah's Life," *Bibliotheca Sacra* 80, no. 318 (April 1923): 265–69; Luckenbill, Ancient Records, 2:152, 185.

[15]Luckenbill, *Ancient Records*, 2:158.

[16]This indicates a time gap of twelve years between 2 Kings 19:8 and 19:9 (see also parallels in Isa. 37:8 and 9). The Bible often has similar time gaps, as between Ezra chaps. 6 and 7, for example.

[17]Tirhakah reigned 690–664 B.C. during Egypt's Twenty-fifth Dynasty.

Many support the idea of two invasions into Judah by Sennacherib, perhaps initially because of some records that seemed to make Tirhakah, the Egyptian king, too young to lead a battle in 701 B.C., the time of the Egyptian defeat at Eltekeh. This seemed to confirm a second invasion as necessary in 688, believed to be the year of Sennacherib's victory over Arabia and of the subsequent slaying of the 185,000 Assyrians by angel of the LORD.

Since that time better analysis of methods of recording historical information has shown Tirhakah's age to be inconsequential, and a shift in the thinking of many has occurred, believing that more than one invasion was unnecessary and even improbable. To uphold this view, Kitchen has noted: "In other words, the biblical narrative (from the standpoint of 681 B.C.) mentions Tirhakah by the title he bore at that time (not as he was in 701)—as is universal practice then and now. Unaware of the importance of these facts, and badly misled by a wrong interpretation of some of Tirhakah's inscriptions, Old Testament scholars have often tumbled over each other in their eagerness to diagnose hopeless historical errors in Kings and Isaiah, with multiple campaigns of Sennacherib and what not—all needlessly."[18]

However, Tirhakah's chronology aside, the return to the conclusion of only one invasion really seems to be an overreaction. Strong argument still stands for two invasions by Sennacherib—one in 701 B.C. and another in 688 B.C.[19] This explanation is much more adaptable to Herodotus's historical accounts.[20] (See the commentary on 36:1 and following.) We see also that 37:9–20 shows basic changes in what Sennacherib

---

[18]Kenneth Kitchen, *The Bible in its World: The Bible and Archaeology Today* (Exeter, England: Paternoster Press, 1977), 114. Others who support the single invasion theory include: John N. Oswalt, *The Book of Isaiah: Chapters 1–39* (Grand Rapids: Wm. B. Eerdmans, 1986), 702; Motyer, *Prophecy of Isaiah*, 284; Edward J. Young, *The Book Of Isaiah*, 3 vols. (Grand Rapids: Wm. B. Eerdmans, 1969), 2:506; Oswalt T. Allis, *The Old Testament: Its Claims and Its Critics* (Philidelphia: Presbyterian & Reformed, 1972), 412.

[19]Others who support the two-campaign theory include: John Bright, *The History of Israel*, 3d. ed. (Philadelphia: Westminster Press, 1981), 298–309; W. F. Albright, "Old Testament History, Including Archaeology and Chronology," *Encyclopedia Americana*, 3:636.

[20]Herodotus, *History*, trans. George Rawlinson, ed. Manuel Komroff (New York: Tudor Publishing Co., 1928), 131.

writes and how Hezekiah responds. Sennacherib says nothing about depending on Egypt (cf. 36:6). He also recognizes that Hezekiah claims to have received a message from God (37:10). Hezekiah responds differently from 37:1–2, where he tore his clothes and sent messengers to Isaiah. This time he goes himself to the temple, spreads the letter out before the Lord, and declares "a straightforward, personal and unequivocal faith."[21] Most important is the fact that, like the preceding robber kings of Assyria, Sennacherib had made a military campaign every year of his reign until 688. Inscriptions of Sennacherib tell of an Arabian campaign in that year.[22] It is logical that this would lead to a campaign against Egypt where Tirhakah would be the defender. But he never engaged Tirhakah, nor did he go near Jerusalem or build a siege ramp against it—just as Isaiah prophesied (37:33)—something Sennacherib did in 701.[23] After 688 B.C. he never made another campaign.[24] This meant there was no treasure or spoils of war being brought into Nineveh and the economy must have suffered greatly during the final seven years of his reign. This was probably the reason his sons assassinated him (2 Kings 19:37).

During the fifteen added years of peace promised to Hezekiah, many of the surrounding nations "brought offerings to Jerusalem for the LORD and valuable gifts for Hezekiah," for they were free from Sennacherib's oppression as well (2 Chron. 32:23). However, even though it was a time of "comfort" (Isa. 40:1), Hezekiah followed the custom of his predecessors and brought his son Manasseh to the throne in 696 B.C. to reign with him. After Hezekiah's death in 686 B.C. Manasseh turned away from God, becoming one of the worst kings in Judah's history. He reintroduced idolatry with its many immoral practices. So many resisted him that he "filled Jerusalem from end to end"

---

[21] J. Alec Motyer, *The Prophecy of Isaiah* (Downers Grove, Ill.: InterVarsity Press, 1993), 280.

[22] Luckenbill, *Ancient Records*, 2:207.

[23] Ibid, 2:143. Sennacherib's records say, "Earthworks I threw up about it [Jerusalem]."

[24] When Sennacherib returned in 688 B.C. he reported victory over the Arabians, and then issued a final edition of his annals ending with the destruction of Babylon in 689. Luckenbill, *Annals of Sennacherib*, 23. The Oriental Institute has a copy. He left no later records except a few building inscriptions at Nineveh and Asshur. Luckenbill, *Ancient Records*, 2:183.

22 / Introduction to Isaiah

with the innocent blood of martyrs (2 Kings 21:16). Ancient Jewish tradition says Isaiah was among this number and Manasseh had him sawn in half (cf. Heb. 11:37).[25]

Chronology Of The Time Of The Prophet Isaiah

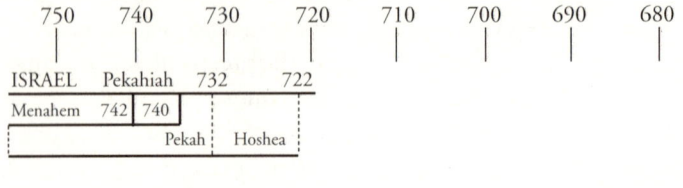

Critical Views Of The Book Of Isaiah

Isaiah began to prophesy in 739 B.C. and continued to be a voice for God during the Assyrian invasions until well into the reign of Manasseh. Because there is a "change of tone and focus at ch. 40, and . . . a similar change at ch. 56,"[26] and because of his mention of Cyrus (44:28; 45:1,13), critics have claimed that

---

[25]For further study on the historical background of the Book of Isaiah see Charles F. Pfeiffer, *Old Testament History* (Grand Rapids: Baker Book House, 1987), 324–70.

[26]John N. Oswalt, *The Book of Isaiah: Chapters 1–39* (Grand Rapids: Wm. B. Eerdmans, 1986), 17.

Introduction to Isaiah / 23

chapters 40 to 66 were not written by Isaiah. Abraham ibn Ezra proposed something like this in the early twelfth century A.D. J. C. Doederlein in A.D. 1775 proposed that these chapters were written by a second or "Deutero-Isaiah" in 540 B.C. when Cyrus was already on the way to Babylon.[27] Duhm and Marti in 1892 each proposed a third, or "Trito-Isaiah," for Isaiah 56 to 66.[28] Soon Isaiah 1 to 39 was also fragmented, as many took from Isaiah most of his book. By 1900, most German critics claimed that Isaiah did not write chapters 40 to 66. Also at that time the writings of S. R. Driver and George Adam Smith popularized the views of the German critics in England and America.[29] By 1950 liberal critics were "virtually unanimous"[30] in their belief in at least a second Isaiah.[31] Gray, for example, said, "The fact that the book of Isaiah is not the work of the prophet Isaiah, but a post-exilic compilation, ought to be the starting-point in all detailed criticism, or interpretation of the book."[32] Conservatives also hastened to affirm that they would not lose their faith if it should turn out that there was a Second Isaiah after all. Kyle Yates, for example, said, "When all the arguments are arrayed on each side of the question we are still left without conclusive proof. The reader is left to choose for himself, knowing that if he accepts the theory of two or three authors, he may still value the material as highly as he could if he were convinced that Isaiah wrote it all."[33] This consensus against the unity of Isaiah still dominates the literature on Isaiah.[34]

---

[27]Robert H. Pfeiffer, *Introduction to the Old Testament*, 3rd. ed. (New York: Harper & Brothers Publishers, 1941), 415.

[28]Ibid., 453. See H. C. Leupold, *Exposition of Isaiah* (Grand Rapids: Baker Book House, 1971), 2:262, for his discounting of the theory of a Trito-Isaiah.

[29]S. R. Driver, *An Introduction to the Literature of the Old Testament*, 7th ed. (Edinburgh, Scotland: T. & T. Clark, 1898), 24–27; George Adam Smith, *The Book of Isaiah* in *The Expositor's Bible,* ed. by W. R. Nicoll (New York: A. C. Armstrong & Son, 1903), 2:7.

[30]John Bright, *The Kingdom of God* (New York: Abingdon-Cokesbury Press, 1953), 136.

[31]Ibid. Some liberals today attribute most of Isa. to disciples writing after 520 B.C.; cf. Wolfgang Roth, *Isaiah* (Atlanta: John Knox Press, 1988), 16. See also B. S. Childs, *Introduction to the Literature of the Old Testament as Scripture* (Philadelphia: Fortress Press, 1979), 316–18.

[32]G. B. Gray, *A Critical and Exegetical Commentary on the Book of Isaiah I–XXXIX* in *The International Critical Commentary* (Edinburgh, Scotland: T. & T. Clark, 1949), xxxii.

[33]Kyle M. Yates, *Preaching from the Prophets* (Nashville: Broadman Press, 1942), 89.

[34]For a good summary of the liberal consensus against the unity of Isaiah see Childs, *Introduction to the Literature,* 316–18.

24 / Introduction to Isaiah

Even though many conservatives were swayed by the liberal arguments, some conservatives recognized that God is able to give true prophecies about Cyrus in advance and that Isaiah 40 to 66 fits Isaiah's time and includes many statements that could not be said about the later exiles or the later Babylon.[35] These include Joseph A. Alexander, Oswald T. Allis, Thomas E. Bartlett, John H. Raven, Merrill F. Unger, George L. Robinson, W. A. Wordsworth, Armand Kaminka, James W. Thirtle, Benjamin R. Downer, J. Wash Watts, Edward J. Young, R. Margalioth, and, more recently, Gleason Archer, Jr., J. Alec Motyer, John N. Oswalt, Willem A. VanGemeren, and Herbert M. Wolf.[36] Watts stated something that is still true: "We cannot afford . . . to dismiss this question of authorship as unimportant. . . . Theoretically, it is easy to say it does not matter. Practically, the effect is tremendous. Commentators' interpretations of the teaching concerning Israel's destiny, concerning the

---

[35]On June 28, 1908, the Roman Catholic Pontifical Biblical Commission affirmed the unity of Isaiah and declared that the hypotheses of a Deutero- or Trito-Isaiah to be untenable. See John E. Steinmueller, *A Companion to Scripture Studies,* vol. II: *Special Introduction to the Old Testament* (New York: Joseph F. Wagner, 1946), 242. Many Catholics today, however, disagree.

[36]Joseph A. Alexander, *Commentary on the Prophecies of Isaiah,* 2 vols. in 1 (1875; reprint, Grand Rapids: Zondervan Publishing House, 1975); Oswald T. Allis, "Book of Isaiah" in *Wycliffe Bible Encyclopedia* (Chicago: The Moody Press, 1975), 1:856–860; idem, *The Unity of Isaiah* (Philadelphia: Presbyterian & Reformed Publishing Co., 1950); Thomas E. Bartlett, *Was There a Second Isaiah?* (Philadelphia: American Baptist Publication Society, 1897); John H. Raven, *Old Testament Introduction* (New York: Fleming H. Revell Co., 1906), 195; Merrill F. Unger, *Introductory Guide to the Old Testament* (Grand Rapids: Zondervan Publishing House, 1951). See especially, G. L. Robinson, *The Bearing of Archaeology on the Old Testament* (New York: American Tract Society, 1941), 102; W. A. Wordsworth, *En-Roeh: The Prophecies of Isaiah the Seer* (Edinburgh, Scotland: T. & T. Clark, 1939); Armand Kaminka, Le Prophète Isaïe (Paris: Librairie Orientaliste, Paul Geuthner, 1925), 53, 75; James W. Thirtle, *Old Testament Problems: Critical Studies in the Psalms and Isaiah* (London: Morgan & Scott, 1916), 237; Benjamin R. Downer, "The Added Years of Hezekiah's Life," *Bibliotheca Sacra* 80, no. 318, 319 (April, July, 1923), 250–71, 360–91; J. W. Watts, *A Survey of Old Testament Teaching* (Nashville: Broadman Press, 1947), 2:150; Edward J. Young, *The Book of Isaiah,* 3 vols. (Grand Rapids: Wm. B. Eerdmans, 1969–72), 1:8; idem, *Who Wrote Isaiah?* (Grand Rapids: Wm. B. Eerdmans, 1958); R. Margalioth (Margulies), *The Indivisible Isaiah* (New York: Yeshiva University, 1964); Gleason L. Archer, Jr., *A Survey of Old Testament Introduction,* rev. ed. (Chicago: Moody Press, 1994), 363–90; J. Alec Motyer, *The Prophecy of Isaiah* (Downers Grove, Ill.: InterVarsity Press, 1993), 25–30; John N. Oswalt, *The Book of Isaiah: Chapters 1–39* (Grand Rapids: Wm. B. Eerdmans, 1986), 18–28; Willem A. VanGemeren, *Interpreting the Prophetic Word* (Grand Rapids: Zondervan Publishing House, Academie Books, 1990), 252; Wolf, *Interpreting Isaiah,* 31–37.

Messiah's work and person . . . [and] the plan of salvation seem to vary with their decisions on this point."[37]

Archaeological discoveries also confirm the fact that Isaiah wrote about the Babylon of his own day.[38] Even so, some liberal critics still ignore the facts and obvious implications of Babylon's importance and its destruction. Some also fail to accept as evidence the important discovery of the Dead Sea Isaiah Scroll coming from before the time of Christ, probably from the second century B.C., that contains all sixty-six chapters. Chapter 40 begins on the last line of the column that completes chapter 39—with no indication that the ancient copyist had any idea that it could have been written by someone other than Isaiah. Liberal critics have supposed that chapters 40 to 66 were not added to Isaiah until the second century B.C. Many liberal critics also ignore the evidence for spiritual revival under Hezekiah in 700 B.C. and its implications of a new faith among Isaiah's audience and a new message that help to account for the few changes we see in Isaiah's style in 40 to 66 (see comments on 36:21 and 40:1).[39]

The primary basis for dividing the Book of Isaiah is historical. The real reason, however, is theological—because of presupposition against the supernatural. The views that propose more than one Isaiah are attempts to disallow the prophetic and the miraculous.

There are two chief historical arguments: One is that Babylon was unimportant and was off the horizon during the Assyrian invasions of Isaiah's day so that Isaiah would have known little about it and would have been concerned even less.[40] The other is that the basic standpoint of chapters 40 to 66 and the passages that mention Babylon in chapters 1 to 39 is that of the Babylonian exile about 540 B.C. or later.[41]

---

[37]Watts, *Old Testament Teaching*, 2:150.

[38]Stanley M. Horton, "A Defense on Historical Grounds of the Isaian Authorship of the Passages in Isaiah Referring to Babylon" (Th.D. diss., Central Baptist Theological Seminary, 1959).

[39]Siebens did recognize that "reform remained effective at least until the end of his reign." A. R. Siebens, "The Historicity of the Hezekian Reform," in *From the Pyramids to Paul*, ed. by L. G. Leary (New York: Thomas Nelson & Sons, 1935), 254.

[40]G. W. Wade, *The Book of the Prophet Isaiah*, in *The Westminster Commentaries*, ed. Walter Lock (London: Methuen and Co., 1911), xliv, 92.

[41]R. B. Y. Scott, "Studia biblica XXIII. Isaiah 1–39," *Interpretation* 12, no. 4 (October 1953): 460.

Babylon *was* prominent in Isaiah's day, however.[42] The Assyrians made it one of their capitals, even sending it some of the tribute they collected until Sennacherib destroyed it in 689 B.C. That destruction caused shock to all the nations around—as their records state—so it would be strange if Isaiah failed to mention it. Babylonians, Medes, and Scythians remembered Babylon's destruction and in 612 B.C. used it as a reason for the destruction of Nineveh.[43]

Many critics have recognized that not everything in 40 to 66 fits the conditions in Babylon during the latter part of the exile.[44] The geographical allusions, the mention of trees native to Palestine, and many historical allusions demand a Palestinian viewpoint and do not fit the later Babylon (e.g., 57:5). The hills and valleys of Judah are in view, never the flat plains of Babylon. Another group of passages (56:7; 60:7; 62:6,9; 65:11; 66:6) clearly shows that the walls of Jerusalem were still standing and the temple and its services were still functioning.[45]

Though Isaiah 40 to 66 has many similarities in style with 1 to 39,[46] liberal critics draw attention to the few differences, especially to its warmth and passion and to its more developed theology, as well as its eschatology and the greater degree of material on comfort versus judgment. One analyst, Y. Radday, put the text of Isaiah through a computer and found linguistic variations, but only one significant difference—less war terminology in 40 to 66. Radday used this to say that one author could not have written the entire Book of Isaiah.[47] However,

---

[42]Young, *Book of Isaiah*, 1:7.

[43]James Frederick McCurdy, *History, Prophecy and the Monuments: Or Israel and the Nations*, 3 vols. in 1 (New York: Macmillan Co., 1911), 2:329.

[44]Harry Bultema, *Commentary on Isaiah*, trans. Cornelius Lambregtse (Grand Rapids: Kregel Publications, 1981), 369–72.

[45]See Archer, *Survey of Old Testament Introduction*, 375–79 for a good survey of "Internal evidence of the composition of Isaiah II in Palestine." He points out that "the whole case for Deutero- or Trito- Isaiah falls to the ground, simply on the basis of the internal evidence of the text itself."

[46]Hobart E. Freeman, *An Introduction to the Old Testament Prophets* (Chicago: Moody Press, 1969), 200–1, recognizes the importance of the similarities in style. Allis also points out that all sixty-six chapters are in "perfectly pure" Hebrew, "without Aramaisms and Babylonian terms which characterize the known post-Exilic books." Allis, "Book of Isaiah," 1:857.

[47]Yehuda T. Radday, *The Unity of Isaiah in the Light of Statistical Linguistics* (Hildesheim, Germany: H. A. Gerstenberg, 1973). See Oswalt, *Isaiah: Chapters 1–39*, 18–19, for questions he raises concerning Radday's methodology.

Introduction to Isaiah / 27

there is good reason for the difference in war terminology. Before 701 B.C., Isaiah was in conflict with the war party in Judah and had to warn them repeatedly. This was no longer true after 701.

The Assyrians defeated the Egyptians at Eltekeh, about thirty-two miles west and slightly north of Jerusalem.[48] The mercenaries Hezekiah hired were scattered. After Hezekiah's healing and the failure of Sennacherib's field commander (Heb. *rab-shakeh*) to take Jerusalem, the war party was discredited and the people took a stand of faith. During Hezekiah's fifteen added years, Isaiah was able to give them comfort. Now that they had seen prophecy fulfilled, the Holy Spirit was able to remind them of the foolishness of idolatry and give them a new message about the salvation of the LORD—through His suffering Servant-Messiah.

Any writer or speaker will show differences in style depending on the subject and the audience. It is also true, as Motyer points out, that Isaiah sometimes used "a high poetic style," especially in chapters 40 to 55, and sometimes "more workmanlike rhythmic prose or somewhat less artful poetry." Furthermore, "These two styles . . . appear throughout the whole book. . . . It is intolerably wooden and unimaginative to deny that one author could produce both styles."[49] It is also true that "at least forty or fifty sentences or phrases . . . appear in both parts of Isaiah, and indicate its common authorship."[50]

The latter part of the Book of Isaiah deals with the evils Manasseh was introducing.[51] Yet Isaiah continued to point ahead to the millennial glories to come and even to the new heavens and the new earth. He never lost the vision of God given to him at the beginning of his ministry in chapter 6—God is the Holy One of Israel and the Lord of history throughout the entire book.

---

[48]Luckenbill, *Annals of Sennacherib*, 31.

[49]Motyer, *Prophecy of Isaiah*, 23.

[50]Archer, *Survey of Old Testament Introduction*, 382. He includes a list, and points out literary resemblances of Isa. 40 to 66 to the eighth century prophet Micah that are "numerous and striking," 382–84.

[51]See 2 Chron. 33:2–10; Allis, "Book of Isaiah," 1:856. There is no evidence that the idolatries and sins Isaiah writes about were common after the return from Babylon. The returnees desired to restore pure worship.

Then, we should not forget that Jesus and the New Testament writers treat the entire book as Isaiah's. Sometimes we could take their words as referring to the book's traditional title. However, "there are other references which clearly imply the personality of the historic Isaiah himself."[52] These include Matthew 3:3; 12:17–18; Luke 3:4; Acts 8:28; Romans 10:16,20. Most conclusive is John 12:38–41, which quotes Isaiah 53:1 and 6:10 as from the same Isaiah.

---

[52]Archer, *Survey of Old Testament Introduction*, 387.

OVERVIEW OF ISAIAH'S MESSAGE

Introduction

Isaiah lived in Jerusalem and had a God-given ministry to its kings, especially to Ahaz and Hezekiah. He was surrounded in his early life by a false, government-aided prosperity that encouraged corrupt luxury accompanied by a downtrodding of the poor and a sensual, immoral, heathen religion (2 Chron. 26:16–20; 27:2; 28:1–27; 29:6–9).

He begins his book with what is often called "The Great Arraignment." Judah was a sinful nation, judged, desolate, and left with a small remnant. God was not only Israel's judge, however; He was also a brokenhearted Father who invited His children, Israel, to return: He would redeem them—if they would be ashamed of their idolatry. The conditions Isaiah describes fits the time of Sennacherib's first invasion, in 701 B.C. Thus the first chapter is an introduction to the whole book.

Isaiah: The Prophet And His Message

Isaiah's name (Heb. *Yesha'yahu*) means "Yahweh [the LORD] saves [or is the source of salvation]." His father Amoz (Heb. *'amots*, "strong") is not mentioned elsewhere in the Bible. Later Jewish tradition speculated that Isaiah was related in some way to the royal family. However, archaeologists have discovered a seal inscribed "Amoz the Scribe." Some believe this means Amoz was a prominent scribe with a high government position.

Since Isaiah came quickly when the king sent for him and since the LORD told him to go out of the city to meet Ahaz (7:3), it seems obvious that Isaiah made Jerusalem his home. Early in his ministry he became well-known as a prophet of God. The Bible calls his wife a prophetess, and though she wrote no books, she must have had an important ministry. He had two sons, *Shear-Jashub* ("a remnant will return") and *Maher-Shalal-Hash-Baz* ("quick to the plunder, swift to the spoil"). Their names highlighted his message to Judah.

Isaiah began prophesying in 739 B.C., the year King Uzziah died. Some suppose he was already a prophet before that time, but there is no evidence of this. Since he records both the death of Hezekiah (686 B.C.) and the death of Sennacherib (681 B.C.) and names the next Assyrian king, Esarhaddon (37:38), he ministered for over sixty years. During the fifteen additional years of peace God gave Hezekiah, Isaiah had opportunity to live quietly and write words of comfort for the people of Judah as he looked ahead to the ministry of the Messiah as the Suffering Servant of the LORD. Then when Manasseh took over and turned away from God, Isaiah's writings dealt with the foolishness of the idolatry Manasseh reintroduced and warned of God's judgment.

The word "prophet" (Heb. *navi'*) comes from an old word meaning "speaker." Throughout the book, Isaiah speaks for God and declares, " 'The word of our God stands forever' " (40:8). Key verses to his message include 6:3; 45:22; 55:6–7; and 59:2. There are many powerful passages in the book. Note especially chapters 1; 6; 40; 49; 50; 53; and 55.

Early Prophecies

Isaiah's prophecies are arranged in a form that keeps showing the contrast between Israel's present sin that requires judgment and the future hope of God's promised restoration. He draws attention to the nations who will come to Jerusalem in peace, seeking God and His word, at a time when God alone will be exalted. But the people of Judah and Jerusalem have done evil to themselves. The leaders have crushed the poor. What they have done will be repaid to them in special judgment.

Isaiah's Vision And Call

After introducing his message, Isaiah introduces himself. He began his ministry the year King Uzziah died as a leper (739

B.C.). As a proud young aristocrat, probably related to the royal family, Isaiah went into the temple courts, probably congratulating himself that he was not a sinner like Uzziah. But a vision of God's majestic glory and holiness led him to see himself as a sinner. Then God provided cleansing and Isaiah responded to God's voice and was commissioned as a prophet to warn a people who would be hardened by his message and would be brought to judgment. However, there would be a change in his ministry after prophecy was fulfilled and judgment came.

God's Angry Hand And His Saving Hand

Isaiah prophesied that because of Judah's sin, God's angry hand of holy, righteous judgment would use Assyria to bring judgment in the near future; but His saving hand would use the Messiah in the distant future. Then God sent Isaiah and his son *Shear-Jashub* ("a remnant will return") to tell King Ahaz of Judah not to be afraid of King Pekah of Israel and King Rezin of Syria, who were threatening to attack Jerusalem and replace him with a puppet king who would help them defy Assyria. God offered Ahaz the privilege of asking for a supernatural sign to confirm His promise, but Ahaz refused because he had already decided to send tribute to Tiglath-Pileser III of Assyria to help himself. God then promised a sign, not for Ahaz, but for the whole dynasty of David. The Messiah, "Immanuel" ("God with us"), would be born to the virgin (see comments on 7:14). God promised that before such a child could reach an age of accountability, the land of those two kings would be forsaken.

Immanuel is again mentioned in 8:8, and the Book of Isaiah gives an enlarging picture of the Messiah, continuing in 9:1–7; 11:1–10; 16:5; 28:16; 32:1–5,15–18; 42:1–12; 49:1–6; 50:4–11; 52:13 to 53:12; 54; 55; and 61:1–11.

Isaiah's second son, *Maher-Shalal-Hash-Baz* ("quick to the plunder, swift to the spoil"), became a further warning that the Assyrians would attack, plunder, and rob Judah soon. In contrast, the virgin-born Son with names that show His deity (Wonderful, Counselor, Mighty God, Father of Eternity, Prince of Peace) would make David's throne eternal.

God would use the Assyrians, without their knowledge, to punish Judah, and in due time they, too, would receive God's judgment. However, the Messiah as a new shoot or branch from the line of David would come in the future with the sevenfold Spirit of the LORD upon Him. He would be a Teacher, a righteous Judge, a Peacemaker filling the earth with the knowledge of the LORD, and a Banner to the Gentile nations who will seek Him. The result will eventually be a return of Israel that will be like a new exodus. Then they will acknowledge God himself as their salvation and will draw water from the wells of salvation with joy, thanksgiving, and shouts of praise.

Judgment On Foreign Nations

Because God is the God of the whole world and sovereign over all nations, Isaiah had a message for other nations. His attention, however, is primarily on their relation to Judah. Babylon, as the leading center of pagan religion in Isaiah's day, is mentioned first. Its judgment would be severe, total, and soon to come. This was fulfilled in 689 B.C. when Sennacherib leveled Babylon and made it a swamp.[1]

Then Isaiah resumes telling more of the king of Babylon who exalted himself and in whom Ahaz put his trust, Tiglath-Pileser III, who was crowned king in Babylon two years before his death. He took prisoners into exile instead of releasing them to go home. He set the example for later kings of Assyria by considering himself greater than any god, even greater than the God of Israel. He was brought down to Sheol, all his glory left behind and not even a proper burial.

Other foreigners upon which God pronounced judgment include Philistia, Moab (for its pride), Damascus (and with it, northern Israel that had forgotten the God of their salvation), Cush, and Egypt. Egypt would have internal discord (fulfilled in Isaiah's day) and would become weak. Yet God would eventually have a witness there, and both Egyptians and Assyrians would eventually worship the LORD.

---

[1] Daniel David Luckenbill, *Ancient Records of Assyria and Babylonia,* 2 vols. (Chicago: University of Chicago Press, 1926–27), 2:152, 243.

When Sargon took the Philistine city of Ashdod,[2] God commanded Isaiah to go naked and barefoot for three years as a sign that Assyria would lead people captive from Egypt and Cush. An additional word against Babylon prophesied that it would become a wilderness. In 689 B.C., Isaiah received the news that Babylon had indeed fallen. Sennacherib had not only destroyed the city but smashed most of its idols.[3] Further prophecies tell of judgment on Edom, Arabia, Jerusalem's treasurer (Shebna), and Tyre.

Judgment And Restoration For Judah

Isaiah is careful to show that God's judgment reveals not His arbitrariness but His righteousness. Nor is judgment an end in itself. It prepares for the demonstration of God's glory that will eventually bring a feast of spiritual things for all nations. This will be necessary before Jerusalem can be transformed into a city of peace. In contrast to the vineyard of bad grapes mentioned in an earlier prophecy, judgment will make Judah a vineyard of good fruit. For Isaiah's day, many lessons must be taught by the Assyrians.

Samaria was ripe for judgment and the people of Judah were hypocritical in their worship of the LORD. They mocked Isaiah's message that was meant to bring them rest and refreshment. They would have to learn the hard way, from the Assyrians. Five woes must come on Jerusalem and Judah because of their hypocrisy, their rebellion against God, their trust in Egypt, and their refusal to trust in the LORD. But in the future day, a King will reign in righteousness. Although judgment must come, God's purpose for Israel would not change. He will restore the land and the people of Israel, giving them salvation, streams in the desert, holiness, and everlasting joy.

Hezekiah And Sennacherib's Invasions

In 701 B.C., Sennacherib destroyed all the fortified cities of Judah except Jerusalem. The Book of Isaiah finishes up the account of Sennacherib's invasions and then tells of Hezekiah's

---

[2]James B. Pritchard, ed., *Ancient Near Eastern Texts Relating to the Old Testament,* 2d ed. (Princeton: Princeton University Press, 1955), 287.
[3]Daniel David Luckenbill, *The Annals of Sennacherib* (Chicago: University of Chicago Press, 1924), 84.

sickness, the miraculous sign of the shadow on the sundial going backward, Hezekiah's recovery, the promise of protection from the Assyrians, and the promise of Hezekiah's fifteen additional years of life. However, that sickness came early after Hezekiah took gold from the temple and paid tribute to Sennacherib so he would bypass Jerusalem.

The news of this prophesied promise of protection against the Assyrians stirred Sennacherib to send an army under his field commander (Heb. *rab-shakeh*), who demanded Jerusalem's surrender and told the people not to listen to Hezekiah and not to put their trust in the Lord. He kept telling them that the gods of the other nations had not delivered them from Sennacherib, implying Sennacherib was greater than any god, even greater than Israel's God. However, the people took a stand of faith, refused to answer or surrender, and put their trust in the Lord. Isaiah prophesied the Assyrians would hear a rumor and leave. The rumor they heard was that the Chaldeans had overrun Babylon. Babylon was more important to Sennacherib than either Jerusalem or Egypt. So both the field commander and Sennacherib with their armies left without taking Jerusalem, just as Isaiah had prophesied.

Though Isaiah does not indicate the interval between 701 and 688 B.C., the context and Assyrian records found by archaeologists indicate that Sennacherib made a second campaign westward after he destroyed Babylon. This time he sent a letter to Hezekiah threatening to take up where he had left off and warning him not to trust in the LORD—whom he treated as no different than the pagan gods of the countries he had conquered already. Hezekiah brought the letter before the LORD. Then Isaiah prophesied that God would defend Jerusalem, that the Assyrians would not enter the city but go back by the way they had come. This was fulfilled when the death angel slew 185,000 of Sennacherib's army. Sennacherib then withdrew, going back to Nineveh the way he had come, as Isaiah had prophesied, and stayed there, until two of his sons assassinated him and another son, Esarhaddon, took the throne.

Isaiah then goes back to the time when kings were sending gifts to Hezekiah because of his healing. Envoys from Babylon came and Hezekiah showed them all his treasures. Isaiah told him this was a mistake, for the time would come when the Babylonians would remember this and take captive some of Hezekiah's descendants.

Comfort And Deliverance

After the people of Jerusalem took a stand of faith and Sennacherib left Jerusalem unconquered, Isaiah called for the people to prepare the way for God to come back to His people. The guarantee of comfort was God's word, and the assurance of the truth of God's word was God himself who created the universe and who is far greater than anyone or anything in it. He is different from idols that have to be fastened in place to keep them from falling over. He is the everlasting God, the Creator, the unwearying Guide for His people. He gives power to the faint, to those who wait for Him.

God will reveal His glory, and He has made Israel His servant. However, Israel as a whole failed, for they sinned and did not accomplish the work they were called to do. But within Israel there was and always has been a godly remnant that is truly God's servant. The remnant will do a work for God, but they cannot do the work that needs to be done—the work of salvation and redemption. God kept telling Israel to stop being afraid. Prophecy has been fulfilled and God will continue to be faithful. He has another Servant, the Messiah, who will accomplish His work of salvation and restoration.

Looking ahead to the time of Israel's exile in Babylonia, Isaiah prophesies of one from the north, Cyrus, who will be God's shepherd, anointed to do the work of sending back the exiles to their land—though Cyrus does not know God. On the other hand, the true Servant upon whom God puts His Spirit will be given as a covenant for the people and a light for the Gentiles. God will rebuke Israel, yet promises to blot out their transgressions for His own sake. They are still God's chosen, and He will pour out His Spirit and His blessing on their descendants. When God restores Israel and makes both peace and judgment, others will recognize there is no other God. He reveals both the past and future and calls everyone in the whole world to turn to Him and be saved.

Isaiah then goes back to the destruction of Babylon in his own day and draws a lesson from the fact that the great gods of Babylon, Bel and Nebo, were loaded on weary beasts and taken into captivity. (Archaeological discoveries show they were carried to Nineveh.)[4] But God says to Israel that they never carried Him—He carried them. His purpose for them will stand.

Then Isaiah goes back to give prophecies about the fall of Babylon, which would take place in 689 B.C. The Assyrians did not destroy Babylon before this time. Babylon thought of itself as a god, but they had to learn that God will not share His glory with another—not with pagan gods, not with Babylon. Sennacherib had taken people from Judah to Babylon to replace the Babylonians he had exiled. Isaiah tells them God prophesied this far in advance, so they could not give credit for their return to idols. Then he calls them to flee. Archaeological records show they did, so there was a prophesied return to Judah fulfilled in Isaiah's day.[5]

Isaiah says nothing more about Babylon or Cyrus after chapter 48. His focus is on the suffering Servant-Messiah. He is the solution to Israel's failure, the assurance of their future joy. Through Him the godly remnant is encouraged. They think God has forgotten them, but He has engraved them on the palms of His hands. He will act and they will be restored. The heavens and earth will pass away, but God's salvation will be forever. Zion will be restored and the good news will be that God reigns.

The high point of the Book of Isaiah describes God's Suffering Servant, who deals wisely. His contemporaries do not understand His suffering. They despise Him and think of Him as smitten by God. But His sufferings are vicarious—completely for others. He bears their sicknesses, pains, sins, and guilt. By His wounds, we are healed. He suffers willingly, and after His atoning death, He lives to see spiritual children and to see the will of God prosper by his power.

The result of the Messiah's suffering, death, and resurrection is growth and blessing for Zion with multitudes added and free

---

[4]Luckenbill, *Ancient Records,* 2:252, 255.

[5]Ibid., 2:152; Benjamin R. Downer, "The Added Years of Hezekiah's Life," *Bibliotheca Sacra* 80, no. 319 (July 1923): 386.

grace for everyone. The call is for everyone who thirsts to come. The greater David, the Messiah, will be a covenant and a witness to all peoples. But Isaiah calls on all to seek the LORD while He may be found. He will have mercy and will abundantly pardon. God assures also that His word will accomplish what He pleases.

Glory For God's People; Judgment For Others

God's blessings are not limited to Israel and to those whose ritual impurities were removed by the cleansing and sacrifices of the Law. Eunuchs could not join in with the temple worship. But God promises to include them in His blessing. Foreigners who turn to the LORD will also be included.

Toward the end of Isaiah's ministry, he had to deal with the failures of leaders in Manasseh's time. They did not contribute to God's purpose, but they could not destroy it. God departs from them, but He does not limit the manifestation of His presence to heaven. He who fills the eternity of time and space also comes to dwell with those of a contrite, humble spirit.

This contrasts with the leaders who go through forms of worship and fast to get their own way, mistreating the poor even while they are fasting. God does not want their kind of fasting. He is looking for a fast from sin, oppression, and greed. Their sins have separated them from God. They confess this and acknowledge they have turned their backs on God. But there was no one to intervene. So God's own arm, His own power, worked salvation. He promised that a Redeemer would come to Zion to those who repent. Then Zion will hear the call to arise and shine for its Light has come. New glory will come. Foreigners will help in Zion's restoration. God will give peace and He will be an everlasting light for them.

The Messiah then speaks, for the Spirit of the Lord is upon Him, anointing Him to preach good news to the poor, the brokenhearted, and the captives. Jesus applied this to Himself at the beginning of His Galilean ministry (Luke 4:17–21).

Isaiah goes on to give further prophecies of Zion's salvation and of the future time when its people will respond to their

Savior. God will rejoice over them, and they will be called the Holy People, the Redeemed of the LORD. Their Messiah will come with garments spattered from having trodden the wine press of God's judgment alone. Judgment must come before the millennial kingdom is established.

Isaiah then praises God for all the good things He has done for His people, even though they rebelled and grieved His Holy Spirit. He prays for deliverance, restoration, and glory. God then promises mercy, blessing, and joy. There will be a new heaven and a new earth, but the present Jerusalem will also have its fulfillment, with joy and many blessings that fit the conditions of wonderful peace prophesied for the Millennium. This will be during the thousand years when Satan will be bound, as the Book of Revelation tells us.

Finally, God draws attention to heaven as His throne and the earth as His footstool. He wants pure worship. He will judge evil and extend peace like a constantly flowing river to Jerusalem. His fame and glory will be declared among the nations. Those who are left after the final judgment will come and worship the LORD, but the judgment of the wicked will be everlasting.

ISAIAH OUTLINE

I. Judgment and Hope 1:1–5:30

   A. Judah: a rebellious people 1:1–31
      1. Title: Isaiah under four kings 1:1
      2. Rebellious people 1:2–4
      3. A desolate land 1:5–9
      4. Unacceptable worship 1:10–15
      5. A call to repentance 1:16–20
      6. Restoration through judgment 1:21–31
   B. The Day of the LORD 2:1–4:6
      1. A future day of peace 2:1–5
      2. Humankind judged, the LORD exalted 2:6–22
         a. Idolatry calls for judgment 2:6–9
         b. Pride calls for judgment 2:10–18
         c. Earth-shaking judgment 2:19–21
         d. Foolish trust 2:22
      3. Judah's evil judged 3:1–4:1
         a. Judah and Jerusalem judged 3:1–3
         b. Resulting chaos and anarchy 3:4–7
         c. Well-deserved judgment 3:8–9
         d. The choice between blessings and disaster 3:10–11
         e. A sorrowful lament 3:12
         f. The LORD passes judgment on leaders 3:13–14
         g. Proud women of Zion judged 3:16–24
         h. Judah's devastation 3:25–26
         i. A result of judgment 4:1
      4. The Branch and the bridal canopy 4:2–6
         a. A day of peace and restoration 4:2–4
         b. A bridal canopy 4:5–6

C. The vineyard and its fruit 5:1–30
  1. The song of the vineyard 5:1–7
     a. A love song 5:1–2
     b. Judgment for putrid grapes 5:3–6
     c. The vineyard explained 5:7
  2. Six woes 5:8–25
  3. Nations under God's control bring judgment 5:26–30

II. The Holy One Exalted 6:1–12:6

  A. Isaiah called to a difficult ministry 6:1–13
    1. Isaiah's vision of God 6:1–4
    2. Isaiah's confession and cleansing 6:5–7
    3. Isaiah commissioned to a difficult ministry 6:8–10
    4. Lasting until only a remnant remains 6:11–13
  B. Rebukes and promises to Judah 7:1–9:7
    1. King Ahaz challenged to trust God 7:1–16
       a. Aram and Ephraim allied against Judah 7:1–9
       b. God offers and promises a sign 7:10–13
       c. The Immanuel sign 7:14–16
    2. God will use Assyria to bring judgment 7:17–8:8
       a. Assyria as God's razor 7:17–25
       b. Maher-Shalal-Hash-Baz 8:1–4
       c. Assyria to come as a flood 8:5–8
    3. How God was with Israel 8:9–18
    4. Judgment on spiritism 8:19–22
    5. Hope for Galilee 9:1–5
    6. The Prince of Peace 9:6–7
  C. Four Reasons for God's Anger 9:8–10:4
    1. Judgment on pride and self-sufficiency 9:8–12
    2. Judgment on a people led astray 9:13–17
    3. Wickedness that consumes because of God's wrath 9:18–21
    4. Woe to unjust rulers 10:1–4
  D. Assyria used and judged 10:5–34
    1. Assyria—God's Rod 10:5–19
       a. Assyria used without knowing it 10:5–11
       b. God will punish Assyria in due time 10:12–19

Isaiah Outline / 41

      2. Hope for the remnant of Israel 10:20–34
         a. A remnant returns to the Mighty God 10:20–23
         b. Assyria's yoke broken 10:24–27
         c. The Assyrian advance 10:28–32
         d. God is in control 10:33–34
    E. A new Branch bears fruit 11:1–12:6
      1. The Spirit-anointed King 11:1–3
      2. The Righteous Judge 11:4–5
      3. The earth changed by the knowledge of the LORD 11:6–9
      4. A new exodus 11:10–16
      5. A day of thanksgiving for Israel and the nations 12:1–6
         a. Praise for salvation 12:1–3
         b. Let the whole world know 12:4–6

III. God Deals With Nations Around Judah 13:1–23:18

    A. Babylon's destruction 13:1–14:23
      1. Judgment soon to come 13:1–22
         a. God's wrath on Babylon 13:1–5
         b. A day of the LORD's wrath is near 13:6–13
         c. Babylon soon to be overthrown 13:14–22
      2. Israel restored but Babylon judged 14:1–23
         a. Compassion on Judah 14:1–2
         b. A taunt against the king of Babylon 14:3–8
         c. Sheol's reception of Babylon's king 14:9–11
         d. The king of Babylon's pride and fall 14:12–17
         e. The king of Babylon lacks a proper burial 14:18–20
         f. Babylon to become a swampland 14:21–23
    B. Judgment on many nations 14:24–17:14
      1. Assyria to be crushed in God's land 14:24–27
      2. Philistia will not escape judgment 14:28–32
      3. Moab 15:1–16:14
         a. Moab's destruction 15:1–9
         b. Moab contrasted to Zion 16:1–5
         c. Moab's pride brought to contempt 16:6–12
         d. Moab to be judged within three years 16:13–14

42 / Isaiah Outline

        4. Judgment on Damascus 17:1–3
        5. The harvest and the gleanings 17:4–11
           a. The remnant of Jacob will be small 17:4–6
           b. A day when people will look to God 17:7–8
           c. A day of desolation 17:9
           d. Punished for forgetting God 17:10–11
        6. Sudden destruction 17:12–14
    C. Cush and Egypt 18:1–20:6
        1. Judgment on Cush 18:1–6
        2. Gifts brought to the LORD 18:7
        3. Judgment on Egypt 19:1–15
        4. A day of smiting and healing for Egypt 19:16–25
        5. Egypt and Cush—a false hope 20:1–6
    D. Fulfillments in Isaiah's day 21:1–23:18
        1. Prophecy of Babylon's fall fulfilled 21:1–10
           a. Babylon attacked 21:1–5
           b. Isaiah receives news of Babylon's fall 21:6–10
        2. Morning and night for Edom 21:11–12
        3. Judgment on Arabia soon to come 21:13–17
        4. Jerusalem judged 22:1–14
        5. Shebna and Eliakim 22:15–25
        6. Lamentation over Tyre's ruin 23:1–18

IV. Judah Deserves God's Judgment 24:1–35:10

    A. The earth polluted, the city desolate 24:1–13
    B. Judgment prepares for God's reign in Jerusalem 24:14–23
    C. Judgment prepares for a millennial banquet 25:1–12
    D. Judgment prepares for restoration and peace 26:1–27:13
        1. A song expressing trust 26:1–11
        2. God alone is worthy to be honored 26:12–27:1
        3. Israel smitten that it might bear fruit 27:2–13
           a. A second vineyard song 27:2–6
           b. Jacob's guilt to be atoned for 27:7–13
    E. Six woes 28:1–33:1
        1. Woe to Ephraim 28:1–29
           a. Drunken leaders 28:1–8

       b. Scoffers to learn the hard way 28:9–22
       c. Natural wisdom comes from the LORD 28:23–29
   2. Woe to Ariel, David's city 29:1–14
       a. Jerusalem to be brought low 29:1–4
       b. Jerusalem's enemies to be frustrated 29:5–8
       c. Ignorance and hypocrisy judged 29:9–14
   3. Woe to those who work in darkness 29:15–24
       a. Foolish planners 29:15–16
       b. Restoration that honors God 29:17–24
   4. Woe to rebellious people 30:1–33
       a. Trusting Egypt will bring shame 30:1–5
       b. An unprofitable trip to an unprofitable nation 30:6–17
       c. God will be gracious and heal 30:18–26
       d. God's control over the nations 30:27–28
       e. Israel will sing when the LORD shatters Assyria 30:29–33
   5. Woe to those who seek Egypt's help 31:1–32:2
       a. Foolish to trust Egypt and not God 31:1–3
       b. God himself will protect Jerusalem 31:4–5
       c. A call for repentance 31:6–7
       d. Supernatural destruction of Assyria 31:8–9
       e. The righteous King 32:1–8
       f. Judgment until the Spirit is poured out 32:9–14
       g. The outpoured Spirit will restore peace 32:15–20
   6. Woe to Assyria 33:1
F. God's purpose in history 33:2–35:10
   1. A prayer for deliverance and God's answer 33:2–24
       a. A plea that exalts God 33:2–6
       b. Sorrow and distress of Judah 33:7–9
       c. The LORD will arise and judge the enemy 33:10–13
       d. Sinners learn a lesson 33:14
       e. Who can dwell with a holy God? 33:15–16
       f. The King is coming 33:17–24
   2. God's wrath on the nations 34:1–17
       a. Judgment on all nations 34:1–4
       b. Special judgment on Edom 34:5–17

3. A Restored land and people 35:1–10
   a. The desert will rejoice 35:1–2
   b. Encouragement for suffering people 35:3–7
   c. The Highway of Holiness 35:8–10

V. Hezekiah and Sennacherib 36:1–39:8

  A. Sennacherib invades in 701 B.C. 36:1–37:8
    1. Judah's cities captured 36:1
    2. Sennacherib's threats 36:2–20
    3. The people obey Hezekiah 36:21
    4. Sennacherib's death prophesied 36:22–37:8

  B. Sennacherib's army decimated and Sennacherib killed 37:9–38
    1. Sennacherib's renewed threats 37:9–13
    2. Hezekiah's prayer and God's response 37:14–35
    3. Isaiah's prophecy fulfilled 37:36–38

  C. Hezekiah's sickness and recovery 38:1–22
    1. A death sentence 38:1
    2. Hezekiah restored 38:2–22

  D. Merodach-Baladan's embassy 39:1–8
    1. Hezekiah shows his treasures 39:1–2
    2. Babylonian exile prophesied 39:3–8

VI. Comfort for Jerusalem and Judah 40:1–48:22

  A. God coming back to His people 40:1–31
    1. Good news for Judah and Jerusalem 40:1–11
    2. God's greatness contrasted to idols 40:12–31

  B. God's glory and His Servant 41:1–42:25
    1. God uses one from the east 41:1–4
    2. The nations and their idols challenged 41:5–29
    3. The Servant of the LORD and His mission 42:1–9
    4. A new song 42:10–13
    5. God will judge and guide 42:14–17
    6. Israel blind and deaf 42:18–25

  C. A redeemed remnant gathered 43:1–45:25
    1. Israel's loving Savior 43:1–7
    2. Israel's witness as God's servant 43:8–13
    3. A new exodus from Babylon 43:14–21

Isaiah Outline / 45

        4. Israel's unfaithfulness 43:22–28
        5. God's Spirit to be outpoured 44:1–5
        6. The foolishness of idolatry 44:6–20
        7. God will redeem and restore Israel 44:21–45:25
           a. Jerusalem to be inhabited 44:21–28
           b. God will use Cyrus to restore Israel 45:1–13
           c. God will save Israel 45:14–25
    D. Babylon's fall 46:1–48:22
        1. The LORD superior to Babylon's deities 46:1–13
        2. No hope for Babylon 47:1–15
        3. Prophecy's witness to the true God 48:1–19
        4. A command to flee from Babylon 48:20–21
        5. No peace for the wicked 48:22

VII. Redemption and the Suffering Servant 49:1–55:13

    A. The Servant brings restoration 49:1–50:11
        1. God's chosen Servant 49:1–7
        2. Restoration brings rejoicing 49:8–26
        3. Israel's sin and lack of response 50:1–3
        4. God's obedient Servant: the Messiah 50:4–9
        5. The choice: rely on God or lie down in torment 50:10–11
    B. The remnant encouraged 51:1–52:12
        1. Remember the Founder and foundation 51:1–8
        2. God assures a joyful return 51:9–16
        3. The cup of God's wrath drained and removed 51:17–23
        4. Jerusalem to be redeemed 52:1–12
    C. The Servant's suffering and atoning death 52:13–53:12
        1. The wise Servant will be exalted 52:13
        2. Astonishing suffering 52:14–15
        3. The Messiah despised and rejected 53:1–3
        4. Suffering for others 53:4–6
        5. Dying for others 53:7–9
        6. An acceptable guilt offering 53:10–12
    D. The Messiah's work brings growth and blessing 54:1–55:13
        1. Joyous growth 54:1–3

46 / Isaiah Outline

      2. The compassionate Redeemer 54:4–8
      3. The covenant of peace 54:9–10
      4. Jerusalem to be reestablished 54:11–15
      5. God's servants to be vindicated 54:16–17
      6. A universal invitation 55:1–2
      7. An everlasting covenant 55:3–5
      8. God will freely pardon the repentant 55:6–9
      9. God's word will bring joy 55:10–13

VIII. Glory for God's People; Judgment on Others 56:1–66:24

    A. Blessing and judgment 56:1–58:14
      1. Blessing includes eunuchs and foreigners 56:1–8
      2. Godless rulers and idolaters deserve judgment 56:9–57:13
        a. Stupid, greedy leaders 56:9–12
        b. Worse judgment will come 57:1–2
        c. Apostates warned of judgment 57:3–6
        d. Persistent idolatry 57:7–10
        e. Idolatry brings no benefit 57:11–13
      3. Restoration and blessing for the contrite 57:14–21
        a. Prepare the way 57:14–15
        b. Comfort and peace for mourners 57:16–19
        c. No peace for the wicked 57:20–21
      4. Hypocritical worship 58:1–2
      5. Hypocritical fasting 58:3–5
      6. God wants fasting from sin 58:6–10
      7. God will guide 58:11–12
      8. The Sabbath brings blessing 58:13–14

    B. Zion's confession, redemption, and glory 59:1–60:22
      1. Sin separates from the Savior 59:1–3
      2. No justice and no peace 59:4–8
      3. Isaiah confesses the people's sins 59:9–15
        a. Walking in darkness 59:9–11
        b. Sins acknowledged 59:12–15
      4. The LORD Himself Will Save 59:16–21
      5. Light and glory come to Zion 60:1–3
      6. Worship restored 60:4–22
        a. Gentiles restore and serve Zion 60:4–7
        b. Sons from afar honor God 60:8–9

Isaiah Outline / 47

   c. Foreigners rebuild and honor Zion 60:10–14
   d. God's purpose to transform Zion 60:15–18
   e. God's people will display His splendor 60:19–22
 C. The Messiah announces His mission 61:1–63:6
  1. Anointed to preach good news 61:1–2
  2. Priests of the LORD 61:3
  3. Happy results 61:4–6
  4. Rejoicing in their inheritance 61:7–9
  5. The Messiah's joy 61:10–11
  6. The Messiah's continuing concern for Zion 62:1–63:6
   a. Zion's future glory 62:1–5
   b. The LORD proves His favor 62:6–9
   c. Zion's Savior will come 62:10–63:6
 D. Isaiah prays for mercy and pardon 63:7–64:12
  1. Praise for God's kindnesses 63:7–15
  2. God is still our Father 63:16
  3. Hardened hearts 63:17–19
  4. Isaiah cries out for God to act 64:1–9
  5. Jerusalem ruined 64:10–12
 E. Mercy, blessing, joy, and judgment 65:1–66:24
  1. God's gracious answer 65:1–7
  2. The remnant will possess the land 65:8–10
  3. God will judge those who forsake Him 65:11–16
  4. A new creation 65:17–25
  5. The earthly temple and its worship are insufficient 66:1–6
  6. Sudden enlargement of Zion 66:7–14
  7. Fiery judgment 66:15–17
  8. God's glory seen 66:18–24

I. JUDGMENT AND HOPE 1:1–5:30

A. Judah: A Rebellious People 1:1–31

1. Title: Isaiah Under Four Kings 1:1

¹The vision concerning Judah and Jerusalem that Isaiah son of Amoz saw during the reigns of Uzziah, Jotham, Ahaz and Hezekiah, kings of Judah.

This verse is the heading for the entire book of Isaiah.[1] It is called a "vision" in the sense that God revealed it to Isaiah in a powerful and dramatic way. The verb "saw" (Heb. *hazah*) is often used of seeing a God-given vision (as in Num. 24:4; 1 Sam. 3:1; Jer. 23:16; Ezek. 7:13,26; Dan. 1:17; Hos. 12:10; Obad. 1; Mic. 3:6; Nah. 1:1; Hab. 2:2–3; etc.). Here it is used to mean a supernatural reception of God's revelatory word. "You must understand that no prophecy of Scripture came about by the prophet's own interpretation. For prophecy never had its origin in the will of man, but holy men spoke from God as they were carried along [led along] by the Holy Spirit" (2 Pet. 1:20–21). Isaiah had a living relationship with God. The Holy Spirit made God's words "vivid, concrete, close, and real" to Isaiah.[2] Like Jesus' words, Isaiah's words were not just his, but the Father's (John 14:10).

The name "Isaiah" means "Yahweh saves" or "the Lord is salvation"[3] and suggests the theme of the book. It is directed to Judah and Jerusalem. Isaiah does prophesy about other nations but only as they relate to Judah and Jerusalem. And it is Jerusalem that commands central attention, for it was and will be the capital city God rules from. In it stood the temple, and in the Millennium the throne of the Messiah will be located there.

---

[1] Edward J. Young, *The Book of Isaiah,* 3 vols. (Grand Rapids: Wm. B. Eerdmans, 1969–72), 1:27–29.

[2] S. H. Widyapranawa, *The Lord is Savior: Faith in National Crisis* (Grand Rapids: Wm. B. Eerdmans, 1990), 3.

[3] David L. McKenna, *Isaiah 1–39,* in *The Communicator's Commentary* (Dallas: Word Books, 1993), 41.

Jewish tradition says Isaiah was related to the kings of Judah. If this is true, it would explain why he was able to go in and out of the palace freely.

Careful study of the biblical accounts and comparison with archaeological discoveries indicate some overlapping in the reigns of the kings mentioned in the verse. David set this pattern of coregency in Israel. Before he died, he brought Solomon to the throne to end the chaotic attempts of others to take the throne. Likewise, many subsequent kings brought a son to the throne as coregent in order to prevent any such confusion.

Uzziah, also called Azariah (2 Kings 14:21), reigned from 790 to 739 B.C. But in 750 he entered the Holy Place of the temple. In human pride he dared to offer incense on the golden altar—something only priests were allowed to do. God judged him by afflicting him with leprosy, and his son Jotham took over the government at that time (2 Chron. 26:21).

Because of turbulent times Jotham (a weak king) brought his son Ahaz to the throne as coruler in 744 B.C. Uzziah died in 739 and Jotham in 731. Jotham had been allowing Ahaz to lead; so when Uzziah died and Isaiah began to prophesy, Ahaz was then the actual ruler. Thus, no prophecies of Isaiah are clearly identified with the reign of Jotham. (See chronology chart, p.22.)

Continued turbulence also prompted Ahaz to bring his son, Hezekiah, to the throne with him in 728 or 727 B.C. When Ahaz died in 715 B.C. Hezekiah began to count the years of his reign over again. His recounting was probably due to the great Passover celebration and spiritual revival at that time.[4] Undoubtedly, Hezekiah wanted revival but could do nothing to encourage it as long as ungodly Ahaz was alive. He considered his coreign with his own father not worth counting. However, he made the mistake of breaking Ahaz's treaty with Assyria. This brought Sennacherib against him in 701 B.C. Hezekiah paid tribute to save Jerusalem. Isaiah then brought God's message of death and judgment. But such judgments of God's are conditional. When Hezekiah repented and prayed, God healed him, promising him deliverance from Assyria and fifteen more years of reign. Hezekiah then brought his son Manasseh to the throne

---

[4]William Foxwell Albright, "The Biblical Period," in *The Jews,* ed. Louis Finkelstein (New York: Harper & Brothers, 1949), 1:42.

(in 696 or 695 B.C.) to reign with him, and lived until 686 B.C.[5]

Isaiah recorded the death of Sennacherib in 681 B.C. Thus, both Isaiah and Sennacherib lived on into the reign of Manasseh.[6] Manasseh, however, turned against God, brought in idolatry, and filled Jerusalem with the blood of martyrs who resisted that idolatry (2 Kings 21:16). Tradition says Manasseh had Isaiah strapped to a log and sawn in half (cf. Heb. 11:37).[7] If Isaiah was about twenty years old when he began to prophesy, he must have been in his eighties when he was martyred. Such a long life was unusual in a time when the average life span was less than thirty-five years. God must have protected him until it was time for his life to be offered like Paul's (2 Tim. 4:6).

2. REBELLIOUS PEOPLE 1:2–4

²**Hear, O heavens! Listen, O earth! For the LORD has spoken: "I reared children and brought them up, but they have rebelled against me.**

Isaiah begins with a message for Judah and Jerusalem. In what is pictured as a court scene, a just and holy God who made the heavens and earth calls on them to witness against Israel. Moses, the fountainhead of Israelite prophecy, had called on the heavens and earth to witness against the people when he set before them the blessings and curses of the covenant (Deut. 30:19; cf. 31:28; 32:1).

The LORD, *Yahweh*,[8] is the self-existent, covenant-keeping, promise-fulfilling God. He had "reared" the Israelites as His children (Exod. 4:22; 15:13; Deut. 24:18; Ps. 77:15 identify

---

[5]Edwin R. Thiele, *The Mysterious Numbers of the Hebrew Kings* (Grand Rapids: Zondervan Publishing House, 1983), 64, 176; Eugene H. Merrill, *An Historical Survey of the Old Testament* (Nutley, N.J.: Craig Press, 1966), 281.

[6]Hobart E. Freeman, *An Introduction to the Old Testament Prophets* (Chicago: Moody Press, 1969), 193.

[7]See Robert H. Charles, "The Martyrdom of Isaiah," in *The Apocrypha and Pseudepigrapha of the Old Testament* (Oxford, England: Clarendon Press, 1913), 2:155–62.

[8]Scholars debate the meaning of the divine name Yahweh. The Heb. writes only the consonants YHWH. It may come from an old form "of the Hebrew verb that means 'becoming,' 'happening,' 'being present.' . . . It is a statement that God is a self-existent being (the I AM or I WILL BE) who causes all things to exist and has chosen to be faithfully present with a people that He has called unto himself." Russell E. Joyner, "The One True God," in *Systematic Theology*, ed. Stanley M. Horton, rev. ed. (Springfield, Mo.: Logion Press, 1995), 134–35.

them as redeemed children, delivered by God's power), guiding them, teaching them, meeting their needs, and establishing His kingdom through them. Now, in spite of God's fatherly provision and tender care for His children,[9] they (the Heb. is in the emphatic position) had "rebelled" against Him, willfully rejecting His fatherly love and guidance.

> ³The ox knows his master, the donkey his owner's manger, but Israel does not know, my people do not understand."

Domestic animals who served the people had more sense than the Israelites. The ox knows whom it belongs to and who gives it direction. The donkey knows who bought it, where to go for food and who provides it (cf. Mal. 1:6). The fact that "Israel does not know" indicates they no longer had a personal relationship with God. They no longer acted like a chosen people, a covenant people. That they did not "understand" indicates that they were no longer able to discern what is true and right. They had forgotten they had been redeemed and no longer recognized God as the source of their strength, reputation, and wealth. They were no longer a witness to the glory of God. But if they had even as much good sense as an ox or a donkey, they would never have rebelled.

> ⁴Ah, sinful nation, a people loaded with guilt, a brood of evildoers, children given to corruption! They have forsaken the LORD; they have spurned the Holy One of Israel and turned their backs on him.

Isaiah responds in grief crying out "Ah" (Heb. *hoi*, "alas") for the sinful, corrupt nation.[10] Their guilt is a heavy load. God wanted them to be a holy people, but they have deliberately continued in the evil doings of their fathers and treated the Holy One of Israel with blasphemous contempt. "The Holy One of Israel" is a term found twenty-nine times in Isaiah and only six times in the rest of the Old Testament. It reflects what Isaiah saw in his inaugural vision (chap. 6) and emphasizes both God's character and His claims on Israel. But Israel has rejected

---

[9]The plural indicates the individual responsibility of each Israelite to God the Father.
[10]Heb. *goy*, a term usually used of Gentiles. Their sin had broken the covenant relation.

those claims. They have turned away, moved away, and separated themselves from Him, rejecting Him completely in total ingratitude. Idol worship may also be implied (as in Ezek. 14:3).

3. A Desolate Land 1:5–9

> ⁵Why should you be beaten anymore? Why do you persist in rebellion? Your whole head is injured, your whole heart afflicted. ⁶From the sole of your foot to the top of your head there is no soundness—only wounds and welts and open sores, not cleansed or bandaged or soothed with oil.

Isaiah now becomes a witness to the consequences of Israel's sin. The nation is like a person who has been viciously mugged by a robber yet does not resist attack, seemingly asking for further beating. Isaiah asks why they want to be hit again. Instead of being a holy people they are like a whipped slave. The "whole head is injured," the "whole heart" (including the mind) is diseased. In other words, the thinking of the people and their leaders is wrong and stubbornly contrary to God's will.

The body, from "the sole of your foot to the top of your head," is covered with open and running wounds. None of these wounds is "cleansed or bandaged or soothed [softened] with [olive] oil." The country is hurting and no one is helping. There seems to be no hope for recovery, and they are willfully headed for further disaster. As McKenna points out, "Isaiah never forgets that sin also has social dimensions."[11]

> ⁷Your country is desolate, your cities burned with fire; your fields are being stripped by foreigners right before you, laid waste as when overthrown by strangers.

Isaiah now lists specific afflictions Israel has suffered. The land of Judah is "desolate": its cities "burned" and its fields "stripped by foreigners" in the presence of Judah's people, who have no power to do anything about it.

The only historical situation this description fits is that of the

---
[11] McKenna, *Isaiah 1–39*, 55.

54 / Isaiah 1:8-9

Assyrian invasion of 701 B.C., when Sennacherib destroyed forty-six cities of Judah.[12] He took more than 200,000 prisoners, not to Assyria as some have assumed, but to Babylonia, to replace the 208,000 prisoners he once took from there.

Archaeologists have discovered a bas-relief more than sixty feet in length adorning the wall of a room in Sennacherib's palace. It pictures the siege of Lachish, a city about thirty miles southwest of Jerusalem.[13] It shows Assyrian soldiers with slings, bows and arrows, spears, battering rams, and scaling ladders attacking the city. The final panel shows Sennacherib on his throne receiving captives and the spoil of Lachish. Its inscription calls Sennacherib "king of the universe." This bas-relief was apparently intended to draw attention to his capture of forty-six walled cities of Judah, with the further intent of drawing attention away from his failure to take Jerusalem (see v. 8).

> ⁸The Daughter of Zion is left like a shelter in a vineyard, like a hut in a field of melons, like a city under siege.

By the mercy of God Jerusalem was not captured. Yet it was left insecure. Isaiah likens it to the temporary structures—branches and mats or poles and awnings—farmers set up in the fields to guard crops. In his "Annals" Sennacherib put it this way: "I devastated the wide province of Judah; the strong, proud Hezekiah, its king, I brought in submission to my feet[14] . . . I shut up Hezekiah like a bird in a cage."[15] (See chaps. 36 and 37 for further details of Sennacherib's campaigns.)

> ⁹Unless the LORD Almighty had left us some survivors, we would have become like Sodom, we would have been like Gomorrah.

Sennacherib was not responsible for a few survivors escaping the devastation. Yahweh, the personal God of Israel, the God of the armies of heaven, limited the destruction in order to save

---

[12]John Mauchline, *Isaiah 1–39* (New York: Macmillan Co., 1962), 51.
[13]A full-size copy of this relief may be seen in the Oriental Museum of the University of Chicago.
[14]Daniel David Luckenbill, *Ancient Records of Assyria and Babylonia,* 2 vols. (Chicago: University of Chicago Press, 1926–27), 2:327.
[15]Ibid., 2:240.

Jerusalem. Had He not done so, it would have been a complete ruin "like Sodom" and "like Gomorrah." But there were survivors. And they could still be saved.

4. Unacceptable Worship 1:10–15

> ¹⁰Hear the word of the LORD, you rulers of Sodom; listen to the law of our God, you people of Gomorrah!

Now Isaiah turns to the people whose sin and rebellion were responsible for God's allowing the devastation. Israel had become Sodom-like rulers and Gomorrah-like people and were worthy of the same destruction as Sodom and Gomorrah. It was only the grace of God that preserved a remnant. This remnant needed to listen to God's law (Heb. *torah*, "instruction").

> ¹¹"The multitude of your sacrifices—what are they to me?" says the LORD. "I have more than enough of burnt offerings, of rams and the fat of fattened animals; I have no pleasure in the blood of bulls and lambs and goats.

Instead of obeying God, the people were simply multiplying their sacrifices to Him. The pagans around them believed that their gods needed sacrifices and that continually-offered sacrifices increased the possibility that their gods would answer their prayers. But the God who made the heavens and the earth does not need anything. He gave the sacrifices of the Law for the benefit of His people—as a means of restoring fellowship with Him and as first steps toward walking with Him.

The "burnt offerings" were intended to express exaltation of God and dedication to His will. The "fat" was an expression of giving Him their best. The "blood of bulls and lambs and goats" was placed on the altar as an atonement—a ransom paid for their forgiveness and deliverance. Practiced without sincerity the sacrifices were an abomination to God. He hates religion when it is just a form and ceremony, lacking any true loving fellowship with Him. The multiplication of these sacrifices made God feel like vomiting.

> ¹²When you come to appear before me, who has asked this of you, this trampling of my courts?

Because their hearts were not reaching out to God in faith and obedience, their continual crowding into the temple was not what God wanted. Their worship was not genuine. All they were doing was wearing out the floor of the temple courts by their "trampling."

> ¹³Stop bringing meaningless offerings! Your incense is detestable to me. New Moons, Sabbaths and convocations—I cannot bear your evil assemblies.

God commanded them to stop "meaningless offerings," worship that was mere form or that was intended to persuade God to let them continue in their own willful ways. God cannot be bribed or deceived. Incense made the temple courts fragrant, but it was repulsive to God. The celebrations at the time of the new moon, the weekly and annual Sabbaths (Lev. 23:1–44), the "convocations" (or assemblies), were all intended to be holy. Yet God saw them as "evil," for He saw their hearts, and He could not stand their religious activities. The Septuagint translates the last part of the verse ("evil assemblies") as "fasting and ritual preparation," which suggests that all their worship activities were repulsive to God.

> ¹⁴Your New Moon festivals and your appointed feasts my soul hates. They have become a burden to me; I am weary of bearing them.

Emphatically, the "New Moon festivals" and the "appointed feasts" of Leviticus 23 no longer honored God, no longer expressed love and dedication to Him, so He hated them. Instead of being a joy to Him and a blessing to the people, these religious holidays had become a heavy "burden" that God was "weary of bearing."

> ¹⁵When you spread out your hands in prayer, I will hide my eyes from you; even if you offer many prayers, I will not listen. Your hands are full of blood;

Hands "spread out," palms upward in an attitude of submission and desiring to receive from the Lord, meant nothing when the people were really seeking their own way and rejecting God's teaching. God cannot look with favor on such false actions.

Multiplying prayers does not get God's attention when hands are "full of blood." This striking expression depicts how the people were oppressing the poor and using violence to get what they wanted.

5. A Call To Repentance 1:16–20

16wash and make yourselves clean. Take your evil deeds out of my sight! Stop doing wrong,

There was still hope. Prayers could still be heard, but the hands spread out in supplication must be cleansed. The people must realize their condition and cry out as David did in Psalm 51. David asked God to wash away all his iniquity and cleanse him from his sin. But God tells Israel they have a part to do. They must wash. But the washing must be more than a symbol or empty form. It must be a sincere repentance that makes a clear break with sinful acts and habits. It must also include an inner change, for God sees the heart. Then they will be able to "stop doing wrong."

17learn to do right! Seek justice, encourage the oppressed. Defend the cause of the fatherless, plead the case of the widow.

Turning from sin and evil is the first step, but it is not enough. It must be followed by good actions. They must "learn to do right." Doing "right" means doing good to others. Seeking "justice" means dealing honestly and fairly. They must not only cease from oppression and correct oppressors but encourage the oppressed. It also means avoiding injury to others and providing for the needs of the unfortunate. Most important, to "seek justice" means actively defending those who cannot defend themselves: specifically orphans and widows, who had no one to stand up for them and who were often victims of schemes and scams (cf. Ps. 85:8–13; Amos 5:24; Mic. 6:6–8; James 1:27).

18"Come now, let us reason together," says the LORD. "Though your sins are like scarlet, they shall be as white as snow; though they are red as crimson, they shall be like wool.

58 / Isaiah 1:19-21

Now the LORD sums up His words that began in verse 10. "Reason together" is a legal term that is part of the court scene. It may mean "let us cease the arguments; let us do something about it." God is taking the initiative. Their sins are indeed "like scarlet"—the deepest kind of red—referring back to the bloody hands of verse 15. It is implied that if they admit, or confess, this they shall become as white as the clearest, brightest white of snow or wool, a white that is white by its nature, indicating that their own nature would be changed by God's grace. This exhortation continues in the following verses.

> ¹⁹If you are willing and obedient, you will eat the best from the land;

God's promise to cleanse and renew their hearts and minds is conditioned upon willing obedience (to the covenant). They must do more than talk about their situation. They must do what God asks. Though foreign invaders were eating the fruit of the land, true repentance would ensure that God would make it possible for His people to enjoy its fruits again. Like the Prodigal Son of Luke 15:11–32, they could come home to God and receive His blessings.

> ²⁰but if you resist and rebel, you will be devoured by the sword." For the mouth of the LORD has spoken.

Continued refusal and rebellion would mean that instead of their eating the fruit, the sword (of the Assyrians) would eat them. The LORD has spoken this, and His divine authority is behind His word. The people must make the choice: obey and eat or rebel and be eaten. The gospel, too, demands a choice. We may have eternal life or eternal death (John 3:16). There is no middle ground. We cannot love God and hold on to our sin at the same time.

6. RESTORATION THROUGH JUDGEMENT 1:21–31

> ²¹See how the faithful city has become a harlot!
> She once was full of justice; righteousness used
> to dwell in her—but now murderers!

God continues His case against Jerusalem. The corruption of Zion has resulted from the people's unfaithfulness to God, their unjust dealings with each other, and the rebellion and corrupt practices of their rulers. This corruption brings a lamentation over the city, which in David's time had begun as a "faithful city." Now it had become like a wife who had sunk to the unfaithful level of a prostitute. Whereas "justice" and "righteousness" had once marked the relationships of its people, now their conduct had sunk to the lowest possible level. The inhabitants had actually become "murderers."[16] What a contrast to the God who loved them and asked them to love Him! (Deut. 6:5; 7:8). We see the same contrast in the New Testament (1 John 3:1,14–15).

> 22Your silver has become dross, your choice wine is diluted with water.

The degeneration of Zion's people is compared to "dross"—ore that has no more precious metal in it and is of no value. It is further compared to "choice wine" (or the Heb. may mean beer, the common drink of the Philistines) that has been mixed with so much water that it is worthless.

> 23Your rulers are rebels, companions of thieves; they all love bribes and chase after gifts. They do not defend the cause of the fatherless; the widow's case does not come before them.

The "rulers," who administered the various state offices and acted as judges deciding lawsuits, were "rebels" against God. They were "companions of thieves," for they would acquit thieves for a bribe. They "love bribes" instead of loving justice and loving people. They were cowards and bullies, beginning their oppression with the weakest and the most helpless, the orphans and widows (often referred to as victims in the Bible). The rulers refused to let a widow bring her case to justice.

> 24Therefore the Lord, the LORD Almighty, the Mighty One of Israel, declares: "Ah, I will get relief from my foes and avenge myself on my enemies.

"Therefore" indicates God will do something about the situation. He now reveals the judgment these conditions demanded.

---

[16]Cf. Hos. 4:1–2 where Hosea sees similar sins in northern Israel. Judah had not learned the lesson from God's judgment on northern Israel.

The three divine titles—"the Lord *[ha'adon]*, the LORD *[Yahweh]* Almighty, the Mighty One of Israel"—emphasize His claims and authority. He is a divine Person, the Lord of the universe. God has been patient, but now His wrath will bring holy vengeance on His enemies, that is, on those who have oppressed the helpless. They who have oppressed the helpless have gotten so bad that He now considers them—a segment of His own people—His foes.

> ²⁵I will turn my hand against you; I will thoroughly purge away your dross and remove all your impurities.

God's hand will assail again; yet in His wrath there is also grace, for it introduces the process of purifying His people from their sinfulness. His judgment is intended to refine and purify, just as metal is refined and its dross (worthless impurities) is removed.

> ²⁶I will restore your judges as in days of old, your counselors as at the beginning. Afterward you will be called the City of Righteousness, the Faithful City."

God's work of chastisement will end in restoration. Judges and counselors (or administrative rulers) will be restored. Yet, no king is mentioned because the LORD is to be their King, as He was before the time of King Saul. They will be faithful to Him. Jerusalem will no longer be a prostitute but will be a righteous and faithful city. This is God's goal and will have its complete fulfillment in the Millennium.

> ²⁷Zion will be redeemed with justice, her penitent ones with righteousness.

The future people of Zion are to be the purified, redeemed remnant that has been converted to the Lord. His attributes of "justice" and "righteousness" will characterize them. This implies they will live in harmony with a concern for the well-being of one another.

> ²⁸But rebels and sinners will both be broken, and those who forsake the LORD will perish.

The people can still choose between serving God or rebelling against Him. Rebels who reject the authority of God's teachings

Isaiah 1:29–31 / 61

and sinners who violate God's law will be removed from among the people by purifying fire (see v. 25). Though God's judgment is directed against the sin, the sinner who chooses to persist in sin receives it as well. In the end the ungodly "will be . . . broken" (by forces from outside Israel) and "will perish" (due to their inner spiritual bankruptcy).

> 29"You will be ashamed because of the sacred oaks in which you have delighted; you will be disgraced because of the gardens that you have chosen.

Idolatry was always involved in Israel's sin of rebellion. On the day of future judgment, sinners will be dumbfounded and humiliated because their false gods cannot help them escape the results of their sins. The "sacred oaks" and "gardens" were places where pagan rites were observed in a religion that involved nature worship and fertility cults (cf. Deut. 12:2; 1 Kings 14:23). Northern Israel had become involved with them and now they were common in Judah.[17]

> 30You will be like an oak with fading leaves, like a garden without water.

In contrast to the tree and the watered garden, to which God often compared His people (Num. 24:6; Ps. 1; Jer. 11; Hos. 14), their fate will be that of the worldly things they had chosen to trust. God rejects the sinful practices of any cult or false religion (no matter what good they may also do). So the whole nation will suffer and wither away (v. 29).

> 31The mighty man will become tinder and his work a spark; both will burn together, with no one to quench the fire."

The "mighty man" is the ruler who sought to draw strength and might from the worship of false gods. All such rulers will be like "tinder"—fuel for the fire which they themselves have set! These wicked rulers will not be part of the remnant that comes through the fire purified. Instead, they will be consumed together with their wickedness. How ironic that "the mighty

---

[17]See also 57:5; 65:3; 66:17,24; Jer. 3:6,13.

man will become tinder and his work a spark." In choosing paganism, the rebellious element—ruler and subject alike—have sown the seeds of their own destruction. Neopaganism can expect nothing different. Once God brings this judgment it will be too late. Nothing will stop the destruction. This anticipates the lake of fire that John saw (Rev. 20:14–15).

STUDY QUESTIONS

1. What are the chief things we know about Uzziah, Jotham, Ahaz, and Hezekiah?
2. Why did God call the heavens and earth to witness against Israel? What had they seen?
3. In what ways had Israel become like Sodom and Gomorrah?
4. What hope did God hold out to the people?

B. The Day Of The Lord 2:1–4:6

1. A Future Day Of Peace 2:1–5

¹This is what Isaiah son of Amoz saw concerning Judah and Jerusalem:

This title is probably for chapters 2 through 12, which many believe were Isaiah's earliest prophecies. Others think the title is for 2:1 through 4:6.¹

Chapter 2 begins with the future universal desire to know God's truth and draws attention to Judah's present privileges as the sole recipients of divine revelation. It goes on to show the advantages of obedience, the judgments brought by disobedience or indifference, and the certainty of the triumph of the word of God. Verses 2–4 are repeated in Micah 4:1–4 with a few variations which the Holy Spirit inspired for the benefit of Micah's rural audience.

---

¹S. H. Widyapranawa, *The Lord is Savior: Faith in National Crisis* (Grand Rapids: Wm. B. Eerdmans, 1990), 11.

Isaiah 2:2-3 / 63

> ²In the last days the mountain of the LORD's temple will be established as chief among the mountains; it will be raised above the hills, and all nations will stream to it.

Israel enjoyed the privilege of worshipping the LORD in Jerusalem. Idolatrous enemies surrounded them in Isaiah's day. But the greatness of the privilege will be fully realized in the millennial age, when "the mountain of the LORD's temple" will be exalted and the whole world will want to go to Jerusalem.

The temple hill, directly north of David's Zion but considered part of it, was not very high, an elevation of about 2,400 feet. So Isaiah pictures its future preeminence figuratively by its exaltation above the rest of the earth's mountains—including all of the high places where pagans worshiped and where Israelites often went astray (cf. Ezek. 40:2).

With that exaltation will come the conversion of people from all nations. God will powerfully draw them to Jerusalem in a great stream. This expectation of the conversion of Gentiles is an important part of Old Testament prophecy (Isa. 40; 45; Jer. 3:17; Amos 9:12; Hag. 2:6–7; Zech. 8:20–22; 14:16–17; cf. Acts 9:15). It is also a fulfillment of the promise given to Abraham of blessing for all peoples on earth (Gen. 12:3; 22:18).

> ³Many peoples will come and say, "Come, let us go up to the mountain of the LORD, to the house of the God of Jacob. He will teach us his ways, so that we may walk in his paths." The law will go out from Zion, the word of the LORD from Jerusalem.

God will cause Gentiles from many nations to encourage one another to go up to Jerusalem to seek the LORD, learn His ways, and make them the basis of their lives as they "walk in his paths." "Law" (Heb. *torah*) is better translated "teaching" or "instruction," and includes the whole of the inspired Word of God. Jerusalem will be the center for the spreading of His Word.

God is now drawing people to himself (cf. John 6:44; 12:32). The Holy Spirit is convicting them and convincing them (John

16:8–11). Thus the conversion of the Gentiles has a preliminary fulfillment in the present Church Age where the gospel is being spread around the world. But the promise will have its complete fulfillment in the Millennium. Then the whole world will be united under the risen and glorified Jesus (Isa. 11:9).[2]

> ⁴He will judge between the nations and will settle disputes for many peoples. They will beat their swords into plowshares and their spears into pruning hooks. Nation will not take up sword against nation, nor will they train for war anymore.

The millennial age will be one of peace because the LORD will be the sovereign Judge. He will decide any dispute between nations or individuals, providing perfect freedom from war and all strife. Instruments of war will be recycled into instruments of agriculture, symbolizing a peaceful life. However, the world must first suffer great judgments. (See Joel 3:10 for a reversal of Isaiah's imagery here, indicating that the Kingdom will be brought in through judgment, that is, the judgments of the Great Tribulation.)

> ⁵Come, O house of Jacob, let us walk in the light of the LORD.

Isaiah's primary message, like that of all the prophets, was to his own people of his own day. He brings the future in to reinforce God's message for the present. Thus, Isaiah goes back and forth between the future and his own time. In the light of the future blessings of God's prophetic word, he exhorts the house of Jacob (which does not really deserve the name "Israel") to come and "walk in the light" of the LORD's teachings and blessings. People from all nations will do it some day. They have the opportunity and privilege of doing it now.[3] (Cf. 1 John 3:3).

The name "Jacob" had the primary meaning of "heel-catcher" because of the circumstances of his birth (see Gen. 25:26). It also had the meaning of "supplanter" or "deceiver" (see Gen.

---

[2]Stanley M. Horton, *The Ultimate Victory: An Exposition of the Book of Revelation* (Springfield, Mo.: Gospel Publishing House, 1991), 219.

[3]So do we. See Stanley M. Horton, "The Last Things," in *Systematic Theology*, ed. Stanley M. Horton, rev. ed. (Springfield, Mo.: Logion Press, 1995), 599.

27:36; cf. Jer. 9:4), a name Esau emphasized. The Angel of the LORD changed his name to "Israel" (Gen. 32:28) meaning "he struggles with God" or "God strives" or "God rules," making him God's fighter and God's prince. God confirmed the new name later (Gen. 35:10). However, Jacob did not always live up to his new name, nor did the nation of Israel.

2. HUMANKIND JUDGED, THE LORD EXALTED 2:6–22

a. Idolatry Calls For Judgment 2:6–9

6You have abandoned your people, the house of Jacob. They are full of superstitions from the East; they practice divination like the Philistines and clasp hands with pagans. 7Their land is full of silver and gold; there is no end to their treasures. Their land is full of horses; there is no end to their chariots.

Israel in Isaiah's day was despising the privilege of being God's chosen people[4] and imitating the pagan nations around them instead. Like the pagans, they were following "superstitions from the East" (Assyria and Babylon) and practicing "divination" (forbidden by the Law, Deut. 18:10,14) borrowed from the Philistines on the west. They were also clasping hands "with pagans" to enter into commercial and matrimonial alliances (also forbidden, Exod. 23:32). Instead of trusting in the Lord they were trusting in horses, chariots (military might), wealth, and idolatry. Because of this God was at the point of abandoning them.

The wealth that filled the land points to the prosperity that developed during the reign of Uzziah and indicates that this prophecy was given before the Syro-Ephraimite war in the days of King Ahaz (7:1–2; see also 2 Kings 16:5; 2 Chron. 28:5).

Isaiah does not condemn the wealth itself but how the people got it. Much of it came through oppressing the poor. The problem was made worse by their trust in wealth and their reliance on the material things it could buy. They were no longer trusting in the LORD. During the time of prosperity king

---

[4]"Chosen" to serve God and carry forward His plan.

Uzziah became powerful, but pride led to his downfall (2 Chron. 26:16). His son Jotham did serve the LORD (2 Chron. 27:6), but Jotham's son Ahaz turned to idolatry (2 Chron. 28:2–4). Pride and trust in material things continued to be a problem in the reign of the next king, Hezekiah.

> ⁸Their land is full of idols; they bow down to the work of their hands, to what their fingers have made.

Along with their land being full of wealth, it is also "full of idols." The presence of idols everywhere shows the depths to which Israel had fallen. The term "idols" may be translated literally "nothings" (cf. Job 13:4; Zech. 11:17). Isaiah's use of this term reveals his contempt for them as nothing more than the work of human hands.

> ⁹So man will be brought low and mankind humbled—do not forgive them.

Calling idols "nothings" does not mean that idolatry is insignificant. Idolatry is a serious matter. Because of it God will humble humankind as a whole (Heb. *'adham*) and individuals in particular *('ish)*. All, regardless of class, had bowed down to idols.

Because Isaiah feels God's indignation at idolatry, he calls on Him not to forgive them. He is not commanding God here. He is simply expressing the inevitable result of idolatry, God's divine judgment.

b. Pride Calls For Judgment 2:10–18

> ¹⁰Go into the rocks, hide in the ground from dread of the LORD and the splendor of his majesty!

Criminals and fugitives would often hide in caves in the limestone rock cliffs of the land of Israel. David did this when King Saul was seeking to kill him (e.g., 1 Sam. 22:1). In other lands people often sought underground refuges. Isaiah now gives an ironic command to those who bowed down to idols. In the future Day of Judgment, let them try to escape in those refuges. But they will not be able to (cf. Rev. 6:15). They trusted in earthly things, but the earth and the rocks will not be able to hide them. They who mocked the "majesty" of the LORD will flee before His glory "when he rises to shake the earth" (Isa. 2:19,21) during the judgments that precede the Millennium.

> **11The eyes of the arrogant man will be humbled and the pride of men brought low; the LORD alone will be exalted in that day.**

When people come face to face with God, all of their human arrogance and pride will suddenly fall. "The LORD alone will be exalted in that day," for no one will be able to stand before the terror and glory of His divine majesty.

"In that day," "on that day," or "the day of the Lord" is strictly prophetical language. New Testament eschatological passages also use such phrases (see 1 Thess. 5:2; 2 Pet. 3:10).

> **12The LORD Almighty has a day in store for all the proud and lofty, for all that is exalted (and they will be humbled),**

That God "has a day in store" is further evidence of the Bible's linear view of history. Ancient pagans had a cyclical view of history, as Hindus do even today. They look at the events of time as repeating themselves forever. Reincarnation apart from Hinduism is such a view of history.

God, however, has a plan with a beginning and an end. Genesis 1:1 emphasizes that the universe had a real beginning. The Book of Revelation shows that some day the universe will end to give way to a brand new heavens and earth.[5] And God will carry out His plan to its consummation.

In addition to the future day of judgment that will bring in the Millennium, the prophets often saw a near day of judgment, a day of judgment especially upon Israel.[6] The near day of judgment (still a day of the LORD) that Isaiah now sees is pictured in terms of a storm sweeping across the land, from the mountaintops in the northeast (v. 13, Bashan) to the harbors in

---

[5]Stanley M. Horton, *Our Destiny: Biblical Teachings on the Last Things* (Springfield, Mo.: Logion Press, 1996), 251.

[6]See Amos 5:18–20 where Amos deals with those in northern Israel who thought a near day of the LORD would exalt them. It would judge them and there would be no escape once it came.

the southwest (v. 16, where the merchant ships were anchored in the Gulf of Aqaba, as in Solomon's day). Such a storm would be most destructive upon elevated objects. Consequently, "all the proud and lofty" and the self-exalted will be humbled.

> **13for all the cedars of Lebanon, tall and lofty, and all the oaks of Bashan, 14for all the towering mountains and all the high hills, 15for every lofty tower and every fortified wall,**

The proud are compared to the cedars of Lebanon. These cedars, unlike the common cedars of North America, are true cedars and were highly regarded as symbols of power and majesty (Ezek. 31:3–9). "The oaks of Bashan" (on the fertile plains northeast of the Sea of Galilee) were the finest oaks, providing wonderful shade, but were often connected with idolatry, especially the idolatry of the rulers.

The mountains and hills west of the Jordan and the towers and fortified walls of the cities refer to the defenses that the people pointed to in pride and trusted as safeguards. They thought they were secure, but God would use invaders to attack them and bring His judgment.

> **16for every trading ship and every stately vessel.**

God would bring judgment also on great merchant ships which were outfitted for long voyages and could go as far as Tarshish (probably Tartessus in Spain at the mouth of the Guadalquivir River[7]). These were like the ships that were the pride of Solomon (1 Kings 9:26; 10:22) and of the Phoenicians. Luxurious, stately pleasure ships would come under God's judgment too.

> **17The arrogance of man will be brought low and the pride of men humbled; the LORD alone will be exalted in that day, 18and the idols will totally disappear.**

Isaiah concludes this section by essentially repeating verse 11. Human pride will be humbled. In verse 18, the singular verb *(halaph)* with the plural "idols" indicates not one idol will remain. The same verb is used in Isaiah 9:10 to mean "replace"

---

[7]Charles F. Pfeiffer, Howard F. Vos, and John Rea, eds., *Wycliffe Bible Encyclopedia*, 2 vols. (Chicago: Moody Press, 1975), 2:1662.

or "supplant." In other words, the Lord alone will be exalted in that day and will wholly supplant the idols.

c. Earth-shaking Judgment 2:19–21

> ¹⁹Men will flee to caves in the rocks and to holes in the ground from dread of the Lord and the splendor of his majesty, when he rises to shake the earth.

The glory and majesty of the LORD will fill idol worshipers with dread and cause them to "flee to caves in the rocks and to holes in the ground" when He "rises" (goes into action) on the Day of Judgment, a day when He will "shake the earth." Their dread of the LORD includes a trembling. They as well as the earth will be shaking.

> ²⁰In that day men will throw away to the rodents and bats their idols of silver and idols of gold, which they made to worship.

Verse 20 develops the thought of verse 18. The awesome glory and majesty of the LORD will cause idol worshipers to throw their idols away in fear before Yahweh to "rodents and bats," that is, to darkness and oblivion. They had given their silver and gold to make their idols they thought would protect them. But their idols will not be able to do anything to stop the terror inspired by God's glory. All that gold and silver will be recognized as lifeless and without value.

> ²¹They will flee to caverns in the rocks and to the overhanging crags from dread of the Lord and the splendor of his majesty, when he rises to shake the earth.

This is parallel to verse 19 and reemphasizes how the terror of the LORD strikes fear into the people (cf. Hos. 10:8, "Then they will say to the mountains, 'Cover us!' and to the hills, 'Fall on us!'"). But losing their trust in idols will not make them trust in the LORD. It will be too late.

d. Foolish Trust 2:22

> ²²Stop trusting in man, who has but a breath in his nostrils. Of what account is he?

Their trust in idols was really a trust in human ability. But human beings, no matter how powerful, are dependent on God for life and breath. They cannot stop God's judgment. Accordingly, the command is to stop depending on human beings and human resources, encouraging a trust in the Lord instead.

3. Judah's Evil Judged 3:1–4:1

In 3:1–15 Isaiah deals with God's judgment on the people of Judah and their rulers. It will bring deportation, chaos, and disaster. Actually, the people bring ruin on themselves, and their sins testify against them. They are guilty, and God's judgment is just.

a. Judah and Jerusalem Judged 3:1–3

¹See now, the Lord, the Lord Almighty, is about to take from Jerusalem and Judah both supply and support: all supplies of food and all supplies of water, ²the hero and warrior, the judge and prophet, the soothsayer and elder, ³the captain of fifty and man of rank, the counselor, skilled craftsman and clever enchanter.

The double title, "the Lord, the Lord Almighty" (Heb. *ha'adon Yahweh tseva'oth*, "the Lord Yahweh of Armies," probably meaning "of the armies of angels") emphasizes the Lord's authority. The Hebrew form of the verb "take" indicates a near and certain fulfillment. God will remove all forms of support (indicated by the masculine and feminine forms of the same Heb. word). That support includes the necessities of food and water. A siege that will last until "all supplies of food and all supplies of water" are gone is implied.

The people have been depending on the support of powerful heroes, mighty warriors. But God will take them away either by death or into captivity by the enemy. He will also take away the officers and enlisted men of the army; judges who decided legal disputes; prophets who were the advisors of the king (but who were disobedient to God and more concerned about public opinion); superstitious soothsayers who were supposed to communicate with the spirit world;[8] wise elders who were advisers to the

---

[8] King Saul had driven most of them out (1 Sam. 28:3), but they were again common.

king; captains of fifty who were lesser officials; men of rank who were haughty, despotic, powerful, and wealthy; expert craftsmen or artisans who produced war materials; and clever enchanters who whispered formulas or magic charms. All these who were considered the backbone of the country will be taken away. Their support will be ineffective and they themselves will be lost.

Second Kings 24:14 tells how Nebuchadnezzar deported all the officers and fighting men as well as all the craftsmen and artisans. We can be sure Sennacherib also included them among the 200,150 captives he claims he deported in 701 B.C. in Isaiah's day.[9]

b. Resulting Chaos And Anarchy 3:4–7

4I will make boys their officials; mere children will govern them.

Because of the moral and spiritual bankruptcy of the people as a whole, God would remove all those with leadership abilities (age, experience, or social status). The leadership, in effect, would be left to boys and children. This probably does not refer to actual children but to adults without experience and understanding, without a sense of responsibility, and without real authority for leadership. These individuals might be careless, capricious, or even ruthless. They might be hoodlums.

5People will oppress each other—man against man, neighbor against neighbor. The young will rise up against the old, the base against the honorable.

The deportation of the leaders and skilled workers will result in a breakdown of society—violence, chaos, and anarchy. People will try to take advantage of each other. Instead of neighborly helpfulness and mutual appreciation, there will be mutual opposition: "man against man, neighbor against neighbor." Instead of respect for the age or the dignity of honorable people, the young will take advantage of the old, and contemptible people will refuse to honor anyone.

---

[9]Daniel David Luckenbill, *The Annals of Sennacherib* (Chicago: University of Chicago Press, 1924), 33.

> ⁶A man will seize one of his brothers at his father's home, and say, "You have a cloak, you be our leader; take charge of this heap of ruins!"

Some people will be sincerely concerned about the chaotic situation. They will make frantic but unsuccessful efforts to restore order in the midst of the chaos. Because they are hungry and poorly clothed, they will seize any man who has good clothes and seems to have some self-respect to try to make him a ruler over the ruined cities of Judah.

> ⁷But in that day he will cry out, "I have no remedy. I have no food or clothing in my house; do not make me the leader of the people."

The man seized will immediately cry out that he has no ability or resources to bind up the wounds of the nation. He has "no food or clothing" in his house. In other words, what he is wearing is all he has. Ordinarily people seek positions of leadership as an honor. But in this pitiful situation, he will refuse to get involved. He knows any attempt at leadership will be fruitless.

c. Well-deserved Judgment 3:8–9

> ⁸Jerusalem staggers, Judah is falling; their words and deeds are against the Lord, defying his glorious presence.

The siege will end in defeat for Israel. Now Isaiah describes the causes of the coming disaster. He uses verb forms of completed action (the Heb. perfect tense), for he presents the future as certain, as sure as if it had already happened. "Jerusalem staggers" and nearly falls. Judah does fall. This actually took place during Sennacherib's invasion in 701 B.C.

Then Isaiah describes the cause of the disaster. It will not come by mere chance. By both "words and deeds" they have rebelled against the Lord. They have defied the "presence" (lit., "the eyes") of the Lord's glory. He sees their rebellion and is hurt by it.

> ⁹The look on their faces testifies against them; they parade their sin like Sodom; they do not hide it. Woe to them! They have brought disaster upon themselves.

These guilty Israelites deserve to hear the Hebrew term *'oy*, "Woe" or "Alas"—a term unique to the prophets and often used to introduce a judgment passage. Jesus also used this prophetic terminology (Matt. 23). The term sets the context for the entire passage. The people no longer have any shame; "they parade their sin." The impudent look on their faces shows their attitude toward God. In fact, they flaunt their sin as the people of Sodom did, and all the people round about see their attitude as well as their degenerate state. Thus God pronounces a woe upon them. They are about to suffer the consequences of their sins, and the "disaster" they have brought "upon themselves" will damage them, not God.

d. The Choice Between Blessings And Disaster 3:10–11

> **10 Tell the righteous it will be well with them, for they will enjoy the fruit of their deeds.**

In the midst of these judgments, God assures "the righteous" (godly people whose conduct and character please Him) that it will be well with them. Here the term "well" is in the emphatic position in the Hebrew. They deserve and will enjoy blessings because of their righteous deeds.

> **11 Woe to the wicked! Disaster is upon them! They will be paid back for what their hands have done.**

In contrast to the reward of the righteous, "disaster," or ruin, will come to the wicked (especially to the corrupt leadership), who are guilty of injustice and wrongdoing. God loves His people, but there is a fundamental law of retribution that the New Testament also recognizes: "Do not be deceived: God cannot be mocked. A man reaps what he sows. The one who sows to please his sinful nature, from that nature will reap destruction; the one who sows to please the Spirit, from the Spirit will reap eternal life" (Gal. 6:7–8).

e. A Sorrowful Lament 3:12

> **12 Youths oppress my people, women rule over them. O my people, your guides lead you astray; they turn you from the path.**

God's heart is broken by our sin (as the Book of Hosea so clearly shows). In the midst of Israel's situation that was leading to disaster, God still recognizes the people as His people. There is a sense of grief as He recognizes that young, inexperienced leaders oppress them like the taskmasters who were slave drivers. Women ruling may refer to women as the power behind the weak rulers. These weak rulers do not warn the people of danger and even encourage them in their rebellion against God and in their idolatry. The Hebrew for "they turn you from the path" can mean "they swallow up the paths of righteousness," that is, they confuse the people about what is right, trying to make it impossible for the people to follow the paths of obedience to God.

f. The LORD Passes Judgement On Leaders 3:13–14

¹³The LORD takes his place in court; he rises to judge the people.

Again Isaiah pictures a court scene. The LORD comes in as the divine Judge. He arises with holy indignation to pass judgment after the people's own sins have witnessed against them. "People" is plural in the Hebrew; however, the context indicates that it is God's people who are in view, possibly the people of both northern Israel and Judah. Nevertheless, there can be an application to all the peoples of the world.

¹⁴The LORD enters into judgment against the elders and leaders of his people: "It is you who have ruined my vineyard; the plunder from the poor is in your houses. ¹⁵What do you mean by crushing my people and grinding the faces of the poor?" declares the Lord, the LORD Almighty.

The primary condemnation is against the rulers and tribal leaders or elders who have oppressed and treated God's people with injustice. Again and again Isaiah emphasizes the responsibilities of leadership. God expected leaders to act justly and teach righteousness. When they failed, they deserved special judgment.

The nation is God's vineyard that He planted (cf. Isa. 5:7; Jer. 12:10; Hos. 10:1), but the leaders have not tended or guarded it. Instead, they have "ruined" it, enriching themselves. They have ruthlessly oppressed the poor (including those without social status or worldly distinction), disregarding their rights, "crushing" them, "grinding" their faces (in the dirt). God confronts them with their guilt.

g. Proud Women Of Zion Judged 3:16–24

> **16**The LORD says, "The women of Zion are haughty, walking along with outstretched necks, flirting with their eyes, tripping along with mincing steps, with ornaments jingling on their ankles.

In a way somewhat parallel to the preceding section, the LORD now addresses the women. God is not overemphasizing the guilt of the women. Only half a chapter out of the sixty-six in this book deals expressly with them. The men showed by their conduct that they were the primary causes of the disaster, but they were not alone. Frivolous, luxury-loving women helped to bring it on (cf. Amos 4:1–3).

When the women of the nation are self-centered, the nation is headed toward destruction. The women contributed to the disaster by their arrogant spirit, haughty attitudes, lustful desires, and flirting gestures. They walked with unnaturally short steps because of ankle chains worn in a prescribed fashion, making the ornaments "on their ankles" jingle. Their whole demeanor and dress served only to draw attention to themselves.

> **17**Therefore the Lord will bring sores on the heads of the women of Zion; the LORD will make their scalps bald."

Because of their pride, God will strike "the heads of the women" with scabby sores, like those of leprosy. Uncleanness will cause disease, which in turn will cause the baldness that will bring their ostracism. Their shame will become obvious to all, and the ruin of the nation will humiliate the proud, wealthy women.

> **18**In that day the Lord will snatch away their finery: the bangles and headbands and crescent necklaces, **19**the earrings and bracelets and veils, **20**the headdresses and ankle chains and

> sashes, the perfume bottles and charms, ²¹the signet rings and nose rings, ²²the fine robes and the capes and cloaks, the purses ²³and mirrors, and the linen garments and tiaras and shawls.

"That day" is a preliminary day of the LORD brought about by Assyrian invasions. The LORD's judgment will be the real cause of the women losing all of their finery—literally from head to toe.

> ²⁴Instead of fragrance there will be a stench; instead of a sash, a rope; instead of well-dressed hair, baldness; instead of fine clothing, sackcloth; instead of beauty, branding.

Not only will the beauty and finery be taken away; instead of the fragrance of perfumes, there will be a rotten stench, probably from pus in open sores and ulcers. Instead of rich, ornamented sashes, they will have a rope around them, like the poorest slave. Instead of beauty, they will be disfigured by burning, branded as slaves. (The Dead Sea Scrolls read "shame" instead of "branding.") It is a picture of women being taken into captivity by the conquering Assyrians in 701 B.C. Most of the people who heard Isaiah give these warnings lived to share in the judgment.

h. Judah's Devastation 3:25–26

> ²⁵Your men will fall by the sword, your warriors in battle.

Now the prophet addresses Judah. The men are victims of war. There are none left to defend the nation or protect the women. 4:1 shows how this affects the women.

> ²⁶The gates of Zion will lament and mourn; destitute, she will sit on the ground.

The gates of Jerusalem are depicted as being in mourning because the crowds that usually gathered there for public meetings and for business are all gone. To "sit on the ground" is an act of mourning the desolate, helpless situation caused by the devastation.

i. A Result Of Judgment 4:1

> ¹In that day seven women will take hold of one man and say, "We will eat our own food and

provide our own clothes; only let us be called by your name. Take away our disgrace!"

As a result of the judgment prophesied in 3:25–26 so few men will be left after the Assyrian assault that most young women will be unprotected and unable to get a husband. As a result, "seven women" will beg "one man" to marry them.[10] Though the law required a husband to provide food and clothing for his wife (Exod. 21:10–11), these women will provide their own—if only the man will let them "be called" by his name, that is, marry them and give them his protection. Hebrew women felt a deep disgrace if they were unmarried or childless.

4. THE BRANCH AND THE BRIDAL CANOPY 4:2–6

In Isaiah, judgment is not the end of God's plan. The rest of this chapter jumps ahead to the new, restored Zion, a Zion purified by suffering. This renewed Zion will be made prosperous and holy, with the LORD dwelling among His people and protecting them. He is a gracious and faithful God.

a. A Day Of Peace And Restoration 4:2–4

²In that day the Branch of the Lord will be beautiful and glorious, and the fruit of the land will be the pride and glory of the survivors in Israel.

The "Branch" (Heb. *tsemach,* "Shoot," "Sprout") of the LORD is a term that later prophets used to refer to the Messiah (Jer. 23:5–6; 33:15–16; Zech. 3:8; 6:12). Scholars have differing opinions here. Some contend it is a collective term for everything the LORD makes grow in marvelous fertility. Others apply it to the restored, spiritually regenerated nation of Israel or the purified remnant.[11] Still others say it is the Messiah and that He will be a fruit-bearing Branch. Certainly nothing here excludes its being applied to the Messiah. It cannot apply to the rem-

---

[10]It is also possible that these are "widows who needed a security and protection. In ancient times the fate of widows was tragic." And it is possible that they were asking to be adopted rather than be taken as wives. Widyapranawa, *Lord is Savior,* 19.

[11]Ibid.

nant, however, for they are the survivors who are distinguished from the Branch here. The Branch will bear fruit that the survivors will enjoy. The fruit will be their "pride and glory."

> ³Those who are left in Zion, who remain in Jerusalem, will be called holy, all who are recorded among the living in Jerusalem.

The remnant will be holy. The remnant referred to here are not the ones left behind after Sennacherib's invasion or after the later Babylonian destruction, but those who are left after the future Day of Judgment. These will be recorded as true citizens of the holy Jerusalem.[12] (See 2:2–3.)

> ⁴The Lord will wash away the filth of the women of Zion; he will cleanse the bloodstains from Jerusalem by a spirit of judgment and a spirit of fire.

The Lord (Heb. *'adonai*) will purge the "women of Zion" from the filth of their sin. "He will cleanse the bloodstains" caused by violence and crimes. A blast of God's righteous judgment will fan the flames of His cleansing fire. God's judgment will restore purity and His Spirit will bring sanctification. Jerusalem will once again be a place where the people will enjoy fellowship with God.

b. A Bridal Canopy 4:5–6

> ⁵Then the LORD will create over all of Mount Zion and over those who assemble there a cloud of smoke by day and a glow of flaming fire by night; over all the glory will be a canopy.

During the Exodus from Egypt, God manifested His glory and presence in a pillar of cloud by day and a pillar of fire by night. The godly remnant is promised a restoration to that original closeness of God's presence. However, there is a difference.

During the Exodus, the cloud rested only over the ark. Now the glory is over the whole of Zion and its people, who assemble for worship there. The whole city is a sanctuary, newly cre-

---

[12]The Book of Life may be implied (cf. Exod. 32:33; Ps. 69:28; Dan. 12:1; Rev. 20:12).

ated by God.¹³ Over it all, God's glory rests like the canopy over a king's throne. "Canopy" might also be compared to that of a marriage ceremony, with God and His people rejoined in love. (See Ps. 19:5; Joel 2:16, translated "chamber" instead of "canopy.") This is God's unconditional promise.

> ⁶It will be a shelter and shade from the heat of the day, and a refuge and hiding place from the storm and rain.

The canopy of glory "will be a shelter and shade from the heat" of a hot, midsummer day. It will be "a refuge and hiding place" from the storm elements, human enemies, the powers of evil, and all the vicissitudes of life. We can have a foretaste of this now through Jesus, our Immanuel ("God with us"), who gives us the Holy Spirit to be with us always.

STUDY QUESTIONS

1. What did Isaiah expect the conversion of Gentiles to encourage Israel to do?
2. What judgment must those who engage in false worship expect?
3. How does the Day of the LORD fit in with the Bible's linear view of history?
4. What will the judgments of the Day of the LORD cause idol worshipers to do?
5. What were the people depending on in Isaiah's day?
6. What would be the result of the deportation of leaders and skilled workers?
7. In what ways does this chapter contrast the reward of the righteous with the judgment of the wicked?
8. Why would God's judgment come on the women?
9. Why would seven women beg one man to marry them?
10. Who is the Branch of the LORD?
11. What does God promise the holy remnant in Jerusalem?

---

¹³"Create" (Heb. *bara'*) always has God as its subject. He alone can create new life.

C. The Vineyard And Its Fruit 5:1–30

1. THE SONG OF THE VINEYARD 5:1–7

   a. A Love Song 5:1–2

¹I will sing for the one I love a song about his vineyard: My loved one had a vineyard on a fertile hillside.

Why does God bring judgment on His chosen people? Isaiah answers by giving us "the song of the vineyard" and its lessons. The song (vv. 1–7) is a parable (or allegory) in which the prophet acts as a singer who sings about "the one" he loves and his loved one's vineyard. The use of the vineyard as a symbol would have gotten the attention of the people of Israel, for fertile vineyards were a joy to them. Eventually the singer gives voice to his loved one, who tells of his disappointment in his vineyard (cf. Matt. 21:33–44). After the song, the prophet explains the symbols and applies them to the relationship between the Lord and His people.

The Hebrew literally says the vineyard is planted in "a horn of a son of oil," that is, on a hillside that has rich soil, a favorable situation, and a sunny aspect. Israelites considered such vineyards very valuable.

²He dug it up and cleared it of stones and planted it with the choicest vines. He built a watchtower in it and cut out a winepress as well. Then he looked for a crop of good grapes, but it yielded only bad fruit.

The loved one did everything possible to insure an excellent crop. Limestone is prevalent in Israel, and the soil is full of stones, so turning over the soil also calls for clearing away stones.[1] He planted "the choicest vines,"[2] a superior variety that normally produces luscious, sweet red grapes.[3] A strong stone

---

[1] Archaeologists have found that the stones were used to build retaining walls supporting flat terraces the vines were planted on. See Carey Ellen Walsh, "God's Vineyard," *Bible Review* 14, no. 4 (August 1988): 45.

[2] The vine is Heb. *soreq*, "rare, choice vine." The term is used only here and in Gen. 49:11 and Jer. 2:21.

[3] Assyrian wall reliefs from Sennacherib's palace in Nineveh depict the capture of Lachish and show freestanding vines low to the ground.

tower was built for a watchman to guard the vineyard and to provide "a shady, cool place to rest."[4] A winepress was ready—two troughs hewed out of the bedrock. The larger, upper one was for trampling the grapes, the lower one was for receiving the juice. The owner of the vineyard did all this preparation with loving devotion and had great expectations. But instead of the good grapes he had a right to expect, the vines bore "only bad fruit" (small putrid grapes). Isaiah's agrarian hearers must have felt the owner's disappointment.

b. Judgment For Putrid Grapes 5:3–6

3"Now you dwellers in Jerusalem and men of Judah, judge between me and my vineyard.

Now the loved one, the owner of the vineyard, calls on the people of Judah and Jerusalem to decide what should be done with his vineyard.

4What more could have been done for my vineyard than I have done for it? When I looked for good grapes, why did it yield only bad?

Without waiting for an answer, the owner of the vineyard asks further rhetorical questions which make it obvious that nothing more could have been done. The owner of the vineyard could not be blamed in any way. His loving preparation and care was complete and unconditional. The implication is that the fault must be in the vineyard itself. Just as no one could accuse Jesus of sin (John 8:46), so no one could accuse the loved one who planted and cared for the vineyard.

5Now I will tell you what I am going to do to my vineyard: I will take away its hedge, and it will be destroyed; I will break down its wall, and it will be trampled.

The owner now pronounces judgment on the vineyard. There is nothing left to do but to destroy it since it failed to produce the good harvest it should have. The owner declares he "will take away its hedge" and "break down its wall,"[5] thus

---

[4]Walsh, "God's Vineyard," 49. She notes also that the tower showed the prestige of the owner. Most vineyards had a *sukkah* ("shelter, temporary hut") as in Isa. 1:8.

[5]Or, "wall" may refer to the retaining walls supporting the terraces. Ibid., 47.

removing protection and allowing intruders to come in and trample it down. Isaiah's hearers would have to admit that the owner's decision is only just.

> ⁶I will make it a wasteland, neither pruned nor cultivated, and briers and thorns will grow there. I will command the clouds not to rain on it."

The owner "will make it a wasteland," no longer pruned, cultivated, or cared for in any way. "Briers and thorns" will choke out the vines and make it an unpleasant place.

That the owner "will command the clouds not to rain on it" makes clear the meaning of the parable. Only God can do that. He is the loved one who planted the vineyard.

c. The Vineyard Explained 5:7

> ⁷The vineyard of the LORD Almighty is the house of Israel, and the men of Judah are the garden of his delight. And he looked for justice, but saw bloodshed; for righteousness, but heard cries of distress.

Now Isaiah explains the parable. The loved one is the Almighty LORD himself. The people of Judah and Jerusalem are His choice vines. He looked for the fruit of justice and righteousness but instead found the putrid fruit of injustice (the law violated by the judges) and a wailing cry for help from the oppressed. The wordplay in the Hebrew is striking: He looked for *mishpat* (justice) and saw *mispach* (lawbreaking); for *tsedaqah* (righteousness) and saw *tse'aqah* (a cry for help).

2. SIX WOES 5:8–25

> ⁸Woe to you who add house to house and join field to field till no space is left and you live alone in the land.

The judgment of verse 2 is shown to be just by the following list of six woes on six forms of rotten, stinking "fruit." The first woe is against land-grabbers who enrich themselves by disregarding the sacred right of land inheritance (cf. Lev. 25:13–34; Mic. 2:2). There is no room left for people of ordinary means to own a house and land. The rich have reduced them to hired servants or sharecroppers. The rich minority own the whole land, God's land—given as an inheritance to all of His people. These land-grabbers made property ownership their god.

> **⁹The Lord Almighty has declared in my hearing:
> "Surely the great houses will become desolate,
> the fine mansions left without occupants.**

The Lord has heard the cry of the poor, dispossessed people and gives a sure word to Isaiah: The mansions of the rich will become "desolate" and empty, for the rich will be forced to leave them because of their sins (cf. Amos 3:15).

> **¹⁰A ten-acre vineyard will produce only a bath of
> wine, a homer of seed only an ephah of grain."**

Just how bad the desolation will be is seen in this verse. "A ten-acre vineyard" is literally a great field that takes ten yoke of oxen to plow in a day. But it will produce "only a bath" (about five and one-half U.S. gallons, or twenty-four liters) of wine (rather, grape juice).

Sowing 220 liters of seed will produce a crop of less than 22 liters of grain. In other words, their crop would amount to only a meager 10 percent of what they sowed. The land-grabbers will end up devastated and hungry. God will judge their greed.

> **¹¹Woe to those who rise early in the morning
> to run after their drinks, who stay up late at
> night till they are inflamed with wine.**

A love of pleasure that involves intemperance and drunken reveling brings the second woe. That they have become alcoholics is shown by their need for "drinks" (Heb. *shekhar*, probably beer) in the early morning. They continue partying and reveling through the day and into the night until they are "inflamed"—totally drunk—with wine.

> **¹²They have harps and lyres at their banquets,
> tambourines and flutes and wine, but they
> have no regard for the deeds of the Lord, no
> respect for the work of his hands.**

They live for the music and wine of their banquets and par-

84 / Isaiah 5:13-15

ties. Thus, they have "no regard" or time for the LORD, His deeds, or His work. They are blind to His acts, His sovereignty, and to the course of events that will bring His work of judgment. They have made pleasure and entertainment their gods.

> ¹³Therefore my people will go into exile for lack of understanding; their men of rank will die of hunger and their masses will be parched with thirst.

Because their leaders have not instructed them in God's law and have not warned them against breaking it, the people lack understanding and "will go into exile." The judgment will fall on both the rulers and the masses of the common people. In contrast to the feasting and partying, the wealthy rulers "will die of hunger" and the common people will die of thirst. As Isaiah 10:5–6 prophesies, God would soon use Assyria to bring this judgment.

> ¹⁴Therefore the grave enlarges its appetite and opens its mouth without limit; into it will descend their nobles and masses with all their brawlers and revelers.

Sh^e'ol,[6] the abode of the wicked dead, which corresponds to the Greek *Hadēs* and the English "hell," is pictured as an insatiable monster ready to swallow up the people who are guilty of sins against God. They spent their time feasting; now Sheol waits to feast on them. The masses who followed their false leaders will descend with them into Sheol, along "with all their brawlers and revelers."

> ¹⁵So man will be brought low and mankind humbled, the eyes of the arrogant humbled.

So all classes of people will be "brought low . . . humbled" (cf. 2:9,17). "The eyes of the arrogant" oppressors—the covetous, unscrupulous people—are singled out for humiliation.

---

[6] Dr. R. Laird Harris of Covenant Seminary told me that the translation of *Sh^e'ol* in the NIV as "the grave" is due to his interpretation. However, examination of such passages as Job 26:6; Pss. 30:3; 49:13–15; 55:15; 88:11–12; Prov. 5:5; 7:27; 9:18; 15:10–11; 27:20; Isa. 38:18 shows it means "hell." In the New Testament it is translated as *Hadēs*, which is always a place of punishment. See Stanley M. Horton, *Our Destiny: Biblical Teachings on the Last Things* (Springfield, Mo.: Logion Press, 1996), 44–51. See also J. Alec Motyer, *The Prophecy of Isaiah* (Downers Grove, Ill.: InterVarsity Press, 1993), 144–45.

> ¹⁶But the Lord Almighty will be exalted by his justice, and the holy God will show himself holy by his righteousness.

The wealthy and the rulers violated the principles of justice and righteousness. But God "will be exalted by his justice" that He upholds when He judges the guilty. He is holy and "will show himself holy" by demonstrating His righteousness. Isaiah later shows that God's righteousness will restore people through His divine grace.

> ¹⁷Then sheep will graze as in their own pasture; lambs will feed among the ruins of the rich.

Those great estates and rich fields seized by the rich will become pasture lands. No one will be there to cultivate them. Lambs (or goats) will roam over the ruins of what the rich once enjoyed.

> ¹⁸Woe to those who draw sin along with cords of deceit, and wickedness as with cart ropes,

Obstinate sinners whose open unbelief defies the Lord bring the third woe. Their loads of sin and wickedness are so heavy that the deceitful cords they use to draw their load are too small, so they have to use "cart ropes."

It is also clear that they are bound to their sin and guilt. The cords that bound them at first have now become unbreakable ropes. Sin enslaves those who yield to it.

> ¹⁹to those who say, "Let God hurry, let him hasten his work so we may see it. Let it approach, let the plan of the Holy One of Israel come, so we may know it."

They mockingly refer to Isaiah's warnings of the coming day of God's judgment. In a sense, they dare God to make good His warnings of future punishment. They are indifferent to Isaiah's prophecies, thinking that because nothing has happened yet, nothing ever will. They do not understand God's timing (cf. 2 Pet. 3:9–10). They despise God because they do not know Him.

> ²⁰Woe to those who call evil good and good evil, who put darkness for light and light for darkness, who put bitter for sweet and sweet for bitter.

86 / Isaiah 5:21-23

Reversing moral distinctions brings the fourth woe. The people and their teachers have become so depraved they consider sin to be normal, and good to be evil. The whole attitude of most of the people had become like confusing bitter and sweet or light and darkness. "Bitter" and "sweet" may be compared to personal morality; "light" and "darkness" to public morality. Theirs is like the attitude of the world today with respect to alcohol, abortion, homosexuality, and other sexual perversions. How sad when people twist the truth! How sad when they laugh at sins that Christ died for. The pursuit of the pleasures of sin can only bring suffering and anguish.

> 21 Woe to those who are wise in their own eyes
> and clever in their own sight.

Conceited people, probably rulers and politicians, receive the fifth woe. They put self and their own wisdom on the throne and imagine they know better than God and His prophet. Isaiah often found himself in conflict with the political advisers of Judah's kings (see 28:9–15; 30:1,10–14). Self-sufficient people who depend on the reasonings of their own finite minds, reject God's will, and selfishly pursue a secular lifestyle are still headed for divine judgment.

> 22 Woe to those who are heroes at drinking
> wine and champions at mixing drinks,

Drunken, corrupt judges deserve the sixth woe. Leaders who should be heroes on the battlefield could boast only of how much wine they could hold and how they excelled at "mixing drinks" (wine with spices, aromatic herbs, and probably drugs) in order to get a greater high. Such indulgence is exalted by them.

> 23 who acquit the guilty for a bribe, but deny
> justice to the innocent.

To support their drugs and drinking, bribery has become a way of life to the judges. Their indulgence in these things makes them insensitive to anything but their own desires. So the innocent poor, who are not able to give them a bribe, cannot get justice from them. With these judges and leaders, "the love of money is a root of all kinds of evil" (1 Tim. 6:10).

> ²⁴Therefore, as tongues of fire lick up straw and as dry grass sinks down in the flames, so their roots will decay and their flowers blow away like dust; for they have rejected the law of the LORD Almighty and spurned the word of the Holy One of Israel.

As a conclusion to the list of woes, God speaks of the release of His wrath. The suddenness of the judgment is compared to straw and dry grass quickly disappearing in flames. The decay of the root and the blowing away of the flowers illustrate the completeness of the ruin. The rejection of the law and instruction of the LORD includes the spurning of His word and their rejection of the prophecies of Isaiah.

> ²⁵Therefore the LORD's anger burns against his people; his hand is raised and he strikes them down. The mountains shake, and the dead bodies are like refuse in the streets. Yet for all this, his anger is not turned away, his hand is still upraised.

As a climax to the six woes, Isaiah now draws a lesson from the past, probably from the great earthquake in the time of Uzziah (Amos 1:1). This was a major disaster, remembered even in the time of Zechariah (Zech. 14:5). It killed so many in such a few minutes that bodies lay in the streets for some time.

Despite the size of that disaster, it was nothing compared to the results of their continued sin. God's anger was not appeased. His hand in Isaiah's day was "still upraised" against Judah for further disaster—that is, to bring the Assyrian invasion described in the following verses.

3. NATIONS UNDER GOD'S CONTROL BRING JUDGMENT 5:26–30

> ²⁶He lifts up a banner for the distant nations, he whistles for those at the ends of the earth. Here they come, swiftly and speedily!

God is about to execute His judgment. The "banner," or flag, the LORD lifts high is a signal for warriors of a distant nation to attack. God has appointed them as agents of His wrath. He will whistle to summon them and they will come swiftly. Assyria and her allies are these foreign warriors. They come from a land that to the Israelites was "at the ends of the earth."

> **27Not one of them grows tired or stumbles, not one slumbers or sleeps; not a belt is loosened at the waist, not a sandal thong is broken.**

The reason the enemy will come so speedily is that they are well-prepared. The warriors are fit, alert, and ready to march. The long march will not wear them out and they will be ready for battle, not sleep, when they reach their objective. Their loose outer garments are belted in preparation for fighting. Their sandals are new—not even a broken sandal strap will impede them. What a contrast to the unprepared, careless, carousing disposition of Judah and its leaders!

> **28Their arrows are sharp, all their bows are strung; their horses' hoofs seem like flint, their chariot wheels like a whirlwind.**

The enemy's equipment is in top shape: arrows sharpened, bows strung (Heb. *d^erukhoth*, "bent") for battle, horses' hooves hard and sound (metal horseshoes were not used in ancient times), multitudes of chariot wheels whirring—making a sound like that of a hurricane or tornado.

> **29Their roar is like that of the lion, they roar like young lions; they growl as they seize their prey and carry it off with no one to rescue.**

The approaching Assyrian armies will be irresistible. The uproar and battle cries of their approach will be like the roaring of a lion. Also, like a lion, they will pounce on their prey and "carry it off." Because of the numbers and equipment of the enemy, Judah will not be able to resist. Once the enemy comes, any human aid they trust in will be nowhere to be found. Hezekiah did look to Egypt for help and hired mercenary soldiers to help defend Judah, but Egypt was defeated and the hired soldiers all fled.[7] The Assyrians then carried off many of the people of Judah into captivity.

---

[7]Daniel David Luckenbill, *Ancient Records of Assyria and Babylonia*, 2 vols. (Chicago: University of Chicago Press, 1926–27), 2:121.

³⁰In that day they will roar over it like the roaring of the sea. And if one looks at the land, he will see darkness and distress; even the light will be darkened by the clouds.

Now, as God is using the Assyrians, another roar, "like the roaring of the sea," will be heard over the land—like a great, unstoppable tidal wave. This time the people of Judah will experience the chaos of being in this hopeless situation. The figures of clouds and darkness show their distress. They will be like a ship in a storm that has lost its bearings and looks for some sign of land or a ray of light and sees none. We must remember, however, that God's purpose for Israel was still redemptive.[8]

STUDY QUESTIONS

1. In what ways was Israel like a vineyard?
2. How do the six woes describe and judge Israel's putrid fruit?
3. What kind of army will God summon to bring judgment on His people?

II. THE HOLY ONE EXALTED 6:1–12:6

A. Isaiah Called To A Difficult Ministry 6:1–13

After giving such a warning, Isaiah goes back to his inaugural vision and call to give his authority for declaring such a dark destiny. First he gives the time and place of the vision and its effect on him, then his commission, and finally the future results of his prophecy.

---

[8]David L. McKenna, *Isaiah 1–39*, in *The Communicator's Commentary* (Dallas: Word Books, 1993), 103.

1. Isaiah's Vision Of God 6:1–4

¹In the year that King Uzziah died, I saw the Lord seated on a throne, high and exalted, and the train of his robe filled the temple.

Some have suggested that Isaiah prophesied before this vision and that it was a confirmation of the call he had previously received. However, the Book of Isaiah is not strictly chronological, and there is no evidence that he prophesied before this time. McKenna suggests that "he summarized his prophecies and stated his themes in the first five chapters to *show the priority of the message over the messenger*. . . . Isaiah is not a prophet on an ego trip. He mentions his name only when it is relevant to a historical happening."[1]

The vision probably came before King Uzziah died in 739 B.C. It was a critical time for both Israel and Judah. Tiglath-Pileser III had established the Neo-Assyrian Empire and was already focusing attention on the West. He would soon conquer northern Syria and make Israel submit. Uzziah, because of his presumption in going into the Holy Place of the temple, became a leper and his office was turned over to his son Jotham.

Isaiah was outside the temple, probably in its courts, when he suddenly saw beyond it. In a vision of the heavenly temple, he saw no curtain, or veil, that would cut off his view of the heavenly throne. The sight of the Lord (Heb. *'adonai*) "high and exalted" on His throne illustrated His sovereignty over all the kings, authorities, and powers in the universe. No one has seen God in His totality, for He is an infinite Spirit (John 1:18; 4:24). But God revealed himself here, possibly through the one Mediator between God and humankind—our Lord Jesus Christ. Isaiah does not describe the form on the throne because it probably defied description. The glory of the Lord being so powerful and awesome, the only thing Isaiah could and did describe were the folds of the great flowing robe covering the floor of the temple.

²Above him were seraphs, each with six wings: With two wings they covered their faces, with

---

[1] David L. McKenna, *Isaiah 1–39*, in *The Communicator's Commentary* (Dallas: Word Books, 1993), 107, McKenna's emphasis.

two they covered their feet, and with two they were flying.

Above the Lord,[2] seraphs were flying. The name *seraph*, meaning "burning one," may indicate the purity of such a being. They reflected the dazzling brilliance of the glory of God to such a high degree that they seemed to be on fire. They are not called angels, and Isaiah saw their faces, hands, and feet. Yet they also had wings: two continually covering the face to indicate their unworthiness to look on God or pry into His divine secrets, two covering the feet and lower part of the body to indicate humility and reverence, and two ready for instant and continual flight to do the will of the Lord.

> [3]And they were calling to one another: "Holy, holy, holy is the LORD Almighty; the whole earth is full of his glory."

We are not told how many seraphs there were, but there must have been several. They kept calling back and forth to each other, "Holy, holy, holy is the LORD Almighty [of hosts, or armies]." The threefold repetition of "holy" gives supreme emphasis to holiness as the central and most essential characteristic of the LORD. "Holy" has the basic meaning of being separated. He is separated from sin and evil. He is transcendent over His universe and separate from it. (This leaves no room for the concept of pantheism.) But He has also separated himself in a positive way—to carry out His divine plan and purpose of redeeming and restoring that will ultimately lead to a new heaven and a new earth. The seraphs proclaim that now His glory, including the manifestation of His power and His holy nature, fills the whole earth. It is also possible that the threefold "holy" reflects the Trinity.[3] The seraphs surely would have known and understood there is a Trinity. John 12:41 speaks of Isaiah's seeing the glory of Jesus. Certainly the Trinity was present in Isaiah's vision, though the concept was never fully revealed in the Old Testament.

---

[2]The Septuagint has *kuklōi autou*, "around him," possibly because the translators wanted to say that God was Lord over the seraphs.

[3]Herbert M. Wolf, *Interpreting Isaiah* (Grand Rapids: Zondervan Publishing House, Academie Books, 1985), 86.

> ⁴At the sound of their voices the doorposts and thresholds shook and the temple was filled with smoke.

As he listened to the seraphs, Isaiah saw the doorposts and thresholds of the temple shake. A fire on the altar began to burn at this point, indicating a sacrifice, and its smoke filled the temple. Smoke may also symbolize the wrath of God kindled against the people Isaiah must prophesy to. In any case, it probably veiled the One on the throne from Isaiah's sight.

2. Isaiah's Confession And Cleansing 6:5–7

> ⁵"Woe to me!" I cried. "I am ruined! For I am a man of unclean lips, and I live among a people of unclean lips, and my eyes have seen the King, the Lord Almighty."

Isaiah was a young aristocrat who, some believe, was probably a little self-righteous, looking down on King Uzziah for his sins. Though unlike the king, yet in God's holy presence, Isaiah suddenly realized he too was a sinner. His "'unclean lips'" attest to an unclean heart and mind and is analogous to having "'unclean hands'" (cf. Ps. 24:4). As Jesus said, "'The things that come out of the mouth come from the heart, and these make a man "unclean"'" (Matt. 15:18). His unholy lips could not utter a prayer for mercy. He was no different from the people around him, for they were all "people of unclean lips," all unworthy to come into the presence of the holy Lord, (the true King).

The people thought it was impossible to see God and live, so Isaiah must have been filled with fear. Surely he never forgot this vision of God's holiness, splendor, and glory. Isaiah's repetition throughout the book of God's name as "the Holy One of Israel" indicates he was always conscious of God's holiness.

> ⁶Then one of the seraphs flew to me with a live coal in his hand, which he had taken with tongs from the altar. ⁷With it he touched my mouth and said, "See, this has touched your lips; your guilt is taken away and your sin atoned for."

The live coal taken by a seraph from the altar was indeed hot, for the seraph took it "with tongs." Yet when it touched Isaiah's lips at the point of his confessed sin,[4] it did not burn but cleansed, for atonement had been made for his sins—they were taken away along with his guilt. He now stood before the LORD as though he had never sinned. He received the full salvation that only God can give, the salvation that is ours through Christ's sacrifice on Calvary. God could give it to him because Christ was going to die and provide an atonement sufficient for all people of all time. But they must confess their sin and guilt as Isaiah had done (cf. Rom. 3:23; 1 John 1:7,9).

3. Isaiah Commissioned To A Difficult Ministry 6:8–10

> [8]Then I heard the voice of the Lord saying, "Whom shall I send? And who will go for us?" And I said, "Here am I. Send me!"

Now that there was nothing between him and his Lord, Isaiah heard the words, "Whom shall I send? And who will go for us?" Some take "us" as the plural of majesty. More likely, it is a reflection of the Trinity. With his sins forgiven, a passionate fire took possession of Isaiah's heart. He replied immediately, offering himself willingly without regard to the nature or difficulty of the mission.

> [9]He said, "Go and tell this people: " 'Be ever hearing, but never understanding; be ever seeing, but never perceiving.'

If Isaiah thought he was called to a grand ministry that would immediately move the nation toward God, he was going to be disappointed. "This people" is an expression that usually implies God's disfavor. His message is a series of imperatives for them to keep hearing but "never understanding," to keep seeing but "never perceiving." In other words, Isaiah must boldly and repeatedly tell the people God's messages of present judgment and future hope. But the people's spiritual and moral condition will render them unable to obey God's law, to receive His instruction, or to acknowledge His sovereign power and authority

---

[4]J. Alec Motyer, *The Prophecy of Isaiah* (Downers Grove, Ill.: InterVarsity Press, 1993), 78.

—even though they see His works which demonstrate that He alone is God.

People are still hardened by their sin (Rom. 3:23), and, as Jesus said, " 'Light has come into the world, but men loved darkness instead of light because their deeds were evil' " (John 3:19). Jesus also quoted Isaiah in order to warn His disciples of people's hardhearted resistance to the truth (e.g., Matt. 13:14–15).

> ¹⁰Make the heart of this people calloused; make their ears dull and close their eyes. Otherwise they might see with their eyes, hear with their ears, understand with their hearts, and turn and be healed."

Instead of bringing present restoration, Isaiah's message will only harden the people further in their rebellion and unbelief. Isaiah will "make the heart of this people [Israel] calloused"—even more unwilling to receive God's message, their ears too dull or deaf to hear. He will close (Heb. *hasha'*, "smear over" or "stick shut") their eyes so they cannot see the truth being presented. Instead of making them realize their hardened condition, they will be hardened further. (This does not mean God purposely hardened their hearts. But Isaiah's preaching would cause their hardened hearts to be exposed and would vindicate God's judgment as just.) Repentance could avert the coming ruin, but the people will not repent.

4. Lasting Until Only A Remnant Remains 6:11–13

> ¹¹Then I said, "For how long, O Lord?" And he answered: "Until the cities lie ruined and without inhabitant, until the houses are left deserted and the fields ruined and ravaged, ¹²until the Lord has sent everyone far away and the land is utterly forsaken.

Isaiah realized his would be a difficult and unpopular ministry. He cried out in anguish, wanting to know "how long" he would have to endure this hardening of the nation. The Lord's answer pointed to a time when destruction would spread across the land, cities would be destroyed, fields would be left desolate, and people would be taken far away. This was fulfilled when Sennacherib destroyed all the walled cities of Judah (2 Kings 18:13) and, according to his records, took 200,150 people captive.

> ¹³And though a tenth remains in the land, it will again be laid waste. But as the terebinth and oak leave stumps when they are cut down, so the holy seed will be the stump in the land."

Sennacherib's destruction would leave a few. But even if only "a tenth" of the people are left, they should expect further destruction—probably meaning the future destruction by the Babylonians under Nebuchadnezzar. The comparison of "the terebinth and oak" portrays the nation as a forest cut down with only a few stumps left. But an important stump will be left—"the holy seed," the remnant from which the new Zion will come.

Some take "the stump" to be the house of David that the Messiah will come from (cf. Isa. 11:1; 53:2). However, the meaning seems to be that though the judgment on sin and rebellion will be severe, there will be revival. Isaiah does not leave a hopeless picture. Israel was still the inheritance of the Lord and He will preserve it by His grace. A partial fulfillment came when the people of Jerusalem took a stand of faith in response to Isaiah's prophecy, and Sennacherib was kept from destroying Jerusalem. From that point on, Isaiah had a changed audience and he was able to give a new message, which appears in chapters 40 to 66. God had not changed His purpose. He would still use His covenant people in His great plan to bless all peoples on earth (see Gen. 12:3).

STUDY QUESTIONS

1. What was Isaiah's response to his vision of God and why did he so respond?
2. How did God remove Isaiah's sin?
3. What would be the results of Isaiah's message?

B. Rebukes And Promises To Judah 7:1–9:7

Isaiah gave these prophecies during a time of political turbulence during the reign of King Ahaz (744–715 B.C.). Nations were rising and falling during this period (see 2 Kings 16:1–20). But God was still in control. Human ambitions could not stand against his power and rule.

1. KING AHAZ CHALLENGED TO TRUST GOD 7:1–16

a. Aram And Ephraim Allied Against Judah 7:1–9

> ¹When Ahaz son of Jotham, the son of Uzziah, was king of Judah, King Rezin of Aram and Pekah son of Remaliah king of Israel marched up to fight against Jerusalem, but they could not overpower it.

King Ahaz "did not do what was right in the eyes of the LORD. He ... made cast idols for worshiping the Baals. He ... sacrificed his sons in the fire" (2 Chron. 28:1–3; cf. 2 Kings 16:2–4). As a result God used the Arameans (Syrians) to defeat him and take prisoners to Damascus. King Pekah of Israel also killed 120,000 soldiers in Judah and took captives to Samaria (2 Chron. 28:5–8).

Israel and Syria (Aram of Damascus) had been enemies but the threat of Tiglath-Pileser's Neo-Assyrian Empire caused them to join in an alliance against him. Egypt encouraged this alliance because it wanted a buffer state between it and Assyria. Apparently, an attempt was made to get Judah to join the alliance, but Ahaz refused. So Rezin and Pekah marched against Jerusalem intending to force Ahaz to join. This attempt failed (2 Kings 16:5), though Judah suffered considerable losses.

> ²Now the house of David was told, "Aram has allied itself with Ephraim"; so the hearts of Ahaz and his people were shaken, as the trees of the forest are shaken by the wind.

The armies of Israel, which is called "Ephraim" after its leading tribe, and Aram regrouped and set up a camp in Israel near the border of Judah about three days' march from Jerusalem. When King Ahaz heard this, he and his people were panic-stricken. They had forsaken their trust in God and had been looking only to their own resources.

The mention of "the house of David" is significant because the purpose of Pekah and Rezin was not only to make Judah join them, but to overthrow the dynasty of David, whom Ahaz was descended from. This would break the covenant God made with David (see 2 Sam. 7:4–17).

> ³Then the LORD said to Isaiah, "Go out, you and your son Shear-Jashub, to meet Ahaz at the end of the aqueduct of the Upper Pool, on the road to the Washerman's Field.

God then commanded Isaiah to meet Ahaz where he was looking over Jerusalem's water supply, making plans for its defense during the siege of Aram and Israel. The presence of Isaiah's son Shear-Jashub (Heb. *she'ar yashuv*, "a remnant will return") was actually a keynote to Isaiah's message, but it was here more of a threat than a promise.[1] Ahaz needed to know that his real danger was not from Samaria or Damascus but from Assyria. Assyria would bring about an exile from which only a remnant, by the grace of God, would return.

> ⁴Say to him, 'Be careful, keep calm and don't be afraid. Do not lose heart because of these two smoldering stubs of firewood—because of the fierce anger of Rezin and Aram and of the son of Remaliah.

The LORD's word to Ahaz was first to warn him to "be careful." Ahaz was thinking of appealing to Tiglath-Pileser III to save the city from Rezin and Pekah, something God did not approve. Ahaz must "keep calm" and stop being afraid. That is, Ahaz should trust God, take no action, and the danger would pass. Even from a purely human standpoint this would have been wise.

Assyria's goal was Egypt. Tiglath-Pileser III normally would take the main road down the coast, and if Jerusalem kept quiet,

---

[1] Strangely enough, some take it as an encouragement to Ahaz. See John H. Hayes and Stuart A. Irvine, *Isaiah: The Eighth-Century Prophet* (Nashville: Abingdon Press, 1987), 123.

it would escape attention. But Ahaz panicked because of enemies swarming near Jerusalem. He could not see anything but the immediate threat from Rezin and Pekah. The fierce anger of those two kings made Ahaz think they were a dangerous fire. But God called them "two smoldering stubs of firewood" that could produce only a little smoke and would soon be extinguished. Indeed, Assyria conquered them soon after this.

> [5]Aram, Ephraim and Remaliah's son have plotted your ruin, saying, [6]"Let us invade Judah; let us tear it apart and divide it among ourselves, and make the son of Tabeel king over it." [7]Yet this is what the Sovereign LORD says: " 'It will not take place, it will not happen,

God assured Ahaz that the plan to depose him would fail. These three verses are all one causal sentence. Rezin and Pekah were wrong in assuming they or anyone else could overthrow the Davidic line and put a puppet king in Jerusalem to cause Judah to join them against Assyria. Syria (Aram) and Ephraim (Israel) were working together, though the plan came from Syria. "Tabeel" ("the bad one") is a Syrian name, so his son may have been a relative of Rezin or of the Tyrian king.

God, however, was in control—not Israel or Damascus. He declared that Rezin and Pekah would not be successful. Ahaz did not need to worry about his throne. But Judah's only hope was to trust in the LORD.

> [8]for the head of Aram is Damascus, and the head of Damascus is only Rezin. Within sixty-five years Ephraim will be too shattered to be a people.

Damascus is the capital of Aram, and its head is "only Rezin." Rezin will never be the head over Jerusalem because the context reveals that Rezin can never be more than he was: Damascus would soon be destroyed by Assyria. Though Tiglath-Pileser III would not destroy Samaria, within sixty-five years Ephraim (Israel) would no longer be a separate people or nation. Samaria was destroyed in 722 B.C. by Shalmaneser V. And sixty-five years later, King Esarhaddon settled foreign colonists in Israel's territory (Ezra 4:2).

> ⁹The head of Ephraim is Samaria, and the head of Samaria is only Remaliah's son. If you do not stand firm in your faith, you will not stand at all.'"

The headship of Judah would never belong to Ephraim, or Pekah. Then God, still speaking to Judah, said that if the people of Judah and Jerusalem did not "stand firm in [their] faith" (Heb. *taʾaminu,* "believe, trust, rely on, have faith") they would not "stand at all" (Heb. *teʾamenu,* "have stability, remain, continue"). The Hebrew uses the hiph'il and niphal form of the verb *ʾaman* as a wordplay. The NIV brings out the pun well in the English translation. It emphasizes that their only hope of escaping the fate of Aram and Israel is to take a stand of faith in God, relying on Him alone.

b. God Offers And Promises A Sign 7:10–13

> ¹⁰Again the LORD spoke to Ahaz, ¹¹"Ask the Lord your God for a sign, whether in the deepest depths or in the highest heights."

When Ahaz did not respond, the Lord spoke to him again, possibly soon after the preceding warning. As a last attempt to make Ahaz heed this warning and exercise faith, God told him to "ask the LORD" for a supernatural sign. God was gracious in reminding Ahaz that He was his God. God had not yet abandoned Ahaz, and He put no limits on the nature of the sign. It could be anything, from the depths of Sheol to the height of heaven; that is, anything in all creation. What wonderful love God was showing!

> ¹²But Ahaz said, "I will not ask; I will not put the LORD to the test."

With mock piety Ahaz refused, pretending it would be against the Law, which forbids putting God "to the test"; that is, demanding God show His power without reason (Deut. 6:16). Asking God for a sign was not a test when God himself made the offer. Furthermore, Ahaz was not concerned about the Law, for he had already discontinued its public observance and closed the temple. His real reason for refusing was that he had already rejected the LORD and made up his mind to ask the

Assyrian king, Tiglath-Pileser, for help—which he soon did (2 Kings 16:7–9). Thus God was testing Ahaz, but with a desire to keep him from sinning (Exod. 20:20). However, because of his own plans, Ahaz was not ready to subject himself to God's will.

> **13 Then Isaiah said, "Hear now, you house of David! Is it not enough to try the patience of men? Will you try the patience of my God also?**

Inspired by the Lord, Isaiah then spoke to the entire Davidic dynasty, not just to Ahaz. The command here is plural. He returns to the singular in verse 16 because what follows it is again specifically directed to Ahaz. King Ahaz, as the current representative, had tested "the patience of men," including Isaiah, and the patience of God as well. Note that Isaiah said "my God." He could not say "your God" because Ahaz had rejected God and His word.

c. The Immanuel Sign 7:14–16

> **14 Therefore the Lord himself will give you a sign: The virgin will be with child and will give birth to a son, and will call him Immanuel.**

Commentators do not agree about the interpretation of this passage, whether it forms a "promise or a warning, or who is meant by the child Immanuel."[2] John Calvin, Bishop Lowth, and the Baptist John Gill were early writers holding a messianic interpretation. Because of the contemporary threat of Assyria, many commentators limit the fulfillment to the near future. Others propose a dual fulfillment, one contemporary and one referring to the birth of Jesus.[3]

In spite of Ahaz's unbelief and his refusal to ask for a sign, the Lord will give a supernatural sign anyhow—but not to Ahaz.[4] The particle "therefore" refers back to verse 13 and indicates God will give a different sort of sign than He offered to Ahaz in

---

[2] O. Kaiser, *Isaiah 1–12,* 100.

[3] For a list of commentaries holding these views see Edward E. Hindson, *Isaiah's Immanuel* (Phillipsburg, N.J.: Presbyterian & Reformed, 1978), 23.

[4] Harry Bultema, *Commentary on Isaiah,* trans. Cornelius Lambregtse (Grand Rapids: Kregel Publications, 1981), 108. Bultema points out that by unbelief, Ahaz "forfeited an immediate sign."

verse 10.[5] It "is no longer a matter of invitation but of prediction."[6] The plural "you" means it will be a sign for the whole house of David.[7] The sign refers not only to a supernatural birth, but to the conditions surrounding that birth as well.

The meaning of "virgin" (Heb. *'almah*) is disputed. It occurs only eight other times in the Old Testament (Gen. 24:43; Exod. 2:8; 1 Chron. 15:20 [plural]; Pss. 46 [superscription; plural]; 68:25; Prov. 30:19; Song of Sol. 1:3; 6:8). But it is never used of a married woman.[8] For example, in Song of Solomon 6:8, its use is distinct from the Hebrew used for married women ("queens") and "concubines" and can mean only "virgin." Another word, *bethulah*, is used of virgins of any age.[9] However, the word used here (*'almah*) seems to be specific to a virgin of marrying age.[10]

The Hebrew particle *hinneh* ("Behold," KJV) directs attention to the importance of the virgin and her son. She is called "the" virgin, indicating a specific virgin in God's plan. She will call her son's name "Immanuel," meaning "God with us," or "the with-us God." Contrary to Jewish tradition no father is mentioned. Yet this omission fits with the fact that the child is virgin-born. Some commentators confine their attention to the immediate context and suppose the child was born to Ahaz or Isaiah.[11] However, Immanuel could not be Hezekiah, for Ahaz appointed him coregent in 728 B.C.[12] and he began his full

---

[5]Hindson, *Isaiah's Immanuel*, 30.

[6]J. Alec Motyer, *The Prophecy of Isaiah* (Downers Grove, Ill.: InterVarsity Press, 1993), 84.

[7]Since Rezin and Pekah were intending to replace the Davidic family with the son of Tabeel, the Davidic covenant was in view, with its promise leading to the Messiah who would make David's throne eternal.

[8]Motyer, *Prophecy of Isaiah*, 85. This is true of nonbiblical literature also. Hindson, *Isaiah's Immanuel*, 39–40, 82.

[9]The Septuagint translates the Heb. *'almah* the Gk. *parthenos*, which means "virgin." Matthew also uses *parthenos* and specifically states, "All this took place to fulfill what the Lord had said through the prophet" (1:22).

[10]If Isaiah had meant "young woman" (RSV), he would have used the term *na'arah* (which the RSV translates as "young woman" elsewhere). See H. Hanke, *The Validity of the Virgin Birth* (Grand Rapids: Zondervan Publishing House, 1963), 24.

[11]Hayes and Irvine, *Isaiah*, 135–36.

[12]Horn says "about 729 B.C." Siegfried H. Horn, "The Divided Monarchy," in *Ancient Israel*, ed. Hershel Shanks (Englewood Cliffs, N.J.: Prentice-Hall, 1988), 129, 131. This is further proof that Hezekiah is not meant by "Immanuel."

reign in 715 when he was twenty-five years old, so he would already be alive at this time (732 B.C.).[13] Neither could the virgin be Isaiah's wife, since his sons are specifically named as his, and this is not said of Immanuel.[14]

Then, in 8:8, the land of Judah is identified as Immanuel's land, which indicates the child Immanuel is the Messiah. In 8:10, Immanuel is the pledge of the survival of Israel.[15] The same virgin-born Son is the wonderful Child in Isaiah 9 and 11. "The Immanuel prophecy comes to a greater fulfillment in the birth of the God-man, who is both the Protector Deliverer and the Divine Warrior. Matthew properly applied this prophecy to Jesus the Messiah (Matt. 1:23)."[16] Note also that Matthew ends his book with Jesus saying, "And surely I am *with you* always, to the very end of the age" (28:20). He continues to be Immanuel, "God with us."

> [15] He will eat curds and honey when he knows enough to reject the wrong and choose the right.

Eating curds (curdled goat's milk) and wild honey shows that the child will be born into poverty. To Ahaz this should have been a warning that the house of David would be reduced to a lowly state as a consequence of Ahaz's policies and those of future kings who followed his example. To the Child it meant that by the time He came to an age of accountability, He would be sharing in the reduced situation of His people.

> [16] But before the boy knows enough to reject the wrong and choose the right, the land of the two kings you dread will be laid waste.

The prophecy of the desolation of Damascus and Israel would be carried out as if the Child were born at that time. But the passage is flexible—the Child does not need to be present at

---

[13] Roth's suggestion that "virgin" is "possibly referring to King Ahaz's still virginal queen-to-be" so that Immanuel is "the future King Hezekiah" does not fit the biblical dating (cf. 2 Kings 16:2; 18:2). Wolfgang Roth, *Isaiah* (Atlanta: John Knox Press, 1988), 46.

[14] For further discussion of the identity of the virgin see Hindson, *Isaiah's Immanuel*, 42–44.

[15] Willem A. VanGemeren, *Interpreting the Prophetic Word* (Grand Rapids: Zondervan Publishing House, Academie Books, 1990), 260.

[16] Ibid.

the destruction Ahaz will witness.[17] Some understand the passage to mean that Immanuel must actually be present to undergo the results of Ahaz's refusal from that moment.[18] Others think that the meaning is that Immanuel at maturity will refuse the policy of Ahaz and choose the way of His heavenly Father (as in the temptation of Jesus). Underlying this passage is the contrast between the Messiah and the degenerate condition of the house of David as embodied in Ahaz.

2. God Will Use Assyria To Bring Judgment 7:17–8:8

a. Assyria As God's Razor 7:17–25

17The Lord will bring on you and on your people and on the house of your father a time unlike any since Ephraim broke away from Judah—he will bring the king of Assyria."

The secession of the ten tribes was a terrible blow to Judah and the kings of David's line. Now God is going to bring on an even worse blow. The Assyrians to whom Ahaz looked for help will eventually bring devastation to Judah.

18In that day the Lord will whistle for flies from the distant streams of Egypt and for bees from the land of Assyria.

"That day" is the day of God's righteous judgment on Judah. Some see the use of the flies and bees to refer to bee culture in Assyria and to the flies that settled on filth in Egypt. The point, however, is that God is in control of Egypt and Assyria. He only has to "whistle" for the Egyptian armies, which will be as ineffective as "flies."

---

[17]Cf. Herbert M. Wolf, *Interpreting Isaiah* (Grand Rapids: Zondervan Publishing House, Academie Books, 1985), 90–92. Wolf suggests "Maher-Shalal-Hash-Baz" (see Isa. 8:1) may have been referred to as "Immanuel" as a rebuke to Ahaz, but that the New Testament applies it in a fuller sense to Jesus. Hindson points out, however, that the name of Maher-Shalal-Hash-Baz "expresses judgment" rather than the blessing implied in the name Immanuel. Hindson, *Isaiah's Immanuel,* 48.

[18]Motyer points out that chaps. 7 to 11 show "a tension between the immediate and the remote." 7:14–16 points to "the immediate threat." 8:11–22 and 11:12–13 point to "the undated future, for before his birth Judah and Israel will be scattered and need regathering." Motyer, *Prophecy of Isaiah,* 87. Motyer adds, "The promise awaited its time but the threat was immediate."

By this time (735 B.C.), Assyria was a dominant world power. God will "whistle" for the armies of Assyria to be His agents, and they will be like a swarm of bees settling down and desolating Israel and Judah. Egypt became the bait that lured Assyria, and Egypt proved to be powerless against them. In 701 B.C., Assyria defeated Egypt at Eltekeh, about thirty-two miles west-northwest of Jerusalem. Trusting in Egypt was also futile.

> **19They will all come and settle in the steep ravines and in the crevices in the rocks, on all the thornbushes and at all the water holes.**

Not even the most remote part of the land will be safe from the Assyrians. The rugged valleys and rock clefts, once strongholds for David, will be invaded by enemy forces. The thornbush hedges that protect the vineyards will be taken over, as will the sources of water.

> **20In that day the Lord will use a razor hired from beyond the River—the king of Assyria—to shave your head and the hair of your legs, and to take off your beards also.**

The king of Assyria will be like a barber's razor that will bring God's judgment. The Assyrian king will be "hired" because Assyria was not God's people in the same sense as Israel. "Hired" also indicates God would be using Assyria only temporarily.

The shaving of the head, the legs, and the beard was the greatest humiliation imaginable in those days. It indicates the complete disgrace and depopulation of all classes. While the "shaving" refers metaphorically to God's use of a foreign power to punish His people, it was also a literal humiliation of the men of Judah taken into captivity.[19]

> **21In that day, a man will keep alive a young cow and two goats.**

The remnant left will be able to maintain only a few livestock. The great herds will be gone, taken as spoil by the invading Assyrians.

---

[19]This was fulfilled in 701 B.C. when Sennacherib, according to his records, took 200,150 captives from Judah. See Daniel David Luckenbill, *The Annals of Sennacherib* (Chicago: University of Chicago Press, 1924), 33; idem, *Ancient Records of Assyria and Babylonia*, 2 vols. (Chicago: University of Chicago Press, 1926–27), 2:120.

Isaiah 7:22-25; 8:1-2

> ²²And because of the abundance of the milk they give, he will have curds to eat. All who remain in the land will eat curds and honey.

Isaiah's reference to an "abundance of . . . milk" is ironic because it is relative to so few people being left to feed. And because there are so few people, vineyards cannot be maintained; the people will have to live on the more easily produced diet of "curds and honey."

> ²³In that day, in every place where there were a thousand vines worth a thousand silver shekels, there will be only briers and thorns. ²⁴Men will go there with bow and arrow, for the land will be covered with briers and thorns. ²⁵As for all the hills once cultivated by the hoe, you will no longer go there for fear of the briers and thorns; they will become places where cattle are turned loose and where sheep run.

Because there are so few people to work the well-tilled vineyards with their many expensive vines, "briers and thorns" will take over. (Note that Jeremiah paid only seventeen shekels for a whole field, Jer. 32:9.) Wild animals will take over the cultivated areas, so they become a place for hunting.

Hills where grain and other crops were grown will be covered with briers and thorns so thick that people will be afraid to walk through them because of the danger of getting scratched and cut. The hills will not be able to grow anything; only cattle and sheep will be able to go there and find something to eat to keep themselves alive.

The people of Judah paid a terrible price for the sin of Ahaz. But God was still faithful to the remnant who remained.

b. Maher-Shalal-Hash-Baz 8:1–4

> ¹The LORD said to me, "Take a large scroll and write on it with an ordinary pen: Maher-Shalal-Hash-Baz. ²And I will call in Uriah the priest and Zechariah son of Jeberekiah as reliable witnesses for me."

After Ahaz refused to listen, God told Isaiah to take a large scroll (probably leather)[20] and write a message on it with "an ordinary pen" in ordinary neatly-written letters that people could easily read. The words of the message mean "hurry-plunder-hurry-plundering."[21] The idea is repeated twice in different Hebrew words for emphasis. It implies that a lightning military campaign will take away the wealth and goods from Damascus and Samaria, though it may imply that Judah would also suffer. Isaiah probably explained this to the two "reliable witnesses," so that when the prophecy was fulfilled they could confirm that the LORD and Isaiah were right. The first witness, Uriah, is identified by some as the one who made the altar for Ahaz patterned after one at Damascus (2 Kings 16:10–11). The second witness, Zechariah, may have been the father-in-law of Ahaz (2 Chron. 29:1,13).

> ³Then I went to the prophetess, and she conceived and gave birth to a son. And the LORD said to me, "Name him Maher-Shalal-Hash-Baz.

Isaiah's wife was a prophetess. Some suppose she was called this out of politeness due to her prophet husband, but there is no such custom in Hebrew culture. Indeed, there are prophetesses in both the Old and New Testaments (Exod. 15:20; 2 Kings 22:14; 2 Chron. 34:22; cf. Acts 21:9; 1 Cor. 11:5). The LORD told Isaiah to give the boy the same cryptic name that Isaiah had written on the scroll, so that his son would be a continuing witness to the truth of the prophecy. The boy is not identified with Immanuel (cf. 7:14). In fact, His fourfold name is in sharp contrast to the fivefold name of the Messiah in the next chapter (9:6).

> ⁴Before the boy knows how to say 'My father' or 'My mother,' the wealth of Damascus and the plunder of Samaria will be carried off by the king of Assyria."

Now the LORD applies the meaning of the fourfold name. Before the boy could say the simplest words, probably within

---

[20]Some take the Heb. to mean a large tablet to be written on with a stylus and put up like a billboard.
[21]I take these words as imperatives. Some take them as participles and translate them as "plunder's hurrying, booty's hastening."

his first year, Assyria would pillage Damascus and Samaria. This parallels what was said of the virgin-born child and makes Isaiah's son a sign—though not the supernatural sign that would be given to the whole house of David in the future.

c. Assyria To Come As A Flood 8:5–8

> ⁵The LORD spoke to me again: ⁶"Because this people has rejected the gently flowing waters of Shiloah and rejoices over Rezin and the son of Remaliah,

God is patient and speaks again through Isaiah to the people after they refused to listen to the message of verse 4. The "waters of Shiloah" are probably the water that flows from the Gihon spring. Zadok the priest anointed Solomon there (1 Kings. 1:39). Rejecting the gentle waters of Shiloah probably meant rejecting God's promises in turbulent times. The people were rejoicing over the deaths of Rezin and Pekah (both died in 732 B.C.) but still not relying on God.

As so often in Isaiah, Pekah is called the son of Remaliah to remind us that Pekah had no right to Israel's throne. He had gained it by assassinating Pekahiah (2 Kings 15:25).

> ⁷therefore the Lord is about to bring against them the mighty floodwaters of the River—the king of Assyria with all his pomp. It will overflow all its channels, run over all its banks ⁸and sweep on into Judah, swirling over it, passing through it and reaching up to the neck. Its outspread wings will cover the breadth of your land, O Immanuel!"

Judah refused the gently flowing waters of Shiloah. Now, like the mighty Euphrates ("the River"), the king of Assyria's magnificent army would flood in with grandeur. Like a flood, he would overflow everything, including Judah. His army would reach "up to the neck." It will not take the head, Jerusalem. Sennacherib's invasion of 701 B.C. fulfilled this prophecy (see chaps. 36 and 37). Like a large bird of prey sweeping over the land, Assyria would destroy the whole of Judah. Yet the land is still Immanuel's land. He guarantees that the land will be

108 / Isaiah 8:9–13

restored in the future. Some critics change "O Immanuel!" to mean "for God is with us," but that does not fit the context. Immanuel is the Messiah; therefore, we have a link between 7:14 and chapters 9 and 11.

3. How God Was With Israel 8:9–18

> ⁹Raise the war cry, you nations, and be shattered! Listen, all you distant lands. Prepare for battle, and be shattered! Prepare for battle, and be shattered! ¹⁰Devise your strategy, but it will be thwarted; propose your plan, but it will not stand, for God is with us.

God will bring judgment on Judah, but that is not all He has planned. When Assyria conquered nations, it often allowed those who were conquered to join its army and recoup some of their own losses at the next place of conquest. Thus, the Assyrian army included troops from many nations. They were all raising the battle cry against Judah. Assyria's army, however, would eventually "be shattered." God would overrule their plan, "for God is with us," which can be translated "on account of Immanuel." The promise of the future Immanuel is the assurance that Jerusalem would survive and the nations who tried to destroy her would eventually fall.

> ¹¹The Lord spoke to me with his strong hand upon me, warning me not to follow the way of this people. He said:

In the Old Testament, the Lord's "strong hand" is often parallel to the Holy Spirit's mighty power. With a mighty anointing upon him, Isaiah was warned "not to follow the way of this people," that is, in their rebellion, unbelief, and distrust of the Lord. Only human, Isaiah must have felt the opposition of unbelievers and cynics. But God anointed and assured him. He must continue to declare the word of the Lord with courage.

> ¹²"Do not call conspiracy everything that these people call conspiracy; do not fear what they fear, and do not dread it. ¹³The Lord Almighty is the one you are to regard as holy, he is the one you are to fear, he is the one you are to dread,

Isaiah's warning against alliance with Assyria, and his warning to Hezekiah not to break that alliance once made, were both considered treason, or "conspiracy," by the war party in Judah.

The verbs here are plural and are addressed to Isaiah and those disciples who would listen to him. They are not to fear or dread what the unbelievers fear, which was the conspiracy of Pekah and Rezin. That was not the real danger for Jerusalem. They must regard the LORD as holy, and have the same kind of fear and respect that recognizes His awesome power and that confesses and forsakes sin.

> ¹⁴and he will be a sanctuary; but for both houses of Israel he will be a stone that causes men to stumble and a rock that makes them fall. And for the people of Jerusalem he will be a trap and a snare.

For those who will trust in Him and respect His holiness, God will be a refuge, a holy place set apart. This implies blessings of peace, joy, and fellowship with Him. But to those who refuse to trust Him, He will become a stumbling stone, causing them to fall.

The same defeat by Assyria awaits both Israel and Judah. Samaria fell in 722 B.C. during the fourth year of Hezekiah's coregency with his father, Ahaz (2 Kings 18:9). Then in 701, the fourteenth year of Hezekiah's full reign, Sennacherib destroyed all the cities of Judah except Jerusalem (2 Kings 18:13). Jerusalem was trapped by the surrounding Assyrian armies until God delivered it.

> ¹⁵Many of them will stumble; they will fall and be broken, they will be snared and captured."

"Many of them" probably refers back to both Israel and Judah (v. 14). Undoubtedly, men of Jerusalem were in the army that faced Sennacherib and some of them were killed or captured.

> ¹⁶Bind up the testimony and seal up the law among my disciples.

The "testimony" and the "law," or instruction, are the written prophecies and teachings God gave Isaiah up to this point. They are to be bound up and sealed to indicate that events have already proved their truth. The binding and sealing would also protect the prophecies from unbelievers who might want to destroy the manuscripts or deny that Isaiah wrote them. Isaiah's disciples were charged to preserve them.

> ¹⁷I will wait for the LORD, who is hiding his face from the house of Jacob. I will put my trust in him.

Isaiah then declares that he will trust the LORD to carry out His plan. Though the LORD hides His face in displeasure "from the house of Jacob," that is, from both Israel and Judah, Isaiah will look beyond the present circumstances and put his trust in God—thus honoring the promises of deliverance.

> ¹⁸Here am I, and the children the LORD has given me. We are signs and symbols in Israel from the LORD Almighty, who dwells on Mount Zion.

Even though the LORD was displeased with Judah, He did not leave them without a witness: The names of Isaiah and his two sons had symbolic meanings that would continue to remind the people of both the promise of salvation and the warnings of judgments. They were given by the Almighty LORD of hosts (armies) to inform the people that His presence was still manifested in the temple on "Mount Zion." ("Mount Zion" here means in Jerusalem, not simply on the Ophel hill, the Zion David conquered before the temple was built on the mountain to the north of it.) God was still able to fulfill His promises; He had not left His people. Thus, Hebrews 2:13 quotes from this verse and applies it to Jesus, who brings a greater fulfillment of God's promises.

4. JUDGMENT ON SPIRITISM 8:19–22

> ¹⁹When men tell you to consult mediums and spiritists, who whisper and mutter, should not a people inquire of their God? Why consult the dead on behalf of the living?

Moses' law prohibited consulting "mediums and spiritists" (cf. Lev. 19:31; 20:6; Deut. 18:11). Yet, those who were probably pro-Assyrian and thus rejected Isaiah's prophecies were putting increasing pressure on the people to do just that, instead of consulting God. How foolish to "consult the dead on behalf of the living."

> ²⁰To the law and to the testimony! If they do not speak according to this word, they have no light of dawn.

"The law" (instruction) and "testimony" again refer to Isaiah's prophecy and teaching (see 5:24). Only if they heed his words from the Lord will they find real light: The "dawn," or future blessing, is only for those who accept God's Word and reject pagan superstition, spiritism, and other idolatrous abominations.[22]

> ²¹Distressed and hungry, they will roam through the land; when they are famished, they will become enraged and, looking upward, will curse their king and their God. ²²Then they will look toward the earth and see only distress and darkness and fearful gloom, and they will be thrust into utter darkness.

The people who reject Isaiah's prophecies will wander through the night of God's judgment. The Assyrian siege will bring hunger. And because they have not trusted God, when the judgment comes, they will not repent. Instead, they will curse their king who has not defended them and their God who has not kept this judgment from them.[23] When they look to the land (the mark of their blessing) and the material elements they have trusted in, they will see only hopeless "distress and darkness." They will be driven away into the "utter darkness" and gloom of exile. Certainly this would mean an inner darkness as well.

Sennacherib's records claim 200,150 of the people of Judah were taken away—an incontestable testimony to the certainty of the prophetic word.

5. Hope For Galilee 9:1–5

> ¹Nevertheless, there will be no more gloom for those who were in distress. In the past he hum-

---

[22]Frank D. Macchia, "Satan and Demons," in *Systematic Theology*, ed. Stanley M. Horton, rev. ed. (Springfield, Mo.: Logion Press, 1995), 196–97.

[23]The Heb. can also mean they will curse their situation by their king and their God.

> bled the land of Zebulun and the land of Naphtali, but in the future he will honor Galilee of the Gentiles, by the way of the sea, along the Jordan—

In contrast to the darkness mentioned in 8:22, a day will come when the gloom will be lifted from the lives of God's people. The territory of Zebulun and Naphtali, which is located between the Sea of Galilee and the Mediterranean Sea, had suffered greatly from Assyrian invasions from 734 to 732 B.C. (2 Kings 15:29). Tiglath-Pileser III made it an Assyrian province, took inhabitants into exile, and brought people from other nations to settle there. He also took Gilead, across Jordan, and annexed part of the plain of Sharon by the Mediterranean Sea. But Galilee, where God's judgment first humbled His people in Isaiah's day, would be honored in the future. This was fulfilled when Jesus ministered and chose His first disciples in Galilee—which was still despised by the people of Jerusalem.[24]

The "way of the sea" was the highway that came southwest, from Damascus down through Galilee and then to the Mediterranean Sea and down the coast toward Egypt.

> ²The people walking in darkness have seen a great light; on those living in the land of the shadow of death a light has dawned.

Galilee, the darkest part of the land—whose future looked the darkest when Isaiah gave this prophecy (about 733–732 B.C.)—would see "a great light."[25] There is an obvious connection between this verse and the "child" of verse 6. Jesus would bring the light of salvation to the Gentiles (Isa. 42:6; 49:6).

> ³You have enlarged the nation and increased their joy; they rejoice before you as people rejoice at the harvest, as men rejoice when dividing the plunder.

In contrast to the small remnant, the nation will be enlarged.

---

[24] Some consider this passage "a continuation of the Immanuel sign (Isa. 7:14; 8:8)." S. H. Widyapranawa, *The Lord is Savior: Faith in National Crisis* (Grand Rapids: Wm. B. Eerdmans, 1990), 51.

[25] "Have seen" is the Heb. prophetic perfect, indicating the certainty of fulfillment.

Joy, prosperity, victory,[26] and peace will come because the "light has dawned" (v. 2).

> ⁴For as in the day of Midian's defeat, you have shattered the yoke that burdens them, the bar across their shoulders, the rod of their oppressor.

The "day of Midian's defeat" refers to Gideon's defeat of the Midianites. God gave Gideon the victory after reducing his army from thirty-two thousand to three hundred (Judg. 7:2–25). Similarly the present deliverance from "their oppressor" will also be performed by the LORD, not by the numbers or ability of the people.

> ⁵Every warrior's boot used in battle and every garment rolled in blood will be destined for burning, will be fuel for the fire.

Uniforms and military equipment which shed blood in war will be cast aside and burned, for the LORD's victory over sin and its strife will be complete. There will be no more desire for war.

6. THE PRINCE OF PEACE 9:6–7

> ⁶For to us a child is born, to us a son is given, and the government will be on his shoulders. And he will be called Wonderful Counselor, Mighty God, Everlasting Father, Prince of Peace.

The Messiah will put an end to oppression and injustice. He will come as a child to us. But He will come first of all to the remnant of Israel who passed through darkness and who will be redeemed. "A son" refers back to 7:14, Immanuel, "God with us." Kingship was symbolized by a scepter on the king's shoulder. The government being "on his shoulders" means He will be king.

The names given indicate His essential characteristics. "Wonderful" and "Counselor" are not joined by ancient Hebrew scholars. "Wonderful" is a noun, and means He will be a supernatural wonder (cf. Exod. 15:11; Judg. 13:18). A counselor was a person with God-given wisdom. Jesus implies He is the "Counselor" when He calls the Holy Spirit " 'another' "[27] Counselor (John 14:16).

---

[26] Plunder could only be divided after a victory.
[27] Gk. *allon*, "another of the same kind."

Some critics wish to interpret "Mighty God" as a "divine" or "godly" hero. However, Isaiah uses the same phrase in 10:21 in a way that can refer only to God. This Son is a divine being.

"Everlasting Father" could be translated "Father [or, "Author"] of Eternity [or, "of the Universe"]." This fits with John 1:3, where the Living Word is the One through whom God made everything that was made (cf. also Heb. 1:2). It also speaks of His faithful, loving care that is everlasting.

He is also the "Prince of Peace," the One bringing true peace—which includes salvation, blessing, wholeness, harmony, and well-being—a peace Jesus gives now (John 14:27), and a peace that will be fully in effect in the Millennium.

> ⁷Of the increase of his government and peace there will be no end. He will reign on David's throne and over his kingdom, establishing and upholding it with justice and righteousness from that time on and forever. The zeal of the LORD Almighty will accomplish this.

The kingdom reflects the character of the Son, given in verse 6. Because He is the divine King, "there will be no end" to His government and peace. It is true that Satan will be released for a short time after the Millennium (Rev. 20:7–10), but he will not be able to overthrow the Lord's kingdom—it will continue into the new heavens and the new earth, the New Jerusalem its eternal capital.

The Son's government will be established "on David's throne," fulfilling the covenant giving David's lineage the throne forever (2 Sam. 7:12–13; cf. Luke 1:32–33). Once the Son comes to reign as the longed-for, legitimate King, He will uphold it forever with divine "justice and righteousness."

The "zeal of the LORD" is the powerful expression of the love and determination that is part of His nature—a determination to fulfill His promises and covenants. Nothing will be able to stop Him, for He is the Almighty LORD of hosts with all power and with the armies of heaven at His command.

STUDY QUESTIONS

1. For what purpose was Isaiah to take Shear-Jashub with him to meet Ahaz?

2. Why did Ahaz refuse to ask for a sign?
3. On what grounds can we apply the sign of the virgin-born child to Jesus?
4. What would be the result of God's using Assyria to bring judgment?
5. What is the significance of the name Maher-Shalal-Hash-Baz?
6. Why did the people accuse Isaiah of conspiracy and treason?
7. What would keep Isaiah's disciples faithful to the Lord?
8. How is the "For" at the beginning of 9:6 related to the preceding verses?
9. What is the significance of each of the names given to the Son in 9:6 and how are they fulfilled in Jesus?

C. Four Reasons For God's Anger 9:8–10:4

The four sections of this prophecy deal with sins of Israel and are each followed by a refrain that confirms that further judgment is necessary. The same conditions were also prevalent in Judah, so there are lessons for them as well. God had already brought judgment on His people, but more is to come. Some statements seem to refer to the past, others to the future; some events in the past reflect what is to come in the future.

1. Judgment On Pride And Self-sufficiency 9:8–12

> ⁸The Lord has sent a message against Jacob; it will fall on Israel. ⁹All the people will know it— Ephraim and the inhabitants of Samaria—who say with pride and arrogance of heart, ¹⁰"The bricks have fallen down, but we will rebuild with dressed stone; the fig trees have been felled, but we will replace them with cedars."

God has sent out his "message" of coming judgment by Amos and Hosea as well as Micah and Isaiah, and the whole nation will soon see it come to pass. The people of Ephraim (Israel) and the capital city of Samaria say "with pride and arrogance" that God's judgment will not humble them. Still defying God, they say they will rise again. This pride and self-sufficiency is the first reason for God's anger.

Clay bricks and sycamore fig beams were ordinary building materials, which an earthquake or enemy battering rams could bring down. In their pride the people thought they could rebuild even better without God. They would use squared stones ("dressed stones") and cedar beams, like those in kings' palaces.

> **11But the LORD has strengthened Rezin's foes against them and has spurred their enemies on. 12Arameans from the east and Philistines from the west have devoured Israel with open mouth. Yet for all this, his anger is not turned away, his hand is still upraised.**

"Rezin's foes" are the Assyrians. The mention of "Arameans from the east" (Syrians) and Philistines probably refers to former invasions, especially during the time of the weak King Menahem, who died in 742 B.C. But these judgments in the past have not satisfied God's anger. They must not think that because they have recovered from past judgments they can do as they please in the future. God's "hand is still upraised" (a refrain that will appear four more times: vv. 12,17,21, and 10:4), ready to strike defiant Israel with further judgments, this time using Assyria.

2. JUDGMENT ON A PEOPLE LED ASTRAY 9:13–17

> **13But the people have not returned to him who struck them, nor have they sought the LORD Almighty.**

Previous judgments have not caused the people to turn to the LORD in repentance or seek Him and His will. Again and again, God called on the people to repent. He was longsuffering, but the people remained defiant—the second reason for God's anger.

> **14So the LORD will cut off from Israel both head and tail, both palm branch and reed in a single day; 15the elders and prominent men are the head, the prophets who teach lies are the tail.**

The time will come when God will no longer tolerate rebellion. He will bring sudden judgment. The leadership—referred to here as "head and tail," "palm branch and reed"—are responsible for the people not seeking the LORD. They will be destroyed "in a single day," possibly at the fall of Samaria in 722 B.C. Rulers are "the head." False prophets also thought they were at the head, influencing the people. But they are just "the tail," wagging to try to please the people. They should have been undergirding the leadership with God's Word. Instead, they misled the leaders with their lies. The false prophets themselves apparently had become politicians seeking money and popularity. The branches of the palm grew high; reeds, on the other hand, grew in the low, swampy places. Together they symbolize that both high and low leaders would be brought down. (Isaiah often used a literary device called merism, expressing an entire range by simply listing the maximum and minimum.)

> **16Those who guide this people mislead them, and those who are guided are led astray. 17Therefore the Lord will take no pleasure in the young men, nor will he pity the fatherless and widows, for everyone is ungodly and wicked, every mouth speaks vileness. Yet for all this, his anger is not turned away, his hand is still upraised.**

The leaders mislead the people, who in turn "are led astray" from the ways of the Lord. Therefore, the Lord's attitude will change toward them. Young people should have been a joy to the Lord, but they too are sinning and displeasing God, living as if He did not exist. Ordinarily, God is the advocate for orphans and widows, but even they are as ungodly and wicked as the rest of the people, speaking the same vile language. Everyone is guilty. God's hand of judgment was "still upraised" to bring more judgment on these degenerate people!

3. WICKEDNESS THAT CONSUMES BECAUSE OF GOD'S WRATH 9:18–21

> **18Surely wickedness burns like a fire; it consumes briers and thorns, it sets the forest thickets ablaze, so that it rolls upward in a column**

> of smoke. ¹⁹By the wrath of the Lord Almighty the land will be scorched and the people will be fuel for the fire; no one will spare his brother.

With leaders taken away in judgment, the land will be in chaos, with wickedness spreading like a forest fire and destroying the country. This is the third reason for God's anger. The holy wrath of God will be another flame that will "scorch" the land. God will use the people themselves as instruments of His wrath against them: In their wickedness, instead of helping each other, they will destroy each other. This civil war extended beyond northern Israel to an unbrotherly attack on Judah.

> ²⁰On the right they will devour, but still be hungry; on the left they will eat, but not be satisfied. Each will feed on the flesh of his own offspring: ²¹Manasseh will feed on Ephraim, and Ephraim on Manasseh; together they will turn against Judah. Yet for all this, his anger is not turned away, his hand is still upraised.

Those who destroy each other will "not be satisfied." They will destroy even their own relatives. Gone will be all traces of brotherly love. Tribal dissension will occur even between the Joseph tribes, who had the birthright from Jacob and should have been enjoying the blessing of Abraham.

They will unite only to turn against the southern kingdom of Judah, as they did during the Syro-Ephraimite war.

Again, God's anger still burns and "his hand is still upraised" to bring more judgment.

4. Woe To Unjust Rulers 10:1–4

> ¹Woe to those who make unjust laws, to those who issue oppressive decrees, ²to deprive the poor of their rights and withhold justice from the oppressed of my people, making widows their prey and robbing the fatherless.

A woe is pronounced on lawmakers who make oppression lawful and easy. They are extortioners who make the poor, oppressed, widows, and orphans their victims. This corruption in the law courts is the fourth reason for God's anger. This injustice contradicted the law of Moses, which made provision for the poor, the weak, and especially for widows and orphans (Deut. 14:29).

> ³What will you do on the day of reckoning, when disaster comes from afar? To whom will you run for help? Where will you leave your riches? ⁴Nothing will remain but to cringe among the captives or fall among the slain. Yet for all this, his anger is not turned away, his hand is still upraised.

The rulers think they have the Law on their side, but Isaiah challenges them. What will they do when the day comes and God renders further judgment? They will be too weak to stand against Him.

It will be a day "when disaster comes from afar" (from Assyria), and who will help them then? It will be too late to seek the Lord, and the riches they gained from wicked practices will not help them. Instead, they will be either tortured captives or "among the slain."

STUDY QUESTIONS

1. What judgment does the Lord promise for Israel and what are the reasons for His wrath?
2. What are the reasons for the woe in 10:1–4?

D. Assyria Used And Judged 10:5–34

1. Assyria—God's Rod 10:5–19

a. Assyria Used Without Knowing It 10:5–11

> ⁵"Woe to the Assyrian, the rod of my anger, in whose hand is the club of my wrath!

Now a woe is pronounced on the Assyrians—the tool God is

using to bring judgment on His own people. God's indignation is represented by the club in Assyria's hand.

> ⁶I send him against a godless nation, I dispatch him against a people who anger me, to seize loot and snatch plunder, and to trample them down like mud in the streets.

God is sending the Assyrians against His own people, who have become a godless nation. The Assyrians will fulfill the meaning of Maher-Shalal-Hash-Baz (see 8:1,3). They will have no mercy as they "trample" down the people and seize their possessions.

> ⁷But this is not what he intends, this is not what he has in mind; his purpose is to destroy, to put an end to many nations.

Assyria will not be aware that they are God's agent bringing His judgment on Israel and Judah. Their purpose is to invade and assimilate nations into the Assyrian Empire, with the plan to dominate the world.

> ⁸'Are not my commanders all kings?' he says.

The self-exalting pride of Assyria is so great that it declares all its army officers to be kings in their own right. They think they are invincible.

> ⁹'Has not Calno fared like Carchemish? Is not Hamath like Arpad, and Samaria like Damascus?

The Assyrian king boasts about his conquests. By about 717 B.C., the chief cities in western Asia Minor had been conquered by Assyria. Carchemish on the Euphrates River, a former capital of the Hittite Empire, was conquered by Sargon II in 717. Calno, about fifty-five miles to the southwest, was conquered by Tiglath-Pileser III in 738 B.C. Arpad was just six miles northwest of Calno, near the modern Aleppo. Hamath was on the Orontes River. Damascus was conquered and destroyed in 732. Samaria was taken and destroyed in 722 by Shalmaneser V (though his son, Sargon II, later tried to take the credit). It looked as if nothing could stop Assyria.

> ¹⁰As my hand seized the kingdoms of the idols,

kingdoms whose images excelled those of Jerusalem and Samaria—

The kings of Assyria exalted themselves above the gods of the countries they conquered, and even above their own gods. A title the Assyrian rulers took for themselves was "King of the Universe." Thus, the Assyrian king believed his power had "seized the kingdoms of the idols," gods who were supposed to be the patrons and protectors of the countries he had subdued.

Pagan kingdoms often made great idols of gold and silver. The Assyrian king knows there are idols in Jerusalem and Samaria—even though God had forbidden them—but their idols are not the beautiful, ornate images of the other countries that Assyria has conquered. The Assyrian speaks of them with contempt. Later, when Sennacherib destroyed Babylon, he had his soldiers smash the idols of Babylon. The two exceptions were the images of Bel and Nebo, which he carried off to Nineveh.[1]

> [11]shall I not deal with Jerusalem and her images as I dealt with Samaria and her idols?'"

The fact that Samaria had already been conquered dates this prophecy after 722 B.C. Samaria's "idols" (Heb. *elilim,* meaning "nothings," "worthless nonentities") had been destroyed. Jerusalem's "images" (Heb. *'atsabbi,* "offensive idols") deserved the same judgment. The Assyrian supposed rightly at this time that most of the people of Jerusalem were trusting in images to protect them. The Assyrians believed their idols were more powerful than the idols of other nations. They also thought their idols were greater than the Lord, the one true God.

B. GOD WILL PUNISH ASSYRIA IN DUE TIME 10:12–19

> [12]When the Lord has finished all his work against Mount Zion and Jerusalem, he will say, "I will punish the king of Assyria for the willful pride of his heart and the haughty look in his eyes.

---

[1] Daniel David Luckenbill, *The Annals of Sennacherib* (Chicago: University of Chicago Press, 1924), 84; *Ancient Records of Assyria and Babylonia,* 2 vols. (Chicago: University of Chicago Press, 1926–27), 2:152, 185, 252.

Though God was using Assyria, when God's work of judgment on Judah is "finished" (snapped like a weaver's thread), the pride of Assyria's king will be punished. He would find he was not dealing with idols or graven images but with the mighty God of heaven and earth.

> ¹³For he says: "'By the strength of my hand I have done this, and by my wisdom, because I have understanding. I removed the boundaries of nations, I plundered their treasures; like a mighty one I subdued their kings. ¹⁴As one reaches into a nest, so my hand reached for the wealth of the nations; as men gather abandoned eggs, so I gathered all the countries; not one flapped a wing, or opened its mouth to chirp.'"

The Assyrian king ascribes his conquest and plunder to his own power and wisdom, not recognizing God's sovereignty. He merged other nations into the Assyrian Empire. It was as easy as robbing eggs from an abandoned nest. Notice the boastful "I" and "my" in these verses. "Mighty one" is a term used by the Hebrews of God (1:24) and by the Assyrian king of his gods. The Assyrian king claimed to be acting as a mighty god in his conquest of other kings.

> ¹⁵Does the ax raise itself above him who swings it, or the saw boast against him who uses it? As if a rod were to wield him who lifts it up, or a club brandish him who is not wood!

The foolishness of the king of Assyria's boasting is compared to an "ax" or a "saw" boasting against the one who uses it, or to a "rod" (a scepter) trying to manipulate the one who lifts it up, or a "club" trying to swing a living person "who is not wood." The point is that the Lord is the living Agent and Assyria is only the staff He is using. Assyria is under God's control even though they do not know it. God is able to use anyone to work out His plan.

> ¹⁶Therefore, the Lord, the LORD Almighty, will send a wasting disease upon his sturdy warriors; under his pomp a fire will be kindled like a blazing flame. ¹⁷The Light of Israel will

become a fire, their Holy One a flame; in a single day it will burn and consume his thorns and his briers.

"Therefore," because of their claims exalting themselves as gods, God will judge Assyria. The double title of "the Lord, the LORD Almighty" again emphasizes His power and control. The Assyrian soldiers were healthy and strong, but God's judgment on them is compared to "a wasting disease" and a fire that consumes thorns and briers. The "single day" in which they are consumed is probably a prophecy of the judgment brought by the angel who put to death 185,000 of Sennacherib's army (Isa. 37:36).

> ¹⁸The splendor of his forests and fertile fields it will completely destroy, as when a sick man wastes away. ¹⁹And the remaining trees of his forests will be so few that a child could write them down.

The Assyrian army is compared to both a charred forest and a sick man; so few trees are left that a child could count them.

This had at least a preliminary fulfillment in the death of the 185,000, and a greater fulfillment when Nineveh was destroyed in 612 B.C. Finally, the ultimate fulfillment was at the end of the Assyrian Empire in 609.

2. Hope For The Remnant Of Israel 10:20–34

a. A Remnant Returns To The Mighty God 10:20–23

> ²⁰In that day the remnant of Israel, the survivors of the house of Jacob, will no longer rely on him who struck them down but will truly rely on the LORD, the Holy One of Israel.

"That day" usually means the Day of the LORD. But the reference to relying "on him who struck them down" seems to refer to the treaty Ahaz made with Assyria. After Assyria brings God's judgment on Israel and Assyria, in turn, is also judged, a righteous remnant will have hope in God.

> ²¹A remnant will return, a remnant of Jacob will return to the Mighty God.

"A remnant will return" (Heb. *sheʿar yashuv*) is the name of

Isaiah's first son (7:3). The remnant includes those left after Sennacherib's invasion of 701 B.C. The return is not from exile or captivity but from sin and rebellion "to the Mighty God" (Heb. *'el gibbor*), one of the names of the Messiah (Isa. 9:6). The remnant is made up of the ones who responded to Isaiah and King Hezekiah and took a stand of faith when God healed Hezekiah and gave him fifteen more years of life (Isa. 38:5–6,21).

> ²²Though your people, O Israel, be like the sand by the sea, only a remnant will return. Destruction has been decreed, overwhelming and righteous. ²³The Lord, the LORD Almighty, will carry out the destruction decreed upon the whole land.

This prophecy was given while the leaders and the people were still rebelling against God, probably before the fall of Samaria in 722 B.C. Thus, it is emphasized again that the judgment will be severe. God had already decreed judgment overflowing with righteousness. The nation will be terribly reduced in numbers and "only a remnant will return." The reduction in numbers must refer to the great numbers taken into exile by the Assyrians. In verse 22, the return may include those returning from that exile. It will be a well-deserved, righteous judgment over "the whole land."

b. Assyria's Yoke Broken 10:24–27

> ²⁴Therefore, this is what the Lord, the LORD Almighty, says: "O my people who live in Zion, do not be afraid of the Assyrians, who beat you with a rod and lift up a club against you, as Egypt did. ²⁵Very soon my anger against you will end and my wrath will be directed to their destruction."

The Lord now offers reassurance that his judgment will take effect against the Assyrians. The people of Zion (Jerusalem) must stop being afraid of Assyria, even though it threatens them as Egypt threatened them (Exod. 1:8–10).

God's use of Assyria is only temporary, for His anger against Zion will soon end. His purpose is to bring about its purification. Then His judgment will turn against the Assyrian Empire and bring about its destruction.

> ²⁶The LORD Almighty will lash them with a whip, as when he struck down Midian at the rock of Oreb; and he will raise his staff over the waters, as he did in Egypt.

Just as God gave the victory against Midian, and as God had Moses raise his rod over the Red Sea to provide a way (Exod. 14:16,19–22), and as the LORD also fought for them (Exod. 14:14), so He will bring His judgment on Assyria. The reference to "the rock of Oreb" may allude to Oreb's escaping the battlefield but dying nevertheless, just as Sennacherib would escape the death angel's judgment on the 185,000 but would be assassinated after he went home (37:37–38).

> ²⁷In that day their burden will be lifted from your shoulders, their yoke from your neck; the yoke will be broken because you have grown so fat.

The burden and yoke Assyria put on Zion's shoulders and neck "will be lifted" off by the LORD. The last phrase, literally, "the yoke will be stripped away [destroyed] on account of olive oil," has been interpreted in several ways. Some interpret the oil to refer to the Assyrian's pride, so that when God's judgment comes on that pride, the Assyrian yoke on Zion will be stripped away. Others take oil to mean well-fed people and thus to refer to Zion becoming "so fat," or prosperous, that they burst the yoke. Still other interpreters suggest the oil refers to the Anointed One, the Messiah; or, since oil was used in anointing priests, kings, and prophets, these interpreters refer to it as the KJV does, to the anointing itself (that is, the anointing given by the Holy Spirit). Another interpretation sees the oil as a preservative, for Jerusalem was preserved from Assyrian destruction.

c. The Assyrian Advance 10:28–32

> ²⁸They enter Aiath; they pass through Migron; they store supplies at Micmash. ²⁹They go over the pass, and say, "We will camp overnight at Geba." Ramah trembles; Gibeah of Saul flees.

> ³⁰Cry out, O Daughter of Gallim! Listen, O Laishah! Poor Anathoth! ³¹Madmenah is in flight; the people of Gebim take cover. ³²This day they will halt at Nob; they will shake their fist at the mount of the Daughter of Zion, at the hill of Jerusalem.

Isaiah depicts an enemy—the Assyrians—approaching Jerusalem from a point about ten miles northeast of the city. They stopped at Micmash, some seven miles north of Jerusalem, to store supplies and baggage; crossed the "pass" (the deep, rocky gorge of the Wadi Suweinit) to Geba, about six miles north-northeast of Jerusalem; and then went on to Nob, on Mount Scopus just north of the Mount of Olives. There, in sight of Jerusalem, they arrogantly threatened it. The other towns mentioned may not have been on the direct line of march, but their people were in panic, screaming and fleeing, knowing that the Assyrian soldiers would ravage the countryside. The exact time of this invasion had not been identified. Sargon II did not come this way or even approach Jerusalem. Sennacherib's records do not indicate that his main army came this way. However, his records indicate his army or armies came up more than one time to Jerusalem in 701 B.C., so this prophecy may have been fulfilled some time during that year.

d. God Is In Control 10:33–34

> ³³See, the Lord, the LORD Almighty, will lop off the boughs with great power. The lofty trees will be felled, the tall ones will be brought low. ³⁴He will cut down the forest thickets with an ax; Lebanon will fall before the Mighty One.

God, the Holy One of Israel, limits what people can do. The forest thickets and the tall, stately cedar trees of Lebanon represent the Assyrian army. The LORD cuts it all down. The stroke of the ax must refer again to the 185,000 Assyrians who were destroyed by the angel. Sennacherib thought he was a "mighty one" (10:13), but he falls before the true "Mighty One."

Some want to apply these verses to the destruction of the proud in Judah, but this is hardly likely. However, the principle can be applied to all godless, secular nations. God can chop down their pride and arrogance.

STUDY QUESTIONS

1. What does God's use of Assyria teach us about His sovereignty?
2. What do you learn about the godly remnant of Israel?

E. A New Branch Bears Fruit 11:1–12:6

1. THE SPIRIT-ANOINTED KING 11:1–3

¹A shoot will come up from the stump of Jesse;
from his roots a Branch will bear fruit.

Isaiah saw God's concern for the righteous remnant, but this remnant would not be able to fulfill His plan of redemption. God let Isaiah look ahead to see another picture of the Messiah, who would fulfill it.

The Assyrians nearly destroyed Judah, but the kings of David's line remained on the throne until the Babylonians came and destroyed Jerusalem and the temple in 586 B.C. The image of a tree cut off close to the roots, leaving only a small stump, depicts the loss of royal power and the lowly condition of the descendants of David. But there was still life in the stump and the roots. From the root of Jesse would come "a Branch" that would "bear fruit." That the Branch comes from the root of Jesse indicates that He would be a second David. David means "Beloved." Thus, when the Father's voice from heaven identified Jesus as His "beloved Son" (Matt. 3:17, KJV), He was implying that Jesus is His second David, the fulfillment of what David represented. Isaiah had already prophesied that the Son would reign on the throne of David (9:7). Now he makes clear that the Son would be a descendant of David as well.

"Branch" (Heb. *netser*) in a feminine form became the name of Nazareth *(netsereth),* so "Jesus of Nazareth" or "Jesus the Nazarene" in the Hebrew would be *Yeshua Hannetseri. Hannetseri* can mean either "the man of Nazareth" or "the man of the Branch." Thus, in God's providence, Jesus brought a fulfillment that Matthew 2:23 recognizes: "He went and lived in a town called Nazareth. So was fulfilled what was said through the prophets: 'He will be called a Nazarene.'"

> ²The Spirit of the LORD will rest on him—the Spirit of wisdom and of understanding, the Spirit of counsel and of power, the Spirit of knowledge and of the fear of the LORD—

"The Spirit of the LORD will rest" on the Branch, just as the Spirit did on Moses, the judges, David, and the prophets—but this time permanently (John 3:34). The Spirit is a gift resting on Him.

The gift of the Spirit along with the six aspects or ministries of the Spirit corresponds to the sevenfold Spirit in Revelation 4:5. "Wisdom" in the Old Testament is practical wisdom that carries out plans to successful completion (cf. Proverbs 8). "Understanding" includes knowledge that enables one to distinguish right from wrong and truth from falsehood. "Counsel" includes the ability to make right decisions and solve problems. "Power" means divine power to carry out his decisions. "Knowledge" here is the knowledge of the character and nature of God and His relationship with humankind. "The fear of the LORD" is a reverence that obeys Him and recognizes His right to our worship and adoration. It is the beginning of wisdom and knowledge (Ps. 111:10; Prov. 1:7). This is in contrast to "those who are wise in their own eyes and clever in their own sight" (Isa. 5:21).

> ³and he will delight in the fear of the LORD. He will not judge by what he sees with his eyes, or decide by what he hears with his ears;

He will "delight in [Heb. *haricho,* "enjoy the smell of"] the fear of the LORD." This may mean He will receive with pleasure the fear of the Lord that is directed to Him.

In addition to being a prophet, He will also be a judge. But unlike human judges, He will not have to depend on external evidence. With divine insight, He will see into the minds and hearts of people (cf. John 2:25). He will know what is true and what is not (cf. Matt. 7:21–23).

2. The Righteous Judge 11:4–5

> ⁴but with righteousness he will judge the needy, with justice he will give decisions for the poor of the earth. He will strike the earth with the rod of his mouth; with the breath of his lips he will slay the wicked.

The poor and the needy, often exploited or neglected, will receive justice and protection because of His righteousness. "Righteousness" (Heb. *tsedeq*) also implies He will put them right with God.

On the other hand, as Judge "He will strike the earth," that is, its ungodly inhabitants, "with the rod of his mouth," which is parallel to "the breath of his lips." The word he speaks will be "the rod" that brings judgment.[1] He needs nothing else to accomplish this. The fulfillment of this looks ahead to the Battle of Armageddon (Rev. 19:15).[2]

> ⁵Righteousness will be his belt and faithfulness the sash around his waist.

The belt and sash symbolize being ready for action. He will not depend on the methods or even the armaments of human warfare. "Righteousness . . . and faithfulness" to God's purpose and promises will be seen in all His actions. He is the example for all leaders.

3. The Earth Changed By The Knowledge Of The Lord 11:6–9

> ⁶The wolf will live with the lamb, the leopard will lie down with the goat, the calf and the lion and the yearling together; and a little child will lead them. ⁷The cow will feed with the bear,

---

[1]Cf. Eph. 6:17 where "the sword of the Spirit . . . is the word of God."
[2]Stanley M. Horton, *The Ultimate Victory: An Exposition of the Book of Revelation* (Springfield, Mo.: Gospel Publishing House, 1991), 282–84.

> their young will lie down together, and the lion will eat straw like the ox. ⁸The infant will play near the hole of the cobra, and the young child put his hand into the viper's nest.

The kingdom must be brought in through judgment (as Daniel 2 depicts). So the judgment of 11:4 is followed by the millennial conditions described in verses 6–9. They will be better than the Garden of Eden. The nature of the animals will be changed and children will not need to be afraid of even poisonous snakes. All the effects of the curse inflicted on the earth because of Adam's sin will be gone. The creation "will be liberated from its bondage to decay and brought into the glorious freedom of the children of God" (Rom. 8:21).

> ⁹**They will neither harm nor destroy on all my holy mountain, for the earth will be full of the knowledge of the Lord as the waters cover the sea.**

God's "holy mountain" means the millennial Jerusalem. It will be free from any that will hurt or destroy, because the whole earth will be changed (see also 65:25). In contrast to the condition of Jerusalem and the world in Isaiah's day, as well as in ours, the personal, saving knowledge of the Lord will be everywhere.

4. A New Exodus 11:10–16

> ¹⁰**In that day the Root of Jesse will stand as a banner for the peoples; the nations will rally to him, and his place of rest will be glorious.**

"The Root of Jesse" means the Messiah not only descends from David but is the real source of the Davidic line. That He "will stand as a banner" means He will be the assurance of victory and the One around whom the nations will rally. "Banner" ("ensign," KJV) is the same word used in the name of God in Exodus 17:15 (Heb. *Yahweh nissi*), "The Lord is my Banner." This is another Old Testament indication that the messianic King will not be an ordinary man but will be divine. When the house of David has recovered its glory in the person of the Messiah, the nations will seek His favor and guidance. His resting place, His home, the millennial Zion, will be glorious. (The

Heb. word *kavod* is the same word used of God's glory.)

> ¹¹In that day the Lord will reach out his hand a second time to reclaim the remnant that is left of his people from Assyria, from Lower Egypt, from Upper Egypt, from Cush, from Elam, from Babylonia, from Hamath and from the islands of the sea.

In that millennial day, the Lord himself will gather the godly remnant of His people "a second time." Verse 16 shows the first time was the Exodus from Egypt where the whole nation was brought out of slavery and into the Promised Land. Some take it that the second time refers to the return from Babylon under the edict of Cyrus. This was only a partial return, for many remained scattered in various directions—as the Books of Ezra, Nehemiah and Esther indicate and as shown in the New Testament (Acts 2:5; James 1:1; 1 Pet. 1:1). However, there was a greater scattering after the destruction of Jerusalem in A.D. 70, and after the Bar Kochba rebellion of about A.D. 132–35. Therefore, "that day" must refer to the restoration at the end of this age. It will be a new and greater exodus.

"Reclaim" (Heb. *qanoth*) can also mean redeem. God's purpose is not only to bring the people back to the land. As was the case in the first exodus, He wants to bring them back to himself (cf. Exod. 19:4). The return will prepare for spiritual renewal.

> ¹²He will raise a banner for the nations and gather the exiles of Israel; he will assemble the scattered people of Judah from the four quarters of the earth.

The "banner for the nations" is the Messiah. Through Him the exiles of Israel and Judah will be gathered, not just from the areas where they were scattered in ancient times, but from the "four quarters," that is, all parts of the earth.

> ¹³Ephraim's jealousy will vanish, and Judah's enemies will be cut off; Ephraim will not be jealous of Judah, nor Judah hostile toward Ephraim.

In Old Testament times, Ephraim and Judah were often quarreling. But all the jealousy and hostility between the tribes was gone after they came back from Babylon. All twelve tribes considered themselves and each other to be Jews. In the Millennium, the tribal associations will be restored as Ezekiel prophesied, though the land will be divided differently (in strips running east and west; Ezek. 48:1–29), and the Prince of Peace will rule over all of them.

> [14] They will swoop down on the slopes of Philistia to the west; together they will plunder the people to the east. They will lay hands on Edom and Moab, and the Ammonites will be subject to them.

Like a mighty eagle, restored Israel will "swoop down" over Philistia on the west and conquer the people on the east. To the east of Judah were Edom, Moab, and Ammon. No nation will be able to frustrate the redemptive purposes of God.

> [15] The LORD will dry up the gulf of the Egyptian sea; with a scorching wind he will sweep his hand over the Euphrates River. He will break it up into seven streams so that men can cross over in sandals. [16] There will be a highway for the remnant of his people that is left from Assyria, as there was for Israel when they came up from Egypt.

There will be a new exodus from Assyria. Just as God dried up the Red Sea (Exod. 14:21), He will use "a scorching wind" to destroy the Euphrates River, leaving seven dry streambeds. These streambeds contrast with the one path through the Red Sea, and their number, seven, indicates a complete work—people can "cross over in sandals" without getting their feet wet. God will make a clear road for the remnant of His people to return from Assyria. The mention of Assyria here may indicate that it is representative of all the places Israel was scattered by its enemies. There was a partial return from Assyria in Isaiah's day, as Esarhaddon's records indicate,[3] but here Isaiah is looking ahead to the millennial day.

---

[3] See comments on 13:14 and 48:20.

5. A Day Of Thanksgiving For Israel And The Nations 12:1–6

a. Praise For Salvation 12:1–3

¹In that day you will say: "I will praise you, O LORD. Although you were angry with me, your anger has turned away and you have comforted me.

This section of Isaiah ends with a thanksgiving hymn. "That day" looks ahead to the millennial reign of the Messiah described in chapter 11. In this hymn, Isaiah expresses the confidence of the redeemed, with the king[4] being the first to give thanks to God. The Hebrew jussive form indicates a request: "Let your anger be turned away." The people have responded, recognizing that His anger brought discipline that really came from His love.

After God's anger is turned away from Israel, they will be full of praise because of the comfort He gives—a comfort that reassures them of His presence and blessing. Isaiah experienced this in chapter 6. There was also a preliminary fulfillment of this after the deliverance from Sennacherib in fulfillment of Isaiah's prophecies (40:1).

²Surely God is my salvation; I will trust and not be afraid. The LORD, the LORD, is my strength and my song; he has become my salvation."

With God's anger turned away, they will individually exclaim that God is "my salvation." "Salvation" includes the ideas of help and prosperity. In "that day" (v. 1) they will be trusting in God, not man, for salvation, deliverance, help, and blessing. Fear will be gone. They will be like the Israelites who saw their enemies drowned in the Red Sea, and they will sing the same song (Exod. 15:2).

The repetition "the LORD, the LORD" (Heb. *Yah, Yahweh*) emphasizes that He is the living and true God, the eternal God, the faithful God who acts in behalf of His people. He is the same One who brought them out of Egypt into the Promised

---

[4]Some take the speaker to be the unified twelve tribes of Israel. S. H. Widyapranawa, *The Lord is Savior: Faith in National Crisis* (Grand Rapids: Wm. B. Eerdmans, 1990), 73.

Land. He will be their strength and song because He will have become their salvation in an even greater way. Salvation, *Yeshu'ah,* is another form of the Hebrew name for Jesus, *Yeshu'a.*

> ³With joy you will draw water from the wells of salvation.

In the hot, dry climate at the edge of the desert water spoke of life and blessing. The "wells of salvation" are not ordinary wells but artesian wells, fountains that never run dry. These wells have their source in God himself (cf. Jer. 2:13; John 4:10,14; 7:38). All of Jerusalem will survive the Assyrian crisis and will draw from the wells. In New Testament times, Jews sang of the wells of salvation during the Feast of Tabernacles, drawing water from the pool of Siloam.

b. Let The Whole World Know 12:4–6

> ⁴In that day you will say: "Give thanks to the LORD, call on his name; make known among the nations what he has done, and proclaim that his name is exalted.

The second part of this magnificent hymn is a stirring call for all of the people to "give thanks to the LORD," and is also a call to invoke or proclaim His name and His glorious deeds. His people are not to keep God's blessings to themselves. All the nations need to know what God has done in saving and rescuing His people. He deserves to have the nations join in praising and honoring Him.

His name represents His nature and character. By declaring that "his name is exalted," they honor Him for the kind of God He is.

> ⁵Sing to the LORD, for he has done glorious things; let this be known to all the world.

The "glorious things" God has done in His divine majesty call for songs of praise accompanied by musical instruments. These songs are not to be sung in private, but in public so the whole world knows. Such music is still a wonderful way to spread the good news of God's power and grace in a dark and gloomy world. Such music stirs faith and hope.

⁶Shout aloud and sing for joy, people of Zion,
for great is the Holy One of Israel among you."

The greatness of "the Holy One of Israel," who is in the midst of the holy, redeemed people of Zion, calls for shouts and singing (Heb. *ronni*, "ringing cries of joy"). This is an appropriate conclusion for chapters 7 to 12. It should stir us to joyful, courageous Christian witness.

STUDY QUESTIONS

1. What can we understand from the fact the Branch is from Jesse's roots?
2. What does the sevenfold Spirit of the LORD do for the Branch?
3. What will be the results of His government and when will this occur?
4. In what ways does the "second time" of 11:11 exceed the first exodus?
5. How does chapter 12 express the confidence of the redeemed?
6. What do the things God has done call for?

III. GOD DEALS WITH THE NATIONS AROUND JUDAH 13:1–23:18

After the wonderful hymn of praise Isaiah goes back to the theme of judgment, recognizing that evil still exists in the world. These chapters deal with foreign nations but not in chronological order and not as separate from God's dealings with Judah and Jerusalem. Foreign nations are involved in God's judgment and deliverance of His people, so messages to God's people are interspersed in the following chapters. Throughout all of them we see the glory of the almighty sovereign God and the reality of His promises. He is the one true God over all the earth.

A. Babylon's Destruction 13:1–14:23

This prophecy concerns the famous, splendid city of Babylon in Isaiah's own day, and not the later Babylon of Nebuchadnezzar.[1] Babylon in Assyrian times was the greatest center of trade and industry in the Tigris-Euphrates valley (see map, Appendix B). Even at the time of Joshua's conquest of Jericho, "a goodly Babylonish garment" was highly prized (Josh. 7:21, KJV).

Even more important, Babylon claimed religious and cultural leadership of the world in Isaiah's day. The state letters of Assyria show that the Assyrians included the gods of Babylon among their own.[2] Bel and Nabu (Nebo) are often mentioned by the Assyrians in lists of gods whose protection they seek or whose honor they declare. A number of times Bel and Nabu are mentioned without any reference to any other god, as if they were the chief or most revered gods of that particular Assyrian king.[3] Babylon dominated Assyria's religion.

Nor was commercial, religious, and cultural leadership Babylon's only claims to greatness. From ancient times it was powerful and well-organized. Assyria, for all its ruthless military might, did not treat Babylon as a state of minor importance.[4] Babylon never did consent to be incorporated into the Assyrian Empire. Tiglath-Pileser III "left their liberties and territory alike unimpaired."[5] Even when Babylon's internal disunity brought her to submit to the Assyrian yoke, Babylon still retained political importance. Even in a later age, Babylon was remembered by Herodotus in his history as "one of the most renowned and strongest cities of Assyria."[6]

---

[1] Most commentaries ignore this and try to apply this prophecy to the conquest of Babylon by Cyrus. Even conservative commentaries do this, for example, David L. McKenna, *Isaiah 1–39*, in *The Communicator's Commentary* (Dallas: Word Books, 1993), 171.

[2] Robert Henry Pfeiffer, *State Letters of Assyria, American Oriental Series*, vol. 6 (New Haven: American Oriental Society, 1935), 14, 49, 55, 78, 98, 106, 109, 112, 129, 138, 182, 193, 209, 214, 221, 224, 233, 234, 236.

[3] Ibid., 3, 29, 58, 137, 151, 220, 238.

[4] Gaston Camille Charles Maspero, *The Passing of the Empires, 850 B.C. to 330 B.C.*, trans. M. L. McClure, ed. A. H. Sayce (London: Society for Promoting Christian Knowledge, 1900), 196.

[5] Ibid., 197.

[6] Herodotus, *History*, trans. George Rawlinson, ed. Manuel Komroff (New York: Tudor Publishing Co., 1928), 66. Herodotus was not a historian in the modern sense. He was a fifth-century B.C. Greek tourist who wrote down what the guides told him. Sometimes they were correct, sometimes not.

Another factor Isaiah knew of, confirming the importance of Babylon, is that Assyrian control was always rather tenuous. The possession of Babylon meant a great deal to Assyria's prestige. Until Sennacherib finally destroyed the city, Assyrian kings had prided themselves on being protectors of Babylon, and they were extremely patient with the people of the city.[7] Some Assyrian kings even sent part of the spoil from their conquests to Babylon instead of sending it all to Nineveh.[8]

No king of Assyria dared to proclaim himself king of Babylon merely on the grounds of having conquered the city. Usually Assyrian kings added the name of a conquered country to a list of those they ruled. Tiglath-Pileser III made Babylon the first great objective in his dream of a world empire. But not until two years before he died do we find the Nimrud Tablet declaring him "king of Babylon."[9]

Assyrian recognition of the Babylonian god Bel (identified with Marduk) as the supreme god made the Assyrian kings fear to disobey the demands of the Babylonian priests of Marduk: A legitimate king of Babylon must be recognized by Marduk. This meant the king must be in Babylon on New Year's Day each year and perform the illustrious but humbling ceremony of taking the hands of Bel-Marduk. Most Assyrian kings did not wish to do this, so they contented themselves with a lesser title. Shalmaneser V, for example, proclaimed himself "the mighty king, king of the universe, king of Assyria, king of the four regions of the world . . . king of Sumer and Akkad," but he was only "viceroy," or vice president, of Babylon.[10] Sargon did the same.[11]

Babylon was the center of world attention in Isaiah's day, and God gave him a heavy message for it. The prophet saw the judgment of Babylon as coming in his own lifetime. However, the destruction of Babylon here is a type, pledge, or precursor of final judgment. Certainly Sennacherib's destruction of Babylon in 689 B.C. must have seemed the height of Assyria's atrocities,

---

[7]Theodore H. Robinson, *A History of Israel* (Oxford: Clarendon Press, 1951), 1:383.
[8]Pfeiffer, *State Letters of Assyria,* 79.
[9]Daniel David Luckenbill, *Ancient Records of Assyria and Babylonia,* 2 vols. (Chicago: University of Chicago Press, 1926–27), 1:283.
[10]Ibid., 1:297.
[11]Ibid, 2:25.

and to Isaiah it must have seemed the climax of God's judgment on the world through the Assyrians.[12]

The prophecy concerning it was probably placed first in this series because of its importance. Babylon, from the time of the tower of Babel, was representative of any world power which rose up in proud disobedience to God. Its fall looked ahead to the final fall of the Babylon-like world system described in chapters 17 and 18 of the Book of Revelation.

1. Judgment Soon To Come 13:1–22

a. God's Wrath On Babylon 13:1–5

¹An oracle concerning Babylon that Isaiah son of Amoz saw:

The word "oracle" or "burden" (Heb. *massa'*) means "something lifted up." It refers to a word, declaration, or pronouncement from God. Isaiah "saw" it; that is, he received it as a prophetic vision or message. It was a weighty message of heavy judgment.

²Raise a banner on a bare hilltop, shout to them; beckon to them to enter the gates of the nobles.

On the bare rocks of a high hill, where signals can easily be seen, God commands a banner to be raised as a signal to gather troops. He also commands a loud call and wave of a hand to encourage them to come, so they will "enter the gates of the nobles," probably the gates of Babylon. They were called "gates of the nobles" because the wealthy, powerful Babylonians considered themselves the aristocrats of the world in that day. Thus, Isaiah anticipated judgment on Babylon.

³I have commanded my holy ones; I have summoned my warriors to carry out my wrath— those who rejoice in my triumph.

"I" is in the emphatic position. God will command and summon warriors whom He has consecrated to carry out His wrath. Babylon's pride and arrogance deserve judgment. Those

---

[12]Cf. Charles Boutflower, *The Book of Isaiah (Chapters I–XXXIX) in the Light of the Assyrian Monuments* (London: Society for Promoting Christian Knowledge, 1930), 90.

who come against her will be exulting in God's majesty, even though they may not know it. They are "holy ones" in the sense that God has consecrated them to fulfill His will, even though they do not know it. Their eagerness for battle compares with the attitude of Assyria in 10:7–12. Their victory will really be God's triumph because He will bring His judgment on them in due time.

> ⁴Listen, a noise on the mountains, like that of a great multitude! Listen, an uproar among the kingdoms, like nations massing together! The LORD Almighty is mustering an army for war.

Sennacherib and the Assyrians claimed victory over Babylon, and his army destroyed it. The Assyrian army was like an avalanche, becoming larger as it advanced: The Assyrians allowed men of conquered cities and nations to join forces with them in order to recoup some of their own losses by taking spoils from the next place of conquest. Thus, Isaiah hears the noise of many "nations massing" for war against Babylon. But God is really in control. Using a wordplay, Isaiah says God is *Yahweh tsᵉvaʻoth* and He is mustering a *tsᵉvaʻ* for war. *Tsᵉvaʻ*, meaning "host" or "army" (plural, *tsᵉvaʻoth*), sometimes refers to earthly armies and sometimes to angelic hosts. Here, God is using an earthly army to bring judgment on Babylon and destroy it.

> ⁵They come from faraway lands, from the ends of the heavens—the Lord and the weapons of his wrath—to destroy the whole country.

As Assyria was the club in God's hand to bring judgment on Israel (10:5), now Assyria and its combined armies from many distant lands become "the weapons" to bring God's judgment on Babylon.

b. A Day Of The LORD's Wrath Is Near 13:6–13

> ⁶Wail, for the day of the LORD is near; it will come like destruction from the Almighty.

The people of Babylon will wail, for the Day of the LORD is soon to come. Using another wordplay, Isaiah says that that day will come as a *shod* (violent destruction) from *Shaddai* (the

Almighty).[13] The wordplay emphasizes that God is able to keep His promises. Here, Isaiah is looking at "the day of the LORD" as imminent.

> [7] **Because of this, all hands will go limp, every man's heart will melt.**

Babylon will not be able to withstand the violent destruction of the coming Day of the LORD. Instead of holding on to weapons to defend themselves, they will be so demoralized that their "hands will go limp," and their courage will vanish as their hearts melt. They will be unable to do anything or think of any way to save themselves.

> [8] **Terror will seize them, pain and anguish will grip them; they will writhe like a woman in labor. They will look aghast at each other, their faces aflame.**

They will be so terrified that they will be out of their senses, convulsed with pain that will seize them like the pangs of "a woman in labor." For years after the Assyrians took control of Babylon, they treated it with respect and honor—until the Assyrian king Sennacherib destroyed it. This sudden, violent destruction shocked and surprised the Babylonians. Their faces became hot, inflamed by the shame of their defeat.

> [9] **See, the day of the LORD is coming—a cruel day, with wrath and fierce anger—to make the land desolate and destroy the sinners within it.**

The destruction of Babylon by Sennacherib in 689 B.C. becomes a type of future judgment that will come in the final Day of the LORD.[14] What Isaiah sees here is the wrath of a holy God being poured out, making "the land desolate" and destroying sinners upon it. "The land" (Heb. *ha'arets*) can also mean "the earth." It may be that beginning with this verse (rather than the next) Isaiah is speaking of the final Day of the LORD.

> [10] **The stars of heaven and their constellations will not show their light. The rising sun will be**

---

[13] The wordplay is more obvious in the ancient Heb., which wrote only consonants.
[14] Stanley M. Horton, *The Ultimate Victory: An Exposition of the Book of Revelation* (Springfield, Mo.: Gospel Publishing House, 1991), 254–56.

darkened and the moon will not give its light.

The future Day of the LORD will involve darkness over all the earth (cf. 5:30; 8:22; Amos 5:18; Matt. 24:29; Rev. 6:12–13). There is no compassion here, only judgment on a world corrupted by sin and evil.

> ¹¹I will punish the world for its evil, the wicked for their sins. I will put an end to the arrogance of the haughty and will humble the pride of the ruthless.

The punishment here is not just for Babylon, but for the entire inhabited earth. God's righteous judgment will be upon the world's evil—the twisted activities of the wicked, the presumption of the proud, and the haughtiness of the tyrants who violently exercise their authority. They will all be humbled and brought to an end because of their evil deeds.

> ¹²I will make man scarcer than pure gold, more rare than the gold of Ophir.

The judgment will fall on individuals and humankind in general. The remnant will be small—it is compared to the scarcity of pure gold, especially "the gold of Ophir." Much of Solomon's gold was brought from Ophir (1 Kings 9:28; 10:11), on a three-year voyage (1 Kings 10:22). The location of Ophir today is unknown. It may have actually been in India, as Jerome and the Septuagint suggest.

> ¹³Therefore I will make the heavens tremble; and the earth will shake from its place at the wrath of the LORD Almighty, in the day of his burning anger.

Therefore, because the world deserves God's judgment, in His fierce anger and wrath He will make the heavens tremble and the earth shake out of its place. Such language was sometimes used of tremendous storms and earthquakes.

c. Babylon Soon To Be Overthrown 13:14–22

> ¹⁴Like a hunted gazelle, like sheep without a shepherd, each will return to his own people, each will flee to his native land.

Isaiah now returns to his own day and gives several aspects of the judgment on Babylon by Sennacherib in 689 B.C. First, those who are not Babylonians will flee to their own lands. The Assyrians settled a number of captive peoples in Babylonia to replace the 208,000 Babylonians Sennacherib claimed he moved out earlier. These probably included most of the 200,150 captives taken from Judah.

Esarhaddon, Sennacherib's son and successor, confirms in his records that when Sennacherib destroyed Babylon, captive peoples fled back to their own lands.[15] The figure of "a hunted gazelle" demonstrates how fast they ran to escape. The "sheep without a shepherd" indicates that their Babylonian overlords were no longer present to confine them.

> **[15] Whoever is captured will be thrust through;**
> **all who are caught will fall by the sword.**

The Babylonians did not escape. Whether they were found hiding in the city or trying to escape, all were killed. The annals of Sennacherib, which describe the destruction of Babylon in 689 B.C., say the public squares were piled high with corpses.[16]

> **[16] Their infants will be dashed to pieces before**
> **their eyes; their houses will be looted and their**
> **wives ravished.**

The Assyrians were merciless and cruel. It was common for them to kill babies, strip valuables from houses, and rape women.[17] When Cyrus and his armies entered Babylon in 539 B.C., there was no fighting and no such atrocities.[18] Cyrus considered himself a deliverer of the cities he conquered and would not have allowed those kinds of behavior. But at this time God withdrew His hand and allowed the Assyrians to show their cruelty toward the people of Babylon.

---

[15] Luckenbill, *Ancient Records,* 2:245.

[16] Daniel David Luckenbill, *The Annals of Sennacherib* (Chicago: University of Chicago Press, 1924), 83.

[17] Thirtle suggested that Ps. 137 reflects the past feelings of captives who returned from Babylon in Isaiah's day. James W. Thirtle, *Old Testament Problems* (London: Morgan & Scott, 1916), 130–131.

[18] James B. Pritchard, ed., *Ancient Near Eastern Texts Relating to the Old Testament,* 2d ed. (Princeton: Princeton University Press, 1955), 316.

Isaiah 13:17–19 / 143

> [17]See, I will stir up against them the Medes,
> who do not care for silver and have no delight
> in gold.

The Assyrians directed eight campaigns against Media shortly before Isaiah's time. When Isaiah was a young man, Tiglath-Pileser III made a more thorough conquest of what he called "the mighty Medes." Then Sargon II received tribute from them and kept them under control.[19]

Assyrians in the time of Sennacherib labeled all Medes and Persians "Madai," that is, Medes.[20] The Medes referred to by Isaiah may be a general term for the combined armies of Sennacherib. Certainly, since Herodotus spoke of the armies of Sennacherib as "the Arabian host"[21] after Sennacherib passed through Arabia in 688 B.C., it is not impossible that Isaiah would specifically recognize the Median contingent of Sennacherib's army in 689. On the other hand, they may be designated as the part of his army that did not want spoil (having no "care for silver . . . no delight in gold"), only revenge. This does not fit the later time of Cyrus. The later armies of the Medes and Persians considered themselves deliverers of Babylon from the misrule of Nabonidus and Belshazzar.[22]

> [18]Their bows will strike down the young men;
> they will have no mercy on infants nor will they
> look with compassion on children.

The cruel treatment and merciless slaughter described in this verse was typical of the Assyrian armies. Cyrus was a different kind of conqueror. He destroyed no Mesopotamian cities. Ancient records show that in 539 B.C. the people of Babylon welcomed his army in by throwing open the city gates. They even gave Cyrus a triumphal entry complete with palm branches.[23]

> [19]Babylon, the jewel of kingdoms, the glory of
> the Babylonians' pride, will be overthrown by
> God like Sodom and Gomorrah.

---

[19]Luckenbill, *Ancient Records*, 1:281; 2:6; Pfeiffer, *State Letters of Assyria*, 76.
[20]E. E. Herzfeld, *Archaeological History of Iran* (London: Humphrey Milford for the British Academy, Oxford University Press, 1935), 9.
[21]Herodotus, *History*, 131, 133.
[22]Cf. Pritchard, *Ancient Near Eastern Texts*, 316.
[23]Ibid., 306.

Babylon, in Isaiah's day, was indeed a "jewel" among ancient kingdoms. The Chaldeans under Merodach-Baladan made it "the glory" of their pride.[24] No one believed anything could destroy it. The world of that day expressed horror and shock at its sudden, total destruction by Sennacherib. The city was leveled, so its destruction compares with that of Sodom and Gomorrah. That the Assyrians are not mentioned here is in line with Isaiah's recognition that a holy God was using the Assyrians to bring His divine judgment. He gives the city no hope at this point.

> [20]She will never be inhabited or lived in through all generations; no Arab will pitch his tent there, no shepherd will rest his flocks there. [21]But desert creatures will lie there, jackals will fill her houses; there the owls will dwell, and there the wild goats will leap about. [22]Hyenas will howl in her strongholds, jackals in her luxurious palaces. Her time is at hand, and her days will not be prolonged.

The verbs (v. 20) are active, not passive. The first part is literally, "It will not sit forever; it will not dwell [continue] from generation to generation."[25] This needs to be connected with the last part of verse 22, where the repetition emphasizes that Babylon's destruction is soon to come. Before her destruction in 689 B.C., Babylon's expectation was of a long, uninterrupted existence. The capture of the city by the Assyrians did not change that expectation. Even Sennacherib treated the city with considerable respect until he finally decided that it must be destroyed.

The emphasis of verse 20 is not on a future state, but on Babylon's current hopes, and on the soon, sudden, and total destruction of Babylon that they did not expect.[26] This was exactly the case in 689 B.C. but not in any other time in Babylon's history. Thus, the meaning is not that the city would never be inhabited. The city was too important to be left in the condition described in these verses, where Arabians and shep-

---

[24]Boutflower, *Book of Isaiah*, 69.

[25]John Calvin, *Commentary on the Book of the Prophet Isaiah*, trans. William Pringle (Grand Rapids: Wm. B. Eerdmans, 1948), 1:427; cf. Joseph A. Alexander, *Commentary on the Prophecies of Isaiah* (Grand Rapids: Zondervan Publishing House, 1953), 1:281.

[26]E. Flecker, *A New Translation of Isaiah* (London: Elliot Stock, 1901), 109.

herds avoided it and where wild animals made it their home. So after a time, Esarhaddon rebuilt it, Nebuchadnezzar enlarged it, Cyrus and Alexander the Great honored it, and it remained a great city for many centuries—only gradually being deserted after Baghdad took the leadership in that part of the world.[27] Today, though Saddam Hussein has tried to restore parts of ancient Babylon, its ruins still remind us that God will destroy evil.

2. Israel Restored But Babylon Judged 14:1–23

a. Compassion On Judah 14:1–2

¹The Lord will have compassion on Jacob; once again he will choose Israel and will settle them in their own land. Aliens will join them and unite with the house of Jacob. ²Nations will take them and bring them to their own place. And the house of Israel will possess the nations as menservants and maidservants in the Lord's land. They will make captives of their captors and rule over their oppressors.

Before continuing with the judgment on Babylon, Isaiah reminds Israel (also called Jacob) that God's purpose has not changed. He is still faithful. His compassion is an intense love full of mercy and affection. Settling the Israelites "in their own land" could also mean providing them with security, peace, and rest. Conditions will be the reverse of what they were in Isaiah's day. Instead of nations taking them captive, nations will restore Israel to its own land. Instead of nations taking possession of Israel, Israel will possess the nations, and the people of the nations will serve Israel. Their captors will be the captives, and Israel will rule over the despots who once oppressed them. God will still use Israel in His divine plan.

b. A Taunt Against The King Of Babylon 14:3–8

³On the day the Lord gives you relief from suffering and turmoil and cruel bondage,

---

[27]Saddam Hussein has tried to restore some of the ruins of ancient Babylon. See McKenna, *Isaiah 1–39*, 173.

There will be a day of relief from the hardship, turmoil, and hard labor that was endured by those taken captive by the Assyrians. Although Nebuchadnezzar later settled Jews in Babylonia, he did not put them through such pain and hard labor. The kingdom of God initiated by Jesus brought relief (Matt. 11:28–30), but the Millennium will bring complete relief.

> **⁴you will take up this taunt against the king of Babylon: How the oppressor has come to an end! How his fury has ended!**

When that day comes, the people will be able to "take up this taunt," a mocking song against the king of Babylon. Though patterned after the royal funeral orations of the day, its content is sharply satirical, revealing the truth about the king.[28] The king is not named because he does not deserve to be remembered.

However, this particular king of Babylon is identified in verses 17–20 as one who did not let his captives return to their homes and did not himself receive a proper tomb-burial like other kings.

These facts fit Tiglath-Pileser III, the only Assyrian king in Isaiah's day who took the title "King of Babylon" and ascended its throne.[29] He established the Neo-Assyrian Empire and instituted the policy of taking people captive to other lands. Before his time, a conqueror would tell the inhabitants of a city how much tax or tribute they had to pay and would then let them go back to rebuild their homes. But Tiglath-Pileser III took people into exile in hope of controlling them better.

His death perfectly fulfilled the prophecies in verses 18–20. He took the title "King of Babylon" in 729 B.C., two years before he died. The details of this passage fit him, but do not fit what we know about later Babylonian kings.[30]

---

[28] John H. Hayes and Stuart A. Irvine, *Isaiah: The Eighth-Century Prophet* (Nashville: Abingdon Press, 1987), 231.

[29] Flecker, *New Translation of Isaiah*, 109. Flecker was one of the first to identify the king here as Tiglath-Pileser III. Boutflower also showed reasonable grounds for it. Boutflower, *Book of Isaiah*, 73.

[30] For further evidence of this see Boutflower, *Book of Isaiah*, 18, 73. See also George Buchanan Gray, *A Critical and Exegetical Commentary on the Book of Isaiah I–XXXIX*, in *The International Critical Commentary* (Edinburgh: T. & T. Clark, 1949), 251; George Livingstone Robinson, *The Book of Isaiah*, rev. ed. (Grand Rapids: Baker Book House, 1954), 51.

> ⁵The LORD has broken the rod of the wicked,
> the scepter of the rulers,

The LORD is truly the One who shatters "the rod [power] of the wicked [guilty people]" and "the scepter [governing authority] of the rulers." He uses them to bring His judgment, but they in turn are judged (cf. 10:12).

> ⁶which in anger struck down peoples with unceasing blows, and in fury subdued nations with relentless aggression.

Tiglath-Pileser III and his cohorts were extreme in their brutalities against nations. Every year the Assyrian armies went out on military campaigns and relentlessly "struck down peoples." No one was able to restrain their cruel aggression. In his records, Tiglath-Pileser said he smashed like pottery all who did not obey him and scattered them to the winds like a hurricane.

> ⁷All the lands are at rest and at peace; they break into singing.

The world rejoices at the death of this oppressor, for now they can enjoy rest and quiet (cf. Nah. 1:15; Zech. 1:11). "Singing" includes shouts of joy.

> ⁸Even the pine trees and the cedars of Lebanon exult over you and say, "Now that you have been laid low, no woodsman comes to cut us down."

Now Isaiah mockingly addresses the departed king via trees of the forest, for even the natural world rejoices. No Assyrian woodsman comes to cut down "the pine trees and the cedars of Lebanon" (cf. 2:13; 10:34; 33:9; 37:24).

c. Sheol's Reception Of Babylon's King 14:9–11

> ⁹The grave below is all astir to meet you at your coming; it rouses the spirits of the departed to greet you—all those who were leaders in the world; it makes them rise from their thrones—all those who were kings over the nations.

In Sheol (not the grave, but hell)[31] the departed spirits are stirred up to meet the king of Babylon. They had retained their personal identity, being recognizable to each other. They included leaders and kings killed by Tiglath-Pileser III and his armies. The leaders are called in the Hebrew *'attudim,* "he goats," comparing them to male goats leading a flock. But now they are reduced to weakness. They are pictured as sitting in darkness on shadowy thrones. They have not changed, but their thrones are meaningless.

> **10They will all respond, they will say to you, "You also have become weak, as we are; you have become like us."**

Tiglath-Pileser III was the most powerful king of his time. He had impressed other kings by his majesty and by his claims of deity. They are amazed that in death he has become as weak and as ineffectual as they.

> **11All your pomp has been brought down to the grave, along with the noise of your harps; maggots are spread out beneath you and worms cover you.**

Tiglath-Pileser III called himself "the great king, the mighty king, the king of the universe." In spite of all his pomp, he has been brought down to Sheol, having become no different than any other sinner. His body has been left without any of the glory he arrayed himself with in life. He is now on a bed of maggots and blanketed with worms. As part of his judgment he has not had a proper burial.

d. The King Of Babylon's Pride And Fall 14:12–17

> **12How you have fallen from heaven, O morning star, son of the dawn! You have been cast down to the earth, you who once laid low the nations!**

The pomp brought down to Sheol is described as a fall "from heaven." The king is called the "morning star, son of the dawn."

---

[31]See Stanley M. Horton, *Our Destiny: Biblical Teachings on the Last Things* (Springfield, Mo.: Logion Press, 1996), 44–51.

Like the morning star that fades in the light of dawn, he has lost all his brilliance now that he is in hell. He who once defeated the nations is now broken in pieces on the ground.

The KJV translates "morning star" as "Lucifer," a term borrowed from the Roman Catholic Latin Vulgate version of the Bible, meaning "light-bearer." Because of the arrogant claims of the king of Babylon, the name Lucifer was applied to the devil by Jerome (translator of the Latin Vulgate)—recognizing that Satan really did fall from heaven (cf. Luke 10:18). Luther and Calvin, however, said that applying the name to Satan here was a great error. Certainly Satan did not become as weak as the people in hell (Isa. 14:9). Nevertheless, Satan was certainly behind the king's pride and arrogance. As a fading morning star, he is in contrast to Christ, the true "bright Morning Star" (Rev. 22:16).[32]

> [13]You said in your heart, "I will ascend to heaven; I will raise my throne above the stars of God; I will sit enthroned on the mount of assembly, on the utmost heights of the sacred mountain.

The king's ascent "to heaven" was only by his arrogance and self-exaltation. Notice the repetition of "I will." In his heart, that is, in his ambitious thoughts, he determined he would ascend to heaven, exalt his throne above the stars of God, and sit in the assembly on top of "the sacred mountain" (Heb. *tsaphon*). Mount Tsaphon ("north") was thought by the pagans to be the seat of the chief gods. The godly people of Jerusalem recognized only one true God and one place on earth where He was manifesting himself—Mount Zion (see Deut. 12:5; Ps. 48:1–2, etc.). Thus, Isaiah's audience would recognize that the king of Babylon was claiming to be greater than any god, even greater than the one true God.

This same arrogance was later displayed by Sennacherib when he sent his chief officer to try to get Jerusalem to surrender and warn them not to listen to their king, Hezekiah, or trust

---

[32]Note that the king's power ended at his fall. Satan's power has not yet ended. Cf. Edward J. Young, *The Book of Isaiah*, 3 vols. (Grand Rapids: Wm. B. Eerdmans, 1969–72), 1:441.

the LORD (36:18–20). Sennacherib was really claiming to be greater than any god, even greater than the God of Israel—whom he classed with the gods of the other nations.

> ¹⁴I will ascend above the tops of the clouds; I will make myself like the Most High."

In his pride, the king of Babylon also said he would ascend above the highest clouds, above where the gods were thought to live. By this act he would put himself on a par with the "Most High" (Heb. *'elyon,* a title that really belonged only to the one true God; cf. Gen. 11:1–4; 14:18–20,22; Dan. 4:17,24–25; 2 Thess. 2:4). What a profound sin this was! It was like the sin of Adam and Eve, the sin of the tower of Babel, and will be the sin of the Antichrist (2 Thess. 2:4).

> ¹⁵But you are brought down to the grave, to the depths of the pit.

Continuing the thought of verses 9–12, the self-exalted king of Babylon who was reaching for the highest point in heaven will be brought down to the lowest part of Sheol—in fact, "to the [inmost] depths of the pit." ("Pit" is used here as a synonym for Sheol.)³³

> ¹⁶Those who see you stare at you, they ponder your fate: "Is this the man who shook the earth and made kingdoms tremble,

Now Isaiah directs our attention to the fact that the body of Tiglath-Pileser III would lie unburied, something considered humiliating by ancient people. This also confirms the fact that Sheol is not in the grave, for the king's body was not in a grave. People will look at his corpse and say with surprise and disgust, "Is this the man who shook the earth and made kingdoms tremble?"

"The man" (Heb. *ha'ish*) means an individual male human being, and is further indication that the primary meaning of this passage applies to Tiglath-Pileser III, not to Satan.

> ¹⁷the man who made the world a desert, who overthrew its cities and would not let his captives go home?"

---

³³*Sh*ᵉ*'ol* is not the grave but the place of departed spirits. See note on 5:14.

In establishing the Neo-Assyrian Empire, Tiglath-Pileser III stripped everything valuable from the territories he conquered, leaving them each as a wilderness, or desert. He also instituted the policy of taking people into exile instead of letting them go back and rebuild their homes.

e. The King Of Babylon Lacks A Proper Burial 14:18–20

> 18 All the kings of the nations lie in state, each in his own tomb. 19 But you are cast out of your tomb like a rejected branch; you are covered with the slain, with those pierced by the sword, those who descend to the stones of the pit. Like a corpse trampled underfoot,

In Bible times, tombs were considered important in honoring the dead. In contrast to all other kings of the time, Tiglath-Pileser III would not be royally buried in a magnificent tomb, or mausoleum. He would be cast out "like a rejected branch," like the blood-soaked clothing of people slain by the sword, "like a corpse trampled underfoot." Ironically, "branch" (Heb. *netser*) is the same word used of the Messiah in 11:1. What a contrast between the shame of the tyrant, the rotten branch who called himself "king of the universe," and the glory of the righteous Branch from the line of David, Jesus, the true King of kings and Lord of lords!

> 20 you will not join them in burial, for you have destroyed your land and killed your people. The offspring of the wicked will never be mentioned again.

The king of Babylon will not have a proper burial because he destroyed his land and slaughtered his people. This charge is leveled against all the kings of Assyria in Isaiah 37:18. The last part of the verse, "the offspring of the wicked will never be mentioned again," can be taken as an imperative: "Don't ever mention the name of this descendant of evil doers, this king of Babylon." Perhaps that is another reason why Isaiah did not mention the name of Tiglath-Pileser III in this passage.

f. Babylon To Become A Swampland 14:21–23

²¹Prepare a place to slaughter his sons for the sins of their forefathers; they are not to rise to inherit the land and cover the earth with their cities.

The command is also to "prepare a place to slaughter his sons" for the guilt of their fathers. They dare not rise "to inherit the land" and fill the face of the inhabited earth with cities—which would serve as symbols of their power and authority.

²²"I will rise up against them," declares the Lord Almighty. "I will cut off from Babylon her name and survivors, her offspring and descendants," declares the Lord.

God's judgment is not merely against the king of Babylon but against Babylon itself. God will cut off its name—that is, its power and authority—and will not leave it a remnant as He promised for Israel.

²³"I will turn her into a place for owls and into swampland; I will sweep her with the broom of destruction," declares the Lord Almighty.

The destruction of Babylon will be such that only lowly animals will inhabit it. God's agent for making it "into swampland" and sweeping the city with the stiff "broom of destruction" was Sennacherib. He razed it in 689 B.C. and dug trenches from the river to flood the city and turn it into a swamp. Older writers usually connected its being flooded with Herodotus's account of the supposed diversion of the Euphrates River by Cyrus.[34] The records of Cyrus are silent about this, however, and because the Babylonians welcomed his army, it would not even have been necessary.

Others have supposed that the city gradually became an uninhabitable marsh, after long ages. But Babylon has not yet become an uninhabitable marsh. The area has become more like a desert since the time of the Seleucids in the third century B.C., but it has orchards and gardens nearby even now. Since the

---

[34]Joseph A. Alexander, *Commentary on the Prophecies of Isaiah,* 2 vols. in 1 (1875; reprint, Grand Rapids: Zondervan Publishing House, 1975), 1:304.

eleventh century A.D., the town of Hilla has been on the southern edge of its site. We know of only one time when Babylon became an uninhabitable marsh—the few years after 689 B.C. when Sennacherib leveled the city and flooded its site.[35]

STUDY QUESTIONS

1. Why does Isaiah start this section on foreign prophecies with Babylon?
2. What characterized Babylon in Isaiah's day?
3. What will enable peoples captive in Babylon to flee back to their own lands?
4. What statements show that Babylon's destruction was soon to come? How was this fulfilled?
5. What evidence from chapter 14 and from archaeology shows that the king of Babylon was Tiglath-Pileser?
6. How did this king exalt himself?
7. What shows this king was only a man?
8. How was the destruction of Babylon fulfilled?

B. Judgment On Many Nations 14:24–17:14

1. Assyria To Be Crushed In God's Land 14:24–27

> ²⁴The LORD Almighty has sworn, "Surely, as I have planned, so it will be, and as I have purposed, so it will stand. ²⁵I will crush the Assyrian in my land; on my mountains I will trample him down. His yoke will be taken from my people, and his burden removed from their shoulders."

At the time Isaiah prophesied, it seemed that nothing could stop Assyria. But God had a firm purpose to break Assyrian

---
[35]Merrill F. Unger, *Unger's Bible Dictionary* (Chicago: Moody Press, 1957), 116.

domination, and this is expressed in strong terminology, like that of an oath.

God committed himself to break and destroy the Assyrian in His own land, the land of Judah. The following year (688 B.C.) the prophecy was fulfilled. Isaiah saw this in 10:12. God's purpose was to punish the Assyrians in due time. The destruction of the 185,000 of Sennacherib's army effectively did that (37:36–37). Sennacherib never made another military campaign during the remaining years of his reign.[1]

> 26This is the plan determined for the whole world; this is the hand stretched out over all nations. 27For the LORD Almighty has purposed, and who can thwart him? His hand is stretched out, and who can turn it back?

Now God's purpose is extended to the whole earth. His hand is "stretched out" to bring judgment on the nations. No human being or earthly power can keep Him from fulfilling His purposes. He is the Lord of history.

2. PHILISTIA WILL NOT ESCAPE JUDGMENT 14:28–32

> 28This oracle came in the year King Ahaz died:

Isaiah now goes back to 715 B.C., the year King Ahaz died. (As in 6:1, the dating is in the year the king died, not the year of the accession of the new king, because the new king was already on the throne as joint ruler with his father.) Ahaz had made the treaty with Assyria in disobedience to God (see chap. 7). Now that he was gone, there was a temptation to break that treaty.

> 29Do not rejoice, all you Philistines, that the rod that struck you is broken; from the root of that snake will spring up a viper, its fruit will be a darting, venomous serpent.

Some take "the rod that struck" Philistia to be the house of David. David had subdued the Philistines. Judah had long kept

---

[1] He left no late records except a few building inscriptions at Nineveh and Asshur. See Daniel David Luckenbill, *Ancient Records of Assyria and Babylonia*, 2 vols. (Chicago: University of Chicago Press, 1926–27), 2:183.

them in check. But with the treaty of Ahaz, Judah became subservient to Assyria. Thus, its power over Philistia was broken. On the other hand, Isaiah may have had the power of Assyria in mind. It seemed to the people that Assyrian power was broken because after Shalmaneser V died in 722 B.C., King Sargon II was busy dealing with revolts in the other end of his empire and was not able to drive Merodach-Baladan out of Babylon at this time. Consequently, it seemed a good time to revolt against Assyria, but it was a mistake to do so. The "root" and "fruit" mean the whole tree (cf. a similar merism at 9:14–15). Out of it will come other vicious Assyrian kings like snakes, each one more venomous than the one before.[2]

> 30The poorest of the poor will find pasture, and the needy will lie down in safety. But your root I will destroy by famine; it will slay your survivors.

"The poorest of the poor" is literally "the firstborn of the poor." It speaks of Israel as God's "firstborn" (Exod. 4:22). "The needy" seems to refer to the people of Jerusalem, but God's judgment will bring famine and death to the Philistines.

> 31Wail, O gate! Howl, O city! Melt away, all you Philistines! A cloud of smoke comes from the north, and there is not a straggler in its ranks.

The "gate" represents the "city," and both words are collective here. So instead of rejoicing, all the cities and people of Philistia should be howling and crying, for they will be melted away, totally demoralized and unable to resist the enemy. The "cloud of smoke . . . from the north" is Assyria coming as a powerful army, leaving the smoke of burning cities behind it. It cannot be stopped, and Judah would be foolish to join with the Philistines in trying to do so.

> 32What answer shall be given to the envoys of that nation? "The LORD has established Zion, and in her his afflicted people will find refuge."

---

[2]Sargon put down Philistine revolts in 719 and 711 B.C.; Sennacherib put down one in 701. Herbert M. Wolf, *Interpreting Isaiah* (Grand Rapids: Zondervan Publishing House, Academie Books, 1985), 116.

Philistine messengers apparently want Hezekiah to join them in rebelling against Assyria. But Jerusalem must declare her trust in God who "established" (Heb. *yissad,* "founded") her. Her "afflicted people"—even the poorest and most humble—will find safe refuge in her. Sargon did not attack Jerusalem, and Sennacherib failed to take it. (See chaps. 36 and 37 for God's dealings with Sennacherib.)

It is also probable that when Ahaz died in 715 B.C., Hezekiah was free to cleanse the temple and celebrate the great Passover described in 2 Chronicles 29:3 to 30:27. He would not have been able to do that while his father was alive. Nor would he have been able to destroy high places and altars in Ephraim and Manasseh before Hoshea was defeated and Samaria taken into exile in 722 B.C. Thus, Hezekiah counted 715 as the true first year of his reign even though he had reigned as king with his father for six years.

3. MOAB 15:1–16:14

Chapters 15 and 16 deal with Moab (descendants of Lot, Gen. 19:36–37) on the east side of the Dead Sea. Moab was subdued by David. Later, the northern kingdom of Israel controlled it from time to time. The form of these chapters is that of a lamentation.

a. Moab's Destruction 15:1–9

> ¹An oracle concerning Moab: Ar in Moab is ruined, destroyed in a night! Kir in Moab is ruined, destroyed in a night!

After the death of Jeroboam II of Israel (753 B.C.), Moab took over some of the cities that were formerly Israelite. Amos prophesied against Moab (Amos 2:1–3). Now Isaiah sees that unexpected, sudden destruction will be widespread, from Ar by the Arnon River in the north (Num. 21:15) to Kir (later known as Kerak) in the south. This probably took place during the reign of the Assyrian king Shalmaneser. The cities of Moab are not mentioned in any clear geographical pattern. This may mean that Shalmaneser fought on several fronts at the same time, or that he sent smaller units to the various cities.

> ²Dibon goes up to its temple, to its high places to weep; Moab wails over Nebo and Medeba. Every head is shaved and every beard cut off.

Dibon, the capital city under King Mesha, was about three miles north of the Arnon River. Its inhabitants will go to its temple devoted to its god, Chemosh, and to its open-air high places on the hill outside the city to weep, or howl. Moab's wailing over the cities Nebo (east of the Jordan River) and Medeba (southeast of the north end of the Dead Sea) shows they are destroyed. Shaved heads and beards were a sign of deep mourning, along with shame because of defeat.

> ³In the streets they wear sackcloth; on the roofs and in the public squares they all wail, prostrate with weeping.

Wearing coarse sackcloth made of black goat's hair was another sign of sorrow, mourning, and disgrace. The housetops and public squares were filled with people crying.

> ⁴Heshbon and Elealeh cry out, their voices are heard all the way to Jahaz. Therefore the armed men of Moab cry out, and their hearts are faint.

Heshbon, east of the Jordan and about fourteen miles southwest of Amman, had been assigned to the Levites (Josh. 21:39). However, it was captured by King Mesha of Moab and was still in Moabite hands in Isaiah's day. Elealeh was about two miles north-northeast of Heshbon. Jahaz was about ten miles southeast of Heshbon.

Moab's soldiers shout in alarm, for they have lost their courage. The whole country was in poor shape.

> ⁵My heart cries out over Moab; her fugitives flee as far as Zoar, as far as Eglath Shelishiyah. They go up the way to Luhith, weeping as they go; on the road to Horonaim they lament their destruction.

"My heart" is parallel to "I will bring" (v. 9). God is grieving over Moab. God's heart is always broken over the sins of people and over the judgment that must come. He seems to have a special place in His heart for Moab, possibly because of

Abraham's intercession for Sodom in Genesis 18 where Abraham's concern was really for Lot, whose daughter became the ancestress of the Moabites. God buried Moses somewhere in Moab (Deut. 34:6). Ruth, the ancestress of David, came from Moab. When Saul pursued David, David took his parents to Moab for protection. God's love still reached out to Moab, even though judgment must come on it.

The people of Moab are fleeing south to Zoar, the little city that escaped the destruction of Sodom and Gomorrah (Gen. 19:21–22). Their flight is rapid, like that of a three-year-old heifer that has never been yoked. Luhith, on the way to Zoar, was a hill, town, or fortress that might offer temporary refuge. Horonaim was another town on the way to Zoar.

> **6The waters of Nimrim are dried up and the grass is withered; the vegetation is gone and nothing green is left.**

The springs of Nimrim, probably the Wadi Numeirah (see Num. 32:3; Josh. 13:27), are toward the southeast end of the major portion of the Dead Sea. They have become arid, desertlike.

> **7So the wealth they have acquired and stored up they carry away over the Ravine of the Poplars.**

The wealth accumulated during prosperous times will have to be moved for preservation beyond the dry Ravine of the Poplars to the south, probably the Wadi Zerek on Moab's southern border.

> **8Their outcry echoes along the border of Moab; their wailing reaches as far as Eglaim, their lamentation as far as Beer Elim.**

The cry for help has penetrated the borders of Moab. Eglaim was probably in southern Moab. Beer Elim ("well of heroes") was on the northern border. The whole country was lamenting because of the destruction.

> **9Dimon's waters are full of blood, but I will bring still more upon Dimon—a lion upon the fugitives of Moab and upon those who remain in the land.**

The waters of Dimon constitute a stream east of the Dead Sea. The Dead Sea Scrolls and the Latin Vulgate read "Dibon" (see 15:2). Jerome said "Dimon" and "Dibon" were used interchangeably. "Dimon" may have been used here for a wordplay with the Hebrew word for blood *(dam)*. Streams running with blood were not enough judgment—for God will send still more. Those who escape the Assyrian army will be attacked by lions. There are some who interpret the lion to be the Assyrian army continuing to attack relentlessly.

b. Moab Contrasted To Zion 16:1–5

> ¹Send lambs as tribute to the ruler of the land, from Sela, across the desert, to the mount of the Daughter of Zion.

Returning to the situation of the people of Moab at the fords of the Arnon River, they are to send lambs "as tribute" (cf. 2 Kings 3:4, where King Mesha of Moab sent 100,000 lambs as tribute to Ahab, king of Israel). Fleeing Moabites would go south of the Dead Sea to Sela, an Edomite fortress on the top of a mountain near Petra (where Edomite remains still exist). Even in that fortress they did not feel safe. From Sela they would send the tribute to Jerusalem, seeking help.

> ²Like fluttering birds pushed from the nest, so are the women of Moab at the fords of the Arnon.

At the fords of the Arnon River the fugitive women of Moab were like birds whose nest has been scattered, leaving them to wander aimlessly. Their pitiful condition shows how much the Moabites need help.

> ³"Give us counsel, render a decision. Make your shadow like night—at high noon. Hide the fugitives, do not betray the refugees.

The Moabite messengers speak. They want Hezekiah and Jerusalem to "give . . . counsel" (carry out a plan), make a governmental decision, and provide a secure hiding place for the fugitives. They urge Jerusalem not to betray them by handing them over to the enemy.

> **⁴Let the Moabite fugitives stay with you; be their shelter from the destroyer." The oppressor will come to an end, and destruction will cease; the aggressor will vanish from the land.**

The Moabites want Jerusalem to let their fugitives live with them, giving them refuge from the destroying Assyrians.

The last part of this verse (as well as v. 5) looks ahead to the future, as Isaiah so often does, and presents a contrast. The Lord lets them know the time is coming when extortion and destruction will cease. The aggressors will perish.

> **⁵In love a throne will be established; in faithfulness a man will sit on it—one from the house of David—one who in judging seeks justice and speeds the cause of righteousness [cf. 11:2–4].**

The throne that "will be established" in steadfast, covenant-keeping love (Heb. *chesed*) is the Messiah's throne. He will sit on it in continual faithfulness in Jerusalem, being the true and rightful heir of David and fulfilling the covenant given to him. He will be a just judge, and diligent in promoting righteousness. The context indicates that the Messiah's rule will extend to the Gentiles. Therefore, this promise applies to Moab.

Some believe this verse means that in Isaiah's day, Hezekiah became a type of the Messiah and was expected to do what was right.

c. Moab's Pride Brought To Contempt 16:6–12

> **⁶We have heard of Moab's pride—her overweening pride and conceit, her pride and her insolence—but her boasts are empty.**

After dealing with the future way of salvation, Isaiah responds to the Moabite request and points to pride as the cause of Moab's destruction. Haughty Moab also rejected the faith expressed in verse 5. Its outbursts of fury were just empty talk.

> **⁷Therefore the Moabites wail, they wail together for Moab. Lament and grieve for the men of Kir Hareseth.**

Moab wails for itself (cf. 15:5,8). All of it wails for the "men" (lit., "raisin cakes"; Heb. *'ashishe*) of Kir Hareseth, the chief city in the southern part of Moab (cf. 15:1). The raisin cakes which they produced were part of their heathen worship (cf. Hos. 3:1). Unhelped by that worship, they can only moan that they are unmercifully beaten and their raisin-producing vineyards are destroyed.

> ⁸The fields of Heshbon wither, the vines of Sibmah also. The rulers of the nations have trampled down the choicest vines, which once reached Jazer and spread toward the desert. Their shoots spread out and went as far as the sea.

Heshbon at the northern border of Moab was once an Israelite city. The destroyer has "trampled down" its fields as well as the grapevines of Sibmah (also called Shebam, near Mount Nebo in the northern part of Moab). The Assyrians and their cohorts ("the rulers of the nations") also destroyed a vineyard which reached northward to Jazer, another former Israelite city (Josh. 21:39) about ten miles west of Amman, eastward to the desert and westward to the Dead Sea. Moab had expanded in all directions but is now destroyed.

> ⁹So I weep, as Jazer weeps, for the vines of Sibmah. O Heshbon, O Elealeh, I drench you with tears! The shouts of joy over your ripened fruit and over your harvests have been stilled.

The phrases "I weep" and "I drench you with tears" show again that the LORD mourns with Moab over the loss of its vineyards and summer fruits that have perished in the shout of battle. He has compassion even though they deserve the judgment (cf. Jesus' compassion for Jerusalem, Luke 13:34).

> ¹⁰Joy and gladness are taken away from the orchards; no one sings or shouts in the vineyards; no one treads out wine at the presses, for I have put an end to the shouting.

No one is rejoicing in the orchards or singing in the vineyards, and no one is trampling on the grapes in the presses, so no juice is flowing into the lower vat. God has put an end to their shout. Some see this as the fulfillment of "I will bring still more upon Dimon" (15:9).

> ¹¹My heart laments for Moab like a harp, my inmost being for Kir Hareseth.

Some interpret this verse as Isaiah speaking, and understand the prophet's reference to his heart (Heb. *me'ay,* "bowels") making a sound like the harp (Heb. *kinnor,* "lyre") for Moab and his inner parts for Kir Hareseth as an expression of sarcasm. However, since God is speaking in verse 10, it seems more likely that God is expressing the deep-seated hurt He feels (cf. His grief and pain in Noah's day, Gen. 6:6; cf. also Jer. 48:36). "Kir Hareseth" in Hebrew is *qir chares. Chares* means a broken piece of pottery, and the name is probably an ironic wordplay on the name of Kir Hareseth (16:7).

> ¹²When Moab appears at her high place, she only wears herself out; when she goes to her shrine to pray, it is to no avail.

It will be obvious when the Moabites go to their high places to worship and to seek help from their chief god, Chemosh, that they will only be tiring themselves out. Their prayers in his holy place will not bring victory. Those who turn away from the LORD to other religious practices will find them totally useless. The LORD is the one true God, the only One who can provide refuge and salvation.

d. Moab To Be Judged Within Three Years 16:13–14

> ¹³This is the word the LORD has already spoken concerning Moab. ¹⁴But now the Lord says: "Within three years, as a servant bound by contract would count them, Moab's splendor and all her many people will be despised, and her survivors will be very few and feeble."

The previous prophecy was made earlier by Isaiah (chap. 15). Now he adds that the Lord will fulfill it "within three years." This means three full years exactly, such as would be stated in a business contract given to someone who was hired for a job.

Within that time, Moab's glory will become of little account. Its remnant will be very small and without power. Assyria fulfilled this prophecy.

Today, Jordanian Arabs occupy that territory. The descendants of Moab were scattered, intermarried (probably with Arabs), and lost their national identity. There are no more Moabites.

4. Judgment On Damascus 17:1–3

¹An oracle concerning Damascus: "See, Damascus will no longer be a city but will become a heap of ruins.

When Isaiah began to prophesy, Damascus was a large, important, wealthy city with a long history. This prophecy of the destruction of Damascus was fulfilled by Tiglath-Pileser III in 732 B.C. and again in 728–727. He plundered the city, deported many of its people, executed its king, Rezin, and made it part of the Assyrian province of Hamath.[3] It had no more significance in Old Testament times. However, "no longer be a city" (Heb. *muṣar meʿir*, "removed from [being] a city") does not mean the destruction would be permanent, but that it would simply be complete at the time. Since there was fertile soil and a good water supply there, the city was rebuilt again and again.

²The cities of Aroer will be deserted and left to flocks, which will lie down, with no one to make them afraid.

The same Assyrian campaign that took Damascus also reached down into the northern part of Moab and took the cities of Aroer. (The Septuagint, however, reads "her cities," that is, the cities under the control of Damascus, not Aroer.) The Bible mentions three cities called Aroer: one in Judah (1 Sam. 30:28), one in Moab (Josh. 12:2), and one in Ammon (Josh. 13:25). If the cities in Moab and Ammon are meant, this would fit the situation after Tiglath-Pileser III partially depopulated the area.

---

[3]Charles F. Pfeiffer, *Old Testament History* (Grand Rapids: Baker Book House, 1987), 334.

> ³The fortified city will disappear from Ephraim,
> and royal power from Damascus; the remnant
> of Aram will be like the glory of the Israelites,"
> declares the LORD Almighty.

Northern Israel had allied itself with Damascus (see 7:5–6). Assyria's campaign of 734–732 B.C. that took Damascus also took the northern part of Israel (referred to here as "Ephraim," after its leading tribe). Thus, Israel had no more defenses on its northern border. Later, in 722, Samaria, its chief fortress, would be destroyed. Damascus and the remnant of Aram will also be without defenses. Their glory will be gone just as the glory of Israel will be gone. This was the word of the LORD Almighty (Heb. *Yahweh tseva'oth*, "the LORD of Hosts [armies]"), the One in ultimate control of the armies of earth and heaven.

5. THE HARVEST AND THE GLEANINGS 17:4–11

a. The Remnant Of Jacob Will Be Small 17:4–6

> ⁴"In that day the glory of Jacob will fade; the fat
> of his body will waste away.

Israel made a terrible mistake by allying itself with Damascus. The false, worldly glory of Jacob (Israel) will be reduced to nothing, like the fat on a starving man.

> ⁵It will be as when a reaper gathers the stand-
> ing grain and harvests the grain with his arm —
> as when a man gleans heads of grain in the
> Valley of Rephaim.

The glory of Israel is further compared to what is left after grain is harvested and the remaining heads of grain are gleaned. "Rephaim" means "ghosts," further emphasizing the tragedy of Israel's downfall. The valley was just southeast of Jerusalem and once had fertile fields of grain.

> ⁶Yet some gleanings will remain, as when an
> olive tree is beaten, leaving two or three olives
> on the topmost branches, four or five on the
> fruitful boughs," declares the LORD, the God of
> Israel.

There will be a remnant, but it will be small. It is compared to the few olives—"two or three . . . four or five"—left after the harvesters have beaten the branches for remaining olives.

b. A Day When People Will Look To God 17:7–8

⁷In that day men will look to their Maker and turn their eyes to the Holy One of Israel.

"That day" is the future Day of the LORD. God has a purpose in allowing Israel's glory to be brought down: to cause people (Heb. *ha'adam*, "the men," i.e., "humankind"—not just Israel, but the whole world), collectively and individually, to look steadfastly to ("have regard for," NASB) their Maker, who is also the Maker of Israel. God also uses Israel to get the world to acknowledge the one true God who is "the Holy One of Israel."

⁸They will not look to the altars, the work of their hands, and they will have no regard for the Asherah poles and the incense altars their fingers have made.

When they turn to God after suffering, they will not look again for help to the pagan altars or to idols. To make an application to his own day, Isaiah specifies that the "Asherah poles" and portable "incense altars" used in heathen worship will no longer be respected. The Law commanded the Israelites to break them down (Exod. 34:13). "Asherah poles" were either wooden images of Asherah or a stylized "tree of life," which stood at the entrances of houses of prostitution (cf. Deut. 16:21). These were brothels devoted to the goddess Asherah, who was considered by the Canaanites to be the mother of Baal and sixty-nine other gods.[4] We can apply this further to the fact that when people stand before God's judgment bench, nothing but trust in the LORD will help.

c. A Day Of Desolation 17:9

⁹In that day their strong cities, which they left because of the Israelites, will be like places abandoned to thickets and undergrowth. And all will be desolation.

---

[4]Some Canaanites considered her to be the consort of Baal. See Wolf, *Interpreting Isaiah*, 120.

Isaiah speaks again of God's judgment. Canaanites were once driven out because of their idolatry. The Law forbade worship in heathen shrines and high places left by the Canaanites. Though Israelites turned to such places many times, whenever they were truly serving the LORD, those places were deserted. In the Day of the LORD, the trust in "strong cities" will be abandoned like idolatrous shrines in times of revival.

d. Punished For Forgetting God 17:10–11

> **[10]You have forgotten God your Savior; you have not remembered the Rock, your fortress. Therefore, though you set out the finest plants and plant imported vines,**

God's judgment will come on Israel because their hearts and minds are no longer focused on their Savior—the One who delivered them out of Egypt, the God who is, and has been, "the Rock," their unfailing fortress. They have been too busy planting gardens[5] for the worship of false gods. The "imported vines" imply foreign alliances that were contrary to God's will. Thus, their forgetting God was a rebellion and a betrayal.

> **[11]though on the day you set them out, you make them grow, and on the morning when you plant them, you bring them to bud, yet the harvest will be as nothing in the day of disease and incurable pain.**

Their setting out (the Heb. may mean fencing carefully) a false garden and bringing the seed to blossom conveys a false hope of a good harvest. The harvest from their heathen worship and entangling alliances will amount to nothing. Instead they will reap God's judgment: "the day of disease and incurable pain."

It is also possible that their planting includes their plans to revolt against Assyria, possibly the revolt that was quelled by Tiglath-Pileser III in 734 B.C.

---

[5]"Finest plants" probably means "plants of the garden of Adonis." William L. Holladay, *A Concise Hebrew and Aramaic Lexicon of the Old Testament* (Grand Rapids: Wm. B. Eerdmans, 1986), 240.

6. Sudden Destruction 17:12–14

¹²Oh, the raging of many nations—they rage like the raging sea! Oh, the uproar of the peoples—they roar like the roaring of great waters!

Isaiah turns to the sudden destruction of the enemy, Assyria. "Oh" (Heb. *hoi*) can mean "alas," and indicates lamentation. There will be an "uproar" of nations like a storm at sea or a river at flood stage. Many nations ("waters") had joined Assyria.

¹³Although the peoples roar like the roar of surging waters, when he rebukes them they flee far away, driven before the wind like chaff on the hills, like tumbleweed before a gale.

The nations united under Assyria will come like a raging flood, but God will rebuke them. Instead of their sweeping everything before them as they expected, the LORD will speak a word and they will be swept away like chaff and tumbleweeds before a wind or a storm.

¹⁴In the evening, sudden terror! Before the morning, they are gone! This is the portion of those who loot us, the lot of those who plunder us.

God's judgment will take place in a night. This prophecy found a fulfillment in the death angel's judgment on the 185,000 of Sennacherib's army (2 Kings 19:35), a judgment deserved because of their terrorizing, looting, and plundering of Judah.

STUDY QUESTIONS

1. How and when was 14:25 fulfilled?
2. What judgment would come on the Philistines and why?
3. What would cause mourning in Moab?
4. Why would God show grief over Moab?
5. What did the Moabites want from Hezekiah and Jerusalem?
6. What were the causes of Moab's destruction?
7. What would happen in three years?

8. How was the destruction of Damascus fulfilled?
9. What will happen to the northern part of Moab and the northern part of Israel at the same time and why?
10. What judgment will come on Assyria?

C. Cush And Egypt 18:1–20:6

1. Judgment On Cush 18:1–6

¹Woe to the land of whirring wings along the rivers of Cush,

Isaiah now moves from the prophecy of judgment on many nations (17:12) to specific woe for Cush. The land of "whirring wings" (Heb. *tsiltsal*, "winged crickets") on both sides of "the rivers of Cush"—the blue and the white Nile—is the land of Cush, which is not modern Ethiopia, but the Sudan, south of Egypt. In the background, we may note that the Cushite pharaoh, Piankhi, invaded the Egypt's Delta about 725 B.C. and brought all but a small part under his control. He was concerned about the many Assyrian attempts to control Phoenician trade with Egypt.

²which sends envoys by sea in papyrus boats over the water. Go, swift messengers, to a people tall and smooth-skinned, to a people feared far and wide, an aggressive nation of strange speech, whose land is divided by rivers.

Isaiah orders messengers to go "by sea," that is, along the Mediterranean coast, in seagoing papyrus boats. They are commanded to go to a people tall or lanky and "smooth-skinned" (or, of bronze skin). These are a people evoking fear "far and wide," a nation expanding and trampling others under foot, and a land "divided by rivers" (Heb. *'asher-baz{^{e}}u n{^{e}}harim*, "whose rivers wash away.") Some take this to have a general application to any land accessible by water. Others take them to be the Assyrians, for their goal was to conquer Egypt and

Cush.[1] Others take the sea to be the Nile River (cf. Nah. 3:8), and the smooth-skinned people to be the Egyptians who, unlike the Semitic peoples, shaved.[2]

> ³All you people of the world, you who live on the earth, when a banner is raised on the mountains, you will see it, and when a trumpet sounds, you will hear it.

The call is to all people in the world. The raising of a banner (flag) and the blowing of a trumpet (ram's horn) was a signal for troops to go into action. Isaiah wants them to be ready to see and hear.

> ⁴This is what the LORD says to me: "I will remain quiet and will look on from my dwelling place, like shimmering heat in the sunshine, like a cloud of dew in the heat of harvest."

Isaiah then hears the LORD's word to him. The time for action had not yet come. God has His timing, and it is a mistake to get ahead of God. The LORD will "remain quiet" and do nothing but "look on" from His dwelling place, the temple, when there is "shimmering [or dazzling] heat in the sunshine," when there is a dewy mist "in the heat of harvest." In other words, the LORD will offer no support to plans of rebellion against Assyria, though He knows what is going on and is still in ultimate control. Hezekiah learned this the hard way when he rejected Isaiah's prophetic warnings and made an alliance with the Cushite king of Egypt.

> ⁵For, before the harvest, when the blossom is gone and the flower becomes a ripening grape, he will cut off the shoots with pruning knives, and cut down and take away the spreading branches.

Yet God has his time for action. He will not allow the harvest. Just as the grapes are beginning to ripen and the enemy is

---

[1] David L. McKenna, *Isaiah 1–39*, in *The Communicator's Commentary* (Dallas: Word Books, 1993), 198.
[2] Herbert Wolf and John Stek, "Isaiah notes," in *The NIV Study Bible*, ed. Kenneth Barker (Grand Rapids: Zondervan Bible Publishers, 1985), 1042.

expecting a harvest, He will take pruning knives and cut down the grapevines. This is what happened to Sennacherib when he expected to take Jerusalem, but instead was stricken by the death angel, who took the lives of 185,000 of his army. The word for the "shoots" of the grapevine (Heb. *zalzal*) seems to be a wordplay on the "whirring wings" (Heb. *tsiltsal*) of verse 1.

> ⁶They will all be left to the mountain birds of prey and to the wild animals; the birds will feed on them all summer, the wild animals all winter.

The Assyrians who flee back to their own land will leave many corpses, which will become a feast for "birds of prey" from the mountains and for "wild animals" of the land. There will be so much carnage that there will be sufficient food for the birds throughout the summer and for the wild animals throughout the winter.

2. Gifts Brought To The Lord 18:7

> ⁷At that time gifts will be brought to the Lord Almighty from a people tall and smooth-skinned, from a people feared far and wide, an aggressive nation of strange speech, whose land is divided by rivers—the gifts will be brought to Mount Zion, the place of the Name of the Lord Almighty.

The people described in 18:2 will send gifts to the almighty Lord of Hosts, "to Mount Zion, the place of the Name of the Lord Almighty [of hosts, armies]." There may have been an initial fulfillment of this in the gifts brought to Hezekiah after God healed him (2 Chron. 32:23). Ultimately, however, the whole world will see the Lord's glory as Jesus is established as the messianic King on Mount Zion.

3. Judgment On Egypt 19:1–15

> ¹An oracle concerning Egypt: See, the Lord rides on a swift cloud and is coming to Egypt. The idols of Egypt tremble before him, and the hearts of the Egyptians melt within them.

Before Assyria came against Judah in 701 B.C. King Hezekiah

was looking to Egypt for help. Egypt once made slaves of God's people and was often their enemy. Egyptians worshiped many gods and believed the sun god was greater than any other god. They also worshiped the pharaoh. Yet this prophecy about Egypt declares that God's power will make Egypt fear Judah (19:1–17). God will be worshiped in Egypt (19:18–22). Egypt and Assyria will unite in worship with Israel; God will make them a blessing. The LORD is coming on a light, swift cloud to Egypt, causing Egypt's idols ("nothings") to tremble and the people of Egypt to lose courage. This was a warning in Isaiah's day for Hezekiah and the people of Judah not to listen to Egyptian encouragement to rebel against Assyria.

> ²"I will stir up Egyptian against Egyptian—
> brother will fight against brother, neighbor
> against neighbor, city against city, kingdom
> against kingdom.

God will stir up internal discord, provoking the Egyptians to fight against each other. This took place in the 740s and 730s B.C., when cities of Egypt turned against each other in suspicion.

> ³The Egyptians will lose heart, and I will bring
> their plans to nothing; they will consult the
> idols and the spirits of the dead, the mediums
> and the spiritists.

Their spirit will be agitated, devastated, in shock, and their advice and plans will be confused by God. With human counselors contradicting themselves, the Egyptians will go to idols (lit., "worthless nonentities"), spirits of the dead, and to those mediums and spiritists who claimed to be possessed by such a spirit.

> ⁴I will hand the Egyptians over to the power of
> a cruel master, and a fierce king will rule over
> them," declares the Lord, the LORD Almighty.

God will hand over the Egyptians to severe masters and a fierce king will rule over them as a dictator. The Cushite (Ethiopian) Pharaoh Piankhi took control of all Egypt. In 715 B.C., he was succeeded by another hard master, Shabako. In 671, Esarhaddon of Assyria conquered Egypt's Delta to

Memphis, and in 663 Ashurbanipal took Thebes, Egypt's capital. God kept handing Egypt over to these and other conquerors.

> [5] The waters of the river will dry up, and the riverbed will be parched and dry. [6] The canals will stink; the streams of Egypt will dwindle and dry up. The reeds and rushes will wither, [7] also the plants along the Nile, at the mouth of the river. Every sown field along the Nile will become parched, will blow away and be no more. [8] The fishermen will groan and lament, all who cast hooks into the Nile; those who throw nets on the water will pine away.

Egypt depended on the Nile for its very life. What the Nile waters could not irrigate was nothing but desert sand. Where the Nile overflowed and where the Nile waters could be used for irrigation, the soil was rich. They could grow two, and in some places, three crops a year. For the Nile to dry up and the many streams, canals, and rivulets in the Delta area to be diminished or dry up was a terrible tragedy. Fish would die and cause a stink. The fish in the Nile were the chief source of protein in the Egyptians' diet. Egyptian history records several times when the Nile was not able to water the land.

> [9] Those who work with combed flax will despair, the weavers of fine linen will lose hope. [10] The workers in cloth will be dejected, and all the wage earners will be sick at heart.

The making of linen cloth from flax was a major industry in Egypt. Workers in flax and linen will be ashamed and grow pale, losing hope.

Although the NIV translates the Hebrew *shahthotheha* as "workers in cloth," or, weavers, it is better translated as "its pillars" which will be crushed (v. 10). The drying up of the land affects everyone, including the pillars or foundations of (Egyptian) society and the most humble day laborers, who will be distressed by this unfortunate turn of events.

> [11] The officials of Zoan are nothing but fools; the wise counselors of Pharaoh give senseless

advice. How can you say to Pharaoh, "I am one of the wise men, a disciple of the ancient kings"?

Zoan (also called Tanis) was a capital city in the Delta of Egypt. Its leaders bragged about their great wisdom. They would be exposed as "fools" (the Heb. here is an exclamation), too stupid to see the results of these actions. Pharaoh's counselors had a reputation for wisdom (cf. Acts 7:22), but they too proved to be as stupid as cattle. Isaiah asks them how they can say they are wise men, sons, or disciples, "of the ancient kings"?

> ¹²Where are your wise men now? Let them show you and make known what the LORD Almighty has planned against Egypt.

If the wise men of Egypt were really wise, they would be able to tell what the LORD Almighty, the LORD of hosts, has purposed for Egypt, and Isaiah challenges them to do so. It is clear they cannot. God has overruled their supposed wisdom.

> ¹³The officials of Zoan have become fools, the leaders of Memphis are deceived; the cornerstones of her peoples have led Egypt astray.

Not only have the leaders at Zoan "become fools," the leaders at Memphis (Heb. *noph*) have false hopes. They should have been "the cornerstones" upholding the "peoples" (Heb. *sh^evateha*, "tribes, districts, provinces") of Egypt. Instead, they made them go astray—a fatal mistake.

> ¹⁴The LORD has poured into them a spirit of dizziness; they make Egypt stagger in all that she does, as a drunkard staggers around in his vomit.

Because the leaders of Egypt were making the people go astray, the LORD increased their going astray by mingling a dizzy, staggering spirit among them.

Consequently, in everything they do they are staggering like a man so drunk that he has vomited upon himself. Such a person could not make wise decisions or lead people in the right direction. Some Bible scholars believe the staggering spirit was a spirit of judgment that mixed itself with their own spirits, controlling them.

> **15There is nothing Egypt can do—head or tail, palm branch or reed.**

Egypt and her leaders have put themselves in a hopeless position from which they cannot extricate themselves. Neither their leaders nor the common people, neither the high nor the low, can do anything about it. The whole situation is out of control.

4. A Day Of Smiting And Healing For Egypt 19:16–25

> **16In that day the Egyptians will be like women. They will shudder with fear at the uplifted hand that the Lord Almighty raises against them.**

Isaiah now looks ahead and gives five prophecies of a future day when Egypt will no longer be a dominant power. Instead, Egypt will be like helpless women, trembling in terror because of the divine hand of judgment God is shaking over them. Isaiah wanted Judah to see how foolish they were to trust Egypt for any help.

> **17And the land of Judah will bring terror to the Egyptians; everyone to whom Judah is mentioned will be terrified, because of what the Lord Almighty is planning against them.**

God will use the land of Judah. Instead of Egypt terrifying Judah, Judah will be a terror to Egypt. The very mention of Judah will "bring terror" because of what God is planning against Egypt. He is a holy God and must judge their sin.

> **18In that day five cities in Egypt will speak the language of Canaan and swear allegiance to the Lord Almighty. One of them will be called the City of Destruction.**

A second promise of the future day is not only judgment but blessing. "Five cities in Egypt" will turn to the Lord and "speak the language of Canaan [Hebrew] and swear allegiance to the Lord." One of these cities will be called "the City of Destruction"—a wordplay on "the City of the Sun," which the Greeks called Heliopolis. This may have had a partial fulfillment when Jews fled to Egypt and settled there after

Nebuchadnezzar destroyed Jerusalem. In New Testament times, a large contingent of Jews settled in Egypt. Complete fulfillment, however, looks ahead to the coming millennial kingdom.

> ¹⁹In that day there will be an altar to the LORD in the heart of Egypt, and a monument to the LORD at its border.

A third prophecy looks ahead to Egypt's coming to the LORD and a future Savior. Not only will there be allegiance to the LORD, but there will also be worship at an altar (a place of reconciliation to God and of pure worship) in the middle of Egypt and at a stone pillar or monument dedicated to the LORD at its border.

As late as 1935, a British Israel cult was proclaiming that the Great Pyramid of Cheops *(Khufu)* was the pillar and that the length of its main passage meant the present age would have its final end in 1936. All such date setting is forbidden by the Bible (see Mark 13:32–33; Acts 1:7; 1 Thess. 5:1–2). The Great Pyramid was built about 1,800 years before Isaiah's time. Isaiah saw the pillar as something in the future.

> ²⁰It will be a sign and witness to the LORD Almighty in the land of Egypt. When they cry out to the LORD because of their oppressors, he will send them a savior and defender, and he will rescue them.

The pillar will be for "a sign and witness" to the LORD in Egypt. Because of oppressors, Egyptians will cry for help to the LORD and He will send them a Savior (Heb. *moshia'*) and a Defender (Heb. *rav*, "one who will contend for them"), a mighty One who "will rescue them."

> ²¹So the LORD will make himself known to the Egyptians, and in that day they will acknowledge the LORD. They will worship with sacrifices and grain offerings; they will make vows to the LORD and keep them.

By his mighty acts the LORD will make himself known to Egypt, and the Egyptians will know the LORD in a personal way, worshiping Him and making vows to Him, which they will carry out with dedication.

> ²²The LORD will strike Egypt with a plague; he will strike them and heal them. They will turn to the LORD, and he will respond to their pleas and heal them.

God will cause His judgment to "strike Egypt" but His purpose will be to heal. The Egyptians will return in repentance to the LORD, and He will be moved by entreaties for them and "will respond . . . and heal them."

> ²³In that day there will be a highway from Egypt to Assyria. The Assyrians will go to Egypt and the Egyptians to Assyria. The Egyptians and Assyrians will worship together.

The fourth prophecy looks forward to a time of peace. In Isaiah's day Egypt and Assyria were enemies. Judah was caught in a vise between them. In the future Day of the LORD this will no longer be so. Instead, a highway (a built-up or elevated roadway) between Egypt and Assyria will provide for both to go back and forth freely. No longer will they fight each other. Instead, they "will worship [the LORD] together," united in spirit because they have been accepted by and united to the LORD.

> ²⁴In that day Israel will be the third, along with Egypt and Assyria, a blessing on the earth. ²⁵The LORD Almighty will bless them, saying, "Blessed be Egypt my people, Assyria my handiwork, and Israel my inheritance."

The fifth prophecy promises a united body that includes Israel, Egypt, and Assyria. Israel "will be the third," for God will speak first of Egypt as His people—though they once refused to let His chosen people go. Then He speaks of Assyria as the work of his hands—though they once worshiped gods made by their own hands. And last, He claims Israel as His inheritance—though many of them would reject the One who alone can make us heirs of God (see Rom. 8:17).

God will bless them all and make them all a blessing to the rest of the world. His ultimate purpose for all the families of the earth has always been blessing (Gen. 12:3). Nations once mortal enemies of one another will become brothers in the LORD and will no longer invade each other. Instead, they will visit with each other as trusted friends. Together they will all become a new people of God with Israel having a central place as God's inheritance. This is far from being fulfilled today. As Isaiah says, it will be so "in that day," the millennial day when Christ shall reign.

5. Egypt And Cush—A False Hope 20:1–6

> ¹In the year that the supreme commander, sent by Sargon king of Assyria, came to Ashdod and attacked and captured it—

Sargon II, mentioned only here in the Old Testament, reigned from 721–705 B.C. Sargon's records tell how Azuri, king of the Philistine city of Ashdod about 713, refused to pay tribute to Assyria and sent messages to neighboring kings to do the same. In this act of rebellion Egypt urged him on. Egypt failed to keep its promises to him, however, and in 711 Sargon's "supreme commander" (Heb. *tartan*) took Ashdod, thirty-three miles west of Jerusalem, near the Mediterranean coast, and made it an Assyrian province.[3]

> ²at that time the Lord spoke through Isaiah son of Amoz. He said to him, "Take off the sackcloth from your body and the sandals from your feet." And he did so, going around stripped and barefoot.

Isaiah had been wearing sackcloth as a sign of mourning over the sins of the people. The Lord told him to take it off and remove his sandals as well. "Stripped" does not mean completely naked here. Rather, it means wearing only a loincloth or an extremely short wraparound tunic. By doing this he was making himself an example of what conquerors such as the Assyrians would do when they stripped their captives of everything they owned, including their sandals.

> ³Then the Lord said, "Just as my servant Isaiah has gone stripped and barefoot for three years, as a sign and portent against Egypt and Cush, ⁴so the king of Assyria will lead away stripped

---

[3] Three fragments naming Sargon and commemorating his victory over Ashdod were discovered there in 1963.

> and barefoot the Egyptian captives and Cushite exiles, young and old, with buttocks bared—to Egypt's shame.

The LORD calls Isaiah "my servant" because of his obedience and faithfulness and because God was using him to give prophecies that declared His power, glory, and eternal plan.

Isaiah's going about "stripped and barefoot" would be a warning and a sign concerning Egypt and Cush. These countries were united at this time (since 715 B.C.), and they believed they could withstand Assyria.

Later, in 701 B.C., the Ethiopian pharaoh Shebitku sent an army against Sennacherib, but it was defeated at Eltekeh, thirty-two miles west-northwest of Jerusalem.[4] Isaiah gave them an object lesson in advance about what would happen to them. The Assyrians would take captives from Egypt and Cush stripped and barefoot into exile. This humiliation, especially with their "buttocks bared" (which would be visible as they bent over), would bring them great shame.[5]

Hezekiah was tempted to trust in Egypt but apparently listened to Isaiah at this particular time and did not join in the Philistine rebellion.[6]

> [5]Those who trusted in Cush and boasted in Egypt will be afraid and put to shame. [6]In that day the people who live on this coast will say, 'See what has happened to those we relied on, those we fled to for help and deliverance from the king of Assyria! How then can we escape?'"

The Philistines along the coast who trusted in Cush and Egypt to help them would be ashamed and afraid. With Cush and Egypt defeated by Assyria, how would they escape? Their cry of despair would be echoed not only by the Philistines but

---

[4]The location of Eltekeh is not certain. Some place it twenty-five miles west of Jerusalem.

[5]Sennacherib claimed he "personally captured alive the Egyptian charioteers with their princes and also the charioteers of the king of Ethiopia." James B. Pritchard, ed., *Ancient Near Eastern Texts Relating to the Old Testament,* 3d ed. (Princeton: Princeton University Press, 1969), 287.

[6]Sargon claimed he received gifts from Judah. See Pritchard, *Ancient Near Eastern Texts,* 287.

also by the people of Judah. There would be no escape unless they trusted in God.

STUDY QUESTIONS

1. What does God want all the people of the world to see?
2. How will God keep the enemies of Israel from their expected harvest?
3. Why was it important for Israel to listen to God's warnings against listening to Egypt?
4. What indicated that Egypt would no longer be a dominant power in that day?
5. What changes will come in Egypt in the future millennial day?
6. What object lesson did Isaiah teach by going around stripped and barefoot?

D. FULFILLMENTS IN ISAIAH'S DAY 21:1–23:18

1. PROPHECY OF BABYLON'S FALL FULFILLED 21:1–10

a. Babylon Attacked 21:1–5

¹An oracle concerning the Desert by the Sea: Like whirlwinds sweeping through the southland, an invader comes from the desert, from a land of terror.

The "sea land" is what the Assyrians called the lower part of the Mediterranean region, especially the part dominated by Merodach-Baladan. The "Desert by the Sea" is what Babylon would become because of God's judgment. "The Sea" is the Persian Gulf southeast of Babylon. Like the destructive windstorms that sweep into Judah from "the southland" (the Negev desert to the south of Beersheba), so there will be terrible

180 / Isaiah 21:2-5

destruction for Babylon coming "from a land of terror," a land to be feared. In Isaiah's day this would be Assyria. The illustration of the whirlwinds from the Negev indicates that the writer was in Judah.[1]

> ²A dire vision has been shown to me: The traitor betrays, the looter takes loot. Elam, attack! Media, lay siege! I will bring to an end all the groaning she caused.

Isaiah sees "a dire vision," that is, a revelation having bad news. The traitor who betrays, the looter who lays waste to everything, is Assyria. Elam is told to attack.[2] In 691 B.C., Elam, who was hired by the priests of Babylon, defeated Sennacherib. Media probably joined in the battle. Then Sennacherib destroyed Babylon in revenge (in 689). The "end [of] all the groaning" indicates a victory over the nation causing the distress and probably indicates Babylon. Or this may refer to Assyria's defeat in 591 B.C.

> ³At this my body is racked with pain, pangs seize me, like those of a woman in labor; I am staggered by what I hear, I am bewildered by what I see. ⁴My heart falters, fear makes me tremble; the twilight I longed for has become a horror to me.

Isaiah's ministry was never easy. When he sees the terrible destruction of Babylon in this vision, it fills him with pain and bewilderment; he cannot continue to look at it. His "heart [mind] falters": shuddering and terrified. The "twilight" he desired was probably the destruction of Babylon, for he already knew it would cause trouble (see 39:6–7). Even so, the vision made him tremble, "a horror" to him. We should feel the same about the destruction of the Babylonian world system prophesied in Revelation 18 and 19.

> ⁵They set the tables, they spread the rugs, they eat, they drink! Get up, you officers, oil the shields!

---

[1] D. Otto Procksch, *Jesaia* (Leipzig, Germany: D. Werner Scholl, 1930), 261.
[2] That is, against Assyria, not Babylon as some suppose. Cf. Charles Boutflower, *The Book of Isaiah (Chapters I–XXXIX) in the Light of the Assyrian Monuments* (London: Society for Promoting Christian Knowledge, 1930), 157–58.

Isaiah sees them in Babylon preparing the table, spreading carpets, eating and drinking—banqueting. They are unprepared for what is coming. Their princes need to get up and "oil the shields" (so arrows and other weapons will glance off them). This phrase speaks of their need to quit their revelry and prepare for war.

b. Isaiah Receives News Of Babylon's Fall 21:6–10

> **6This is what the Lord says to me: "Go, post a lookout and have him report what he sees. 7When he sees chariots with teams of horses, riders on donkeys or riders on camels, let him be alert, fully alert."**

In another vision concerning Babylon, God's word to Isaiah was to post a lookout and have him report what he sees. When he sees chariots, teams of horses, and riders on donkeys or camels, he must pay strict attention. They will be bringing important news.

> **8And the lookout shouted, "Day after day, my lord, I stand on the watchtower; every night I stay at my post.**

The Hebrew text says "A lion *['aryeh]* cried out"[3] (cf. KJV and NASB). The Dead Sea Scrolls as well as the Syriac read "the seer *[haro'eh]* cried out" or shouted. The seer would be the "lookout." Like a lion he stood in his strength on the watchtower all day and remained standing as a sentinel all night.

> **9Look, here comes a man in a chariot with a team of horses. And he gives back the answer: 'Babylon has fallen, has fallen! All the images of its gods lie shattered on the ground!'"**

The lookout calls out to "a man in a chariot," drawn by a team of horses, who answers back that "Babylon has fallen. . . . All the images of its gods lie shattered on the ground!" This is not a prophecy; rather, it is a record of how Isaiah received the news of the destruction of Babylon in 689 B.C. by Sennacherib.[4]

---

[3]Millar Burrows, ed., et al., *The Isaiah Manuscript and the Habakkuk Commentary* (New Haven: American Schools of Oriental Research, 1950), 1: Plate 16, line 22.

[4]Oswald T. Allis, "Book of Isaiah," in *Wycliffe Bible Encyclopedia* (Chicago: Moody Press, 1975), 1:857.

He was the "traitor" and "looter" of 21:2.[5] This refers to Assyria, as in Isaiah 33:1.

Sennacherib boasted of his ability to destroy nations (37:11), and Hezekiah recognized him as a destroyer of images (37:19). Sennacherib's records show that he was angry with the priests of Babylon and had his soldiers smash the images,[6] except for those of Bel and Nebo, which he carried off to Nineveh (Isaiah 46).

We know of no other time when the images of Babylon's gods were shattered by a conqueror. Sargon did not do it; he entered Babylon peacefully and honored its gods.[7] Cyrus did not do it; he was a polytheist who, according to his own records, honored the gods of Babylon. He even interpreted his entrance into Babylon as a victory for Babylon's gods.[8]

In the New Testament, "Babylon" becomes the term for the entire world system that is destined to fall during the Great Tribulation at the end of the age (Rev. 14:8; 18:2). Since ancient Babylon involved a political, commercial, and religious system, so the apostle John sees the fall of those aspects of the present world system.[9]

> **10 O my people, crushed on the threshing floor,
> I tell you what I have heard from the LORD
> Almighty, from the God of Israel.**

The grain does not represent Isaiah's people crushed on the threshing floor, as the NIV takes it and as others think.[10] The Hebrew is literally "my threshing" and "the son of my threshing floor," in apposition to "I tell you what I have heard." "The son of my threshing floor" means the floor piled high with grain, picturing a great harvest—representing Isaiah's prophecies.[11] Isaiah means that Babylon has fallen exactly as he prophesied.

---

[5] Boutflower, *Book of Isaiah*, 154.

[6] Daniel David Luckenbill, *Ancient Records of Assyria and Babylonia*, 2 vols. (Chicago: University of Chicago Press, 1926–27), 2:152, 185.

[7] Ibid. 2:35

[8] Boutflower, *Book of Isaiah*, 149.

[9] J. Alec Motyer, *The Prophecy of Isaiah* (Downers Grove, Ill.: InterVarsity Press, 1993), 175–76. Motyer recognizes that this refers to 689 and that Isaiah also looks ahead "to the eschatological Babylon and the day of the Lord."

[10] For example, David L. McKenna, *Isaiah 1–39* in *The Communicator's Commentary* (Dallas: Word Books, 1993), 213.

[11] The news of the destruction of Babylon would not have made Isaiah call them "my threshing" meaning "my people."

Isaiah 21:11-15 / 183

This is the harvest of all his labors. This is the vindication and fulfillment of prophecies he gave long before. Later, Isaiah draws attention to the fact that the people have seen prophecy fulfilled (41:22–24,26–27), in contrast to the ineffectiveness of idols.

2. Morning And Night For Edom 21:11–12

> **11**An oracle concerning Dumah: Someone calls to me from Seir, "Watchman, what is left of the night? Watchman, what is left of the night?" **12**The watchman replies, "Morning is coming, but also the night. If you would ask, then ask; and come back yet again."

"Dumah" ("silence") is a symbolic name for Edom, south of the Dead Sea, where Esau's descendants lived. "Seir" is the mountain range of Edom, used collectively in this passage for the whole country. The watchman is asked how late it is in the night. The response is that the morning is coming, but also the night. That is, there will be a brief respite from trouble, but more trouble is on the way and will surely come (cf. Isa. 34:5–15). However, Isaiah does not leave them without hope. They can "come back yet again." This may imply that even they can come back to God and repent.

3. Judgment On Arabia Soon To Come 21:13–17

> **13**An oracle concerning Arabia: You caravans of Dedanites, who camp in the thickets of Arabia,

Arabia would be next after the destruction of Babylon. The Dedanites were important merchants of Arabia (cf. Ezek. 27:20; 38:13). Because of a sudden attack, they will go to "the thickets of Arabia" to hide from the terrible Assyrians. Sennacherib conquered Arabia in 688 B.C., after he had destroyed Babylon the year before.[12]

> **14**bring water for the thirsty; you who live in Tema, bring food for the fugitives. **15**They flee from the sword, from the drawn sword, from the bent bow and from the heat of battle.

---

[12] Boutflower, *Book of Isaiah*, 10, 149.

They will need to bring water to thirsty fugitives. People of Tema, midway between Damascus and Mecca, would need to meet fugitives with bread. They will be fleeing from both the swords and arrows of intense battle. In his records Sennacherib said he took one thousand camels from the queen of the Arabs in 688 B.C. and the Arabs left their tents and fled to an area where there were no feeding or drinking places.[13]

> **16This is what the Lord says to me: "Within one year, as a servant bound by contract would count it, all the pomp of Kedar will come to an end.**

Isaiah gives another prophecy specifying an exact period of time (cf. 16:14): within a full year "the pomp [Heb. *k^{e}vod*, "glory"] of Kedar," the tribe of northern Arabia, would be destroyed, ruined. This was fulfilled in 688 B.C., one year after Sennacherib destroyed Babylon.[14] With Babylon out of the way Sennacherib was ready to move toward Egypt. This time he went through Arabia instead of following the easier route down the Mediterranean coast. His records tell how he defeated the Arabians and added "King of Arabia" to his long list of titles. Egyptians, according to the Greek historian Herodotus, later referred to him by this, his latest title.[15]

> **17The survivors of the bowmen, the warriors of Kedar, will be few." The LORD, the God of Israel, has spoken.**

The tribe of the Kedar Arabians was well-known and wealthy. Its defeat will leave few of their celebrated archers and soldiers. The Arabians probably would not believe this prophecy. But it was given and guaranteed by the LORD and was fulfilled in every detail, as confirmed by the testimony of Sennacherib's annals.

4. JERUSALEM JUDGED 22:1–14

In 22:1–14, Isaiah turns to Jerusalem with a series of four prophecies. The "Valley of Vision" may refer to a valley by

---

[13] George A. Barton, *Archaeology and the Bible,* 7th ed. (Philadelphia: American Sunday-School Union, 1941), 472.

[14] Boutflower, *Book of Isaiah,* 10, 149.

[15] Herodotus, *History,* trans. George Rawlinson, ed. Manuel Komroff (New York: Tudor Publishing Co., 1928), 131, 133.

Jerusalem (perhaps the Valley of Hinnom on the west) where God gave Isaiah supernatural visions (cf. Joel 3:2,12). However, the message that follows is to the whole city of Jerusalem. It may be that standing on the Mount of Olives and looking down, Jerusalem would appear to be in a valley. This would mean Isaiah received his visions there.

> ¹An oracle concerning the Valley of Vision: What troubles you now, that you have all gone up on the roofs, ²O town full of commotion, O city of tumult and revelry? Your slain were not killed by the sword, nor did they die in battle.

It may be that the people have gone up to the housetops shouting and rejoicing because they escaped the judgment that the Assyrians brought on Ashdod and other Philistine cities (see 20:1). More likely, however, they were rejoicing because Sennacherib accepted tribute from Hezekiah and left Jerusalem untouched as he moved on toward Lachish (2 Kings 18:14–16). They thought they had escaped the destruction coming on Judah's other cities. But their rejoicing was not justifiable. They had put their trust in gold and silver instead of in the Lord.[16]

> ³All your leaders have fled together; they have been captured without using the bow. All you who were caught were taken prisoner together, having fled while the enemy was still far away.

Judean leaders fled even before the Assyrians attacked. Some were captured and executed.

> ⁴Therefore I said, "Turn away from me; let me weep bitterly. Do not try to console me over the destruction of my people."

Isaiah warned the people but they did not listen. He could not join their revelry on the rooftops, for he knew the results of Hezekiah's tribute were only temporary. He wanted to be left alone to mourn the prophesied destruction of his beloved peo-

---

[16] In 705 B.C. Sargon was killed in a battle with barbarian Cimmerians at Tabal. His death encouraged "widespread revolt throughout the empire. In Syria-Palestine, Hezekiah was one of the prime movers behind the rebellion." J. Maxwell Miller and John H. Hayes, *A History of Ancient Israel and Judah* (Philadelphia: Westminster Press, 1986), 353.

ple. None of the prophets were cold pronouncers of doom. Like Isaiah, they loved their people and their hearts were broken over judgment coming upon them.

> ⁵The Lord, the LORD Almighty, has a day of tumult and trampling and terror in the Valley of Vision, a day of battering down walls and of crying out to the mountains.

It was a sad day when the people of Judah joined the fight against Assyria. They had failed to listen to what the Lord said in the Valley of Vision. The result was noise, violence, terror, and confusion. Walls of the cities of Judah were not able to withstand the Assyrian attack.

> ⁶Elam takes up the quiver, with her charioteers and horses; Kir uncovers the shield.

East of Assyria, Elam provides a contingent of bowmen, chariots, chariot drivers, and horses as reinforcements for the Assyrian army. Kir provides foot soldiers with their shields uncovered and ready for battle. Many nations have joined Assyria.

> ⁷Your choicest valleys are full of chariots, and horsemen are posted at the city gates;

Judah's situation was hopeless. The enemy had filled her "choicest valleys," including the Kidron on the east of Jerusalem and the Hinnom on the west and south, with chariots and posted horsemen at "city gates" throughout the country. Judah could not defend itself against such a vast army.

> ⁸the defenses of Judah are stripped away. And you looked in that day to the weapons in the Palace of the Forest;

Assyria had already taken the fortified outposts of Judah's cities. Any allies they trusted in were also already defeated.

The Hebrew verb may mean that God had also removed His protective covering from Judah because they no longer trusted Him to be their Guardian. Jerusalem's leaders "looked . . . to the weapons" instead; that is, they trusted in the weapons stored in the "Palace of the Forest" built by Solomon (1 Kings 7:2–5).

> ⁹you saw that the City of David had many breaches in its defenses; you stored up water in the Lower Pool.

Jerusalem was not prepared for an attack or a siege. The "breaches in its defenses" needed to be repaired. Water was essential if there was to be a siege, so water was stored "in the Lower Pool," probably the Pool of Siloam, about two hundred yards below the Gihon spring (2 Kings 20:20; 2 Chron. 32:30). Hezekiah led a concerted effort to prepare for war.

> ¹⁰You counted the buildings in Jerusalem and tore down houses to strengthen the wall.

Hasty preparations for defense included tearing down houses for stones "to strengthen the wall" (a desperate and shameful measure that made some of Jerusalem's citizens homeless). There were plenty of other sources of stone in the vicinity of Jerusalem (cf. 2 Chron. 32:5). However, workmen undoubtedly were afraid to go outside the city walls.

> ¹¹You built a reservoir between the two walls for the water of the Old Pool, but you did not look to the One who made it, or have regard for the One who planned it long ago.

"The two walls" may have been at the bottom of the Tyropoeon Valley, between David's Zion and the hill to the west. The description of Hezekiah's defense measures is given in 2 Kings 20:20 and 2 Chronicles 32:3–8. They included the construction of the Siloam tunnel under the city of Jerusalem to bring water from the Gihon spring to the Pool of Siloam, thus giving Jerusalem a protected water supply.

But in these hasty preparations, they did not look to the LORD. They were putting their confidence in what they could do instead of what He wanted. They were committing one presumptuous sin after another.

> ¹²The Lord, the LORD Almighty, called you on that day to weep and to wail, to tear out your hair and put on sackcloth.

God wanted the people of Jerusalem to humble themselves and repent with evidences of their sorrow—not because of the danger from the Assyrians, but because they had turned from the LORD.

> ¹³But see, there is joy and revelry, slaughtering of cattle and killing of sheep, eating of meat and drinking of wine! "Let us eat and drink," you say, "for tomorrow we die!"

The people ignored Isaiah, engaging in fatalistic revelry and feasting. They did not see any hope of defeating the Assyrians, so they decided to enjoy what time they had left. Paul would endorse that sort of lifestyle too—if there were no resurrection (1 Cor. 15:32).

> ¹⁴The LORD Almighty has revealed this in my hearing: "Till your dying day this sin will not be atoned for," says the Lord, the LORD Almighty.

Some sins "will not be atoned for." Like other such warnings, however, the reason for this lack of atonement was their refusal to repent. Thus, an implied hope was still there if they should repent.

5. Shebna And Eliakim 22:15–25

> ¹⁵This is what the Lord, the LORD Almighty, says: "Go, say to this steward, to Shebna, who is in charge of the palace:

Now Isaiah, for the only time in his book, gives a prophecy against a particular person in Jerusalem. Shebna, a corrupt, self-sufficient official, was manager of the royal household and keeper of the keys, including the keys to the royal treasuries. He was possibly a foreigner since his name is Aramaic, not Hebrew. He rose in power by learning how to please the king. The term "steward" comes from a root word meaning "to be of use." He had made himself useful. But he himself owned nothing and was directly accountable to the king.

> ¹⁶What are you doing here and who gave you permission to cut out a grave for yourself here, hewing your grave on the height and chiseling your resting place in the rock?

Shebna was using his stewardship to advance himself. By preparing a tomb high up on a rock face, he was bestowing on himself the honor and place in history due a king. He was not a true servant and he was betraying the king's trust. (Some commentators take this as a sarcastic reference to his directing the digging of the Siloam tunnel [see v. 11 and commentary], but it was not "on the height.")

> [17]"Beware, the LORD is about to take firm hold of you and hurl you away, O you mighty man.

Because Shebna had misused his position, the LORD was about to take him down and cast him out. He is sarcastically called a "mighty man." It has been suggested that he may have been the chief one to persuade Hezekiah to seek an alliance with Egypt.[17]

> [18]He will roll you up tightly like a ball and throw you into a large country. There you will die and there your splendid chariots will remain—you disgrace to your master's house!

"Like a ball," Shebna would be thrown where he would die outside the city, possibly in exile. He would be buried without any royal pomp. He was a disgrace to the palace of Hezekiah, where he was in charge. His "splendid chariots" were part of his attempt to honor himself as royalty.

> [19]I will depose you from your office, and you will be ousted from your position.

God would take him from office. Apparently, Shebna had a change of heart and later accepted a lower position as secretary (36:3). The complete fulfillment of God's judgment on him may have come after his eventual demotion.

> [20]"In that day I will summon my servant, Eliakim son of Hilkiah. [21]I will clothe him with your robe and fasten your sash around him and hand your authority over to him. He will be a father to those who live in Jerusalem and to the house of Judah.

---

[17]S. H. Widyapranawa, *The Lord is Savior: Faith in National Crisis* (Grand Rapids: Wm. B. Eerdmans, 1990), 129.

At this time, Eliakim was a true servant of the Lord. God would put him in Shebna's place, give him Shebna's symbols of office—the robe and the sash—and let him be "a father" to the people of Jerusalem and Judah. He was commissioned to love and care for them. This implies he would be accountable, just as Shebna was.

> 22I will place on his shoulder the key to the house of David; what he opens no one can shut, and what he shuts no one can open.

Eliakim would become what we might call the prime minister, exercising the powers of government in the name of the king, much as Joseph did for Pharaoh (Gen. 41:41–44). He was the palace administrator when Sennacherib's chief officer threatened Jerusalem in 701 B.C. Eliakim's authority was nearly unquestioned. The phrases "key to the house of David" and "what he opens no one can shut" depict his power. Jesus, the King of kings, now holds the key to the house of David (Rev. 3:7), fulfilling the Davidic covenant, which promised a man for the throne forever.

> 23I will drive him like a peg into a firm place; he will be a seat of honor for the house of his father. 24All the glory of his family will hang on him: its offspring and offshoots—all its lesser vessels, from the bowls to all the jars.

God's purpose was to make Eliakim's position firm, like a tent peg driven in "a firm place." He would hold the business of the palace securely against the winds of adversity. He would be like an honorable seat for all his family, and the glory and reputation of his family would "hang on him" and what he did (as upon a wall peg).

> 25"In that day," declares the Lord Almighty, "the peg driven into the firm place will give way; it will be sheared off and will fall, and the load hanging on it will be cut down." The Lord has spoken.

Unfortunately, Isaiah had to add an addendum to this prophecy. God saw that Eliakim would not prove worthy of his office. The burden would be too great for him and, in turn, he too would be cut down. Apparently, Eliakim was more concerned about the house of his father (his relatives) than he was about the house of Judah and the house of his master, Hezekiah. The people began to trust in him rather than in the LORD. The Hebrew here, however, could be translated as a warning that if people trusted in Eliakim instead of in the LORD—and in his human weakness Eliakim let them—the LORD would have to cut him down. Our trust must be in God, not in any man or woman.

6. Lamentation Over Tyre's Ruin 23:1–18

> ¹An oracle concerning Tyre: Wail, O ships of Tarshish! For Tyre is destroyed and left without house or harbor. From the land of Cyprus word has come to them.

This is the last of Isaiah's prophecies concerning foreign nations. David had a good relationship with Hiram, king of Tyre. Tyre supplied both skilled craftsmen and materials for the building of Solomon's Temple (1 Kings 5:1–12,18).

Tyre's influence was not always good, however, especially in the spiritual realm. Jezebel, the wife of King Ahab, was the daughter of the king of Sidon. She eventually used Ahab to introduce Baal worship. She even tried to root out the worship of the LORD and substitute the worship of the Baal of Tyre (1 Kings 16:31–33; 18:19; 19:2).

Tyre, a great commercial city, was located on an island less than a mile off the Phoenician coast. Originally it was two small islands, which were joined together by Hiram in the time of David. The plain of Tyre, on the coast, was fifteen miles long and two miles wide. Tyre was about one hundred miles north of Jerusalem. It was proud of its world trade and symbolized a mercenary, materialistic spirit.

Tarshish was probably Tartessus, on the southwest coast of Spain, west of Gibraltar. Hiram of Tyre may have founded it as a Phoenician colony. The "ships of Tarshish" were large trading vessels capable of traveling to Tarshish, whether they actually went that far or not.

192 / Isaiah 23:2–4

The island of Cyprus (Kittim) hears the news of Tyre being overpowered and sends word to the ships planning to go there. The city yielded to Sargon in Isaiah's day. Later, it was besieged by Nebuchadnezzar and became subject to him. Then in 332 B.C., Alexander the Great built a ramp made of earth and stone from the mainland turning the island into a peninsula. Then he destroyed the city. It was rebuilt, however, and recovered its prosperity. In New Testament times it had become a Greek-speaking city and a Christian church was established there (Acts 21:3–6).

> **²Be silent, you people of the island and you merchants of Sidon, whom the seafarers have enriched.**

Tyre was a busy international port once filled by the seagoing merchants of, among others, Sidon, twenty-two miles to the north. Tyre and Sidon are told to "be silent," implying Sidon must cease its trading with Tyre. All business was to come to a standstill. Tyre dominated Sidon in Isaiah's day, and many of Sidon's people contributed to Tyre's growth by moving there after Sidon was destroyed by sea raiders about 1200 B.C.

> **³On the great waters came the grain of the Shihor; the harvest of the Nile was the revenue of Tyre, and she became the marketplace of the nations.**

Tyre's ships on the "great waters" of the Mediterranean Sea transported crops and goods from Shihor in the Nile Delta and from the fertile valley of the Nile, bringing great revenue to Tyre through international trade.

> **⁴Be ashamed, O Sidon, and you, O fortress of the sea, for the sea has spoken: "I have neither been in labor nor given birth; I have neither reared sons nor brought up daughters."**

Sidon, the mother-city of Tyre, is to receive shame because of the silence, the disappointing cessation of business. Isaiah sees the waters of the Mediterranean personified and hears it speaking. The sea had been the livelihood of Tyre and Sidon.

Some take the "fortress of the sea" to be literal as it speaks of the loss of children. Others take the fortress to be Tyre, and others, the island of Cyprus, which after submitting to Sargon II could not contribute to Tyre and Sidon's business, nor could Tyre to theirs.

> ⁵When word comes to Egypt, they will be in anguish at the report from Tyre.

Egypt will writhe in pain and anguish when they hear the news of the conquest. Their grain was carried by Tyre's ships to ports around the Mediterranean. Egypt, dominated by Cush (Ethiopia), was against Assyria. This Assyrian takeover of Phoenicia and Cyprus would affect their trade, and thus, their income. They would also lose their source of timber as well as resin (used for mummification).

> ⁶Cross over to Tarshish; wail, you people of the island.

The destruction of Tyre caused its people to become refugees. This verse may mean that refugees were going to Tarshish in Spain (at that time a prosperous colony of Tyre; cf. v.1), causing that city to wail. "Island" here may refer to the far islands and coasts of the Mediterranean (cf. 40:15).

> ⁷Is this your city of revelry, the old, old city, whose feet have taken her to settle in far-off lands?

Tyre was about two thousand years old in Isaiah's day. It was a joyous, exultant city because of its growth, its trade, its wealth, and its colonizing enterprises around the Mediterranean (which included Carthage, the city that challenged Rome).

> ⁸Who planned this against Tyre, the bestower of crowns, whose merchants are princes, whose traders are renowned in the earth? ⁹The LORD Almighty planned it, to bring low the pride of all glory and to humble all who are renowned on the earth.

Tyre founded colonies ruled by kings, so Isaiah called it "the bestower of crowns." Princes and people of high worldly honor contributed to its trade and its wealth. Tyre thus became proud and God planned to bring it down. His purpose was to show how polluted self-exalting human glory is and how contemptible those honored by a pagan world really are.

> ¹⁰Till your land as along the Nile, O Daughter of Tarshish, for you no longer have a harbor.

"Till" (Heb. *'ivri*, "pass over" or "traverse"[18]) is interpretation, taking Isaiah to mean that Tarshish can now cultivate its own land without being dominated by Tyre. The translation "traverse" (cf. NAB) indicates that because Tyre's power is broken, the people of Tarshish can pass through its vicinity as freely as the Nile passes through Egypt. "You no longer have a harbor [dockyard, wharf]" could also be translated, "no more strength," meaning, "no more restraint" (like that of a girdle; see NASB, incl. margin). Tarshish is free, no longer subject to Tyre. "No more harbor" is the more difficult translation.[19]

> ¹¹The LORD has stretched out his hand over the sea and made its kingdoms tremble. He has given an order concerning Phoenicia that her fortresses be destroyed.

"The LORD stretched out His hand" indicates judgment, which agitates the kingdoms. Phoenicia ("the merchant city," KJV) is literally Canaan, which includes Phoenicia.[20] His judgment will destroy its "fortresses"—its places of refuge.

> ¹²He said, "No more of your reveling, O Virgin Daughter of Sidon, now crushed! "Up, cross over to Cyprus; even there you will find no rest."

Because of Sidon's contributions to Tyre, the city could be called the "Daughter of Sidon." Tyre, once exalted, is now oppressed; but not yet conquered, it is called "Virgin." Its refugees will cross over to Cyprus but will find "no rest," no place of refuge, there. This may refer to the fact that Assyria controlled Cyprus and restricted Tyre's ships from landing there.

---

[18] *The Prophets* (Philadelphia: Jewish Publication Society of America, 1978), 400.

[19] Most scholars are inclined to accept the more difficult translation.

[20] The Heb. *kena`an* can also mean tradesmen, so the meaning may be that God has commanded tradesmen to destroy Tyre's strongholds.

> ¹³Look at the land of the Babylonians, this people that is now of no account! The Assyrians have made it a place for desert creatures; they raised up their siege towers, they stripped its fortresses bare and turned it into a ruin.

Isaiah looks ahead again to the destruction of the land of the Babylonians (Chaldeans) by the Assyrians. What Sargon did to the Chaldeans in 710–709 B.C. (when he demolished their capital city, Dur-Yakin, and took away 90,000 captives) and what Sennacherib did to Babylon in 703 B.C. (when he took away 208,000 captives and later leveled it in 689 B.C.) were warnings. Refugees from Tyre would not be able to find comfort or rest wherever Assyria was in control.

> ¹⁴Wail, you ships of Tarshish; your fortress is destroyed!

This repetition from verse 1 indicates the conclusion of this section. This passage, however, adds that there is no more "fortress," no place of strength. In other words, Tyre is no longer a fortress that can provide security for its ships.

> ¹⁵At that time Tyre will be forgotten for seventy years, the span of a king's life. But at the end of these seventy years, it will happen to Tyre as in the song of the prostitute:

Tyre will fall into oblivion "for seventy years." "The span of a king's life" is literally "the days of one king" and refers to the fact kings kept daily records (cf. 1 Kings 14:29; Esther 6:1). The seventy years may have been fulfilled between Sennacherib's 701 B.C. campaign and the recovery of Tyre about 630, after Assyria's power began to wane. Then Tyre would try to recover but would be unchanged, as in the song of the prostitute in verse 16.

> ¹⁶"Take up a harp, walk through the city, O prostitute forgotten; play the harp well, sing many a song, so that you will be remembered."

The song speaks of an old prostitute who goes about the city trying to gain back customers by singing songs that they would remember. The comparison of Tyre to an old prostitute indicates it will show no pity, compassion, or love. Its only concern will be to turn a profit.

> ¹⁷At the end of seventy years, the LORD will deal with Tyre. She will return to her hire as a prostitute and will ply her trade with all the kingdoms on the face of the earth.

God "will deal with Tyre," that is, He will bring himself into the situation to allow Tyre to be restored. However, Tyre will continue to act "as a prostitute," seducing other nations for profit, taking financial advantage of them by her dishonest commercial operations.

> ¹⁸Yet her profit and her earnings will be set apart for the LORD; they will not be stored up or hoarded. Her profits will go to those who live before the LORD, for abundant food and fine clothes.

Looking ahead, God promises that after judgment the restored Tyre will be able to provide food and clothing for the people who "live before the LORD," that is, the restored people of Jerusalem in the Millennium. Because God will make this possible, Tyre's "profit and . . . earnings will be set apart [Heb. *qodesh*, "a holy thing"]" for the LORD. This implies Tyre will be consecrated to a service the way the priests were.

Since everyone in the millennial Zion will be called holy (4:3), this may mean that Tyre's provisions will be for all the people of Jerusalem. Since Tyre's supplies "will not be stored up or hoarded" in a treasury, the provisions for Jerusalem in the millennial age will be plentiful and obtainable (cf. 60:5–9; 61:6–7).

STUDY QUESTIONS

1. How does Isaiah react to his vision of the destruction of Babylon?
2. When were images of Babylon's gods shattered?
3. What would happen to Edom and Arabia?
4. Why did Isaiah want to be left alone?

5. What hasty preparations for defense did Jerusalem make?
6. What preparation did they fail to make?
7. Why would Shebna be replaced by Eliakim and with what results?
8. How did suppression of Tyre's trade affect Sidon, Egypt, Tarshish, and Cyprus?
9. What would happen to Tyre and what would be the results of its restoration?

IV. JUDAH DESERVES GOD'S JUDGMENT 24:1–35:10

In these chapters Isaiah sees alternating visions of judgment on sinners and praise to God by the redeemed.

A. The earth polluted, the city desolate 24:1–13

> ¹See, the LORD is going to lay waste the earth and devastate it; he will ruin its face and scatter its inhabitants—

The word "earth" can mean "land," but the parallelism with "world" (v. 4) shows that this judgment involves a disordering of the whole world. This looks ahead to end-time events, especially the judgment of the Great Tribulation (cf. 1 Thess. 5:1–3,9; Rev. 8; 9; 15; 16; 18; 19).

> ²It will be the same for priest as for people, for master as for servant, for mistress as for maid, for seller as for buyer, for borrower as for lender, for debtor as for creditor.

No one will escape this judgment. It will affect all of society and each person impartially. From the highest to the lowest, all will suffer.

> ³The earth will be completely laid waste and

> totally plundered. The LORD has spoken this word.

The earth will be devastated. Armies will rob and plunder everything. God has spoken, and His word will be fulfilled.

> ⁴The earth dries up and withers, the world languishes and withers, the exalted of the earth languish.

The earth is metaphorized. It withers and suffers blight. Some take the "exalted of the earth" to be the Assyrians. Others take them to be the Israelites—with the whole world suffering also because of their sin.

> ⁵The earth is defiled by its people; they have disobeyed the laws, violated the statutes and broken the everlasting covenant.

The judgment that falls on the earth is the result of defilement "by its people." Isaiah then identifies their sins: They have disobeyed (abolished) God's instructions, violated His rules, and broken the regulations given to Noah (Gen. 9:1–16).

They have refused to recognize any covenant relationship with God. They want no fellowship with Him (cf. 2 Thess. 2:9–12). This becomes the condition of the whole world in the last days.

> ⁶Therefore a curse consumes the earth; its people must bear their guilt. Therefore earth's inhabitants are burned up, and very few are left.

Because of the people's sin, a curse devours the earth. They are reaping what they sowed (cf. Gal. 6:7). The judgment is not arbitrary, for the people bear "their [own] guilt," not another's. God is just and cannot leave sin unpunished; the people "must" bear the burden of their guilt. God's anger burns against them and few people are left (cf. Zech. 5:3–4; Rev. 19:11–21). Today, such worldwide destruction is possible.

> ⁷The new wine dries up and the vine withers; all the merrymakers groan.

"New wine" (i.e., grape juice) has dried up. Grapevines are withered. The "revelry" of 22:1–2 has changed to groaning.

Grape juice was a symbol of harmless pleasures.

> **8The gaiety of the tambourines is stilled, the noise of the revelers has stopped, the joyful harp is silent.**

The rejoicing and laughter accompanied by tambourines and harps has ceased.

> **9No longer do they drink wine with a song; the beer is bitter to its drinkers.**

"Wine" will not loosen them up and cause them to sing. "Beer" (and other alcoholic beverages) will make them feel bitter instead of exhilarated.

> **10The ruined city lies desolate; the entrance to every house is barred.**

"The ruined city" (Heb. *qiryath tohu*, "city of nothingness or emptiness;" possibly generic for the cities of the world or of the land rather than a specific city) is without inhabitants and is broken down. (*Tohu* is the word used in Genesis 1:2 for the state of the earth before God gave it inhabitants.) Every house is closed up against entry. It is a picture of total desolation.

> **11In the streets they cry out for wine; all joy turns to gloom, all gaiety is banished from the earth.**

Outside in the streets—or outside the city—there is wailing because of a lack of wine. All the joy that delights merrymakers has darkened as when the day is done. "All gaiety," including the joy of laughter, has gone.

> **12The city is left in ruins, its gate is battered to pieces.**

"The city" is probably collective for cities in general (cf. v. 10). The devastation left in the city by God's judgment is horrible. The desolate gates have been "battered to pieces." The city is no longer livable and there is no protection. A preliminary fulfillment of this took place when Sennacherib destroyed forty-six cities of Judah.

> **13So will it be on the earth and among the**

> nations, as when an olive tree is beaten, or as when gleanings are left after the grape harvest.

The remnant left after this judgment on the world will be small, like the few olives left on the tree after they beat its branches or the few grapes left after the gleaners have gone through and picked what the harvesters left (cf. 17:6).

STUDY QUESTIONS

1. How is chapter 24 related to chapters 13 to 23?
2. What is this time of world judgment called in the New Testament?
3. What will happen to all who do not repent and turn to God?
4. What city is ruined?

B. Judgment Prepares For God's Reign In Jerusalem 24:14-23

> ¹⁴They raise their voices, they shout for joy;
> from the west they acclaim the LORD's majesty.

In contrast to the lack of joy among those suffering God's judgment, the godly remnant shout about the LORD's majesty, and they shout joyously "from the west" (Heb. *miyyam*, "from the sea"). See Revelation 18:20 where there is a similar command to rejoice because of God's righteous judgment.

The initial occasion of the shouts may have been the death of Sargon in 705 B.C., which people recognized was judgment brought about by God's sovereignty. Another occasion may have been the rejoicing of other nations after the healing of Hezekiah and the defeat of Sennacherib (cf. 2 Chron. 32:22-23).

> ¹⁵Therefore in the east give glory to the LORD;
> exalt the name of the LORD, the God of Israel,
> in the islands of the sea.

The shouts of joy from the west cause Isaiah to call for people to respond "in the east" by glorifying the LORD's name in isles and the coastlands, and in all parts of the inhabited earth. All humankind needs to praise and glorify the one true God, the God of Israel.

> ¹⁶From the ends of the earth we hear singing: "Glory to the Righteous One." But I said, "I waste away, I waste away! Woe to me! The treacherous betray! With treachery the treacherous betray!"

From "the ends [Heb. *kᵉnaph*, "wing"] of the earth," that is, from its outermost parts, the song comes, "Glory to the Righteous One," that is, to God who has revealed His righteousness both in judgment and in forgiveness and restoration. The same term is used of the Suffering Servant in 53:11 (NASB).

But the vision of the future does not cause Isaiah to rejoice. He knows that judgment must come before restoration and millennial joys. However, he is shocked by what he sees coming. The prophets were not compassionless doomsayers. "I waste away" and "Woe to me!" are expressions of Isaiah's feelings. Even though he foresaw the future shouts of joy, the sins of the people and the terrible curse and judgment on the earth and its people break his heart (the Heb. has noticeable alliteration in these phrases).

Betrayal and treachery are indeed deserving of judgment.[1] Nevertheless, the thought of judgment makes Isaiah feel intense sorrow. (Compare his reaction in 6:5 and 22:4.)

> ¹⁷Terror and pit and snare await you, O people of the earth.

Terror (Heb. *pachad*), a pit (Heb. *pachat*), and a snare, or set trap (Heb. *pach*), are waiting for the inhabitants of the earth. It is not by accident that the results of sin will catch up with them. (Note the alliteration in the Heb. words.)

> ¹⁸Whoever flees at the sound of terror will fall into a pit; whoever climbs out of the pit will be

---

[1] "The treacherous betray! With treachery the treacherous betray" could be translated "The faithless who acted faithlessly have been betrayed in turn." *The Prophets* (Philadelphia: Jewish Publication Society of America, 1978), 403.

> caught in a snare. The floodgates of the heavens are opened, the foundations of the earth shake.

There will be no escape from God's judgment. (Cf. Amos 5:18–19, which depicts similar attempts at evasion that only go from bad to worse.) Isaiah concludes this thought by describing "the floodgates of the heavens" being opened and the "foundations of the earth" shaking. This reminds us of what happened in Noah's flood (Gen. 7:11; 8:2), as well as in the great earthquake of Uzziah's day (Amos 1:1). God's judgment will bring a radical change.

> ¹⁹The earth is broken up, the earth is split asunder, the earth is thoroughly shaken. ²⁰The earth reels like a drunkard, it sways like a hut in the wind; so heavy upon it is the guilt of its rebellion that it falls—never to rise again.

Five expressions emphasize the severity of the earth quaking: The earth splits, breaks up, reels, trembles, and sways—"like a hut in the wind," like the temporary structure (branches and mats or poles and awnings) set up by the farmer from which to guard his field crops (cf. 1:8).

Earthquakes, tornadoes, thunderstorms, and hurricanes will bring judgment. Rebellion weighs so heavily on the earth that it will "never . . . rise again," which shows that the judgment is on humankind and the present evil world system. It also may picture the earth spinning off its orbit and being destroyed.[2] God will create a new heavens and earth (65:17; Rev. 21:1).

> ²¹In that day the LORD will punish the powers in the heavens above and the kings on the earth below. ²²They will be herded together like prisoners bound in a dungeon; they will be shut up in prison and be punished after many days.

A day of the LORD's judgment is coming when He will punish the satanic forces, "the powers in the heavens" (cf. Eph. 6:11–12; Jude 6; Rev. 12:7–9; 20:1–3,11–15). The same judg-

---

[2]David L. McKenna, *Isaiah 1–39*, in *The Communicator's Commentary* (Dallas: Word Books, 1993), 241.

ment will fall on all in high authority, "the kings on the earth." They will be "herded together like prisoners" and kept in a prison pit, unable to control their own destinies. "After many days," a long time, in prison, they will be judged and punished.

> ²³**The moon will be abashed, the sun ashamed; for the LORD Almighty will reign on Mount Zion and in Jerusalem, and before its elders, gloriously.**

The full moon and sun will turn red in shame (cf. Matt. 24:29). They are ashamed because people worshiped them instead of the LORD, who alone "will reign on Mount Zion and in Jerusalem." In the presence of the elders of His people His glory will be manifest (cf. Exod. 24:9–10). This anticipates the vision of God's glory John saw in Revelation 4:4 where "the elders in some way represent the Church."[3] What a glorious hope true believers have!

STUDY QUESTIONS

1. Who will shout for joy and why?
2. What groups will be punished?

C. Judgment Prepares For A Millennial Banquet 25:1–12

> ¹ **O LORD, you are my God; I will exalt you and praise your name, for in perfect faithfulness you have done marvelous things, things planned long ago.**

The vision of the LORD's reigning gloriously inspires Isaiah to praise Him. He recognizes the LORD as his God in a personal way. The presence of God no longer frightens him as it did in chapter 6. Now he exalts God, praising His name for all the

---

[3]Stanley M. Horton, *The Ultimate Victory: An Exposition of the Book of Revelation* (Springfield, Mo.: Gospel Publishing House, 1991), 76.

wonderful things He has done. Plans that God made "long ago" were fulfilled by Him.

> ²You have made the city a heap of rubble, the fortified town a ruin, the foreigners' stronghold a city no more; it will never be rebuilt.

God's judgment has made cities ("city" here is collective) a heap of stones and impregnable fortified cities a ruin. The fortified palaces of foreigners are no longer the citadels they once were, and they will never be rebuilt (cf. Nah. 1:8–9 for a similar prophecy against Nineveh; Mal. 1:3–5 for a similar prophecy against Edom). This tells us that God will defeat everyone who opposes His glorious, righteous purpose.

> ³Therefore strong peoples will honor you; cities of ruthless nations will revere you.

These judgments prepare the way for several results: "Strong peoples" will repent and glorify God; cities of powerful, violent, and hostile nations will repent and fear God.

> ⁴You have been a refuge for the poor, a refuge for the needy in his distress, a shelter from the storm and a shade from the heat. For the breath of the ruthless is like a storm driving against a wall

They will praise God, recognizing that He has been "a refuge" and defense "for the poor . . . for the needy in his distress," where they seem pressed from all sides. God is always concerned about poor, needy, and helpless people.

God has also been a "shelter from the storm and a shade from the heat." His protection is needed, "for the breath of the ruthless," the violent nations, is like a cloudburst beating against a wall. The world still has many violent nations and we still need His protection.

> ⁵and like the heat of the desert. You silence the uproar of foreigners; as heat is reduced by the shadow of a cloud, so the song of the ruthless is stilled.

God defeats and silences (Heb. *takhniʾa*, "you humble, you

subdue") the proud war cries, the "uproar," of foreign armies that oppose Him. They become as silent as the heat in a waterless desert. As heat is lessened by clouds, so "the song of the ruthless," the violent, the tyrant, "is stilled" by the LORD.

> ⁶On this mountain the LORD Almighty will prepare a feast of rich food for all peoples, a banquet of aged wine—the best of meats and the finest of wines.

The judgment prepares for a feast that will take place after Christ returns. It will be a gift from the LORD—a great millennial banquet on Mount Zion "for all peoples," that is, for the saved from every language, tribe, and nation (cf. Rev. 7:9). This is another picture of what is prepared for those who come to the LORD (cf. 2:2–4).

The "feast of rich food" (the Heb. means dishes made with olive oil) represents high quality. "Aged wine," or "wines on the lees" (KJV), is one word in the Hebrew *(sh^emarim)*, usually translated "lees" or "dregs" of wine. See Jeremiah 48:11–12 where Moab is compared to dregs, where the taste and the scent have not changed. This may indicate that the root meaning of *sh^emarim* ("things kept" or "things preserved") is in mind. The "best of meats," literally "rich food filled with marrow," implies the best kind of nourishment. The "finest of wines" means they are filtered or refined, not that they are alcoholic. God has reserved wonderful blessings for those who are faithful (cf. Ps. 22:26–29).

> ⁷On this mountain he will destroy the shroud that enfolds all peoples, the sheet that covers all nations;

The "shroud," or "covering" (KJV), that overshadows or is woven over the peoples and nations may refer to everything that keeps people from seeing the glory of God. Or it may refer to a veil that represents mourning over sin and its sorrowful results that affect even the innocent. For those who come to Mount Zion, God will swallow up that covering.

> ⁸he will swallow up death forever. The Sovereign LORD will wipe away the tears from all faces; he will remove the disgrace of his people from all the earth. The LORD has spoken.

There were many deaths caused by Assyria in Isaiah's day, and many tears due to the Assyrians taking over two hundred thousand captives and transplanting them in other lands. Isaiah looks ahead to the fulfillment of God's promise to "swallow up death" in victory. Then there will be no more death, and God, as a loving Father, will "wipe away the tears from all faces" (cf. 1 Cor. 15:54; Rev. 21:4). This will be possible because He will take away "the disgrace of His people." It implies the work of Christ and the restoration that will come when He returns to establish His millennial kingdom.

> ⁹In that day they will say, "Surely this is our God; we trusted in him, and he saved us. This is the LORD, we trusted in him; let us rejoice and be glad in his salvation."

"In that day," the Day of the LORD's restoration of the kingdom, everyone who has "trusted in Him" (Heb. *qiwwinu lo,* "waited expectantly for him") will have a wonderful testimony. This includes not just Israel who will return to the LORD, but people from all nations (cf. v. 6). They will all rejoice in the LORD's salvation (cf. 1 Cor. 1:7; 1 Thess. 1:9–10; 2 Tim. 4:8; Titus 2:13).

> ¹⁰The hand of the LORD will rest on this mountain; but Moab will be trampled under him as straw is trampled down in the manure.

"The hand of the LORD" means the power of the LORD. In Ezekiel, it is often parallel to the Spirit of the LORD. The Spirit "will rest," that is, He will settle down to stay. God's people will never have to worry or be afraid again.

Moab often caused trouble for Judah and Jerusalem (2 Kings 13:20), and here represents all God's enemies. In contrast to Zion, Moab will be "trampled down" as straw in manure, that is, as something worthless. (Cf. the judgment on the wicked, haughty, adulterous people of Moab in chaps. 15 and 16.)

> ¹¹They will spread out their hands in it, as a swimmer spreads out his hands to swim. God will bring down their pride despite the cleverness of their hands.

The comparison to swimming in manure indicates that

Moab, which represents the sinful world and the enemies of God's people, will try to save itself, but its efforts will be futile. They cannot get rid of their sin and guilt by swimming in manure, that is, by continuing their sinful practices. Their pride will be brought down, and "the cleverness of their hands," or the wealth gained by human skills, will not save them.

> ¹²He will bring down your high fortified walls and lay them low; he will bring them down to the ground, to the very dust.

God will bring down and demolish the fortresses Moab trusted in. Moab apparently sided with Assyria in Isaiah's day and may have been used by Assyria against Judah.[1] In the future judgment God will "bring down" all the defenses human beings put up against Him.

STUDY QUESTIONS

1. What does Isaiah praise the Lord for?
2. What will God do for all the peoples of the earth?
3. What will God do for His people and how will they respond?
4. What is the point of the mention of Moab?

D. Judgment Prepares For Restoration And Peace 26:1–27:13

1. A Song Expressing Trust 26:1–11

> ¹In that day this song will be sung in the land of Judah: We have a strong city; God makes salvation its walls and ramparts.

---

[1] Moab did declare its loyalty to Assyria and apparently sent soldiers to accompany Sennacherib on his march against Judah. See J. Maxwell Miller and John H. Hayes, *A History of Ancient Israel and Judah* (Philadelphia: Westminster Press, 1986), 359.

"In that day" refers to the coming millennial day when Judah and Jerusalem will have a God-given song to sing. The song is a song of praise preparing Jerusalem for its transformation into a city of peace as God fulfills His redemptive purpose.

His salvation will be better than physical walls and "ramparts," or bulwarks (fortifications that slope on the inner side in order to give greater resistance to attempts to batter them down). He will protect His people. He is sufficient.

> ²Open the gates that the righteous nation may enter, the nation that keeps faith.

The city will be prepared by God for His people. The prophet calls for the gates to be opened for "the righteous nation" that keeps, or guards, faith (or, true, faithful, reliable things). "Nation" (Heb. *goi*) is often used of Gentiles. Here, it means any people who are right with God.

> ³You will keep in perfect peace him whose mind is steadfast, because he trusts in you.

God provides "perfect peace" (Heb. *shalom shalom;* repeated to emphasize the genuineness of the peace). In the midst of difficulties and stress, God will keep those in true peace (including spiritual well-being) whose minds (including thoughts, impulses, and tendencies) are unshakable and undeviating because their trust is in God. They believe and do not doubt—for the doubter "is like a wave of the sea, blown and tossed by the wind" (James 1:6)

> ⁴Trust in the LORD forever, for the LORD, the LORD, is the Rock eternal.

Those with steadfast trust in God call on others to "trust in the LORD forever." Our faith and trust in the LORD must be continuous. A one-time expression of faith, or trust, is not enough. He will not fail us because He is "the Rock eternal." The figure of the LORD as a "Rock" speaks not only of strength, but of protection, security, and permanence (see 17:10). Everlasting strength and help are parts of His very nature. The repetition "the LORD, the LORD" (Heb. *Yah, Yahweh*) draws attention to the faithfulness of His covenant-keeping name and character.

Isaiah 26:5-8 / 209

> ⁵He humbles those who dwell on high, he lays the lofty city low; he levels it to the ground and casts it down to the dust.

God is not only a Rock, He is active. Judgment must prepare the way for restoration. What God did in bringing down the pride of Moab and leaving its cities in total ruin, He will do to the pride of all the lofty cities of the world.

> ⁶Feet trample it down—the feet of the oppressed, the footsteps of the poor.

Though God's people are "oppressed" (afflicted) and "poor" (helpless and insignificant), they will walk in triumph on the ruins that God will bring about, a triumph they could not achieve themselves.

> ⁷The path of the righteous is level; O upright One, you make the way of the righteous smooth.

Isaiah now returns to the time of waiting for the LORD. The path of "the righteous" (those right with God) is a level way. That is, God makes it orderly, upright, and straight toward its goal. The LORD who is the "upright One" makes the path "smooth," cleared of obstacles. This does not mean we never have difficulties, problems, or struggles, but God sees us through them. He makes a way when there seems to be no way. All we need do is walk with Him.

> ⁸Yes, LORD, walking in the way of your laws, we wait for you; your name and renown are the desire of our hearts.

Those who are expectantly waiting for the LORD, trusting in Him, walk in the path of His "laws" (Heb. *mishpatekha*, "decisions"). This can mean that either they live in obedience to His Word, or they are faithful in the midst of the judgments that are beginning to come on the earth. The desire for the name of the LORD is a desire to see His nature and character manifest. It is also a desire to see Him in personal manifestation. They want also to see His nature held in remembrance, His past revelations of who He is.

> ⁹My soul yearns for you in the night; in the morning my spirit longs for you. When your judgments come upon the earth, the people of the world learn righteousness.

The change to the first person singular shows that the prophet had that same expectant desire even "in the night." The phrase "my spirit longs for you" indicates the inner depths of his desire after the Lord.[1]

Longing for Him "in the morning" includes the idea of seeking Him often or constantly. God's "judgments [that] come upon the earth" are the motivation for doing this, and the testimony of obedient seekers of the Lord becomes a means whereby the inhabitants of the earth "learn righteousness." This will have its future and more complete fulfillment after the judgments of the Great Tribulation (cf. Rev. 15:4).

> ¹⁰Though grace is shown to the wicked, they do not learn righteousness; even in a land of uprightness they go on doing evil and regard not the majesty of the Lord.

The wicked, however, are not ready to "learn righteousness," even when God shows them gracious favor and goodness. In "a land of uprightness," where God's truth is evident, they still act unjustly, doing evil and refusing to recognize "the majesty of the Lord." God's judgments are necessary, though the wicked cannot see how righteous and just they are.

> ¹¹O Lord, your hand is lifted high, but they do not see it. Let them see your zeal for your people and be put to shame; let the fire reserved for your enemies consume them.

The Lord will lift up His hand to act, that is, to bring judgment, but they will not "see [recognize] it." But Isaiah calls on God to "let them see . . . and be put to shame." He wants God's zeal for His people to be seen and wants God's holy fire to devour His enemies (who are also enemies of God's people).

---

[1]Timothy Munyon, "The Creation of the Universe and Humankind," in *Systematic Theology*, ed. Stanley M. Horton, rev. ed. (Springfield, Mo.: Logion Press, 1995), 240.

2. GOD ALONE IS WORTHY TO BE HONORED
26:12–27:1

> ¹²LORD, you establish peace for us; all that we have accomplished you have done for us.

Now all the godly remnant in Judah confess what God has done for them. In contrast to the judgment on the wicked, God will appoint peace for His people and establish it. God has done everything for them. His salvation is wholly His work.

> ¹³O LORD, our God, other lords besides you have ruled over us, but your name alone do we honor.

"Other lords" would include Pharaoh and the various rulers who subjugated Israel during the time of the judges.[2] But the people honor God alone. God is the Lord of history and has been faithful and has made His people keep His name in remembrance as their only true Leader.

> ¹⁴They are now dead, they live no more; those departed spirits do not rise. You punished them and brought them to ruin; you wiped out all memory of them.

Those former lords considered themselves gods, but they were merely men—and "they live no more." They are departed spirits in Sheol, and they shall not rise, or be resurrected, with the righteous, who will rule and reign with Christ during the Millennium. God visited judgment on them, "brought them to ruin," and caused memory of them to fade. Who honors the name and memory of the pharaoh of the Exodus? Scholars disagree about the identity of even that particular pharaoh.

> ¹⁵You have enlarged the nation, O LORD; you have enlarged the nation. You have gained glory for yourself; you have extended all the borders of the land.

It is for His glory that God has "enlarged the nation." He has extended it to the ends of the earth. That is, He has enlarged it

---

[2] Some commentators believe Isaiah was referring to current kings such as Tiglath-Pileser and Sargon.

not because of who the Israelites are but because of who He is. (There was some expansion of Judah's territory in Isaiah's day, but Isaiah looks ahead to something greater in the Millennium. Then they will truly recognize God's glory.)

> ¹⁶Lord, they came to you in their distress; when you disciplined them, they could barely whisper a prayer.

Isaiah "reminds" the Lord of how the Israelites sought God in times of trouble. They could hardly whisper, but as they did give a whisper of prayer, God "disciplined them" and brought them back to himself. This repeatedly occurred during the time of the judges. It also occurred in an abortive revolt of 712 to 711 B.C.

> ¹⁷As a woman with child and about to give birth writhes and cries out in her pain, so were we in your presence, O Lord.

Now, in Isaiah's own time, he and his people have endured suffering in the Lord's presence. Because of His judgments, they have cried out like a woman in the pangs of birth.

> ¹⁸We were with child, we writhed in pain, but we gave birth to wind. We have not brought salvation to the earth; we have not given birth to people of the world.

When a child is born the pain turns to joy. But in the suffering of this people there has been no birth, no good results—only wind, only pain. There has been no deliverance, no salvation in the land, and the world's rulers, the Assyrians, have not fallen. God would deal with the Assyrians in due time (10:12), but that time had not yet come.

> ¹⁹But your dead will live; their bodies will rise. You who dwell in the dust, wake up and shout for joy. Your dew is like the dew of the morning; the earth will give birth to her dead.

In contrast to the wicked who are brought "down to the dust" (v. 5), the dead who belong to the Lord ("your dead") will live. To God's people, death does not mean the end. Isaiah expects his dead body to rise with them. Some apply this to the restoration of national Israel (as in Ezek. 36 and 37), but the language is too individualistic here. There will be a call for God's people to "wake up and shout for joy." Like David (Ps. 23:6), they already had a hope of dwelling in the house of the LORD forever. Like Asaph (Ps. 73:24), they expected God to guide them in this life with His counsel and afterward take them into the glory of heaven. Like Solomon, they expected the path of life to lead to the place above for the wise (those that fear and worship the LORD) in order to avoid Sheol beneath (that is, hell). But Isaiah's prophecy adds another hope—the hope of resurrection (cf. Dan. 12:2).

"Dew" is symbolic of God's blessing and favor. The KJV has "dew of herbs." In 2 Kings 4:39 "herbs" refers to the mallow *(Malva rotundifolia),* a plant sensitive to light. However, it is better translated here as "lights" (NASB margin), meaning a fullness of light that comes when the morning sun appears above the horizon. It speaks of a fullness of life here when the graves in the earth break open and the dead rise (cf. Job 19:26; Ps. 16:10; Dan. 12:2; John 5:28–29; 1 Cor. 15:50–53; Phil. 3:21; 1 Thess. 4:16–17).

> ²⁰Go, my people, enter your rooms and shut the doors behind you; hide yourselves for a little while until his wrath has passed by.

The gates will be open in that glad millennial day (v. 2). But now the call is for God's people to go into their rooms and shut the door "for a little while," until the judgment "has passed by," literally "passes over" (the same word used of the Passover in Exod. 12:12,23). The rooms are taken by some to be those mentioned by Jesus in John 14:2 and would thus indicate being in heaven during the time of judgment. Others compare it to Matthew 6:6, where Jesus instructs His listeners how to pray "in secret." Here it seems to indicate that God's people will escape the terrible wrath and judgment of God (cf. 1 Thess. 5:9), which will not last long.

> ²¹See, the LORD is coming out of his dwelling to punish the people of the earth for their sins. The earth will disclose the blood shed upon her; she will conceal her slain no longer.

The reason for God's people shutting their doors (and thus closing themselves in with the LORD) is God will come "to punish the people of the earth for their sins," for all their crookedness and wrongdoing. A type of this is the judgment on the Assyrians. The earth will cooperate by disclosing the blood and the bodies of the slain. Nothing will be hidden from God.

> ¹In that day, the LORD will punish with his sword, his fierce, great and powerful sword, Leviathan the gliding serpent, Leviathan the coiling serpent; he will slay the monster of the sea.

"Leviathan" is a term used of several sea creatures or river monsters, such as the whale (Ps. 104:26) and the crocodile (Job 41:1). As the "gliding serpent," it seems to refer to Assyria on the Tigris River. As the "coiling serpent," it seems to refer to Babylon on the Euphrates. The "monster" (Heb. *tannin*) is parallel to Rahab, "the afflicter," or "the arrogant," a name for Egypt (cf. 30:7). "The sea" in this case refers to the Nile River.

These three nations were the chief enemies of Israel in Isaiah's day. Together they are representative of all the enemies who are against God and His people. Isaiah saw a day coming when God would punish them "with His sword." The repetition emphasizes the supernatural character of the punishment. Their chastisement is a foretaste of the complete punishment to come on all ungodly nations during the Great Tribulation at the end of this age.

3. ISRAEL SMITTEN THAT IT MIGHT BEAR FRUIT 27:2–13

a. A Second Vineyard Song 27:2–6

> ²In that day—"Sing about a fruitful vineyard:

"That day" looks ahead to what God will do in the distant future. This is another song of a vineyard. "Fruitful" ("red wine," KJV) is translated "pleasant" in Isaiah 32:12 and in Amos 5:11. It is a vineyard of beauty and delight. (Some Heb. manuscripts do have *chamar*, "wine that is foaming as it ferments"; however, this does not fit the idea of a vineyard.) It produces a good harvest of sweet grapes, in contrast to the putrid grapes of the vineyard in chapter 5.

> ³I, the LORD, watch over it; I water it continually. I guard it day and night so that no one may harm it.

The LORD is the guardian of the vineyard. His care, provision, and protection are continual. His faithful love has waited until Israel would put their trust in Him.

> ⁴I am not angry. If only there were briers and thorns confronting me! I would march against them in battle; I would set them all on fire.

In contrast to the vineyard of chapter 5 God now has no anger or resentment at all against this vineyard. If briars and thorns appear He will root them out and burn them. This may mean He will purify His people.

> ⁵Or else let them come to me for refuge; let them make peace with me, yes, let them make peace with me."

All is not hopeless for the "briars and thorns" (v. 4) that are against God. God invites them to come to Him "for refuge," as a stronghold, a place of refuge. He wants all adversaries to repent and "make peace" with Him. The way of salvation is always open, even to those who seem like unpleasant, irritating briars and thorns. We can come to God as a loving Father and He will nurture us.

> ⁶In days to come Jacob will take root, Israel will bud and blossom and fill all the world with fruit.

Jacob, the supplanter and deceiver, was changed when he wrestled with the angel and was given the new name of "Israel" (Gen. 32:24–28). In the coming days of the millennial kingdom, the nation of Israel that had its origin in Jacob will be changed and be like a vine whose every part—root, bud, blossom, and fruit—is beautifully developed. God will restore and prosper Israel. As a result, the whole world will be blessed by its "fruit." The fruit implies righteousness that will influence others. In this way we have a fulfillment of the promise to Abraham in Genesis 12:3. As chapters 9 and 11 have shown, the greater Seed of Abraham, who is also the greater Son of David, will make this possible.

b. Jacob's Guilt To Be Atoned For 27:7–13

> ⁷Has [the LORD] struck her as he struck down those who struck her? Has she been killed as those were killed who killed her?

Looking back over Israel's history, did God ever strike them the way He struck down their enemies, as, for example, the way He drowned the entire Egyptian army at the Red Sea? Did He ever slay them the way He slew the 185,000 of Sennacherib's army? The answer is no. No matter how they failed or how often they turned from the LORD, God always left a remnant of His people Israel. He was gracious to them and loved them. He still does.

> ⁸By warfare and exile you contend with her—
> with his fierce blast he drives her out, as on a
> day the east wind blows.

God's judgments on Israel in the past were severe, like a blast of "the east wind" from the desert. "By warfare" ("in measure," KJV) translates a Hebrew word used only here and probably means "by chasing away" or "by scaring away." God's purpose was never to destroy them completely, but to deal with them in a way that would bring them back to himself. Assyrians under Tiglath-Pileser, and later under Sargon, took people of northern Israel into exile. Then Sennacherib took people of Judah into exile. They were God's "fierce blast."

> ⁹By this, then, will Jacob's guilt be atoned for, and this will be the full fruitage of the removal of his sin: When he makes all the altar stones to be like chalk stones crushed to pieces, no Asherah poles or incense altars will be left standing.

God's love and care for His people includes discipline and suffering. He will deal with them so that their "guilt [will] be atoned for" and their sin taken away. Part of this will involve disposing of false worship, so the Asherah poles (symbols of Asherah worship, which included prostitution) and incense altars "will [not] be left standing." Hezekiah did do away with false worship (2 Kings 18:4). The "altar stones" that are "crushed to pieces" either may be altars for false worship or may represent the old sacrificial system that will be done away with. Only then could Israel become the pleasant, fruitful vineyard of verse 2.

> ¹⁰The fortified city stands desolate, an abandoned settlement, forsaken like the desert; there the calves graze, there they lie down; they strip its branches bare.

Some commentators take "the fortified city" to mean Jerusalem, but in this connection it is probably a collective for the cities of this world (cf. 25:2), the strongholds of the enemies of God and His people. Their defenses will not save them from the judgment of God. Nothing will be left of them (cf. Rev. 16:19), so "calves [will] graze" where they were.

> ¹¹When its twigs are dry, they are broken off and women come and make fires with them. For this is a people without understanding; so their Maker has no compassion on them, and their Creator shows them no favor.

In the deserted cities, when branches are stripped bare, women will come and use the twigs for fires. Those left after the judgment are people "without understanding," having no insight into spiritual truths or into the ways of God. Though God created them, though God formed them with care like that of a skillful potter, He will show them "no favor." They had no understanding of God because they have so dulled their minds and hearts that even His saving grace does not reach them.

> ¹²In that day the LORD will thresh from the flowing Euphrates to the Wadi of Egypt, and you, O Israelites, will be gathered up one by one.

"That day," the Day of Judgment, will also bring restoration. God will bring a harvest, threshing the grain from the chaff, a gathering of good wheat. He will gather "from the flowing Euphrates to the Wadi [stream bed that is dry except in the rainy season] of Egypt" (the Wadi El-Arish at the border of Egypt), that is, from the whole area that was once held by Solomon in the days of his greatness. The true people of Israel will be gleaned one by one and restored to the land. Though God's intent is to restore the nation of Israel, He will also be concerned about the salvation of each individual, "one by one" (cf. Jesus' parables of the Lost Sheep, the Lost Coin, and the Lost Son in Luke 15).

> **13And in that day a great trumpet will sound. Those who were perishing in Assyria and those who were exiled in Egypt will come and worship the LORD on the holy mountain in Jerusalem.**

"A great trumpet" will be blown. It will call people home to worship—people who are outcasts, homeless, harassed, and perishing in Assyria. It will also cause exiles in Egypt to come and "worship the LORD on the holy mountain in Jerusalem." Assyria was the place where exiles of Israel were in Isaiah's day, although Egypt had been the place of their slavery in Moses' day. These two countries represent all the places in the world where Israel suffers. From them will come not only Israel but others who will worship the LORD (cf. Isa. 2:2–3).

STUDY QUESTIONS

1. What lessons from the song can be applied to today?
2. What reasons does Isaiah give for seeking the Lord?
3. What will happen to the oppressors of Israel?
4. How does 26:19 relate to Job 19:26? Psalm 16:10? Daniel 12:2?
5. What does leviathan symbolize?
6. How is the prophetic song of 27:2–6 different from the song of the vineyard in chapter 5?
7. What judgments are about to overtake Israel?
8. What hope is given to the future remnant?

E. Six Woes 28:1–33:1

1. WOE TO EPHRAIM 28:1–29

   a. Drunken Leaders 28:1–8

> ¹Woe to that wreath, the pride of Ephraim's drunkards, to the fading flower, his glorious beauty, set on the head of a fertile valley—to that city, the pride of those laid low by wine!

The Book of Isaiah now goes back to the time before Assyria conquered the northern kingdom of Israel and took Samaria in 722 B.C.[1] God's prophetic word to the northern kingdom of Israel is that it is ripe for judgment. "Woe" warns them.

The Northern Kingdom is called "Ephraim" because Ephraim was its leading tribe. Their leaders are drunkards in a feast honoring Samaria as a "wreath," a victor's crown. They imagine that it is impregnable and that their power and position give them privilege to indulge themselves.

But the wreath is fading, as is the beautiful city of Samaria on a steep hill at the head of its prosperous valley. The leaders are "laid low" (Heb. *halume*, "overcome") by wine. Their pride that led to carousing leaves them unprepared for the judgment that is coming. Drunkenness and intoxicating pride both demand God's judgment (cf. Isa. 5:11–17).

> ²See, the Lord has one who is powerful and strong. Like a hailstorm and a destructive wind, like a driving rain and a flooding downpour, he will throw it forcefully to the ground.

Ironically, the "powerful and strong" one that the Lord will use is Assyria. The coming of the Assyrian army under Shalmaneser is compared to the violent destruction of both a hailstorm and a flood.

> ³That wreath, the pride of Ephraim's drunkards, will be trampled underfoot.

Ironically, the wreath, a symbol of victory—the victor's crown—and a symbol of the pride of the drunkards of

---

[1]Oswald T. Allis, "Book of Isaiah," in *Wycliffe Bible Encyclopedia* (Chicago: Moody Press, 1975), 1:859.

Ephraim, "will be trampled underfoot." Israel will be completely defeated. Assyria will fulfill God's judgment on Samaria.

> ⁴That fading flower, his glorious beauty, set on the head of a fertile valley, will be like a fig ripe before harvest—as soon as someone sees it and takes it in his hand, he swallows it.

Samaria is compared first to a fading flower, then to a first-ripe fig. As soon as a person sees such a fig, he picks it, pops it into his mouth, and swallows it. Just so, God will not postpone the judgment, and there will be nothing left of Samaria. This prophecy was fulfilled when Shalmaneser besieged Samaria for three years and the city fell in 722 B.C.

> ⁵In that day the LORD Almighty will be a glorious crown, a beautiful wreath for the remnant of his people.

Again Isaiah looks to the future millennial day as a contrast to Israel's present situation. The LORD himself will become a glorious victor's crown and a beautiful wreath or diadem to the remnant of all Israel—a stark contrast to the self-exalting pride and wreaths of fading flowers of Ephraim's drunkards (v. 1)!

> ⁶He will be a spirit of justice to him who sits in judgment, a source of strength to those who turn back the battle at the gate.

In all decisions the LORD, as "a spirit of justice," will give His strength to enable all those who will be judges or rulers to do what is right. He will also be strength for those who take the battle to the enemy's city gates (or the meaning may be those who at their own city gates defend from the enemy).

> ⁷And these also stagger from wine and reel from beer: Priests and prophets stagger from beer and are befuddled with wine; they reel from beer, they stagger when seeing visions, they stumble when rendering decisions.

These who have the LORD as their strength will supersede the former rulers, priests, and prophets. In Isaiah's day they were so drunk from wine and beer that they could not see the right, so they made mistakes in their judgment (cf. Amos 4:1; 6:1,6).

Instead of being filled with the Spirit of God, they were filled with wine and other fermented drink (Lev. 10:9–10; Num. 11:24–25,29; cf. Eph. 5:18).

> ⁸All the tables are covered with vomit and there is not a spot without filth.

Their extreme drunkenness is absolutely filthy and disgusting. This may picture Samaria as in verse 1. They are staggering drunkenly toward destruction.² More likely, however, it jumps ahead to a later time at a banquet table where the leaders of the war party in Jerusalem were celebrating the return of messengers to Egypt. These messengers came with the promise of help against Assyria. The mere thought of their drunken celebration was abhorrent to Isaiah.

b. Scoffers To Learn The Hard Way 28:9–22

> ⁹"Who is it he is trying to teach? To whom is he explaining his message? To children weaned from their milk, to those just taken from the breast?

The leaders of the war party, along with the priests and prophets who support them, begin to mock Isaiah: They want him to know they are not babies and do not need his advice. They are claiming a mature understanding of the world situation in their day, which they suggest God's prophet does not possess.

> ¹⁰For it is: Do and do, do and do, rule on rule, rule on rule; a little here, a little there."

They mock his message as if it were baby talk, repeating syllables, like reciting ABC's (Heb. *tsau latsau, tsau latsau, qau laqau, qau laqau, ze'er sham, ze'er sham*). They contended that Isaiah was treating them as if they were little children. Actually, his message was simple and clear.

Many unbelievers today are like them. They do not consider the Bible to be logical, or they say it is out-of-date. We need to

---

²Some take this to mean "the sacred tables in the sanctuary where sacrifices are offered" by drunken priests. David L. McKenna, *Isaiah 1–39*, in *The Communicator's Commentary* (Dallas: Word Books, 1993), 272.

witness to the truth of the Scriptures, not only by our words but by our lives.

> ¹¹Very well then, with foreign lips and strange tongues God will speak to this people,

Isaiah responds by saying that if they do not learn the lesson by heeding the simple message in their own language, God will use people of another language to teach them. The Assyrians, with their Akkadian language, are in view.[3]

> ¹²to whom he said, "This is the resting place, let the weary rest"; and, "This is the place of repose"—but they would not listen.

God's message through Isaiah was intended to bring rest—including security and rejuvenation—to his people, but they refused to listen.

> ¹³So then, the word of the L<small>ORD</small> to them will become: Do and do, do and do, rule on rule, rule on rule; a little here, a little there—so that they will go and fall backward, be injured and snared and captured.

Therefore, the word of the L<small>ORD</small> will continue to be a simple message and it will be fulfilled by the Assyrians. But the message will only harden the hearts of those who rejected it. God will let them continue with their plans, but they will fail in their purposes and will be defeated, trapped, and captured.

> ¹⁴Therefore hear the word of the Lord, you scoffers who rule this people in Jerusalem.

---

[3] "Lest the Corinthians jump to the conclusion that there was no place for speaking in tongues in the public worship, Paul [in 1 Corinthians 14:21–22] quickly draws their attention to Isaiah 28:11. In the context of Isaiah's prophecy proud Israelites were saying that Isaiah was treating them like spiritual babies and they resented it. Isaiah then made it clear that because of their unbelief, the message meant for blessing would bring judgment. God would send foreign conquerors whose language they would not understand, but whose actions would make it clear that these Israelites were separated from God, cut off from His blessing and under His judgment. Paul applies this to speaking in tongues (languages) which they did not understand. So speaking in tongues is necessary as a judgment sign to unbelievers, making them realize that they are separated from God and cannot understand God's message." Stanley M. Horton, *I & II Corinthians* (Springfield, Mo.: Logion Press, 1999) 137–38.

God has a further word for the powerful rulers or princes in Jerusalem who were mocking God's word and God's prophet in an arrogant, cynical way.

> ¹⁵You boast, "We have entered into a covenant with death, with the grave we have made an agreement. When an overwhelming scourge sweeps by, it cannot touch us, for we have made a lie our refuge and falsehood our hiding place."

Their "covenant with death" and their secret agreement with Sheol (hell, not the grave[4]) was actually a covenant with Egypt for help against the overwhelming scourge of Assyria (cf. 8:7; 10:5). They had rejected their covenant with the Lord and were confident in human ability, perhaps encouraged by those who depended on occult practices for guidance. However, they were really making lies their refuge and hiding under falsehood. Unbelievers do the same today and make fools of themselves in God's eyes.

> ¹⁶So this is what the Sovereign LORD says: "See, I lay a stone in Zion, a tested stone, a precious cornerstone for a sure foundation; the one who trusts will never be dismayed.

In contrast to their foolish refuge of lies and falsehood, God is laying in Zion a foundation of stone, a tested stone, a precious, valuable stone, "a sure foundation."

God himself is the foundation Stone (see 8:14; 17:10; cf. Gen. 49:24). He was present as the foundation for the future fulfillment of His divine plan and the kingdom to come. When Hezekiah took a stand of faith, he was like a cornerstone who would stand firm (cf. 36:15,18,21; 37:15–20). But Jesus Christ is the ultimate fulfillment, for He is the Stone the builders rejected (Ps. 118:22; Matt. 21:42) and He is the One on whom the Church is built (Acts 4:11; Rom. 9:33; 10:11; 1 Cor. 3:11; Eph. 2:20; 1 Pet. 2:4–8). Those who believe and trust in God will not have to hurry here and there seeking human help or fleeing from human enemies. Because of their faith in God, they will rest in Him and enjoy His peace.

---

[4]See note on 5:14.

> ¹⁷I will make justice the measuring line and righteousness the plumb line; hail will sweep away your refuge, the lie, and water will overflow your hiding place.

The "measuring line" measured horizontally. The "plumb line" (Heb. *mishqaleth*) was actually a level used to check horizontal accuracy[5] (not a modern plumb line). When a wall is tested by the measuring line and the level is crooked, the wall must be torn down. The lies and schemes of the Jerusalem princes, who planned rebellion against Assyria and trusted in Egypt, will be tested by God's justice and righteousness. They will find out how fragile their refuge of lies is.

> ¹⁸Your covenant with death will be annulled;
> your agreement with the grave will not stand.
> When the overwhelming scourge sweeps by,
> you will be beaten down by it.

Their "covenant with death" and secret "agreement with the grave" (hell, not the grave; see v. 15) will not stand when the scourge of Assyria overflows their land. All will be swept away and the scoffers will be defeated.

> ¹⁹As often as it comes it will carry you away;
> morning after morning, by day and by night, it will sweep through." The understanding of this message will bring sheer terror.

The Assyrians will repeatedly pass through the land and will bring terror to those who mocked Isaiah's message of rest and refreshing. This will bring an end to their mocking, for God's word, "this message," will prove true and its fulfillment will terrify them.

> ²⁰The bed is too short to stretch out on, the blanket too narrow to wrap around you.

They rejected God's offer of a resting place for the weary (v. 12). The bed and the blanket they chose (for rest and refreshing) refer to the lies and falsehood of verse 15 and involved

---

[5]William L. Holladay, *A Concise Hebrew and Aramaic Lexicon of the Old Testament* (Grand Rapids: Wm. B. Eerdmans, 1971), 222.

breaking treaties they had made. They trusted in Egypt, but Egypt's help would not be sufficient to protect Judah from Assyria.

> ²¹The LORD will rise up as he did at Mount Perazim, he will rouse himself as in the Valley of Gibeon—to do his work, his strange work, and perform his task, his alien task.

The LORD is the same God who gave David victories over the Philistines "at Mount Perazim" (see 2 Sam. 5:17–23; 1 Chron. 14:11–16), victories that secured David's control over Jerusalem, the new national capital. He is the same God who made the sun stand still "in the Valley of Gibeon" so Joshua could have a victory over the Amorites (Josh. 10:10–14) and continue the conquest of the Promised Land.

Now God will do something "strange," an "alien task"—He will bring judgment on the same people He gave victories to.

> ²²Now stop your mocking, or your chains will become heavier; the Lord, the LORD Almighty, has told me of the destruction decreed against the whole land.

Isaiah pleads with the people not to show themselves to be mockers, scoffers, or scorners (cf. v. 14) lest their chains "become heavier." God has decreed destruction on "the whole land," or the whole earth (the Heb. may mean either "earth" or "land"). The destruction will come; it was too late to change that. Nevertheless, they could still turn to the LORD and stop its gathering force. So also the destruction of the Great Tribulation will come at the end of this age. That cannot be changed. But believers need to be issuing a last call to repentance.

c. *Natural Wisdom Comes From The LORD 28:23–29*

> ²³Listen and hear my voice; pay attention and hear what I say.

Isaiah does not want the people to keep mocking the message. Four imperatives call them to pay careful attention to God.

> ²⁴When a farmer plows for planting, does he plow continually? Does he keep on breaking up and harrowing the soil? ²⁵When he has lev-

eled the surface, does he not sow caraway and scatter cummin? Does he not plant wheat in its place, barley in its plot, and spelt in its field? ²⁶His God instructs him and teaches him the right way.

Isaiah draws a lesson from agriculture to show that God has restoration in mind, not simply judgment and destruction. By a series of rhetorical questions Isaiah reminds the people of a practical wisdom that comes from God: No one plows merely for the sake of plowing; they prepare the ground according to the type of seed, according to its needs. "Caraway" is probably black cummin (Lat. *Nigella sativa*). "Cummin" *(Cuminum cyminum)* is a plant of the carrot family with aromatic seeds. "Rye" (KJV), or "spelt," is emmer wheat *(Triticum sativum)*, which has split kernels.

> ²⁷Caraway is not threshed with a sledge, nor is a cartwheel rolled over cummin; caraway is beaten out with a rod, and cummin with a stick. ²⁸Grain must be ground to make bread; so one does not go on threshing it forever. Though he drives the wheels of his threshing cart over it, his horses do not grind it. ²⁹All this also comes from the Lord Almighty, wonderful in counsel and magnificent in wisdom.

Continuing the lesson, Isaiah points out that the various seeds and grains are not threshed in the same way. Neither does one keep threshing grain intended for bread; it "must be ground." If a person kept on threshing, the grain would be scattered and never ground. This practical wisdom also "comes from the Lord," the true Source of "wonderful . . . counsel and magnificent . . . wisdom." The application of these two lessons, or parables, is that God will carry forward His purposes to their proper end. He is also concerned about purifying, not destroying. God will bring out of the purifying process a righteous remnant. Isaiah wants the scoffers to know that all this calls for praise to God for His wisdom and guidance.

2. Woe To Ariel, David's City 29:1–14

a. Jerusalem To Be Brought Low 29:1–4

¹Woe to you, Ariel, Ariel, the city where David

settled! Add year to year and let your cycle of festivals go on.

Isaiah may be still talking to the mockers. "Ariel" may mean "lion of God" as a symbolic name for Jerusalem, the city of David. Others take it to mean "altar hearth,"[6] the top of the altar where fire continually consumed the sacrifices, and thus represented the sacred city of Jerusalem.

By telling the people to "add year to year" and to let the "cycle of festivals" (the feasts of Lev. 23 with their sacrifices and offerings) go on, Isaiah is saying that time may pass and their religious forms and ceremonies may continue. Those feasts were legitimate but had become meaningless because the people had no genuine faith or trust in the LORD. The ceremonies will not stop the judgment from coming.

> ²Yet I will besiege Ariel; she will mourn and lament, she will be to me like an altar hearth.

The drunken leaders of Jerusalem and their people thought God would never let anything happen to them because the city was sacred. Yet God will "besiege" (oppress, distress) Jerusalem, and its inhabitants will mourn and sorrow because God will turn it into a place where His judgment fire consumes with terrible heat, an "Ariel" (see v. 1 and commentary).

> ³I will encamp against you all around; I will encircle you with towers and set up my siege works against you.

God will use the Assyrians; however, the real Person behind the besieging of Jerusalem (in 701 B.C.) will be the LORD.

> ⁴Brought low, you will speak from the ground; your speech will mumble out of the dust. Your voice will come ghostlike from the earth; out of the dust your speech will whisper.

Their pride and self-confidence will be brought down, and their strength will be gone so that their voice will be like the mumbling voice of a ghost whispering weakly out of the dust. Their refuge of lies will be of no avail.

---

[6]Cf. Ezek. 43:15–16.

b. Jerusalem's Enemies To Be Frustrated 29:5–8

> ⁵But your many enemies will become like fine dust, the ruthless hordes like blown chaff. Suddenly, in an instant,

After judging Judah and Jerusalem, Yahweh has greater judgment for Jerusalem's enemies. The Assyrians were indeed ruthless. The "fine dust" and "blown chaff" speak of complete and sudden judgment.

> ⁶the LORD Almighty will come with thunder and earthquake and great noise, with windstorm and tempest and flames of a devouring fire.

God is in control. He can use the forces of nature to bring His judgment.

> ⁷Then the hordes of all the nations that fight against Ariel, that attack her and her fortress and besiege her, will be as it is with a dream, with a vision in the night—

God will deliver Jerusalem. After the deliverance the great throng of their enemies will seem like a dream that is past, even though the threat and the distress were real at the time. For the enemies it will be a nightmare. The primary reference is to the deliverance from Sennacherib. Psalm 126 was probably written after that deliverance.[7]

> ⁸as when a hungry man dreams that he is eating, but he awakens, and his hunger remains; as when a thirsty man dreams that he is drinking, but he awakens faint, with his thirst unquenched. So will it be with the hordes of all the nations that fight against Mount Zion.

Dreams can be disappointing, so the nations that fight against Mount Zion will be disappointed. Assyria is in mind here. They felt frustration when they failed to conquer and destroy Jerusalem. But the principle holds true for other nations as well.

---

[7] "When the Lord brought back the captives to Zion" (Ps. 126:1) uses Heb. that is similar to the restoring of Job's prosperity (Job 42:10) and the restoring of fortunes in Ps. 14:7. So the psalmist was talking about restoring prosperity rather than the return of captives.

c. Ignorance And Hypocrisy Judged 29:9–14

> ⁹Be stunned and amazed, blind yourselves and be sightless; be drunk, but not from wine, stagger, but not from beer.

Isaiah now returns to the woe on Ariel. He tells the people of Jerusalem almost sarcastically to be "stunned," or stupefied, and to be "amazed," or marvel in an indecisive way. But though they are stunned, they do not pay attention. They are drunk and stagger, but not (as in 28:7) from wine or beer (implying an even worse spiritual condition)—they are stubbornly resisting Isaiah's message. In effect, they have chosen to blind themselves to the truth (cf. 1 John 1:6) because of their trust in Egypt.

> ¹⁰The LORD has brought over you a deep sleep:
> He has sealed your eyes (the prophets); he has covered your heads (the seers).

Their spiritual condition is the problem. They act drunk and stagger because the LORD will pour out a spirit of "deep sleep" on them. He will close and seal the "eyes" of the false prophets and cover the "heads" of the seers, both of whom claim to be spiritual leaders, so they cannot see what is right. The people and their leaders will be totally insensitive to God's will (cf. 6:9–10). Their hearts, which they have hardened against God, will be made harder.

> ¹¹For you this whole vision is nothing but words sealed in a scroll. And if you give the scroll to someone who can read, and say to him, "Read this, please," he will answer, "I can't; it is sealed."

All God-given revelation had become to the people like the words of a scroll that is sealed. If it is given to a person who knows how to read, he refuses because the book is sealed. He does not care enough about what God says to break the seal and read it.

> ¹²Or if you give the scroll to someone who cannot read, and say, "Read this, please," he will answer, "I don't know how to read."

If the scroll is carelessly given to someone who doesn't know how to read, he does not have enough concern over God's revelation to get someone to read it to him. It is a terrible thing when leaders and people are unconcerned about God's Word.

> [13] The Lord says: "These people come near to me with their mouth and honor me with their lips, but their hearts are far from me. Their worship of me is made up only of rules taught by men.

Behind this indifference to God-given revelation is the hypocrisy of religion that is merely external and obedience that is superficial. In their worship, they mouth the proper words and repeat prayers they have learned by rote, but their hearts are far from God (cf. Ezek. 33:31–32; Matt. 6:7; 15:8–9; Mark 7:6–15). They are all spiritually blind.

> [14] Therefore once more I will astound these people with wonder upon wonder; the wisdom of the wise will perish, the intelligence of the intelligent will vanish."

Because of this hypocrisy and spiritual blindness, God will do something amazing and supernatural that will destroy human wisdom and intelligence and cause it to vanish because it is ineffective. Isaiah probably had in mind the Israelites' trust in Egypt and their plan to rebel against Assyria.

Paul quoted this verse in writing to the Corinthians, going on to say, "Where is the wise man? Where is the scholar? Where is the philosopher of this age? Has not God made foolish the wisdom of the world? For since in the wisdom of God the world through its wisdom did not know him, God was pleased through the foolishness of what was preached to save those who believe. Jews demand miraculous signs and Greeks look for wisdom, but we preach Christ crucified: a stumbling block to Jews and foolishness to Gentiles, but to those whom God has called, both Jews and Greeks, Christ the power of God and the wisdom of God. For the foolishness of God is wiser than man's wisdom, and the weakness of God is stronger than man's strength" (1 Cor. 1:20–25). And godless people today still think they can solve the world's problems.

3. WOE TO THOSE WHO WORK IN DARKNESS 29:15–24

a. Foolish Planners 29:15–16

> [15] Woe to those who go to great depths to hide

their plans from the LORD, who do their work in darkness and think, "Who sees us? Who will know?"

Another woe shows that not only are the Israelites indifferent to God-given revelation, they think they can actually cover up their plans so that the LORD will not see them. They keep their works in the dark, untouched by the light of God's truth (cf. John 3:19), and they do not believe anyone knows them or what they are doing. They want to carry out their plans as if they are in control, not God. They are foolish to think they can hide from God.

> ¹⁶You turn things upside down, as if the potter were thought to be like the clay! Shall what is formed say to him who formed it, "He did not make me"? Can the pot say of the potter, "He knows nothing"?

Isaiah says, ironically, they "turn things upside down." Their egotistical attitudes and thinking are stupid perversity, the opposite of the truth. It is like a clay pot saying to the potter, "You didn't make me," or "You don't know what you are doing." The clay can do nothing of itself. It is the potter who gives it worth.

b. Restoration That Honors God 29:17–24

> ¹⁷In a very short time, will not Lebanon be turned into a fertile field and the fertile field seem like a forest?

God has not changed His plans, however. He will turn things right-side up. In a little while (as God looks at time), Lebanon, which was heavily forested in Isaiah's day, will "be turned into a fertile field" (Heb. *lakkarmel,* "into the Carmel"—an orchard with fruit trees and grape vines, like the Mt. Carmel of Isaiah's day). The Carmel (i.e., Mt. Carmel) will seem like a forest or park. Both will be changed by the LORD.

> ¹⁸In that day the deaf will hear the words of the scroll, and out of gloom and darkness the eyes of the blind will see.

People will also be turned around. Even the deaf will hear and obey the words of the scroll of divine revelation. The blind, who are blinded to the truth by obscurity and darkness, will see. The truth and the works of God will be made real to them. Restored fellowship with God is implied.

> ¹⁹Once more the humble will rejoice in the LORD; the needy will rejoice in the Holy One of Israel.

Because of this restoration the humble and meek, people of no reputation, will have new and greater joy in the LORD. The needy and poor, who have no influence in this world, will rejoice in the true God who is the Holy One of Israel, the God who has dedicated himself to the carrying out of His plan and purpose of redemption (cf. Rom. 11:25–27).

> ²⁰The ruthless will vanish, the mockers will disappear, and all who have an eye for evil will be cut down—

When God makes things right, He will make an end of "the ruthless" (lit., "tyrant") who use wealth and position to get what they want no matter who may be hurt (probably including the Assyrians as the initial fulfillment).[8] Those who mock, or scoff, at God's Word and biblical standards of morality will be destroyed and disappear. Those who want to make trouble and see evil become rampant will be cut down.

> ²¹those who with a word make a man out to be guilty, who ensnare the defender in court and with false testimony deprive the innocent of justice.

God will cut off legal professionals who trick innocent people into saying words that make them seem guilty, trap the defender in court who opposes what is evil, or get the case of the "innocent" (Heb. *tsaddiq*, "righteous," "just") dismissed on a pretext.

> ²²Therefore this is what the LORD, who redeemed Abraham, says to the house of

---

[8]Because the Heb. *'arits*, "tyrant" is singular, some take it to mean Satan. McKenna, *Isaiah 1–39*, 286. However, the singular probably should be taken as a collective for all ruthless tyrants.

Jacob: "No longer will Jacob be ashamed; no longer will their faces grow pale.

The LORD is the same God who redeemed Abraham, saving him by grace through faith. God made promises to Abraham (Gen. 12:3) and He will carry them out. Jacob, looking down from heaven, will not "be ashamed," neither will his face[9] grow pale from any fear that the promises might not be fulfilled. Jacob's people will be transformed.

> 23When they see among them their children, the work of my hands, they will keep my name holy; they will acknowledge the holiness of the Holy One of Jacob, and will stand in awe of the God of Israel.

The reason for the lack of shame and fear is that the people of Israel are not only Jacob's descendants, they are also "the work" of God's hands. He will cause them to repent and will purify the nation—both Judah and Israel. Then they will treat God's name as holy, recognizing that God is truly "the Holy One of Jacob." They will stand in reverential awe before Him as their God, the God of Israel.

> 24Those who are wayward in spirit will gain understanding; those who complain will accept instruction."

God's work of purifying the nation will transform them. Instead of being rebellious, they will have discernment. Instead of murmuring as their ancestors did in the wilderness (see Num. 11:1), they will "accept instruction" with an eagerness to know God's Word and will. God is still working toward this—now through Jesus Christ and the gospel proclaimed in the power of the Holy Spirit.

4. WOE TO REBELLIOUS PEOPLE 30:1–33

a. Trusting Egypt Will Bring Shame 30:1–5

> 1"Woe to the obstinate children," declares the LORD, "to those who carry out plans that are

---

[9]The Heb. is singular. The NIV takes "Jacob" to mean the people of Israel so uses the plural here.

> not mine, forming an alliance, but not by my
> Spirit, heaping sin upon sin;

After dealing with general principles in the previous two chapters, Isaiah comes now with a woe that is pronounced specifically on those who go down to Egypt for help. Some see this as referring to Hoshea's embassy to So (probably Osorkon IV) when Hoshea ceased paying tribute to Assyria in about 726 B.C. (2 Kings 17:4). However, the situation fits the time of Hezekiah better, when Sennacherib was on the way to attack him in 701 B.C. (2 Kings 18:21).

The LORD calls them "obstinate" (Heb. *sor^erim*, "rebels"). They stubbornly reject Him and refuse to seek His help. They could seek the protection and covering of the Holy Spirit (cf. Zech. 4:6). Instead, they are determined to carry out plans to form an alliance (Heb. *linsokh massekhah*, "pour out a drink offering"[10] as the concluding act of a treaty or alliance, "a covering") with Egypt. "Heaping sin upon sin," they not only reject the LORD's help, they seek the help of Egypt.

> ²who go down to Egypt without consulting me;
> who look for help to Pharaoh's protection, to
> Egypt's shade for refuge.

The embassy sent to Egypt did not pray or seek God's guidance. They were determined to depend on the strength or stronghold of Pharaoh and to take refuge in Egypt's shadow instead of God's (cf. Ps. 91:1–2). The "Pharaoh" was the Ethiopian Shabako (716–702 B.C.) or his successor, Shebitku (702–690 B.C.).

> ³But Pharaoh's protection will be to your
> shame, Egypt's shade will bring you disgrace.

Instead of strength, their trust in Pharaoh will bring shame. Instead of refuge in the shadow of Egypt, there will be confusion and disgrace (cf. 36:6). God knew that Egypt was losing its power and would not be able to stop Assyria or help Judah.

> ⁴Though they have officials in Zoan and their
> envoys have arrived in Hanes,

---

[10]Not the ordinary word for "drink offering." This comes from a root word meaning "to cover," because of the purpose of this drink offering.

Zoan was in the Delta and Hanes[11] was on the Nile, probably about fifty miles south of Memphis. They were key cities in the united Egypt under the Twenty-fifth (Ethiopian) Dynasty. The "officials" and "envoys" may be either those of Hezekiah or those of the Pharaoh. The point seems to be that the treaty is in effect.

> ⁵everyone will be put to shame because of a people useless to them, who bring neither help nor advantage, but only shame and disgrace."

God's word is that all the people of Judah will be "put to shame." Egypt cannot help or profit them, but will bring only "shame and disgrace." This was fulfilled in 701 B.C. at Eltekeh, west of Jerusalem, when Sennacherib defeated the Egyptian army.

b. An Unprofitable Trip To An Unprofitable Nation 30:6–17

> ⁶An oracle concerning the animals of the Negev: Through a land of hardship and distress, of lions and lionesses, of adders and darting snakes, the envoys carry their riches on donkeys' backs, their treasures on the humps of camels, to that unprofitable nation,

This message deals with the donkeys and camels that were carrying baggage for the envoys to Egypt as well as the gifts seeking its favor and protection. They were being taken on a difficult route—full of "hardship and distress," through the Negev desert (the same desert south of Judah where the Israelites spent forty years)—to Egypt. They could have taken the easier coastal route, but this was a secret mission, and they probably wanted to avoid the Philistines along the coast. Consequently there was danger from lions, poisonous adders (or vipers) and fiery, darting serpents. The poor donkeys and camels suffered through this journey for nothing.

> ⁷to Egypt, whose help is utterly useless. Therefore I call her Rahab the Do-Nothing.

Egypt's "help" is of no value and will come to nothing. "Rahab" has the meaning of "arrogance" and "boastfulness,"

---

[11] Hanes was called Heliopolis by the Greeks.

but Egypt cannot live up to its proud boasting, for she has no power against Assyria. Thus she is worthy of the name "Rahab the Do-Nothing" (Heb. *shaveth*, "that sits still").

> ⁸Go now, write it on a tablet for them, inscribe it on a scroll, that for the days to come it may be an everlasting witness.

Because the people of Judah and Jerusalem did not listen to Isaiah's warnings, God gave him a command to write them "on a tablet" where the public could see it and be witnesses. He must also inscribe them "on a scroll," which would be preserved for future generations. His writings would become a part of God's Word into eternity—His unchangeable Word.

> ⁹These are rebellious people, deceitful children, children unwilling to listen to the Lord's instruction.

It was important that the message be written, for the people were faithless (disappointingly so), refusing to hear and obey the teaching of the Lord. They could not be trusted to pass it on by word of mouth.

> ¹⁰They say to the seers, "See no more visions!" and to the prophets, "Give us no more visions of what is right! Tell us pleasant things, prophesy illusions.

These rebellious, "deceitful children" (v. 9) told the seers to stop seeing supernatural truths and visions. They told the prophets to stop prophesying (speaking for God about His righteous demands). Instead, they wanted to hear "pleasant [and inoffensive] things." They even wanted them to prophesy "illusions"—deceptions and unimportant things that would allow them to do as they pleased. The same attitude can be seen in the last days of this age (2 Tim. 4:3–4). Too many do not want expository preaching that declares the truth of God's Word. We can be thankful God commanded His Word to be written down.

> ¹¹Leave this way, get off this path, and stop confronting us with the Holy One of Israel!"

They wanted the prophets to leave the way prescribed by God, turn aside from the path of righteousness, and not bother them with the Holy One of Israel. They were looking for an easy religion. It is sad when preachers lead people astray. It is even worse when people are determined to lead preachers astray.

> ¹²Therefore, this is what the Holy One of Israel says: "Because you have rejected this message, relied on oppression and depended on deceit,

Isaiah did not listen to the people but gave God's answer. It was severe. He is indeed the "Holy One of Israel." They didn't want to be bothered by Him, but they could not dispose of Him. He knew how they had despised and spurned His prophetic word, how they had put their trust in a people who oppressed them, and how they rejected His holiness in their perverted religion.

> ¹³this sin will become for you like a high wall, cracked and bulging, that collapses suddenly, in an instant.

Because of their twisted, perverted attitudes and sins, they would be like a wall that is "cracked and bulging," about to break, ready to collapse "in an instant." They will be unprepared.

> ¹⁴It will break in pieces like pottery, shattered so mercilessly that among its pieces not a fragment will be found for taking coals from a hearth or scooping water out of a cistern."

God's judgment will be severe: He will break the walls so completely that there will not be a broken piece big enough to take embers from one fire to light another or to scoop water from a cistern.[12] In other words, even the remnants of the wall will serve no useful purpose. As Isaiah already has said, God would use the ruthless Assyrians to accomplish it.

> ¹⁵This is what the Sovereign LORD, the Holy One of Israel, says: "In repentance and rest is your salvation, in quietness and trust is your strength, but you would have none of it.

---

[12] Because of infrequent rains, they used cisterns to conserve water supply.

God wanted to save them. He had already pleaded with them to return in repentance and to rest in Him (cf. 28:12), and thus be saved from their enemies. He had asked them to be quiet before Him and put their confidence in Him, for this would bring strength. His grace was available, but they "would have none of it."

> ¹⁶You said, 'No, we will flee on horses.' Therefore you will flee! You said, 'We will ride off on swift horses.' Therefore your pursuers will be swift!

Instead of trusting God, the people put their trust in horses. With swift horses (probably from Egypt), they planned to escape the judgment. God said they would indeed flee, but if they thought they could be swift, their pursuers would be swift as well—implying they would not escape. They did not realize what the Assyrians could do to them.

> ¹⁷A thousand will flee at the threat of one; at the threat of five you will all flee away, till you are left like a flagstaff on a mountaintop, like a banner on a hill."

God promised through Moses that if the Israelites would live in obedience to Him and His instructions, five would chase a hundred (of their enemies) and a hundred would chase ten thousand (Lev. 26:8). But God also warned that the reverse could be true (Deut. 32:30). Now through Isaiah He warns the Israelites again that "a thousand will flee at the threat of one" and that they would all flee "at the threat of five." What would be left would be like "a banner on a hill": There were once people there, but nothing much is left—a result of their forsaking God.

c. God Will Be Gracious And Heal 30:18–26

> ¹⁸Yet the LORD longs to be gracious to you; he rises to show you compassion. For the Lord is a God of justice. Blessed are all who wait for him!

In spite of the necessity of judgment, God's purpose for His people has not changed. Therefore He will wait until after the judgment in order "to be gracious." He will then rise to exalt himself by revealing His nature as merciful and compassionate. He is a God of justice, so the judgment on His people will be just. Those "who wait for Him" are the purified remnant. They will be blessed in due time if they wait faithfully for Him and His mercy.

> ¹⁹O people of Zion, who live in Jerusalem, you will weep no more. How gracious he will be when you cry for help! As soon as he hears, he will answer you.

In Isaiah's day the people would weep. Because of God's grace, the day would come when the people of Zion in Jerusalem would "weep no more." Then God will hear their cry and answer them without any delay.

> ²⁰Although the Lord gives you the bread of adversity and the water of affliction, your teachers will be hidden no more; with your own eyes you will see them.

There will be a period of calamity when adversity will be their bread and affliction their drink—which may imply the scant rations during a siege. Although the NIV reads "teachers" (the Heb. *morekha* may be taken as singular or plural), it is better here to take it as singular (the Heb. *yikkaneph,* for NIV "be hidden," is better taken as "hide himself," and is singular). Thus, the time will come when their Teacher (the Lord, cf. Joel 2:23 where the same Heb. word is used [see NIV margin], translated "former rain," KJV) will not hide himself any more, and they will no longer be blinded by sin but will have eyes to see Him. An intimation of the Incarnation may be seen here, since the most popular title for Jesus among the people was "Teacher."

> ²¹Whether you turn to the right or to the left, your ears will hear a voice behind you, saying, "This is the way; walk in it."

The people will no longer reject the word of the Lord, but they will individually hear a "voice" (Heb. *davar,* "word") behind them because He cares for each one. The voice will not only tell them the way, but will correct them whenever they turn away in one direction or the other. Isaiah later identifies "the way" as the way of holiness (35:8). We can still hear this voice if we are sensitive to the Holy Spirit.

> ²²Then you will defile your idols overlaid with silver and your images covered with gold; you will throw them away like a menstrual cloth and say to them, "Away with you!"

When they walk in the way of holiness guided by the word of the LORD, their whole attitude will change. The images used to seek guidance, expensive images painstakingly made, will be recognized as defiled, worthless, and will be totally rejected.

> ²³He will also send you rain for the seed you sow in the ground, and the food that comes from the land will be rich and plentiful. In that day your cattle will graze in broad meadows.

Along with spiritual blessings, the land will be restored to fruitfulness. God will give needed rain for great harvests, and there will be large pastures where the cattle may feed and safely roam.

> ²⁴The oxen and donkeys that work the soil will eat fodder and mash, spread out with fork and shovel.

There will be plenty of fodder that has been spread out and sifted for the oxen and young donkeys to eat. Even they will eat only the best.

> ²⁵In the day of great slaughter, when the towers fall, streams of water will flow on every high mountain and every lofty hill.

The once barren mountains and hills will be well-watered in the day of the LORD's victory (cf. 2:12–18). The towering ones will fall. Initially, this refers to the destruction of the Assyrians. But "the day of great slaughter" will find its ultimate fulfillment in the battle of Armageddon (Rev. 16:16; 19:11–21).

> ²⁶The moon will shine like the sun, and the sunlight will be seven times brighter, like the light of seven full days, when the LORD binds up the bruises of his people and heals the wounds he inflicted.

Judgment will darken the sun and moon. But they will be restored to even greater brilliance in the day of the LORD's triumph, a day that will bring the restoration and healing of the LORD's people. Unusual astral phenomena are often used to describe future events. Such is the case with Isaiah, who describes the coming Day of the LORD as a day when these light sources will fail (13:10; 24:23). He uses the opposite, intensification of light of the heavenly bodies, to describe the Messianic Age (see also 60:19–20). It should be observed, however, that this manner of reference to the heavenly bodies is not unique to Isaiah. It is like the common prophetical phrases "Day of the LORD," "In/On that day," and "Woe/Alas" in this sense (cf. Joel 2:31; Amos 8:9; Mic. 3:6; Hab. 3:11; Mal. 4:2; Matt. 24:29; Luke 21:25; Acts 2:20; Rev. 6:12; 7:16; 8:12; 9:2; 21:23; 22:5, etc.).

d. God's Control Over The Nations 30:27–28

> **27**See, the Name of the LORD comes from afar, with burning anger and dense clouds of smoke; his lips are full of wrath, and his tongue is a consuming fire.

Now Isaiah returns to his own day, when God was about to deal with the Assyrians and the nations allied with them. The "Name of the LORD" represents His character and nature, and so means the LORD himself. He is coming as a storm and from afar His name is signaled. His anger is compared to thick, rising smoke, also a figure of the coming judgment of God in 14:31 (this usage also appears in 34:10). This is common terminology among the prophets (Joel 2:30; Matt. 12:20; Rev. 9:17–18; 18:9,18; 19:3). It is used in a way similar to "fire" in both Testaments as a symbol of God's judgment. His lips speak abundantly of His indignation, and "his tongue is as a consuming fire." That is, He speaks the word and the judgment falls.

> **28**His breath is like a rushing torrent, rising up to the neck. He shakes the nations in the sieve of destruction; he places in the jaws of the peoples a bit that leads them astray.

His breath is like a flood that overwhelms "up to the neck." He will sweep away the Assyrians, sifting them and their allied nations as with a "sieve," disposing of all that is false and worthless. Then, a "bit" (or bridle) will lead them astray instead of guiding them in the right way. God will allow them to go in the wrong direction. They cannot escape His judgment.

e. Israel Will Sing When The LORD Shatters Assyria 30:29–33

> ²⁹And you will sing as on the night you celebrate a holy festival; your hearts will rejoice as when people go up with flutes to the mountain of the LORD, to the Rock of Israel.

With Assyria judged, God's people will sing in the night as they keep a holy feast. Passover was kept at night. Their hearts will respond with rejoicing as when people playing flutes go up to "the mountain of the LORD," the temple mountain—not just going to the temple, but going into the presence of the One who is "the Rock of Israel": Israel's Strength, Refuge, Fortress, and Protector.

> ³⁰The LORD will cause men to hear his majestic voice and will make them see his arm coming down with raging anger and consuming fire, with cloudburst, thunderstorm and hail.

Isaiah now continues the message of judgment with Assyria in view. God in His majesty will cause His glorious, majestic voice to be heard. He will demonstrate what bringing down His arm (symbolizing His power) will do, with raging anger, consuming fire, crashing thunder, a cloudburst, and hailstones.

> ³¹The voice of the LORD will shatter Assyria; with his scepter he will strike them down.

God will use His majestic voice to shatter the Assyrians. They were God's rod which He used to punish Israel and Judah (10:5). But now it is their turn to be judged (cf. 10:12).

> ³²Every stroke the Lord lays on them with his punishing rod will be to the music of tambourines and harps, as he fights them in battle with the blows of his arm.

The LORD's rod on Assyria is a "punishing [Heb. *muṣadah*,

"foundation"] rod," founded to punish Assyria. Every stroke of the rod will be accompanied by tambourines and harps, indicating the joy of victory. "In battle with the blows of his arm" could also be translated "battles of shaking or sieving" to indicate God's purpose to purify His people as well.

> ³³Topheth has long been prepared; it has been made ready for the king. Its fire pit has been made deep and wide, with an abundance of fire and wood; the breath of the LORD, like a stream of burning sulfur, sets it ablaze.

"Topheth" was a place of burning in the Valley of Hinnom, probably involving human sacrifice to Molech and other pagan rites.[13] The name has the Hebrew vowels of the word "shame." It serves much the same function as the Aramaic "Gehenna" which is a sobriquet for the lake of fire.[14]

Assyria is heading for a shameful funeral pyre. The funeral pyre is already prepared in a large pit and is large enough to take care of the Assyrians. God's breath, "like a stream of burning sulfur," will set it on fire. Burning sulfur is used concerning the lake of fire in the New Testament and speaks of terrible judgment (Rev. 19:20).

5. WOE TO THOSE WHO SEEK EGYPT'S HELP 31:1–32:2

a. Foolish To Trust Egypt And Not God 31:1–3

> ¹Woe to those who go down to Egypt for help, who rely on horses, who trust in the multitude of their chariots and in the great strength of their horsemen, but do not look to the Holy One of Israel, or seek help from the LORD.

God now has another specific woe for the war party in Hezekiah's time. Egypt had offered to help because they wanted to stop Assyria. So Judah's representatives were going to Egypt to accept the offer; they were accustomed to relying on

---

[13]See 2 Kings 23:10; Jer. 7:31; 19:11–14.
[14]See Stanley M. Horton, *Our Destiny: Biblical Teachings on the Last Things* (Springfield, Mo.: Logion Press, 1996), 230–33.

horses and chariots, thinking that if they had many with strong horsemen, they would be victorious. This strategy seemed wise to them. But they did not look to the LORD. They had no desire to be in His presence, nor did they worship Him from their hearts.

> ²Yet he too is wise and can bring disaster; he does not take back his words. He will rise up against the house of the wicked, against those who help evildoers.

The politicians who sought Egypt's help had questioned God's ways and wisdom (29:14–16). But God is the One who is truly wise. He will "bring disaster," that is, judgment. He has given His word—and because He does not change, He will not take back His words. His words are always trustworthy and true (Rev. 22:6). Now He declares He will "rise up" against the wrongdoers, those who seek help from Egypt, and against the help these evildoers are expecting from Egypt.

> ³But the Egyptians are men and not God; their horses are flesh and not spirit. When the LORD stretches out his hand, he who helps will stumble, he who is helped will fall; both will perish together.

Isaiah now gives further reasons why human reason cannot be relied on. The Egyptians are merely human, "not God." Their horses are "flesh," having only temporary physical life, they are not "spirit." Judah needed to know how frail the Egyptians were and how insufficient their horses would be. The LORD is in control. When He moves in power ("stretches out his hand"), Egypt, who helps, will stumble, and Judah, who is helped, will fall: They will "perish together."

b. God Himself Will Protect Jerusalem 31:4–5

> ⁴This is what the LORD says to me: "As a lion growls, a great lion over his prey—and though a whole band of shepherds is called together against him, he is not frightened by their shouts or disturbed by their clamor—so the LORD Almighty will come down to do battle on Mount Zion and on its heights.

Isaiah reminds the people that the LORD has spoken personally to him. Like a lion growling over its prey, the LORD regards His possession Zion. The "band of shepherds" are the Egyptians who are seeking to protect Judah from the Assyrians—against God's will. The LORD will fight against Zion, against their plans, thus bringing defeat to the Egyptians. And He will use the Assyrians to do this.

> ⁵Like birds hovering overhead, the LORD Almighty will shield Jerusalem; he will shield it and deliver it, he will 'pass over' it and will rescue it."

But it is not God's purpose to let the Assyrians destroy Jerusalem. "Like birds hovering overhead," He will protect Jerusalem. His compassion will save Jerusalem this time.

The war party wanted the strength of a great army of horses and chariots and they despised God's power. They thought of God's power as nothing more than a few little birds against a great army. But His power is greater than any other. He hovers over the city of Jerusalem to protect it.¹⁵

c. A Call For Repentance 31:6–7

> ⁶Return to him you have so greatly revolted against, O Israelites.

God calls the people of Israel to repent, to turn back to Him. The Hebrew indicates deep apostasy. They are in a deep pit, but they can still change their thinking and their way of life.

> ⁷For in that day every one of you will reject the idols of silver and gold your sinful hands have made.

Isaiah looks ahead to the Day of the LORD, when idols ("no-gods") of gold and silver will be rejected as products of sin.

d. Supernatural Destruction of Assyria 31:8–9

> ⁸"Assyria will fall by a sword that is not of man; a sword, not of mortals, will devour them. They

---

¹⁵Many saw an application of this verse in World War I when British General Edmund Henry Allenby's planes flew over Jerusalem, delivering it from the Turks.

will flee before the sword and their young men
will be put to forced labor.

Now in Isaiah's own day, "Assyria will fall by a sword," but not of any individual man. They will be devoured by the sword, but not of humankind. Human armies, such as the armies of Egypt, would not accomplish it.

Assyria's destruction would be supernatural, as was the case when Sennacherib lost 185,000 soldiers to the death angel in 688 B.C. (37:36; 2 Kings 19:35). The Assyrian young men who left after the destruction of the 185,000 were actually "put to forced labor." Sennacherib lived seven more years and never made another military campaign, instead forcing his soldiers to work on his building projects in Nineveh.[16]

9Their stronghold will fall because of terror; at sight of the battle standard their commanders will panic," declares the LORD, whose fire is in Zion, whose furnace is in Jerusalem.

Assyria's "stronghold" (Heb. *ṣal'ô*, "its rock"), including its strength and the king they trust in, will pass away in terror. The princes of Assyria will desert their flag and be shattered.[17] They have defied the LORD, whose holy presence is like a consuming fire in Jerusalem. There the altar symbolizes forgiveness for the repentant and judgment for God's enemies.

e. The Righteous King 32:1–8

1See, a king will reign in righteousness and rulers will rule with justice.

After telling of God's judgment, Isaiah again looks to the future when the Messiah-King (chaps. 9 and 11) "will reign in righteousness" and rulers will make their decisions "with justice," in line with the principles of His righteousness.

2Each man will be like a shelter from the wind and a refuge from the storm, like streams of

---

[16]Daniel David Luckenbill, *Ancient Records of Assyria and Babylonia,* 2 vols. (Chicago: University of Chicago Press, 1926–27), 2:183. See comments on 37:37.

[17]See J. Maxwell Miller and John H. Hayes, *A History of Ancient Israel and Judah* (Philadelphia: Westminster Press, 1986), 386–87.

water in the desert and the shadow of a great
rock in a thirsty land.

Each person, each ordinary citizen, will be like their King. Some take it that they will become rocks, like God who is our Rock and Refuge. But the Messiah-King will be the "man" who will protect as from the wind and the storm (or inundation), and will provide water. He will be as refreshing as the shade of a "great rock" in an exhausted, thirsty land. He truly cares for His people.

> ³Then the eyes of those who see will no longer be closed, and the ears of those who hear will listen.

He will change the people's perception, which will transform every aspect of society. Eyes that were once willfully closed in self-deception (29:9) will be open and see the truth. Ears that once refused to listen will hear and obey. They will become true disciples of (students of, learners who follow) the Lord.

> ⁴The mind of the rash will know and understand, and the stammering tongue will be fluent and clear.

The hearts and minds of those who are hasty and rush ahead will discern and understand true knowledge. Those who are stammerers and hesitate to speak will be quick to speak, clearly and plainly. They will be ready to spread the truth with wisdom.

> ⁵No longer will the fool be called noble nor the scoundrel be highly respected.

Worldly society often honors fools (godless, amoral people) as noble. They may even honor the unscrupulous who manage to get into high positions. But this will all be changed.

> ⁶For the fool speaks folly, his mind is busy with evil: He practices ungodliness and spreads error concerning the LORD; the hungry he leaves empty and from the thirsty he withholds water.

Here we see the true nature of the godless fool. He characteristically "speaks folly": sin, sacrilege, and stupidity. His heart and mind cause him to be "busy with evil": causing trouble for others and offending God. He "practices ungodliness," spreads perverted error concerning the LORD, and keeps food from the hungry and water from the thirsty (cf. 1 Sam. 25:11,25; Jer. 17:11; Prov. 3:27,28).

> ⁷The scoundrel's methods are wicked, he makes up evil schemes to destroy the poor with lies, even when the plea of the needy is just.

The instruments and methods of the scoundrel are evil. He "makes up evil schemes [plots, including infamous treatment, prostitution, and incest] to destroy the poor with lies" and the needy whose cause is just and right. Manipulation of legal processes by perjury may be implied.

> ⁸But the noble man makes noble plans, and by noble deeds he stands.

Those who are noble in their attitude toward God and liberal in their attitude toward others counsel and plan honorable deeds, and in these they rise up and stand. They are acceptable before God (cf. Ps. 24:3–4).

f. Judgment Until The Spirit Is Poured Out 32:9–14

> ⁹You women who are so complacent, rise up and listen to me; you daughters who feel secure, hear what I have to say!

Isaiah has warned the leaders, prophets, fools, and scoundrels. The women also need to listen to the prophet's voice, for they are at ease. They are complacent about sin, content with things as they are (cf. 3:16–26; Amos 4:1), and "feel secure" (confident, unconcerned) about Isaiah's warnings, trusting that things will never change. Amos indicates that men were the same in Samaria (Amos 6:1). By calling on the women to "rise up and listen," Isaiah recognizes the power they are able to exercise.

> ¹⁰In little more than a year you who feel secure will tremble; the grape harvest will fail, and the harvest of fruit will not come.

After a few days more than a year, these confident women will no longer be secure but upset and trembling in fear. The grape harvest will certainly fail, and the ingathering of the summer fruit will come to nothing. (See Amos 4:1 for the attitude of the women toward wine.)

> ¹¹Tremble, you complacent women; shudder, you daughters who feel secure! Strip off your clothes, put sackcloth around your waists.

These "complacent women" are commanded to shudder (or tremble), strip, and put nothing but a coarse cloth around their waists. This was common treatment of people taken captive or made slaves. They must prepare for the results of their sin.

> ¹²Beat your breasts for the pleasant fields, for the fruitful vines

They will lament, beating their breasts because of what will happen to their fields and vineyards when the enemy comes.

> ¹³and for the land of my people, a land overgrown with thorns and briers—yes, mourn for all houses of merriment and for this city of revelry.

Because the invading army will take the people captive and strip the fields, no cultivation will occur; the fields will lay uncultivated, becoming full of thorny briers instead of good crops. Thorny briers will also spring up in the "houses of merriment" and in the wild, haughty city (a collective for the towns of Judah) so full of revelry. They would be destroyed by the Assyrians (2 Kings 18:13).

> ¹⁴The fortress will be abandoned, the noisy city deserted; citadel and watchtower will become a wasteland forever, the delight of donkeys, a pasture for flocks,

Fortified palaces will be unattended, for the servants and the guards will be captured and slain or taken into exile. (Some commentators understand this verse as referring to Samaria when it was taken in 722 B.C.) The city will fall silent, its crowds gone. The "citadel" (Heb. *'ophel*) and the watchtower will become bare fields, or wasteland, "forever" (Heb. *'ad-'olam*, which may mean "for a long time"; and as the next v. shows, it is not "forever"). The deserted fields will be a joy only to wild donkeys and a pasture for flocks of sheep and goats, probably brought in by neighboring Bedouin tribes.

g. The Outpoured Spirit Will Restore Peace 32:15–20

15till the Spirit is poured upon us from on high, and the desert becomes a fertile field, and the fertile field seems like a forest.

The results of God's judgment on Israel and Judah are not final. A better day is coming—a day of renewal, salvation, and prosperity. But that day will not come until after the Spirit of the Lord will be poured out in Pentecostal fullness "from on high" (from heaven, as God's gift). The desert will become a fertile field (Heb. *karmel*, "garden land" or "orchard"), and the garden land will seem like a forested park (cf. 29:17).

There is indeed an outpouring of the Spirit that began on the Day of Pentecost (Joel 2:28; Acts 1:8; 2:4). But there will be an even greater outpouring of the Spirit when Jesus returns to establish His millennial kingdom on earth.

16Justice will dwell in the desert and righteousness live in the fertile field.

With "justice . . . in the desert" and "righteousness . . . in the fertile field," the renewal of the world by the Holy Spirit will be complete. This seems to mean that the pollution caused by sin and greed, as well as the pollution of the atmosphere, will be cleared away by the Spirit. The earth will be renewed to prepare for millennial joys.

17The fruit of righteousness will be peace; the effect of righteousness will be quietness and confidence forever.

Because there will be a righteousness where people are right with God and with each other, there will be peace, quiet rest, and confident security in the LORD. This harmonious well-being is quite different from the false security felt by the sinners in Isaiah's day. Modern Israel still awaits that day.

> ¹⁸My people will live in peaceful dwelling places, in secure homes, in undisturbed places of rest.

Instead of meaningless complacency, God's people will live in peaceful homes, homes of trust and confidence. Homes will be secure resting places that are undisturbed, cheerful, and untroubled.

> ¹⁹Though hail flattens the forest and the city is leveled completely,

Isaiah now returns to the woe that began this section. Isaiah's audience must be reminded that the judgment must come before the restoration. "Hail" will be an agent of judgment. "The forest" refers to the earth that is infected by sin. "The city" is the world of people who have turned their backs on God.

> ²⁰how blessed you will be, sowing your seed by every stream, and letting your cattle and donkeys range free.

"Blessed" (Heb. *'ashre*) includes the idea of a fullness of happiness, spiritual fulfillment, and a good life—all from God. The picture of sowing in a well-watered land and farm animals virtually tending themselves speaks of the good life to the agricultural community of Isaiah's day. The principle seen here—after the judgment comes the blessing—is in many Bible passages about judgment and millennial blessings.

6. Woe To Assyria 33:1

> ¹Woe to you, O destroyer, you who have not been destroyed! Woe to you, O traitor, you who have not been betrayed! When you stop destroying, you will be destroyed; when you stop betraying, you will be betrayed.

After reminding Israel of God's promise, Isaiah again contrasts God's blessing with another prophecy of His judgment. The woe here is directed against Assyria. (Assyria's immoral treachery and destructive, robber tactics will be seen again in the end times.)

In its prime, Assyria was able to march through country after country without fear of retaliation. It would make treaties and break them, betraying any trust put in it during its efforts to make vassal states. But its time would come; it would, in turn, be destroyed by treachery and betrayal (cf. Matt. 26:52). Nineveh was destroyed in 612 B.C. by a combination of Babylonians and Medes. Then with the additional help of Scythians, they brought Assyria to a final end in 606 B.C.

STUDY QUESTIONS

1. How have the people of Israel disregarded the Law?
2. What lesson would the Assyrians teach Israel and why?
3. How does 1 Corinthians 14:21 apply Isaiah 28:11–12?
4. Why was Israel's covenant with death foolish?
5. Where is the ultimate fulfillment of the cornerstone found?
6. What conclusion can be drawn from 28:23–29?
7. In what ways does the name "Ariel" fit Jerusalem?
8. What was God's purpose in these judgments?
9. Why will even the educated not understand God's word?
10. What was the real cause for the formalism the people had fallen into?
11. What hope will the future day bring?
12. For what reasons was it wrong for Judah to go to Egypt for help?
13. How else did the people express their rebellion against the Lord?
14. What hope did God give them and why did they refuse?
15. What would be the result of the "bread of adversity"?
16. What assurance did God give that He would overthrow the Assyrian army?
17. What further reasons show it was wrong for Judah to seek help from Egypt?
18. Who would defend Jerusalem and what results would follow?
19. Whose reign does Isaiah foresee and what will his reign be like?
20. Why does Isaiah give special warning to "complacent women"?

21. What will be the work of the Spirit in the future kingdom age?
22. Who is the destroyer and what will happen to it?

F. God's Purpose In History 33:2–35:10

1. A Prayer For Deliverance And God's Answer 33:2–24

a. A Plea That Exalts God 33:2–6

²O LORD, be gracious to us; we long for you. Be our strength every morning, our salvation in time of distress.

Isaiah interjects a plea to the LORD for help and deliverance. There was still a godly remnant in Jerusalem waiting for the LORD to move graciously in their behalf. They looked to the LORD to be their strength (Heb. *z^eroa'*, "arm") and help "every morning." They trusted Him to be their salvation[1] in "time of distress," when they were pressed from every side. Even Hezekiah had turned back to the Lord (2 Kings 19:3–4).

³At the thunder of your voice, the peoples flee; when you rise up, the nations scatter.

The noise of an approaching army makes people flee. But when God reveals how exalted He is, "at the thunder of [His] voice," people flee and nations scatter. God is greater than any force humankind can produce. Throughout Israel's history He had scattered nations; He would scatter the armies of the Assyrians in the same way (cf. Num. 10:35; Ps. 68:1). John the Revelator indicated the "sharp sword" of Jesus' mouth would similarly destroy the armies of the Antichrist (Rev. 19:15).

⁴Your plunder, O nations, is harvested as by young locusts; like a swarm of locusts men pounce on it.

---
[1] The Heb. *y^eshu'ah* can also mean deliverance.

The figure of locusts and their larvae swarming in and stripping every green plant indicates how quickly and how completely the battle will be over.

The picture of people pouncing on the spoil may describe what happened after the destruction of Sennacherib's army. It may also represent the way people will enter into the blessings of the LORD's victory over the Antichrist and his armies (Rev. 19:19–20).

> ⁵The LORD is exalted, for he dwells on high; he will fill Zion with justice and righteousness.

The LORD's victory will exalt himself and show how high He is—the true God who dwells in heaven. By His victory He will fill Zion with His own "justice and righteousness." This is His resolute purpose and He will carry it out. Isaiah implies the people will praise Him, recognizing how exalted He is.

> ⁶He will be the sure foundation for your times,
> a rich store of salvation and wisdom and
> knowledge; the fear of the LORD is the key to
> this treasure.

In contrast to the times of distress (v. 2), God's millennial time will be characterized by stability (security brought about by the faithfulness of God) and a treasury of, literally, "salvations." (The plural in the Heb. indicates a fullness of all that salvation means and includes our full inheritance in Christ: our new bodies and our reigning as kings and priests with Him.) There will also be a fullness of "wisdom and knowledge," no doubt the gift of the Messiah (11:2). No longer will ignorance and lack of wisdom cause anyone to go astray. The "fear of the LORD" will not be a mere human emotion. It will be a gift He has as a treasure to be given to those who love Him and honor His awesome holiness.

b. Sorrow And Distress Of Judah 33:7–9

> ⁷Look, their brave men cry aloud in the streets;
> the envoys of peace weep bitterly.

Now Isaiah comes back to his own times when the Assyrians were destroying the cities of Judah and threatening Jerusalem

(701 B.C.). Judah's "brave men" (Heb. *'er'ellam*, "heroes")[2] weep openly in the streets because they cannot stop the enemy. Their envoys who sought peace weep bitterly because Assyria has broken the treaty Hezekiah made that was supposed to protect Jerusalem (2 Kings 18:14–16). This may also refer to the officials mentioned in Isaiah 36:3,22.

> ⁸The highways are deserted, no travelers are on the roads. The treaty is broken, its witnesses are despised, no one is respected.

"The highways are deserted" because of the violence of the enemy—no merchants bringing needed goods. The enemy (Sennacherib) has broken the treaty, rejected and despised the witnesses, and not respected or valued any person. Peace and security are gone and everyone is afraid to venture out.

> ⁹The land mourns and wastes away, Lebanon is ashamed and withers; Sharon is like the Arabah, and Bashan and Carmel drop their leaves.

The land withers and suffers blight (cf. 24:4). The Assyrian armies ruined farmland. Lebanon with its beautiful mountains and cedar forests, the fertile plain of Sharon on the coast south of Mount Carmel, the level fields of Bashan northeast of the Sea of Galilee—all have become like the Arabah desert south of the Dead Sea; the leaves of the trees and plants of Carmel's garden land wither and drop. The Assyrians have ravaged the land.

> *c. The Lord Will Arise And Judge The Enemy*
> *33:10–13*

> ¹⁰"Now will I arise," says the LORD. "Now will I be exalted; now will I be lifted up.

The time comes when God sees it is enough and He rises up in judgment that will exalt Him. God has His time, and He is always on time.

> ¹¹You conceive chaff, you give birth to straw; your breath is a fire that consumes you.

---

[2]Some take this to mean priests.

The Assyrians made their decisions in the past. Now they must suffer the consequences. Reaping those consequences is compared to bringing to birth what had been conceived earlier. Because they had made their plans without consulting the LORD, the result will be chaff and straw. Their own breath, or spirit, will be the fire that devours them.

> ¹²The peoples will be burned as if to lime; like cut thornbushes they will be set ablaze."

God's judgment on the Assyrian armies (which were made up of a multitude of peoples) will be intense, like the burning of lime, and quick, like the burning of dried thorn bushes.

> ¹³You who are far away, hear what I have done; you who are near, acknowledge my power!

If Sennacherib had kept his treaty and left Jerusalem because of the tribute Hezekiah gave him, the people would have thought they were saved by their own wisdom. But when Sennacherib broke the treaty and the situation seemed hopeless, God answered prayer. Thus it was obvious God was the One to trust.

Further, because God will judge all nations and because He has shown the availability of His grace by great deliverances, those "far away" (the Gentiles) and "near" (the people of Judah) need to pay attention to what He has done and acknowledge His mighty power.

d. Sinners Learn A Lesson 33:14

> ¹⁴The sinners in Zion are terrified; trembling grips the godless: "Who of us can dwell with the consuming fire? Who of us can dwell with everlasting burning?"

What God has done has indeed been observed by the sinners in Zion. The godless (who were living as if there were no God) are shaking with fear and ask who can live in the presence of the "consuming fire" of God's unchangeable holiness.

e. Who Can Dwell With A Holy God? 33:15–16

> ¹⁵He who walks righteously and speaks what is right, who rejects gain from extortion and

keeps his hand from accepting bribes, who stops his ears against plots of murder and shuts his eyes against contemplating evil—

The answer to their question calls for the kind of lifestyle the Old Testament emphasizes and the Holy Spirit makes possible for born-again believers. God wants to see everyone continuing to live in full righteousness. He wants us to keep speaking "what is right," rejecting any kind of exploitation of others (this would include fraud, gambling, lotteries, etc.).

He also wants us to refuse bribes, to refuse to listen to anything that would injure others, to refuse to look with favor on anything displeasing to Him.

> [16]this is the man who will dwell on the heights, whose refuge will be the mountain fortress. His bread will be supplied, and water will not fail him.

The person who lives in that kind of full righteousness will "dwell on the heights"—in fellowship with the LORD—having security like that in high, strong cliffs and inexhaustible provision of daily needs.

f. The King Is Coming 33:17–24

> [17]Your eyes will see the king in his beauty and view a land that stretches afar.

The person who lives in that kind of fellowship with the LORD will now personally "see the king in his beauty." Because the king is not named, some suppose it is Hezekiah after his healing and during his fifteen added years of life (2 Kings 20:6). But the connection with the preceding verse indicates that the King is the Messiah (see 32:1; cf. Ps. 45:1–7). He will reign to far distances, to the ends of the earth. Seeing His peace and blessing is implied.

> [18]In your thoughts you will ponder the former terror: "Where is that chief officer? Where is the one who took the revenue? Where is the officer in charge of the towers?"

In that day each person's mind will "ponder the former terror": such as was caused by the Assyrians. They will be asking where is the "chief officer," that is, the "scribe" (Heb. *sopher*) who wrote down the names of those taken captive, where is "the one who took the revenue," weighing out and recording the tribute, and where is "the officer" writing down the number of the towers demolished (or to be demolished)? The enemy terror will be gone.

> **19You will see those arrogant people no more, those people of an obscure speech, with their strange, incomprehensible tongue.**

The lessons taught by the Assyrians with their foreign language and strange, stammering tongue (28:11) will not need to be learned again. The arrogant Assyrians will be punished for their sins.

> **20Look upon Zion, the city of our festivals; your eyes will see Jerusalem, a peaceful abode, a tent that will not be moved; its stakes will never be pulled up, nor any of its ropes broken.**

When they see the King (v. 17), they will be able to see Zion, the city where they came into the presence of the LORD to celebrate the festivals (Passover, Pentecost, and Tabernacles—the pilgrimage feasts which called for them to come to Jerusalem, Exod. 23:14–17). The holy city will be a quiet, peaceful place. Isaiah compares it to "a tent that will not be moved," for its "stakes will never be pulled up," and its security to tent ropes that will never be broken.[3] This, to the ancient Israelite, pictured an ideal state. Only the Messiah can bring in such peace.

> **21There the LORD will be our Mighty One. It will be like a place of broad rivers and streams. No galley with oars will ride them, no mighty ship will sail them.**

Most importantly, "the LORD will be our Mighty One," present with His people in majesty. The lack of shipping in the "broad rivers and streams" seems to indicate they have all they need because the LORD is there (cf. Ps. 46:4–5; Ezek. 47:1–5).

---

[3]The people in Jeremiah's time thought this applied to Jerusalem in their day. They thought they could sin and reject Jeremiah's prophecies and God would never let anything happen to Jerusalem. This was a misapplication of the prophecy.

There will be no necessity to search the world for its riches as Solomon's ships did (1 Kings 10:22).

> ²²For the LORD is our judge, the LORD is our lawgiver, the LORD is our king; it is he who will save us.

The LORD is sufficient for every need: He is Judge, Lawgiver, and King. Isaiah emphasizes that He will save, deliver, and give all the blessings of His salvation. Praise is implied in this verse. He is worthy of all praise!

> ²³Your rigging hangs loose: The mast is not held secure, the sail is not spread. Then an abundance of spoils will be divided and even the lame will carry off plunder.

Some commentators understand this verse as a description of Assyria in terms of a ship that "enters the holy waters of Zion" and becomes shipwrecked.[4] Rather, the verse returns to Isaiah's day and pictures Jerusalem as a ship in bad shape because of Assyrian attacks, yet victorious, dividing the spoil. Though it limps along, it carries off the plunder. The previous verse gives the secret of their victory: God is King.

> ²⁴No one living in Zion will say, "I am ill"; and the sins of those who dwell there will be forgiven.

Isaiah now looks ahead. Because God is King in the future millennial age and will provide divine health, no inhabitant of Jerusalem will say, "I am ill." All their sin and guilt will also be "forgiven" (Heb. $n^e su'$, "lifted up," that is, taken away through the atonement that God will provide through Jesus who would be lifted up on the cross). There will be total well-being for individuals and for society as a whole.

2. GOD'S WRATH ON THE NATIONS 34:1–17

a. Judgment On All Nations 34:1–4

> ¹Come near, you nations, and listen; pay attention, you peoples! Let the earth hear, and all

---

[4]S. H. Widyapranawa, *The Lord is Savior: Faith in National Crisis* (Grand Rapids: Wm. B. Eerdmans, 1990), 210.

that is in it, the world, and all that comes out of it!

The call in 33:13 for those far and near to listen is followed by another call that is even more comprehensive. Now not only are all the people of the world to listen, but "all that is in it" and "all that comes out of it." The future judgment will affect people, the animal world, and the plant world. Tremendous changes will take place.

> **2The LORD is angry with all nations; his wrath is upon all their armies. He will totally destroy them, he will give them over to slaughter.**

God is longsuffering but the time will come when His rage will be ready to explode upon all nations.[5] "His wrath," His hot anger, will be against their armies. He "will totally destroy them" (Heb. *hecherimam*, "dedicate them to God's judgment," that is, to complete destruction, like Jericho; Josh. 6:17). There will be total slaughter (cf. Rev. 19:21).

> **3Their slain will be thrown out, their dead bodies will send up a stench; the mountains will be soaked with their blood.**

Those struck dead will be "thrown out," given no proper burial, so that their bodies will be left to stink and decay. This was considered a terrible disgrace. As sinners they suffer the results of their sin. The picture of mountains "soaked [Heb. *namassu*, "melted"] with their blood" indicates the sanguinary erosion of the soil by the sudden death of so many.

> **4All the stars of the heavens will be dissolved and the sky rolled up like a scroll; all the starry host will fall like withered leaves from the vine, like shriveled figs from the fig tree.**

The judgment will affect all creation. The stars will "be dissolved" (Heb. *namaqqu*, "dwindle away"). The rolling up of a scroll meant the closing of a book. The stars and planets will fall to ruin like fading leaves (cf. Rev. 6:12–14) or dried up figs. The

---

[5]These will be the nations that are left after the Church is taken out at the time of the resurrection and rapture.

God who created the heavens and earth can dissolve all the galaxies. The fulfillment of this will prepare the way for a new heaven and earth (Rev. 20:11; 21:1).[6]

b. Special Judgment On Edom 34:5–17

> [5]My sword has drunk its fill in the heavens; see, it descends in judgment on Edom, the people I have totally destroyed.

Now God speaks. His "sword" is used to attack individuals. His divine sword has brought judgment in heaven (on satanic forces) and then focuses on Edom as representative of the enemies of God's people. God "totally destroyed" them (lit., they are under God's "ban"—doomed to destruction). Edom (descendants of Esau) refused to let the Israelites under Moses go through their territory (Num. 20:14–21) and often showed animosity toward Israel. Obadiah condemned them for antagonistic conduct when the Arabians and Philistines attacked Judah and Jerusalem in 845 B.C. (2 Chron. 21:16–17). He also treated them as representative of all nations who will suffer judgment in the Day of the LORD (Obad. 15–16). Amos spoke of the destruction of Edom in like manner (1:11–12). After the depredations of Assyrians and Babylonians "the Edomites gradually shifted across the Arabah . . . where they became known as the Idumeans. By the fourth century B.C., . . . Edomite territory . . . had come under the domination of . . . the Nabataeans," an Arab people who settled there.[7] (Among the descendants of the Idumeans was King Herod.)

> [6]The sword of the LORD is bathed in blood, it is covered with fat—the blood of lambs and goats, fat from the kidneys of rams. For the Lord has a sacrifice in Bozrah and a great slaughter in Edom.

The blood and the fat of sacrifices were always devoted to the LORD. The fat was considered the best part of the meat (cf. Lev.

---

[6]Stanley M. Horton, *The Ultimate Victory: An Exposition of the Book of Revelation* (Springfield, Mo.: Gospel Publishing House, 1991), 301, 307.
[7]Keith N. Schoville, *Biblical Archaeology in Focus* (Grand Rapids: Baker Book House, 1982), 485.

3:9–11,14–16). For these sinners whose sacrifices were meaningless, the blood and fat only nourished His sword, making it more ready to bring judgment. Edom's capital, Bozrah, about twenty-seven miles southeast of the Dead Sea, was singled out for special judgment.

> ⁷And the wild oxen will fall with them, the bull calves and the great bulls. Their land will be drenched with blood, and the dust will be soaked with fat.

Even the wild oxen will be killed with the bull calves and bulls that would normally be sacrificed.⁸ The land will drink up their blood, "and the dust will be soaked with fat"—for the sacrifice will be judgment, not redemption.

> ⁸For the LORD has a day of vengeance, a year of retribution, to uphold Zion's cause.

God has a day of "vengeance" (Heb. *naqam*, "recompense"), a year of "retribution" or settlement of claims on behalf of Zion, for Zion has a "cause," a case against Edom. This implies judgment on all who are enemies of God and His Word.

> ⁹Edom's streams will be turned into pitch, her dust into burning sulfur; her land will become blazing pitch!

Edom often opposed Israel and Judah (Obad. 10). Edom's streams becoming "pitch" and its very dust becoming "burning sulfur" means that the land of Edom would become like Sodom and Gomorrah.

> ¹⁰It will not be quenched night and day; its smoke will rise forever. From generation to generation it will lie desolate; no one will ever pass through it again.

The ruin of Edom is emphatically declared to be forever. People will not live there or even continue to pass through it. Probably even in the Millennium it will remain as a constant reminder to people of God's holy judgment.

---

⁸Some take the wild oxen and bulls to symbolize the armies of the nations and their leaders.

> ¹¹The desert owl and screech owl will possess it; the great owl and the raven will nest there. God will stretch out over Edom the measuring line of chaos and the plumb line of desolation.

Unclean birds (probably various species of owls, jackdaws, and ravens) will live there. God will stretch over the land "the measuring line [cf. 28:17; Amos 7:7–8] of chaos" (Heb. *tohu*, "emptiness") and "the plumb line of desolation" (Heb. *'avne bohu*, "formless stones" in contrast to building stones). *Tohu* and *bohu* are the same words used in Genesis 1:2 to describe the state of the earth before God gave it form (dry land, continents) and began to fill the emptiness with living creatures. The land of Edom did become a wilderness but its final judgment is still to come.

> ¹²Her nobles will have nothing there to be called a kingdom, all her princes will vanish away.

None of the nobles will be there to proclaim the kingdom of Edom, and all its princes will be gone.

> ¹³Thorns will overrun her citadels, nettles and brambles her strongholds. She will become a haunt for jackals, a home for owls.

With no people present, weeds, wild animals, and birds will take over the decaying ruins of palaces and fortresses. Edom will no longer be a kingdom.

> ¹⁴Desert creatures will meet with hyenas, and wild goats will bleat to each other; there the night creatures will also repose and find for themselves places of rest. ¹⁵The owl will nest there and lay eggs, she will hatch them, and care for her young under the shadow of her wings; there also the falcons will gather, each with its mate.

Wild animals and birds will live there, mating and raising their young undisturbed by humans. There is some dispute among scholars as to the identity of some of the animals. All we know for certain is that some of them are night creatures.

> ¹⁶Look in the scroll of the LORD and read: None of these will be missing, not one will lack her mate. For it is his mouth that has given the order, and his Spirit will gather them together.

To the command to listen (34:1), Isaiah now adds a command to "look in [Heb. *dirshu,* "seek"] the scroll [book] of the LORD and read." The reference seems to be regarding the preceding verses. Isaiah wrote down his prophecies. They came from his mouth by God's Holy Spirit, and by the same Spirit they would be fulfilled.

Edom was later taken over by the Arabs and then, in A.D. 106, by Rome.[9] Petra (Sela), its most famous city, is still a ruin. God's judgment on the nations during the Great Tribulation will just as surely come.

> ¹⁷He allots their portions; his hand distributes them by measure. They will possess it forever and dwell there from generation to generation.

God has cast the lot for them and given it to them by the measuring line (cf. v. 11; 28:17; Amos 7:7–8), that is, given it to the wild animals and unclean birds for an inheritance. It will be theirs forever.

3. A RESTORED LAND AND PEOPLE 35:1–10

a. The Desert Will Rejoice 35:1–2

> ¹The desert and the parched land will be glad; the wilderness will rejoice and blossom. Like the crocus,

Another beautiful revelation of future glory and blessing follows the prophecy of judgment. In contrast to the devastation that will happen to Edom, the people of God will see the desert and the dry land rejoicing with new life, blossoming like the "crocus" (or asphodel, a lily with long sprays of blossoms). Some apply this to the return from Babylon under Zerubbabel, but no such restoration took place at that time. The judgment on the earth prepares for the millennial blessings.

---

[9] Schoville, *Biblical Archaeology,* 485.

> ²it will burst into bloom; it will rejoice greatly and shout for joy. The glory of Lebanon will be given to it, the splendor of Carmel and Sharon; they will see the glory of the LORD, the splendor of our God.

God's people will see a mass of flowers and the very desert shouting ecstatically with joy. The "glory of Lebanon" is its forests. The "splendor of Carmel and Sharon" is their fertility and wonderful fruit. By seeing all this in the desert, God's redeemed people will be seeing the glory of the LORD, "the splendor of our God" that clothes the land.

b. Encouragement For Suffering People 35:3–7

> ³Strengthen the feeble hands, steady the knees that give way;

The commands here imply that God's people need strength to claim what He has provided for them. "Feeble hands" implies discouragement and lack of power and ability. "Knees that give way" indicates weakness that keeps people from moving ahead for God.

> ⁴say to those with fearful hearts, "Be strong, do not fear; your God will come, he will come with vengeance; with divine retribution he will come to save you."

Those with dismayed or terrified hearts need to have someone tell them to be strong, to stop being afraid, for God is present. He will come "with vengeance" for what His people have suffered and "with divine retribution" for what their enemies have done to them. For He will come, save, and transform them. Changed hearts and lives will be even more supernatural than the desert blossoming (see v. 2).

> ⁵Then will the eyes of the blind be opened and the ears of the deaf unstopped.

Then blind eyes and deaf ears will be opened. Jesus used this passage as evidence that He is the Messiah (Matt. 11:4–5; Luke 7:22). Presently divine healing brings only a foretaste of this. However, when He returns there will be further fulfillment.

Then healing will be more than temporary; the body will experience full redemption (Rom. 8:23).

> ⁶Then will the lame leap like a deer, and the mute tongue shout for joy. Water will gush forth in the wilderness and streams in the desert.

The lame person will jump like the fallow deer and the tongue of the dumb will shout for joy. The restoration will see water gushing like artesian wells in the desert and streams in the Arabah desert, south of the Dead Sea.

> ⁷The burning sand will become a pool, the thirsty ground bubbling springs. In the haunts where jackals once lay, grass and reeds and papyrus will grow.

Burning desert sand will be replaced by pools of water and dry thirsty ground will have artesian springs. In what was the home of jackals there will be grass, reeds, and papyrus rushes—a complete change, a God-given miracle.

c. The Highway Of Holiness 35:8–10

> ⁸And a highway will be there; it will be called the Way of Holiness. The unclean will not journey on it; it will be for those who walk in that Way; wicked fools will not go about on it.

God's purpose in creating streams in the desert is to bless people. Through this restored land will be a great "highway" (cf. 19:23), named the "Way of Holiness." No unclean person will travel on it. No wicked fools will wander around on it (or, the meaning may be that no simpleton will be confused and go astray on it; see Exod. 23:4 where the verb is used of a donkey wandering off). Actually, it will be for all the redeemed, for they are all clean (John 15:3), and no one who travels on it, even a simpleton, will go astray or encounter danger. How different from the highways in ancient times often used by armies of enemies and where robbers sometimes lurked (cf. the Parable of the Good Samaritan, Luke 10:30–37).

> ⁹No lion will be there, nor will any ferocious

Isaiah 35:9–10 / 267

**beast get up on it; they will not be found there.
But only the redeemed will walk there,**

In Isaiah's day the rough footpaths through the desert were threatened by dangerous wild animals. All that will be changed. No lion or "ferocious beast" will be there to threaten those who travel on the Highway of Holiness. Only the redeemed of the LORD shall travel on it. The "redeemed" are those ransomed or bought back by the *go'el*, the "Kinsman Redeemer." The primary responsibility of the *go'el* was to redeem his close relative from difficulty, danger, or debt. One aspect of this was to restore the property and rights of a widow. This was accomplished by the nearest male relative taking her as a wife. In the Book of Ruth, Boaz became the *go'el*. When God is recognized as the *go'el* of His people, He stands up for them and vindicates them. Especially in Isaiah (and the Psalms, Jeremiah, Hosea, and Zechariah) God as the *go'el* redeemed His people from the slavery of Egypt and continues to ransom or redeem them, sweeping away their offenses "like a cloud" and their sins "like the morning mist." Then He calls, "Return to me, for I have redeemed you" (44:22). Whenever there is repentance and the Spirit is poured out in the seasons of refreshing, as promised in Acts 3:19, we can have a foretaste of the blessings of the Highway of Holiness He will provide in the Millennium.[10]

[10]and the ransomed of the LORD will return. They will enter Zion with singing; everlasting joy will crown their heads. Gladness and joy will overtake them, and sorrow and sighing will flee away.

The redeemed are further defined as those "ransomed of the LORD." He is the Redeemer who paid the price for their redemption and delivers them from the bondage of sin. They will return and enter Zion with ringing shouts of joy, and eternal joy will be on their heads—a better crown than a crown of gold. Joy that exults and delights will "overtake" them. They will not have to seek joy; it will catch up with them.

---

[10]The Gk. of Acts 3:19 indicates these times of refreshing are available until Jesus comes again.

Trouble that torments or produces sighing, or groaning, will "flee away." Nothing will disturb the joy of the redeemed. God will have done a complete restoration of both the people and the land. The results of sin will have been removed.

STUDY QUESTIONS

1. On what grounds does the godly remnant base their petitions in 33:2–9?
2. What are the characteristics of the godly person in 33:14–16?
3. Who is the king and what do we learn in the latter part of chapter 33 about the kingdom?
4. What will be involved in the final judgment of the earth?
5. What is implied by the dissolving of the stars and how could this be fulfilled?
6. What is the significance of judgment on Edom?
7. Why does Isaiah mention the book of the LORD in 34:16–17?
8. What applications of chapter 35 can we make to today?
9. How does 35:5–6 apply to the ministry of Jesus? (See Matt. 11:4–5; Luke 7:22).
10. What in chapter 35 looks ahead to the Millennium?
11. What is the relationship between God's vengeance and His salvation?
12. What connection do you see between 32:15 and 35:6–10?

V. HEZEKIAH AND SENNACHERIB 36:1–39:8

Chapters 36 to 39 have sometimes been called the Book of Hezekiah. Much of what is written here is also found in 2 Kings 18:13 to 20:21. The facts are recorded here as a witness to the truth of Isaiah's prophecies.

A. Sennacherib Invades In 701 B.C. 36:1–37:8

1. JUDAH'S CITIES CAPTURED 36:1

¹In the fourteenth year of King Hezekiah's reign, Sennacherib king of Assyria attacked all the fortified cities of Judah and captured them.

From Assyrian records it is clear that Sennacherib's invasion was in 701 B.C. Because Hezekiah reigned with his father, Ahaz, the sixth year of that coreign was 722 B.C. (2 Kings 18:10). However, when Ahaz died in 715 B.C., Hezekiah began to reign in his own right, starting the count of his reign over again; thus the twenty-nine years of his reign lasted to 686.

Second Chronicles 29:3 tells us, "In the first month of the first year of his reign, he opened the doors of the temple of the LORD and repaired them." This was followed by a great revival and the celebration of the Passover. None of this would have been allowed by the wicked King Ahaz. His death made possible the inauguration of a new era, and 715 B.C. was declared to be Hezekiah's first year—thus "the fourteenth year" was 701 B.C., the fourth year of the reign of Sennacherib.

As long as Sargon was on the throne of Assyria, Hezekiah accepted the treaty his father had made (2 Kings 16:7) and continued to pay tribute. But when Sennacherib came to the Assyrian throne in 705 B.C. and found it necessary to give his attention to the Chaldean usurpation of Babylon—which was east, in the opposite direction from Israel—Hezekiah decided to break with Assyria, and sent no more tribute (2 Kings 18:7).

Because Egypt under Piankhi seemed to have gained strength, Hezekiah made an alliance with Egypt for their mutual protection against Assyria. At the same time, he defeated the Philistines and took control of their territory as far as Gaza (2 Kings 18:8).

After only six months, however, Sennacherib regained control of Babylon, driving out Merodach-Baladan, and headed west. His real objective was the wealth of Egypt but he was taking control of countries on the way. He gave Judah special attention because, according to his records, Hezekiah tried to stop him. When the Philistine King Padi of Ekron attempted to keep the city from joining Hezekiah's revolt against Assyria, Hezekiah put him in chains and imprisoned him in Jerusalem.[1]

But Sennacherib's annals tell how he conquered Ekron, defeated an Egyptian army at Eltekeh (about thirty-two miles west-northwest of Jerusalem), scattered the other mercenary troops Hezekiah had hired, and then turned his attention to the "fortified cities of Judah" (attacking and capturing them all).[2] Sennacherib's annals state that he captured 46 of them plus many unwalled villages and took 200,146 people captive.[3]

Second Kings 18:14–16 adds that while Sennacherib was besieging Lachish, about thirty miles southwest of Jerusalem, Hezekiah sent a message to him saying, "I have done wrong. Withdraw from me, and I will pay whatever you demand of me." Sennacherib demanded three hundred talents (about ten metric tons) of silver and thirty talents of gold, which Hezekiah paid by taking all the silver from the temple of the LORD as well as from the treasuries of the royal palace and by stripping the gold from the doors and doorposts of the temple. Sennacherib also wrote that he forced Hezekiah to give up Padi, who was then restored to his throne in Ekron.[4]

It must have been at this time that Hezekiah became sick and was told by Isaiah that he was going to die (38:1; see 2 Kings 20:1). The Bible in both 2 Kings and Isaiah finishes up the history of Sennacherib's campaigns and then returns to Hezekiah's sickness as a background for the coming of the envoys from Merodach-Baladan, who had proclaimed himself king of Babylon for the third time. But Hezekiah's prayer and tears brought God's promise of fifteen more years and the assurance that God would deliver him and Jerusalem "from the hand of the king of Assyria" (38:5–6). Hezekiah declared this to the people to encourage them to put their faith in the LORD.

---

[1] Daniel David Luckenbill, *Ancient Records of Assyria and Babylonia*, 2 vols. (Chicago: University of Chicago Press, 1926–27), 2:119–20.

[2] Ibid., 2:121.

[3] Daniel David Luckenbill, *The Annals of Sennacherib* (Chicago: University of Chicago Press, 1924), 33.

[4] Luckenbill, *Ancient Records*, 2:120.

2. Sennacherib's Threats 36:2–20

²Then the king of Assyria sent his field commander with a large army from Lachish to King Hezekiah at Jerusalem. When the commander stopped at the aqueduct of the Upper Pool, on the road to the Washerman's Field, ³Eliakim son of Hilkiah the palace administrator, Shebna the secretary, and Joah son of Asaph the recorder went out to him.

Sennacherib had his spies and soon knew about Hezekiah's sickness and recovery. When Sennacherib heard that Hezekiah was telling the people God would deliver them, he apparently decided he had made a mistake in leaving a fortified city behind. So, like so many worldly dictators, he broke his treaty and sent his "field commander" (Heb. *rab-shakeh;* "Rab-shakeh," KJV) with a large army to Jerusalem. They stopped outside the wall (vv. 11–12) and Eliakim (who was in charge of the palace), Shebna (who was the secretary, probably the secretary of state), and Joah (the recorder, or secretary, who kept the official records) went out to meet him. They probably dared to do this on the strength of the previous treaty made with Sennacherib.

⁴The field commander said to them, "Tell Hezekiah, "'This is what the great king, the king of Assyria, says: On what are you basing this confidence of yours? ⁵You say you have strategy and military strength—but you speak only empty words. On whom are you depending, that you rebel against me?

The field commander called Sennacherib "the great king." But he did not refer to Hezekiah as king. Then he proceeded with Sennacherib's message, trying to break down by ridicule the confidence and trust Hezekiah had placed in the LORD.

Sennacherib was right in that Hezekiah's "strategy and military strength" had already proved meaningless before his armies. He was really saying that Hezekiah was foolish to depend on anyone to help him in his rebellion against Sennacherib.

⁶Look now, you are depending on Egypt, that splintered reed of a staff, which pierces a man's

> hand and wounds him if he leans on it! Such is Pharaoh king of Egypt to all who depend on him.

Sennacherib was also right in saying that it was foolish to depend on Egypt. He probably knew that Isaiah had warned the people not to trust in Egypt. The comparison of leaning on a "splintered reed" (one that would not only break but would pierce the hand of the one leaning on it) symbolized that Pharaoh was not only unable to help but would also take advantage of those who depended on him and would turn against them.

> ⁷And if you say to me, "We are depending on the LORD our God"—isn't he the one whose high places and altars Hezekiah removed, saying to Judah and Jerusalem, "You must worship before this altar"?

Sennacherib knew what was going on in Jerusalem and sharply criticized Hezekiah, really mocking God as well. During the great revival, Hezekiah had taken away the shrines and high places, which were formerly dedicated to Baal (see 2 Kings 18:1–4). The Israelites had turned them into places for worship of the LORD, but they adulterated that worship by including the pagan gods of the shrines. Such worship was an abomination to the LORD and Hezekiah was right in destroying these shrines (cf. Deut. 12:2–14). Sennacherib, however, missed the point. The demand to offer sacrifices only at the temple in Jerusalem was intended to be a witness to the pagan world that there was only one true temple because there is only one true God.

However, those shrines had been popular before the revival, and Sennacherib hoped there was still enough feeling for them among the common people that they could be encouraged not to listen to Hezekiah.

> ⁸"'Come now, make a bargain with my master, the king of Assyria: I will give you two thousand horses—if you can put riders on them!

The field commander then asked Hezekiah to "make a bargain" with Sennacherib: He would get two thousand horses if he could set riders on them. Yet this offer was a mockery. The field commander knew Jerusalem did not have enough soldiers left to put two thousand of them on horses. This was really an invitation to surrender and to join Sennacherib's army as it continued toward Egypt. (It was common for the Assyrians to invite conquered people to join their army and recoup losses at the next place of conquest.)

> ⁹How then can you repulse one officer of the least of my master's officials, even though you are depending on Egypt for chariots and horsemen?

The field commander emphasizes that Jerusalem could not withstand even a small unit led by the least of Sennacherib's officers. Surrender and joining the Assyrian army would be a much better prospect than "depending on Egypt for chariots and horsemen."

> ¹⁰Furthermore, have I come to attack and destroy this land without the LORD? The LORD himself told me to march against this country and destroy it.'"

Part of the psychological warfare of ancient kings was to declare that the gods of the people they were attacking had sent them to do it. Cyrus did this when he was approaching Babylon, claiming that their gods Bel and Nebo had sent him to deliver them from the misrule of Nabonidus and Belshazzar. Cyrus was successful in this and the people of Babylon threw open the gates and welcomed his army in, giving Cyrus himself a triumphal entry complete with palm branches.[5]

But Sennacherib was not as subtle. He claimed that the LORD had sent him to destroy Judah. No doubt he knew of Isaiah's earlier prophecies, where God said Assyria was a rod in His angry hand (10:5); however, he did not pay attention to the rest of the prophecy, which was against Assyria. Thus, he was misrepresenting the truth in an attempt to intimidate the people. All he wanted was for Jerusalem to surrender.

---

[5]James B. Pritchard, ed., *Ancient Near Eastern Texts Relating to the Old Testament*, 2d ed. (Princeton: Princeton University Press, 1955), 306, 315–16.

> **11**Then Eliakim, Shebna and Joah said to the field commander, "Please speak to your servants in Aramaic, since we understand it. Don't speak to us in Hebrew in the hearing of the people on the wall."

Aramaic was the language of trade, commerce, advanced education, and of political communication between countries from before the time of Abraham down to the time of Alexander the Great. The delegation from Hezekiah asked the field commander to speak in Aramaic because they did not want to agitate the people of Jerusalem who were sitting on the wall and who would spread the field commander's threats throughout the city. But that is exactly what the field commander wanted. He was hoping that he could throw the people into a panic so they would call for surrender.

> **12**But the commander replied, "Was it only to your master and you that my master sent me to say these things, and not to the men sitting on the wall—who, like you, will have to eat their own filth and drink their own urine?"

The field commander's reply was even more threatening and crude. He saw that Hezekiah and the Jerusalem leaders did not intend to give in. Therefore he and his army would besiege Jerusalem and cut them off from supplies until there was nothing else to eat or drink.

> **13**Then the commander stood and called out in Hebrew, "Hear the words of the great king, the king of Assyria! **14**This is what the king says: Do not let Hezekiah deceive you. He cannot deliver you! **15**Do not let Hezekiah persuade you to trust in the LORD when he says, 'The LORD will surely deliver us; this city will not be given into the hand of the king of Assyria.'

The words of the field commander clearly show that Hezekiah's sickness came after his giving of tribute.[6] Before that

---

[6]Note that Isaiah finishes up the account of Sennacherib's invasions before telling of Hezekiah's sickness. The account of the sickness also prepares for chap. 39 where Merodach-Baladan hears of the sickness.

time he was trusting in Egypt and not in the LORD. The inclusion of gold and silver from the temple also showed he was not trusting in the LORD when he made the treaty with Sennacherib. Hezekiah's healing and God's promise made the difference (see chap. 38). But Sennacherib tried to break down the confidence of the people in God's promise by saying that Hezekiah could not deliver them and that they must not let Hezekiah persuade them to trust in the LORD. He was really calling Hezekiah a deceiver who would not be able to help them. However, he failed to recognize that the Lord is faithful and He is able to deliver.

> [16]"Do not listen to Hezekiah. This is what the king of Assyria says: Make peace with me and come out to me. Then every one of you will eat from his own vine and fig tree and drink water from his own cistern, [17]until I come and take you to a land like your own—a land of grain and new wine, a land of bread and vineyards.

Again the field commander tells the people not to listen to Hezekiah. If they would make peace with Sennacherib, he would let them live in peace until he returned from this campaign, undoubtedly expecting to return triumphantly from Egypt. Then he would carry out the Assyrian policy of displacing and resettling whole populations. He promised that he would take them to a land as good as their own, where they could grow grapes and wheat as they did in the land of Judah. He probably had Babylonia in mind, for he had just removed 208,000 people from there, and it was Assyrian practice to move other people in to take the place of those captives who were displaced. In this way the Assyrians hoped to disorient and demoralize a people—so they would give up any tendency to rebel.

> [18]"Do not let Hezekiah mislead you when he says, 'The LORD will deliver us.' Has the god of any nation ever delivered his land from the hand of the king of Assyria? [19]Where are the gods of Hamath and Arpad? Where are the gods of Sepharvaim? Have they rescued Samaria from my hand? [20]Who of all the gods of these countries has been able to save his

land from me? How then can the LORD deliver Jerusalem from my hand?"

Again Sennacherib's message refers to Hezekiah's declaration of the promise of 38:6. He reminds Jerusalem that the cities of Hamath on the Orontes River and Arpad in northern Syria and Sepharvaim were all conquered and their gods did not help them. Even Samaria became an Assyrian province in 722 B.C. and some of the inhabitants of Sepharvaim were moved to it. But in his arrogance he still missed the point. He could not imagine that the God worshiped in the little country of Judah could be greater than the gods worshiped in the countries he had already conquered. The gods of those countries had not been able to save their lands from the great king of Assyria. Sennacherib implies that he is greater than any god. Therefore, he suggests that the LORD cannot be any different and cannot save Jerusalem from him. He was also suggesting that it would go much better with Jerusalem if they would surrender.

3. THE PEOPLE OBEY HEZEKIAH 36:21

21But the people remained silent and said nothing in reply, because the king had commanded, "Do not answer him."

The people made no answer to these taunts and threats. Hezekiah had commanded them not to answer. By obeying the king and thus trusting God along with him, they took a new stand of faith. God would indeed deliver them.

The people of Judah who hoped they could defeat the Assyrians by making an alliance with Egypt had been discredited. The Egyptians were no help. The mercenary soldiers that Hezekiah had hired were scattered. Now in Jerusalem a new heart and spirit awaited Isaiah. He was soon able to give them the comfort of chapter 40 and following. (The new attitude of his audience and the new message accounts for the change in style and vocabulary.)

4. SENNACHERIB'S DEATH PROPHESIED 36:22–37:8

22Then Eliakim son of Hilkiah the palace administrator, Shebna the secretary, and Joah

son of Asaph the recorder went to Hezekiah,
with their clothes torn, and told him what the
field commander had said.

The threats of Sennacherib were serious. The field commander had a large army ready to besiege Jerusalem. The three who had met with the field commander then tore their clothes—probably they tore open the front of their tunics as a sign of grief and debasement because of Sennacherib's blasphemy. Then they reported to Hezekiah what the field commander had said.

> ¹When King Hezekiah heard this, he tore his clothes and put on sackcloth and went into the temple of the LORD.

Hezekiah tore his clothes also and put on coarse black sackcloth made of goat's hair as a further recognition of the seriousness of the situation. He knew that his father, Ahaz, and the recent war party that had trusted in Assyria were wrong. He realized his only hope was in the LORD. So he went publicly into the temple to seek the promised help of the LORD. He wanted the people to know he still believed God's promise.

> ²He sent Eliakim the palace administrator, Shebna the secretary, and the leading priests, all wearing sackcloth, to the prophet son of Amoz. ³They told him, "This is what Hezekiah says: This day is a day of distress and rebuke and disgrace, as when children come to the point of birth and there is no strength to deliver them. ⁴It may be that the LORD your God will hear the words of the field commander, whom his master, the king of Assyria, has sent to ridicule the living God, and that he will rebuke him for the words the LORD your God has heard. Therefore pray for the remnant that still survives."

The delegation that had gone to the field commander and the leading priests followed Hezekiah's example and put on sackcloth. The king then sent them to Isaiah, "the prophet son of Amoz," with a message recognizing their danger, the disgrace threatened by the field commander, and their inability to help themselves. The comparison of a mother without "strength to deliver" a child meant that they were in a hopeless situation. In such a case, both the mother and baby would die.

Their one hope, however, was in the LORD. Hezekiah recognized that Sennacherib's words delivered by the field commander were really ridiculing the living God (in contrast to the dead gods of wood, metal, and stone). Hezekiah hoped God would hear and rebuke Sennacherib. Recognizing that Isaiah was in touch with God,[7] Hezekiah asked him to "pray for the remnant." It was too late to pray for the deliverance of the other cities of Judah but there was still a remnant surviving in Jerusalem.

> **5When King Hezekiah's officials came to Isaiah, 6Isaiah said to them, "Tell your master, 'This is what the LORD says: Do not be afraid of what you have heard—those words with which the underlings of the king of Assyria have blasphemed me.**

The servants of Hezekiah then sought out Isaiah and his word from the LORD. Isaiah had a comforting word. They must tell Hezekiah to stop being afraid of the message by which the "underlings" (Heb. *na'are*, "boys" without discernment) of Sennacherib had blasphemed the LORD.

> **7Listen! I am going to put a spirit in him so that when he hears a certain report, he will return to his own country, and there I will have him cut down with the sword.'"**

God would put a spirit in Sennacherib and he would hear a certain report and return to his own land. The "report" was the news that Merodach-Baladan was again taking over in Babylon. Babylon was more important to Sennacherib than Jerusalem or even Egypt, so he would return to his own land, which included Babylon as one of his capitals. Eventually he would die in his own land. Sennacherib in 688 B.C. would threaten Hezekiah and Jerusalem again, but an angel of the LORD would see to it that he would not come near Jerusalem and would return to Nineveh where he would die (see 37:36–38).

---

[7]Note in v. 4 that these representatives of the state and temple say "the LORD *your* God," not "*our* God."

⁸**When the field commander heard that the king of Assyria had left Lachish, he withdrew and found the king fighting against Libnah.**

When there was no surrender, the field commander returned and found Sennacherib fighting against Libnah. (Lachish had been taken and destroyed. From Lachish he went to Libnah.) Then Sennacherib heard the report about Merodach-Baladan taking over Babylon and rushed back to Nineveh and to Babylon. He celebrated this 701 B.C. campaign, however, by commissioning artists to picture it. Archaeologists have found a great wall relief in Sennacherib's palace at Nineveh that pictured the capture of Lachish and its people.⁸ It shows a file of men and women coming out of the city with burdens on their backs. Ahead of them are captives being impaled on sharpened stakes. Another group carries sacks and other articles in their hands. Some are giving up tribute or spoil.⁹ The records of Sennacherib's second campaign state quite clearly that he killed some captives and deported the rest at that time.¹⁰ Since Sennacherib had already directed that some of the tribute brought to Nineveh be taken to Babylon, and since he needed to put down the revolt in Babylon, it is reasonable to believe that Sennacherib took the prisoners from the cities of Judah to Babylon.¹¹

STUDY QUESTIONS

1. What had Sennacherib accomplished in Judah before he sent his field commander with a large army to Jerusalem?
2. Why did Sennacherib say Hezekiah was deceiving the people of Jerusalem?

---

⁸A full-size copy of this can be seen in the Oriental Museum of the University of Chicago.

⁹Charles Marston, *The Bible Comes Alive* (New York: Fleming H. Revell, n.d.), 226–28; James C. Muir, *His Truth Endureth: A Survey of the Beginnings and of Old Testament History in the Light of Archaeological Discoveries* (Philadelphia: National Publishing Co., 1937), 187.

¹⁰Luckenbill, *Ancient Records*, 2:118.

¹¹James W. Thirtle, *Old Testament Problems: Critical Studies in the Psalms and Isaiah* (London: Morgan & Scott, 1916), 134–35; Benjamin R. Downer, "The Added Years of Hezekiah's Life" *Bibliotheca Sacra* 80, no. 319 (July 1923): 269; Robert Henry Pfeiffer, *State Letters of Assyria, American Oriental Series,* vol. 6 (New Haven: American Oriental Society, 1935), 79.

3. What did Sennacherib think of himself and of the Lord?
4. How did the people respond to the field commander's message and why is this significant?
5. Why did Hezekiah send people in sackcloth to Isaiah?
6. What message did the Lord give and how was it fulfilled?
7. What evidence is there for a second campaign of Sennacherib in 688 B.C.?

B. Sennacherib's Army Decimated And Sennacherib Killed 37:9-38

1. SENNACHERIB'S RENEWED THREATS 37:9–13

⁹Now Sennacherib received a report that Tirhakah, the Cushite king [of Egypt], was marching out to fight against him. When he heard it, he sent messengers to Hezekiah with this word:

There is a time gap of about twelve years between 37:8 and 37:9. Old Testament writers would often complete one account and then go back and give details of an earlier event. This was done frequently in the Book of Kings. (See also Ezra 4, where Ezra tells of his attempt at rebuilding the city, how it was stopped, and then goes back to the earlier rebuilding of the temple.) Now, Isaiah jumps ahead at this point to 688 B.C. and concludes the account of Sennacherib and Hezekiah.

Isaiah also skips over the events between 701 and 688 B.C. Sennacherib's records show he was in Babylon in 700, not in a weakened state but with a powerful army.[1] He drove out Merodach-Baladan and continued to wage war there until he finally destroyed Babylon in 689 B.C. It would seem strange if Sennacherib—so relentless in returning again and again to Babylon, even after a disastrous defeat in 691 B.C.—would leave Hezekiah shut up "like a caged bird" in Jerusalem and never come back.[2]

---

[1] Daniel David Luckenbill, *The Annals of Sennacherib* (Chicago: University of Chicago Press, 1924), 35.

[2] George S. Goodspeed, "Sennacherib's Invasion of Judah," *Cumberland Presbyterian Quarterly* 1 (June 1902): 95.

Fragmentary inscriptions of Sennacherib tell of an Arabian campaign. This is confirmed by an inscription of Esarhaddon, who tells how Sennacherib carried off the gods of the king of Arabia and brought them to Assyria.[3] Thus, after the destruction of Babylon in 689 B.C., Sennacherib was free to go west toward Egypt. But this time he went through Arabia and down through the southern part of Judea. After conquering Arabia and proclaiming himself king of Arabia, he forced some of the conquered Arabs into his army and moved to meet Tirhakah. This is confirmed in that Herodotus, the Greek historian,[4] says the Egyptians called Sennacherib "king of Arabia," which was his latest title.[5]

Tirhakah first arrived in Egypt in 690/689 B.C. at the age of twenty, when his brother Shebitku summoned him to reign with him. He coreigned with Shebitku until 684 and continued to reign until 664 B.C.

After defeating Arabia, Sennacherib apparently intended to go to Jerusalem and then down the coast to Egypt. When Tirhakah set out to meet Sennacherib's forces, however, Sennacherib shifted his attention from Judah. But he did not want Hezekiah to think he was absolved. So he sent messengers to Hezekiah.

> [10]"Say to Hezekiah king of Judah: Do not let the god you depend on deceive you when he says, 'Jerusalem will not be handed over to the king of Assyria.'

Again Sennacherib blasphemed God and denied Isaiah's prophecy (38:6). He called God a deceiver and said Hezekiah should not trust in Him. Sennacherib fully expected to take Jerusalem this time.

> [11]Surely you have heard what the kings of Assyria have done to all the countries, destroying them completely. And will you be delivered?

---

[3]Daniel David Luckenbill, *Ancient Records of Assyria and Babylonia,* 2 vols. (Chicago: University of Chicago Press, 1926–27), 2:158, 207.

[4]Herodotus was not a historian in the modern sense. He was a tourist who wrote down what the guides told him.

[5]Herodotus, *History,* trans. George Rawlinson, ed. Manuel Komroff (New York: Tudor Publishing Co., 1928), 131, 133.

By saying that the kings of Assyria have destroyed all countries ("placed all the lands under the ban"; see comment on 34:2), Sennacherib was saying that they were destroyed by consigning them to his god. He was saying also that the God of Israel could not prevent this from happening to Jerusalem. Sennacherib was doing his best to shake Hezekiah's faith in the LORD.

> ¹²Did the gods of the nations that were destroyed by my forefathers deliver them—the gods of Gozan, Haran, Rezeph and the people of Eden who were in Tel Assar?

He adds that the "gods of the nations" his forefathers (i.e., the previous kings of Assyria) had destroyed could not deliver them. The nations named were in western Mesopotamia.

> ¹³Where is the king of Hamath, the king of Arpad, the king of the city of Sepharvaim, or of Hena or Ivvah?"

He repeats the list of gods (called "kings") from the previous message (36:19) with the additions of Hena and Ivvah. The latter may be the same as Avva in Babylonia (2 Kings 17:24).

2. Hezekiah's Prayer And God's Response 37:14–35

> ¹⁴Hezekiah received the letter from the messengers and read it. Then he went up to the temple of the LORD and spread it out before the LORD.

Hezekiah shows a different attitude from that which he had shown some ten years earlier, when Sennacherib's field commander made his threats. He has seen prophecy fulfilled. This time he did not tear his clothes or put on sackcloth or send messengers to entreat Isaiah. He took the letter immediately and spread it before the LORD.

> ¹⁵And Hezekiah prayed to the LORD: ¹⁶"O LORD Almighty, God of Israel, enthroned between the cherubim, you alone are God over all the kingdoms of the earth. You have made heaven and earth.

This time Hezekiah himself prays, recognizing the LORD as the almighty God of Hosts, the God of Israel "enthroned between the cherubim": the most holy place in the temple. He recognized Him alone as God (a theme of Isaiah), not only the one true God "over all the kingdoms of the earth," but the Creator of heaven and earth as well. Hezekiah thus approached in an attitude of faith that honored God for who He is.

> ¹⁷Give ear, O LORD, and hear; open your eyes, O LORD, and see; listen to all the words Sennacherib has sent to insult the living God.

He asks God to give full attention to what Sennacherib has said in defiance of "the living God." By calling God "living," Hezekiah recognizes that God is different from the idols, different from all the false gods of the other nations. He trusts God and wants God honored.

> ¹⁸"It is true, O LORD, that the Assyrian kings have laid waste all these peoples and their lands.

Hezekiah does not deny that Assyria destroyed all these other countries.

> ¹⁹They have thrown their gods into the fire and destroyed them, for they were not gods but only wood and stone, fashioned by human hands.

Hezekiah realized these idols were not God but "only wood and stone, fashioned by human hands." He undoubtedly knew what Isaiah had said about them (see 2:8,20; 31:7). Furthermore, he knew that Sennacherib destroyed the gods of other nations. This was especially true of the many minor gods of Babylon that were smashed in 689 B.C.[6] (This is another confirmation that the letter was written on a second western campaign of Sennacherib in 688 B.C.)

> ²⁰Now, O LORD our God, deliver us from his hand, so that all kingdoms on earth may know that you alone, O LORD, are God."

---

[6] Luckenbill, *Ancient Records*, 2:152, 185.

Hezekiah wants deliverance from Sennacherib not merely for Jerusalem's sake but as a witness to "all kingdoms on earth" that God is Yahweh—the God who brought Israel out of Egypt, the faithful God, the covenant keeper, the God who was and is and always will be. There is no other God.

> 21Then Isaiah son of Amoz sent a message to Hezekiah: "This is what the LORD, the God of Israel, says: Because you have prayed to me concerning Sennacherib king of Assyria, 22this is the word the LORD has spoken against him: "The Virgin Daughter of Zion despises and mocks you. The Daughter of Jerusalem tosses her head as you flee.

God's answer came through Isaiah. God calls Jerusalem "virgin" because it was still unconquered and would remain unconquered by the Assyrians. She has despised and ridiculed them shaking her head in disdain as they retreated. This taunt probably refers to Sennacherib's abandoning his original campaign in 701 B.C., in fulfillment of an earlier prophecy of Isaiah's (37:5–7).

> 23Who is it you have insulted and blasphemed? Against whom have you raised your voice and lifted your eyes in pride? Against the Holy One of Israel! 24By your messengers you have heaped insults on the Lord. And you have said, 'With my many chariots I have ascended the heights of the mountains, the utmost heights of Lebanon. I have cut down its tallest cedars, the choicest of its pines. I have reached its remotest heights, the finest of its forests.

Sennacherib had sent his servants to defy not just Hezekiah but the Lord. His statements meant that he thought that he was able to cut down Lebanon's tallest cedars and its choicest pines, and that he would take over the trees of its garden land. That is, he would triumph in every battle.

> 25I have dug wells in foreign lands and drunk the water there. With the soles of my feet I have dried up all the streams of Egypt.'

The digging of wells and drinking from them may refer to his campaign through Arabia.[7] Now that he was getting close to Egypt, he bragged that nothing could stop him. With the soles of his feet he could dry up all the branches and canals of the Nile River, that is, as easily as a farmer might dam up a little irrigation ditch by pushing up a little dirt. Egypt would be an easy prey.[8]

> [26]"Have you not heard? Long ago I ordained it. In days of old I planned it; now I have brought it to pass, that you have turned fortified cities into piles of stone.

Sennacherib thought he was acting like a god. But the true God is the one who "ordained" the events. Like the potter forming a vessel, He shaped the circumstances that made it possible for Sennacherib to destroy cities (see 10:5–11, which tells how God used Assyria as His "rod" to bring judgment). Nothing is outside the Lord's sovereignty.

> [27]Their people, drained of power, are dismayed and put to shame. They are like plants in the field, like tender green shoots, like grass sprouting on the roof, scorched before it grows up.

It was God's superintendence that permitted the inhabitants to be so "drained of power" (Heb. *qitsre-yad,* lit. "short of hand") that they were shattered with terror and ashamed. They became like "tender green shoots" that could easily be cut down or wither, especially true of the grass that might spring up on the mud-covered reed matting that made up the flat roofs of their houses.

> [28]"But I know where you stay and when you come and go and how you rage against me.

God knew exactly what Sennacherib was doing and the way he was working himself up, raging against God.

---

[7]William Foxwell Albright, "Old Testament History, Including Archaeology and Chronology," in *The Encyclopedia Americana* (New York: American Corporation, 1953), 3:636.

[8]The Heb. *'achriv* is a hiphil imperfect form indicating incomplete action. Sennacherib had not yet been to Egypt but he considered his conquest of Egypt as good as done.

> ²⁹Because you rage against me and because your insolence has reached my ears, I will put my hook in your nose and my bit in your mouth, and I will make you return by the way you came.

Because Sennacherib was working himself into a rage against God and because he was, in his insolence, untroubled about what God could do to him, God would now act: "I will put . . . my bit in your mouth," turning Sennacherib back the way he came, back through Arabia, so he would not come to Jerusalem as he threatened he would do. God is in control.

> ³⁰"This will be the sign for you, O Hezekiah: "This year you will eat what grows by itself, and the second year what springs from that. But in the third year sow and reap, plant vineyards and eat their fruit.

To encourage Hezekiah, God promised a sign. In the remainder of the year and in the year following (which was probably about to begin) they would eat what grew up of itself, but in the third year they would be able to "sow and reap" fields of grain and plant vineyards and eat the grapes.

> ³¹Once more a remnant of the house of Judah will take root below and bear fruit above.

And like the crops, the remnant of the people of Judah would prosper.

> ³²For out of Jerusalem will come a remnant, and out of Mount Zion a band of survivors. The zeal of the LORD Almighty will accomplish this.

The remnant—people who were spared or delivered—would go out of Jerusalem. God would always have a remnant. This is a very important teaching of Isaiah. God's own zeal would see to it, and He has the power to accomplish it.

> ³³"Therefore this is what the LORD says concerning the king of Assyria: "He will not enter this city or shoot an arrow here. He will not come before it with shield or build a siege ramp against it.

Sennacherib would not enter Jerusalem. He could not get close enough to shoot an arrow or hold a shield to protect himself from Jerusalem's defenders. Nor would he "build a siege ramp against it." He had done some of these activities in 701 B.C., but he would not do so this time.

> ³⁴By the way that he came he will return; he will not enter this city," declares the LORD.

God's word was clear, definite, and emphatic. He repeats His assertion (from v. 29) that Sennacherib would return by the way he came (that is, through Arabia) and he would not come to Jerusalem.

> ³⁵"I will defend this city and save it, for my sake and for the sake of David my servant!"

God would rescue Jerusalem—not because its people deserved it but because of the covenant He had made with David (cf. 2 Sam. 7).

3. Isaiah's Prophecy Fulfilled 37:36–38

> ³⁶Then the angel of the LORD went out and put to death a hundred and eighty-five thousand men in the Assyrian camp. When the people got up the next morning—there were all the dead bodies!

That night the angel of the LORD killed 185,000 of the Assyrian army. When the remainder awoke early the next morning, they found them not dying (as if by plague) but "dead." It seems that Sennacherib never encountered Tirhakah. Because the Egyptians could not imagine such sudden death except by a plague, they spread a story that mice ate the bowstrings of the Assyrians, implying a bubonic plague.

> ³⁷So Sennacherib king of Assyria broke camp and withdrew. He returned to Nineveh and stayed there.

Up to that time, Sennacherib had made a military campaign every year of his reign, issuing an annual report of his exploits. Though he lived seven more years he never made another one.

Instead, he summarized his exploits, concluding with the capture and destruction of Babylon in 689 B.C. He made a number of copies, several of which archaeologists have discovered.[9] Apart from it, there remain only a few minor building inscriptions, probably where he had a few repairs made. This must have been shocking to the people of Nineveh, for they depended on the spoils of war for their prosperity.

In his one earlier defeat in 691 B.C. Sennacherib recorded a few wagon loads he had captured and tried to pretend it was a victory. But with the death of the 185,000, there was nothing but total defeat, and no ancient pagan king ever recorded anything as a defeat. Just as the drowning of the Egyptians at the Exodus is not recorded in Egyptian records, so this defeat was not recorded by Sennacherib. However, the fact he made no more campaigns attests the biblical record.

> **38One day, while he was worshiping in the temple of his god Nisroch, his sons Adrammelech and Sharezer cut him down with the sword, and they escaped to the land of Ararat. And Esarhaddon his son succeeded him as king.**

In 681 B.C., Sennacherib was bowing prostrate, worshiping in the temple of Nisroch, his god. Two of his sons "cut him down with the sword." Then they escaped into Ararat (ancient Armenia, now part of modern Turkey). The Babylonian chronicle recorded the death of Sennacherib and the accession of his son Esarhaddon.

STUDY QUESTIONS

1. How was Hezekiah's response to Sennacherib's letter in 688 B.C. different from his response to the field commander's threats in 701 B.C.?
2. Why was God going to defend Jerusalem and how was this fulfilled?

---

[9]Luckenbill, *Annals of Sennacherib,* 23.

C. Hezekiah's Sickness And Recovery 38:1-22

1. A Death Sentence 38:1

> ¹In those days Hezekiah became ill and was at the point of death. The prophet Isaiah son of Amoz went to him and said, "This is what the LORD says: Put your house in order, because you are going to die; you will not recover."

Many have speculated on the date of Hezekiah's sickness. However, the fact that Hezekiah was not trusting God when he gave tribute to Sennacherib, but did trust Him after that and declared God's promise of 38:6 shows that the sickness took place in 701 B.C.[1] Isaiah came to him with a strong command to set his house in order, for he would die. This was probably after Hezekiah attempted to save Jerusalem by taking the gold from the temple and giving it to Sennacherib as tribute. He was trusting in what he could do instead of trusting in what God could do. Worse, the gold of the temple belonged to God; Hezekiah had gone too far.

2. Hezekiah Restored 38:2-22

> ²Hezekiah turned his face to the wall and prayed to the LORD,

Hezekiah knew that God was long-suffering and that when repentance was offered, God would have grounds not to send the prophesied judgment. So he prayed.

> ³"Remember, O LORD, how I have walked before you faithfully and with wholehearted devotion and have done what is good in your eyes." And Hezekiah wept bitterly.

Asking God to "remember" does not mean Hezekiah thought God had forgotten. Rather, he wanted God to enter into the sit-

---

[1] Some agree. See David L. McKenna, *Isaiah 1–39*, in *The Communicator's Commentary* (Dallas: Word Books, 1993), 361; Charles F. Pfeiffer, *Old Testament History* (Grand Rapids: Baker Book House, 1987), 369; Siegfried H. Horn, "The Divided Monarchy," in *Ancient Israel*, ed. Hershel Shanks (Englewood Cliffs, N.J.: Prentice-Hall, 1988), 135.

uation and do something about it. He made his claim on the grounds that he had lived before the LORD in faithfulness and with "wholehearted devotion," doing good in God's sight (cf. 2 Kings 18:3). He had indeed reestablished the temple service and called for a great celebration of the Passover at the beginning of his full reign and had done much to get rid of idolatry (2 Chron. 29:36; 30:1 to 31:1). Then Hezekiah poured out his heart in weeping before God. The tears indicated a humble, repentant spirit.

> **⁴Then the word of the LORD came to Isaiah: ⁵"Go and tell Hezekiah, 'This is what the LORD, the God of your father David, says: I have heard your prayer and seen your tears; I will add fifteen years to your life.**

God, through Isaiah and in line with His covenant with David, told Hezekiah He had heard his prayer and seen his tears, and gave him the promise of "fifteen [more] years" of life. God's grace was truly beyond Hezekiah's expectation.

Thus, he lived to 686 B.C., with his son Manasseh sharing the throne as coruler during the last ten years of his reign. This was a time of blessing and revival.

> **⁶And I will deliver you and this city from the hand of the king of Assyria. I will defend this city.**

The promise to rescue Hezekiah and Jerusalem from the "hand" (Heb. *kaph*, "palm of the hand") of Sennacherib, out of what seemed sure control, was indeed fulfilled. God did "defend this city."

> **⁷"'This is the LORD's sign to you that the LORD will do what he has promised: ⁸I will make the shadow cast by the sun go back the ten steps it has gone down on the stairway of Ahaz.'" So the sunlight went back the ten steps it had gone down.**

God's promise was confirmed by a supernatural sign. Hezekiah's father, Ahaz, had constructed a sundial that consisted of steps whereby the sun's shadow would show the time of day. The shadow would go backward "ten steps." A British scholar, James W. Thirtle,[2] suggested that Psalms 120 to 134, the fifteen songs of steps ("degrees," KJV; "ascents," NIV, RSV), were added by Hezekiah's scribes to the temple collection of psalms to celebrate the fifteen added years of Hezekiah's life, just as the "men of Hezekiah" copied out additional proverbs of Solomon and added them to the collection in the Book of Proverbs (Prov. 25:1).

Thirtle also suggested that since ten of these psalms are not ascribed to David, those ten may refer to the ten steps that the shadow went backward. Psalm 126 does fit 701 B.C., when there was a restoration of prosperity after Sennacherib left and when the people sent gifts to Hezekiah because of his healing (2 Chron. 32:23).

McKenna suggests that Ahaz may have brought the idea for the sundial from Damascus when he was seeking help from Assyria. "If so, God's choice of Ahaz' sundial to give a sign to Hezekiah is another direct refutation of Sennacherib's power and Assyrian idolatry."[3]

> [9]A writing of Hezekiah king of Judah after his illness and recovery: [10]I said, "In the prime of my life must I go through the gates of death and be robbed of the rest of my years?"

After his recovery, Hezekiah recorded his thoughts and feelings. When he was told he would die, he saw it as premature, coming in what should have been the middle of his life, depriving him of the long life he expected.

He also understood that because it was God's judgment, he would go through the "gates of death" (Heb. $b^e sha'are\ sh^e ol$, "within the gates of Sheol," the place of the wicked dead) where he would be unable to communicate with God.

> [11]I said, "I will not again see the LORD, the LORD, in the land of the living; no longer will I look on mankind, or be with those who now dwell in this world.

Hezekiah was grieved that he would not be "in the land of

---

[2]James William Thirtle, *Old Testament Problems: Critical Studies in the Psalms and Isaiah* (London: Morgan & Scott, 1916), 44–45, 133, 135, 167.
[3]McKenna, *Isaiah 1–39*, 365.

the living" to see or experience the presence of the LORD, nor would he look on the inhabitants of this world. He would be cut off from life as he knew it.

> [12]Like a shepherd's tent my house has been pulled down and taken from me. Like a weaver I have rolled up my life, and he has cut me off from the loom; day and night you made an end of me.

His dwelling place would be "pulled down" or moved, like a temporary shepherd's tent being carried away from him. His life was like a weaver's cloth, finished and rolled up. He would be "cut off" the way a weaver snips a thread from the loom. He expected that before the day turned to night, God would make an end of him.

> [13]I waited patiently till dawn, but like a lion he broke all my bones; day and night you made an end of me.

Hezekiah soothed himself until morning (cf. Ps. 131:2). But he still expected God "like a lion" to judge him, breaking all his bones. He felt the wrath of God hovering over him and still expected that God would surrender him to death before the day's end.

> [14]I cried like a swift or thrush, I moaned like a mourning dove. My eyes grew weak as I looked to the heavens. I am troubled; O Lord, come to my aid!"

He kept chattering on like birds, moaning like a dove, but this made him weaker. His very eyes became weak and weary as he kept looking "to the heavens," seeking the Lord's forgiveness and asking Him to step in and alleviate his suffering.

> [15]But what can I say? He has spoken to me, and he himself has done this. I will walk humbly all my years because of this anguish of my soul.

God's answer brought a sudden change. What could Hezekiah say to the promise of verses 5 and 6? God had spoken. God himself healed him. He would "walk humbly," as in a solemn procession (cf. Ps. 42:4; Eph. 5:15), because of the experience of facing death.

> **16Lord, by such things men live; and my spirit finds life in them too. You restored me to health and let me live.**

"Such things" refers to the elements or stages that made up Hezekiah's humbling himself before God. Hezekiah made this humbling the life of his spirit, so that he was an example to others. Truly God had healed him and made him live.

> **17Surely it was for my benefit that I suffered such anguish. In your love you kept me from the pit of destruction; you have put all my sins behind your back.**

God had a purpose in allowing him to be sick and experience the bitterness of facing death. It was for his benefit (including his peace and well-being) and for the blessing of wholeness. It was an experience of God's love and grace, for God literally kept him "from the pit of destruction" (that is, from hell). In addition, God completely forgave him. Since God is everywhere, for Hezekiah to say "you have put all my sins behind your back" means God put them out of existence, just as if they never were. Thus, all of Hezekiah's guilt was gone as well.

> **18For the grave cannot praise you, death cannot sing your praise; those who go down to the pit cannot hope for your faithfulness.**

Hezekiah could have gone down to "the grave," (actually Sheol, hell, the place of the wicked dead). There would be no praise or thanks to God in that place. Those who go down to "the pit" (again, Sheol) under the judgment of God could not hope for God's faithfulness. They are cut off from any fellowship with God forever.

> **19The living, the living—they praise you, as I am doing today; fathers tell their children about your faithfulness.**

"The living," those restored to full life (as was Hezekiah, after his tears and the forgiveness of his sins), will give thanks and praise to God. Such an experience needs to be passed on from father to child, continually making known God's faithfulness.

> ²⁰**The LORD will save me, and we will sing with stringed instruments all the days of our lives in the temple of the LORD.**

Hezekiah recognizes that God continues to be ready to deliver him. So he will join others "in the temple of the LORD," and together they will worship in music as long as they live. God had brought Hezekiah new life; he would make it a life of praise to God. His fifteen additional years would be a time of giving thanks and of revival.[4]

> ²¹**Isaiah had said, "Prepare a poultice of figs and apply it to the boil, and he will recover."**

Now, in preparation for chapter 39, Isaiah goes back to the time when Hezekiah was sick. At that time, as a token or point of contact to help him express his faith, Isaiah had the court physicians put a "poultice of figs" on the boil or inflammation. God, however, would do the healing.

> ²²**Hezekiah had asked, "What will be the sign that I will go up to the temple of the LORD?"**

Isaiah also goes back to remind us of the miraculous sign (v. 8; see the fuller account in 2 Kings 20:7–11). Hezekiah's healing was in answer to prayer and was indeed miraculous. He was healed—body, soul, mind, and spirit. No wonder he sang with joy as he worshiped in the temple.

STUDY QUESTIONS

1. What is the background of Hezekiah's sickness?
2. On what grounds did God give Hezekiah fifteen more years?
3. What assurance did God give Hezekiah?
4. What did Hezekiah emphasize in his response?

---

[4]A. R. Siebens, "The Historicity of the Hezekian Reform," in *From the Pyramids to Paul,* ed. L. G. Leary (New York: Thomas Nelson & Sons, 1935), 254.

D. Merodach-Baladan's Embassy 39:1–8

1. Hezekiah Shows His Treasures 39:1–2

¹At that time Merodach-Baladan son of Baladan king of Babylon sent Hezekiah letters and a gift, because he had heard of his illness and recovery.

"At that time" refers to 701 B.C. With Sennacherib busy in the west, Merodach-Baladan took advantage of the help of the anti-Assyrian party in Babylon and, joined by a Chaldean prince, Shuzubu,[1] took control as king of Babylon and stirred up revolt. He sent an embassy, with "letters and a gift," to Hezekiah, probably hoping that his sickness and God's promise of deliverance would keep Sennacherib in the west.

However, Sennacherib left his western campaign and in 700 B.C. defeated Shuzubu, causing Merodach-Baladan to flee to Elam. Then he placed his eldest son on the throne that had been occupied by Merodach-Baladan.[2] Nevertheless, Merodach-Baladan, along with others, kept Sennacherib in a constant struggle over Babylon, until he finally destroyed it in 689 B.C.[3]

Merodach-Baladan's gift was a token of respect, almost reverence—the same word for "gift" (Heb. *minchah*) is the name of the sacrifice called the "grain offering" (Lev. 2:1; "meat offering," KJV)—for he had heard of the great sign of the shadow turning back on the steps of the sundial.[4] He was not the only one to send a gift, however. "Many brought offerings to Jerusalem for the LORD and valuable gifts for Hezekiah king of Judah. From then on he was highly regarded by all the nations" (2 Chron. 32:23). They realized that the departure of

---

[1] Raymond Philip Dougherty, *The Sealand of Ancient Arabia* (New Haven: Yale University Press, 1932), 61; cf. Albert T. Olmstead, "The Chaldean Dynasty," *Hebrew Union College Annual* 2 (1925): 30.

[2] Daniel David Luckenbill, *The Annals of Sennacherib* (Chicago: University of Chicago Press, 1924), 35.

[3] Daniel David Luckenbill, *Ancient Records of Assyria and Babylonia*, 2 vols. (Chicago: University of Chicago Press, 1926–27), 2:154–55.

[4] See 2 Chron. 32:31; Charles Boutflower, *The Book of Isaiah (Chapters I–XXXIX) in the Light of the Assyrian Monuments* (London: Society for Promoting Christian Knowledge, 1930), 141.

Sennacherib in fulfillment of Isaiah's prophecy meant they did not need to be afraid of him any longer either.

> ²Hezekiah received the envoys gladly and showed them what was in his storehouses—the silver, the gold, the spices, the fine oil, his entire armory and everything found among his treasures. There was nothing in his palace or in all his kingdom that Hezekiah did not show them.

Hezekiah may have been flattered. He rejoiced over the envoys from Merodach-Baladan and showed them all his treasures and armaments. These must have included the gifts from other kings and nations. Then he gave them a tour of the palace and the country of Judah.

2. Babylonian Exile Prophesied 39:3–8

> ³Then Isaiah the prophet went to King Hezekiah and asked, "What did those men say, and where did they come from?" "From a distant land," Hezekiah replied. "They came to me from Babylon."

Isaiah asked two questions: He wanted to know what the envoys said and where they came from. Hezekiah answered only the second question. The envoys must have wanted him to recognize Merodach-Baladan as the legitimate king of Babylon. However, Hezekiah said only that they came from a distant country—Babylon. Hezekiah knew how important that city was, and he was delighted that a gift had come from there.

> ⁴The prophet asked, "What did they see in your palace?" "They saw everything in my palace," Hezekiah said. "There is nothing among my treasures that I did not show them."

Hezekiah admitted he had shown the envoys everything, which was neither necessary nor wise. Undoubtedly the report went back to Babylon and the leadership of Babylon took note: There was treasure to be had in Jerusalem and Judah.

> ⁵Then Isaiah said to Hezekiah, "Hear the word of the Lord Almighty: ⁶The time will surely

> come when everything in your palace, and all that your fathers have stored up until this day, will be carried off to Babylon. Nothing will be left, says the Lord.

Isaiah had a severe word from God, the almighty Lord of the armies of heaven. Hezekiah's pride over all his treasures was sin; God's judgment would fall. The Babylonians would remember the wealth in Jerusalem. The time would surely come when everything in Jerusalem's royal palace and treasuries would be "carried off to Babylon" (cf. Mic. 4:10). This was fulfilled by Nebuchadnezzar in three invasions, in 605, 597, and 586 B.C.

> ⁷And some of your descendants, your own flesh and blood who will be born to you, will be taken away, and they will become eunuchs in the palace of the king of Babylon."

Hezekiah's descendants would also be taken to Babylon and be made eunuchs in the service of Babylon's king. This was fulfilled and probably included Daniel and his friends, since there was only one royal family of Judah. (See Dan. 1:3.)

> ⁸"The word of the Lord you have spoken is good," Hezekiah replied. For he thought, "There will be peace and security in my lifetime."

By saying that the word of the Lord was "good," Hezekiah meant it was appropriate for what he had done, and he humbly submitted to it. He also recognized that the prophecy was for the distant future. This encouraged him to rest on the previous prophecies of Isaiah that assured him of peace and God's faithfulness in his own time.

STUDY QUESTIONS

1. What was wrong with Hezekiah's treatment of the messengers from Merodach-Baladan?
2. What would be the results of Hezekiah's actions?

VI. COMFORT FOR JERUSALEM AND JUDAH 40:1–48:22

A. God Coming Back To His People 40:1–31

"The specific application of this chapter to the return from Babylon has no foundation in the text itself, but is supposed by some to be implied in the relation of this chapter to the one before it which contains a prediction of the exile. . . . But the promise in itself considered is a general one of consolation, protection, and change for the better, to be wrought by the power and wisdom of Jehovah. . . . The reference to idolatry proves nothing with respect to the date of the prediction, although more appropriate in the writings of Isaiah than of a prophet in the Babylonian exile."[1]

1. GOOD NEWS FOR JUDAH AND JERUSALEM 40:1–11

¹Comfort, comfort my people, says your God.

Chapters 40 to 66 have sometimes been called "The Book of Comfort," for they speak of deliverance, redemption, and glory.[2] The fact that chapters 36 to 39 form a historical prologue to chapter 40 helps to show that the message of comfort in chapter 40 is directed to the people of Jerusalem in 700 B.C. after Sennacherib's withdrawal. The war party had been discredited by the failure of Egypt to help. The people of Jerusalem had taken a stand of faith (36:21). Isaiah's prophecies had been fulfilled. Thus, the people's hearts were changed and they became a different audience. Now he could give a different message.

On the basis of differences in the message, some have concluded that this portion of Isaiah derives from another author in a different time period.[3] A modern scholar in Haifa, howev-

---

[1] Joseph A. Alexander, *Commentary on the Prophecies of Isaiah*, 2 vols. in 1 (1875; reprint, Grand Rapids: Zondervan Publishing House, 1975), 2:93.

[2] Ecclesiasticus 48:24 identifies Isaiah as the one who "consoled the mourners of Zion."

[3] See Introduction, pp. 22–23. See also R. K. Harrison, "The Historical and Literary Criticism of the Old Testament," in *Biblical Criticism: Historical, Literary and Textual* (Grand Rapids: Zondervan Publishing House, 1980), 30–33; Hobart E. Freeman, *An Introduction to the Old Testament Prophets* (Chicago: Moody Press, 1969), 196–203.

er, put the Book of Isaiah through a computer to see if there was any significant difference in style and vocabulary between Isaiah 1 to 39 and 40 to 66. He found only one: Chapters 40 to 66 had significantly less war terminology.[4] This accurately reflects the realities of the fifteen additional years of Hezekiah's life, during which peace prevailed. Therefore, Isaiah was able to give a message of comfort from the LORD.

This was not wishful thinking, nor was it merely comfort in sorrow but comfort that brings joy.[5] Before Sennacherib's invasion Isaiah would have agreed with Solomon's complaint: "Again I looked and saw all the oppression that was taking place under the sun: I saw the tears of the oppressed—and they have no comforter; power was on the side of their oppressors—and they have no comforter" (Eccles. 4:1). But now God commissioned him to give a message of comfort, restoration, and peace. The words in Hebrew are plural imperatives, so the command is for all the prophets, priests, and leaders to declare the message of comfort. What follows in 40 to 66 is a "magnificent mini-OT theology . . . with its key personage the servant of the Lord from the seed of Abraham and David."[6]

> ²Speak tenderly to Jerusalem, and proclaim to her that her hard service has been completed, that her sin has been paid for, that she has received from the LORD's hand double for all her sins.

God's message was to the heart and mind of the people of Jerusalem. It announced that her time of "hard service" (a word used of compulsory service to pay off a debt) was finished; her punishment was accepted as sufficient. She had received "double for all her sins." Some take this to be a double portion of judgment, but it could also mean a double pardon given by the grace of God. The word "double" (Heb. *kiphlayim*), however, is from a root that means "to fold double," so it may simply mean

---

[4]Yehuda T. Radday, *Isaiah and the Computer* (Hildesheim, Germany: H. A. Gerstenberg, 1973). Dr. Radday was Senior Lecturer in Bible and Hebrew Language at the Technion, Israel Institute of Technology, Haifa.

[5]George A. F. Knight, *Servant Theology* (Grand Rapids: Wm. B. Eerdmans, 1984), 7.

[6]Walter C. Kaiser, Jr., *Toward an Old Testament Theology* (Grand Rapids: Zondervan Publishing House, Academie Books, 1978), 48, 205.

that each side matches: Thus the pardon takes care of all the sins. All the sins and guilt are gone.

> ³A voice of one calling: "In the desert prepare the way for the LORD; make straight in the wilderness a highway for our God.

A human voice is calling out in the wilderness commanding the people to "prepare the way for the LORD," to make a straight highway in the desert for God. This has nothing to do with people returning to the land of Israel. This highway is like one mentioned in many ancient Near Eastern records. The context is of emissaries of a great conquering king going before him and preparing a road sufficiently magnificent for a powerful monarch. It is also similar to the millennial roads referred to in 11:16; 19:23; 35:8; 45:2 (cf. 43:19; 62:10). They are to prepare the road for the King of kings by pushing every obstacle out of the way.

The road is for God to come back to His people—to come to their aid. There was a fulfillment in Isaiah's day in God's deliverance of Jerusalem and in spiritual revival as Jerusalem rose to new life made possible by fulfilled prophecy. The New Testament recognizes a further fulfillment in the ministry of John the Baptist as he spiritually prepared the way for the ministry of Jesus by calling for repentance (Matt. 3:3).

> ⁴Every valley shall be raised up, every mountain and hill made low; the rough ground shall become level, the rugged places a plain.

The road is to be made level, with valleys filled, mountains made low, and all uneven, rough or rugged places smoothed out into a plain. This is a metaphor emphasizing that God's visit "requires *moral* preparation."[7]

> ⁵And the glory of the LORD will be revealed, and all mankind together will see it. For the mouth of the LORD has spoken."

The "glory of the LORD" is the full weight of His presence and power, the revelation of who He is. When God comes back

---

[7] Walter C. Kaiser, Jr., *The Christian and the "Old" Testament* (Pasadena, Calif.: William Carey Library, 1998), 185, Kaiser's emphasis.

to His people all the people of the world, "all mankind together" (Heb. *kol basar,* "all flesh"), will see His glory (cf. 6:3). This verse implies they will also experience glory. This is the word of the LORD, spoken in heaven and then on earth. We need to pass the word on and recognize God's universal reign.

> ⁶A voice says, "Cry out." And I said, "What shall I cry?" "All men are like grass, and all their glory is like the flowers of the field.

A second voice commands someone to "cry out," to proclaim. A third voice asks what to proclaim.⁸ The answer is, "all men [all humankind] are like grass"; that is, their lives on earth are temporary (cf. Ps. 90:5–6). Their "glory" (Heb. *chasdo,* "covenant love and faithfulness") is like a wild flower that soon withers. All human power and glory is so temporary!

> ⁷The grass withers and the flowers fall, because the breath of the LORD blows on them. Surely the people are grass.

The "breath of the LORD" was the giver of life in the beginning (Gen. 2:7). However, it also brings judgment and death. "Breath" here is the same word translated "Spirit."

"The people" usually refers to God's people. "Surely" emphasizes that they too are part of all flesh; they too are "grass": No matter how rich, famous, or powerful they might seem, they will all fade away.

> ⁸The grass withers and the flowers fall, but the word of our God stands forever."

Though grass withers and the flowers fade and fall, nations and empires rise and fall, human beings come and go, one thing is certain—"the word of our God stands forever." It alone is always reliable and trustworthy. Jesus put it even more strongly, " 'Heaven and earth will pass away, but my words will never pass away' " (Matt. 24:35).

---

⁸The Dead Sea Scroll of Isa. has "she" instead of "I," apparently referring to Jerusalem (cf. v. 2). However, "I" seems preferable, referring to the prophet who has been speaking in the name of the Lord. Cf. Paul D. Hanson, *Isaiah 40–66* (Louisville: John Knox Press, 1995), 23.

> [9]You who bring good tidings to Zion, go up on a high mountain. You who bring good tidings to Jerusalem, lift up your voice with a shout, lift it up, do not be afraid; say to the towns of Judah, "Here is your God!"

Another voice calls to Zion. However, rather than good tidings being brought "to Zion" (as the NIV translates), Zion is to take the good tidings to others (cf. NASB, NKJV). Zion needs to be on a high mountain proclaiming it. Jerusalem needs to shout out the good news with strength and without fear. The good news is directed to the ruined "towns of Judah," torn down by Sennacherib's armies (cf. 2 Kings 18:12). Instead of looking at their circumstances, they need to look to God—the great, good God who has delivered Jerusalem. He is the God who fulfills prophecy. His word is good news and Zion must not keep it to herself. We too need to look to the God that these chapters show is "beyond all comparison."[9]

> [10]See, the Sovereign LORD comes with power, and his arm rules for him. See, his reward is with him, and his recompense accompanies him.

God will come as a strong One, the LORD (Yahweh, the faithful, covenant-keeping God). "His arm" represents His power in action—ruling and in control. "His reward" is the reward He receives for His victory, and "his recompense" that accompanies Him is His own people for whom He won the victory. They could not win it for themselves.

> [11]He tends his flock like a shepherd: He gathers the lambs in his arms and carries them close to his heart; he gently leads those that have young.

In this time of victory and salvation the LORD comes not only with strength and power but with the gentle tenderness of a good shepherd who loves to tend his flock. His strong arm not only rules but also "carries," tenderly, the lambs, as He "gently leads" those with young. God cares for the needs and problems

---

[9]Kaiser, *Christian and the "Old" Testament*, 185.

of every individual in a personal way. Those who trust Him do not need to be afraid.

2. God's Greatness Contrasted To Idols 40:12–31

¹²Who has measured the waters in the hollow of his hand, or with the breadth of his hand marked off the heavens? Who has held the dust of the earth in a basket, or weighed the mountains on the scales and the hills in a balance?

Now Isaiah begins a series of parallel rhetorical questions that draw attention to God's almighty power as the Creator.[10] Sennacherib had declared he was greater than any god (36:20). But he was defeated by the Sovereign Lord, who came with power (v. 10) and tenderly shepherded His people. Now the Lord answers the questions of any who might still have doubts. The one who carries the lambs is so great that all the oceans of the world are no more than "waters in the hollow of his hand." He determined its measure exactly. He marked the heavens off with just "the breadth of his hand," measured the dust of the earth "in a basket" (or a small measuring cup), and "weighed the mountains on the scales and the hills in a balance." All this implies measuring them to suit His purpose or the function He intended. This is awesome and should encourage us to trust the future to the Lord.

¹³Who has understood the mind of the Lord, or instructed him as his counselor?

The second question is: Who has enough understanding to determine the measure of God's "mind" (Heb. *ruach,* "Spirit"), that is, who regulated Him, measured His mind, or is able to tell Him what to do? Pagan gods, like heathen kings, depended on counselors. But the Spirit of God has all wisdom. He needs no one to teach Him.

¹⁴Whom did the Lord consult to enlighten him, and who taught him the right way? Who was it

---

[10]Allis points out that "Isaiah is fond of the rhetorical question. It occurs more than fifty times in his prophecies." Oswalt T. Allis, *The Old Testament: Its Claims and Its Critics* (Philadelphia: Presbyterian & Reformed, 1972), 51.

that taught him knowledge or showed him the path of understanding?

The LORD does not need to consult anyone, for no one has more enlightenment and perception than He, nor does He need instruction. The path of justice, knowledge, and understanding are His already; He knows what to do, how to do it, and when to do it.

> ¹⁵Surely the nations are like a drop in a bucket; they are regarded as dust on the scales; he weighs the islands as though they were fine dust.

Isaiah next sums up the greatness of God in a series of comparisons. All the nations of the world are like a drop left on the edge of a bucket after it is emptied and shaken, a drop that is hardly worth noticing.

They are also like the film of dust that accumulates on scales between weighings, which does not really affect the weighing. "Islands" refers to the whole of the continents and islands of the earth—its entire land mass—which amount to mere dust that doesn't settle. What a striking picture of the greatness and power of God!

> ¹⁶Lebanon is not sufficient for altar fires, nor its animals enough for burnt offerings.

If a person was to look for an offering sufficient to exalt the LORD, worthy of His greatness, neither the forests of Lebanon would be sufficient to burn it nor would all its animals be sufficient to compose it. He is worthy of more than anything the earth can provide or that human beings can do.

> ¹⁷Before him all the nations are as nothing; they are regarded by him as worthless and less than nothing.

Isaiah summarizes by saying that "all the nations are as nothing" before Him (that is, in relation to Him). They are "less than nothing" and worthless emptiness compared to Him. Isaiah saw this when God gave him prophecies about the death of Sennacherib after he made such bold claims about his superiority to the gods of the nations he had conquered (36:18–20).

> ¹⁸To whom, then, will you compare God? What image will you compare him to?

After describing the greatness of God, Isaiah asks, "To whom . . . will you compare God? What image will you compare him to[or, "display him with"]?" No image made by human hands can represent His greatness and glory.

Isaiah said this in the midst of a world that believed in the significance of idols. The Assyrians and Babylonians depended on them. New Age followers need to hear this message today. So do those who put anything "equal to or higher than God"—other persons, ideas, institutions, money, sports, possessions.[11]

> ¹⁹As for an idol, a craftsman casts it, and a goldsmith overlays it with gold and fashions silver chains for it.

Isaiah shows how preposterous idolatry really is. The idol may be made of wood, stone, metal, or clay. A metalworker melts a cheaper metal such as iron and pours it into a form. After it cools, the goldsmith overlays it with beaten-out plates of gold. Then the silversmith makes "silver chains" to hold it up. After all, it would be terrible if a gold-plated god fell over. Pagans believed a god or a spirit lived in the idol. But in reality the idol was nothing except what human hands made of it.

> ²⁰A man too poor to present such an offering selects wood that will not rot. He looks for a skilled craftsman to set up an idol that will not topple.

A person too poor to bring gold and silver for such a purpose chooses the wood of a tree that "will not rot." It would be terrible for a god to rot. He then gets a skilled craftsman to carve out an idol with a broad flat base so it will not wobble. Who would want a wobbly god, a god that will fall over?

> ²¹Do you not know? Have you not heard? Has it not been told you from the beginning? Have you not understood since the earth was founded?

Isaiah chides the idolaters with four questions chiastically

---

[11] Kaiser, *Christian and the "Old" Testament*, 187.

arranged (that is, in an a-b-b-a style). Surely, they should know and understand. They should hear what has been told (cf. Exod. 20:3–4). God is the Creator who has revealed himself from the beginning. (Cf. Ps. 19:1, "The heavens declare the glory of God.") He has been present since the earth was founded, ever since the events of Genesis 1.

> **22He sits enthroned above the circle of the earth, and its people are like grasshoppers. He stretches out the heavens like a canopy, and spreads them out like a tent to live in.**

"He sits enthroned above the circle [disk, sphere] of the earth." From His point of view, the people who live on the earth are as tiny as grasshoppers. The "heavens" (the whole universe) are no more than gauze spread out as a filmy tent to live in.

> **23He brings princes to naught and reduces the rulers of this world to nothing.**

He causes "princes" (including all kinds of dignitaries) to come to nothing and the earth's "rulers" (Heb. *shoph^{e}te*, "judges") to virtually disappear. They may think they are determining things, but God is really in control. (Cf. Isa. 10:12.)

> **24No sooner are they planted, no sooner are they sown, no sooner do they take root in the ground, than he blows on them and they wither, and a whirlwind sweeps them away like chaff.**

The earth's dignitaries and judges may think they are set, rooted, but all God has to do is blow on them. Then "they wither" and His judgment takes them away like a tornado.

> **25"To whom will you compare me? Or who is my equal?" says the Holy One.**

Now God himself repeats the question Isaiah asked in verse 18. There is no other God. How could any other god be equal to the God who fills and transcends the universe? The very idea of comparing anything or anyone else to the God who is "the Holy One" is ridiculous.[12]

---

[12]Note how Isaiah repeatedly praises God as the Holy One (41:14,16,20; 43:3,14; 47:4; 48:17; 49:7; 54:5; 55:5).

> ²⁶Lift your eyes and look to the heavens: Who created all these? He who brings out the starry host one by one, and calls them each by name. Because of his great power and mighty strength, not one of them is missing.

Isaiah again uses a rhetorical question to draw attention to God as the Creator. One should be able to look up at the vastness of the starry heavens and realize that no little tin god could have created "all these." God produces and rules them all and knows them individually. Modern astronomers have run out of names for stars and just give most of them a number. But God calls "each by name" (cf. Ps. 147:4). They demonstrate the greatness of His might, strength, and power; not one of them escapes His knowledge. Surely He knows and cares for us individually as well (cf. Matt. 10:30–31). The New Testament reveals further that God made all these creations through the Living Word, Jesus (John 1:3; Heb. 1:2), and by Him they all consist, or "hold together" (Col. 1:16–17).[13]

> ²⁷Why do you say, O Jacob, and complain, O Israel, "My way is hidden from the LORD; my cause is disregarded by my God"?

Now Isaiah speaks to the nation as Jacob, then as Israel (see Gen. 32:28). This should remind them of His promises. How can they say that this great God who names the stars does not know what they are doing or that He has forgotten His promises and overlooked the justice due to them? This may have been spoken specifically to discouraged people surrounded by the ruined cities of Judah in 700 B.C.

> ²⁸Do you not know? Have you not heard? The LORD is the everlasting God, the Creator of the ends of the earth. He will not grow tired or weary, and his understanding no one can fathom.

Isaiah challenges the people. From God's dealings with them in the past they should have known. From God's past revelation they should have listened and learned. He is "the everlasting

---

[13] Isaiah draws attention to God as Creator about twenty times. Note especially 44:24.

God, the Creator of the ends of the earth," that is, of the entire earth—without any exception. He is never tired or weary. His understanding, including His insight and intelligence, is unsearchable, beyond anything human beings can comprehend. Nothing that the pagans worshiped could be compared to Him. The word "everlasting" (Heb. *'olam*) "comes from the root meaning 'hidden.' And so it speaks of the mists of the past, . . . and looks toward the mists of the future, into which man's mind cannot even begin to pry."[14]

> ²⁹He gives strength to the weary and increases the power of the weak.

God gives "strength" (power and vigor) to those who are tired. To those who have no physical strength, He "increases" fully their power. As the apostle Paul said, "That is why, for Christ's sake, I delight in weaknesses, in insults, in hardships, in persecutions, in difficulties. For when I am weak, then I am strong" (2 Cor. 12:10).

> ³⁰Even youths grow tired and weary, and young men stumble and fall;

Boys may become "tired and weary." Even vigorous "young men" (Heb. *bachurim*, "chosen athletes") may become like the cross-country runner who gives out before making the goal, stumbling and falling.

> ³¹but those who hope in the LORD will renew their strength. They will soar on wings like eagles; they will run and not grow weary, they will walk and not be faint.

But those who "hope in the LORD" (Heb. *qowe YHWH*, "wait for the LORD," as in Pss. 27:14; 37:7,34; 130:5–6) do not set out in their own strength. Instead, they keep their hope in the LORD and patiently keep trusting Him for grace and help (cf. Isa. 30:15). Then when He moves they move along with Him. From Him they keep gaining new strength. They soar "on wings like eagles," mounting over circumstances. They run and do not "grow weary"; they walk and do not become "faint."

---

[14]Knight, *Servant Theology*, 25.

God is indeed their complete source of strength—physical, inner, and spiritual. Nothing the pagans worshiped could do this for them.

STUDY QUESTIONS

1. What was involved in the comfort promised to Jerusalem?
2. What is the significance of the highway in 40:3–5?
3. What characteristics of God do you find in chapter 40?
4. Why does God challenge the people?
5. What can the people expect from Him?

B. God's Glory And His Servant 41:1–42:25

1. GOD USES ONE FROM THE EAST 41:1–4

¹"Be silent before me, you islands! Let the nations renew their strength! Let them come forward and speak; let us meet together at the place of judgment.

God, the Lord of history, continues. In a new courtroom scene (see 1:2,18; 3:13) He calls the "islands" (including coastlands), that is, the inhabited parts of the earth, to keep silence before Him. He who is the source of strength for those in Israel who hope in Him (40:31) wants "the nations" (Heb. *'ummim*, "peoples") to turn to Him. Let them also "renew their strength" from God as their source. God calls them to approach Him and join together for a decision that is appropriate (in conformity with the truth). Do they have the same power and wisdom that God has?

²"Who has stirred up one from the east, calling him in righteousness to his service? He hands nations over to him and subdues kings before him. He turns them to dust with his sword, to windblown chaff with his bow.

Isaiah 41:3–4

God is the one who "stirred up one from the east." This conqueror is not named. Jews, up until the time of ibn Ezra in the twelfth century A.D., thought he was Abraham. Others suggested Joshua or the nation of Israel. Ibn Ezra suggested Cyrus the Great, the king of Persia (559–530 B.C.). Cyrus is named in 44:28 and 45:1. What is said about him confirms that Cyrus is meant here, though he may be taken as a type of the Messiah, who will give the ultimate victory.

Cyrus conquered Babylon and made decrees that sent Jews back to rebuild their temple (2 Chron. 36:22–23; Ezra 1:1–2,7–8; 5:13; 6:3). That he comes "from the east" shows that Isaiah is in Palestine as he speaks. God, the Righteous One, calls this one from the east "to his service" (Heb. *l^eraglo*, "to His feet"), that is, to follow and serve Him (in battle). God will give him victory and rulership that will be unstoppable, not because he is righteous but because he will be doing what is right by fulfilling God's purpose and plan. "Chaff" speaks of God's judgment—carried out by this one from the east.[1]

> ³He pursues them and moves on unscathed, by a path his feet have not traveled before.

That he will pursue them indicates they flee before him. That he passes beyond "unscathed" (Heb. *shalom*, "in peace") means that after he conquers them, he does not destroy them. Cyrus was an unusual conqueror. He destroyed no Mesopotamian cities. He considered himself a deliverer rather than a pillager, as the Assyrians and Babylonians were. The last phrase, "a path . . . not traveled before," may mean he did not take the normal route to Babylon. Cyrus did take a circuitous route. Or it may mean " 'his feet (scarcely) touch the ground.' So fast does he advance that he goes like the wind."[2]

> ⁴Who has done this and carried it through, calling forth the generations from the beginning? I, the LORD—with the first of them and with the last—I am he."

---

[1] See 41:25, which mentions that he comes from the north. Cyrus did come from the east and then from the north.

[2] George A. F. Knight, *Servant Theology* (Grand Rapids: Wm. B. Eerdmans, 1984), 28.

God is the one who acts in history. He was with the first generation, calling them by name (proclaiming His truth to them), and He will be with the last generation. He is the LORD *(Yahweh),* the eternal, covenant-keeping God; He alone is God. He is active and He alone is really in control.

2. THE NATIONS AND THEIR IDOLS CHALLENGED 41:5–29

> ⁵The islands have seen it and fear; the ends of the earth tremble. They approach and come forward;

"The islands" (or coastlands, the inhabited parts of the earth) are invited to draw near to the one true God, but they tremble in fear. They look at what Cyrus is doing and turn away from God. From "the ends of the earth," from lands most distant from Jerusalem, they shake in fear. Then they come forward, joining together against Cyrus, not realizing God is behind what Cyrus is doing.

> ⁶each helps the other and says to his brother, "Be strong!"

Instead of turning to the one true God who has revealed himself, they join together and try to help and encourage one another, trusting in what human strength can do.

> ⁷The craftsman encourages the goldsmith, and he who smooths with the hammer spurs on him who strikes the anvil. He says of the welding, "It is good." He nails down the idol so it will not topple.

What people can do is make idols. They are moved by fear, so each one involved in the process of making an idol encourages the next one to use his best skill. They observe their work and say "It is good," but they have to fasten it with nails "so it will not topple." They hope the manufactured, unmoving idol will help them in the midst of the fears and difficulties of life. What a contrast to the mighty God who made us and made the universe!

> ⁸"But you, O Israel, my servant, Jacob, whom I have chosen, you descendants of Abraham my friend,

God now speaks to Israel in a personal, intimate way. In contrast to the idol worshipers, Israel is God's servant, chosen by Him to do a work (cf. Exod. 19:5–6). They are descendants of Abraham, the one to whom God gave the promise. "My friend" is literally "the one loving me." God loved Abraham, and Abraham responded by loving God (see 2 Chron. 20:7; James 2:23; cf. 1 John 4:19). Even though God calls them by the old name of "Jacob," the deceiver and supplanter, they are still His chosen people.

> ⁹I took you from the ends of the earth, from its farthest corners I called you. I said, 'You are my servant'; I have chosen you and have not rejected you.

Abraham was called from Ur of the Chaldees. Israel was brought out of Egypt. God who made the nation of Israel His servant and chose them has not and will not reject them or treat them as refuse. He cares about their feelings.

> ¹⁰So do not fear, for I am with you; do not be dismayed, for I am your God. I will strengthen you and help you; I will uphold you with my righteous right hand.

The idol makers tried to encourage each other. But God is the one who encourages His people: "Do not fear, for I am with you." They are to stop looking this way and that in fear, not knowing where to find help and safety. He is their God. He promised to help them and "uphold" them (grip them firmly and support them) with His "righteous right hand" (implying He will lead them). He will carry out His righteous purpose with a mighty power that assures victory.

> ¹¹"All who rage against you will surely be ashamed and disgraced; those who oppose you will be as nothing and perish. ¹²Though you search for your enemies, you will not find them. Those who wage war against you will be as nothing at all.

God will bring to shame those "who rage against" His people. They think they are fighting Israel but they are really fighting God. God will make them hang their heads in shame. He will make those who think they have a case against Israel become like "nothing," and they will perish. Then they will not be found, for they will no longer exist on earth.

> ¹³For I am the LORD, your God, who takes hold of your right hand and says to you, Do not fear; I will help you.

God declares who He is. He is the LORD, their God. He keeps saying, "Do not fear [lit., stop being afraid]; I will help you." In all circumstances, no matter how difficult or baffling, He wants them to act with courage and faith. (Though directed to Israel, all believers can claim this; cf. Heb. 13:5)

> ¹⁴Do not be afraid, O worm Jacob, O little Israel, for I myself will help you," declares the LORD, your Redeemer, the Holy One of Israel.

By calling the people of Israel the "worm Jacob," God is reminding them of how weak and helpless they are (cf. Ps. 22:6; Job 25:6). Being afraid is natural, but God again tells them to stop: He will help them. He is their Redeemer (Heb. *go'el*), the Holy One of Israel.

Beginning with this verse, God is recognized as Redeemer thirteen times in Isaiah. In Israel the *go'el* was the kinsman-redeemer, who was also the avenger of blood (cf. Lev. 25:48–49; Num. 35:19–27; Ruth 2:1; 3:2,9–13; 4:1–11). As the "Holy One of Israel," God has dedicated himself to carry out His purposes for Israel in relation to His great plan of redemption.

> ¹⁵"See, I will make you into a threshing sledge, new and sharp, with many teeth. You will thresh the mountains and crush them, and reduce the hills to chaff.

God will make the insignificant worm into "a threshing sledge"—two heavy wooden planks nailed together by two crosspieces and having sharp pieces of iron (like spikes) underneath. It was dragged over the cut grain stalks to break them up and prepare them for winnowing the grain. Israel is compared to a sledge powerful enough to break up mountains and pulverize hills.

> ¹⁶You will winnow them, the wind will pick them up, and a gale will blow them away. But you will rejoice in the LORD and glory in the Holy One of Israel.

The threshed grain was thrown up with a scoop and the wind would blow the chaff away, letting the grain fall to the ground. Israel will not have to get rid of its enemies. God will "blow them away" like a mighty wind. Then Israel will rejoice in the LORD, making their boast in Him.

> ¹⁷"The poor and needy search for water, but there is none; their tongues are parched with thirst. But I the LORD will answer them; I, the God of Israel, will not forsake them.

Aridity has always been a problem in much of the Middle East. When the wretched, unfortunate poor and the oppressed needy are about to die of thirst, the LORD will answer them and meet their need. He will always be there for them.

> ¹⁸I will make rivers flow on barren heights, and springs within the valleys. I will turn the desert into pools of water, and the parched ground into springs.

He will meet their need abundantly in every place: Miraculously, He will open rivers "on barren heights" and make "springs within the valleys," turning the desert into a reed pool of water and the dry country into a place out of which water comes. He is the same God who gave Israel water from the rock during the Exodus (Exod. 17:6; Num. 20:11; Deut. 8:15).

> ¹⁹I will put in the desert the cedar and the acacia, the myrtle and the olive. I will set pines in the wasteland, the fir and the cypress together,

God will put a variety of trees in the desert and in the "wasteland" (Heb. *ba'aravah*, "in the Arabah," the dry area south of the Dead Sea). "Together" can also mean "all at the same time," that is, miraculously, as part of the restoration by the Holy Spirit in the Millennium.

> ²⁰so that people may see and know, may consider and understand, that the hand of the

LORD has done this, that the Holy One of Israel
has created it.

What God does and how He does it in this restoration will be a witness to the poor and needy (of v. 17). Together they will see, know, pay attention to, and understand with insight that the mighty power, or "hand of the LORD," did this; "the Holy One of Israel has created it." The word "create" in the Old Testament always has God as the subject. He alone can create— He alone can fulfill this prophecy.

> 21"Present your case," says the LORD. "Set forth
> your arguments," says Jacob's King.

In another court scene, God, as "Jacob's King" (as Israel's real King), tells the idolaters to bring their case and any strong arguments or proofs they might have for their gods.

> 22"Bring in [your idols] to tell us what is going to
> happen. Tell us what the former things were, so
> that we may consider them and know their final
> outcome. Or declare to us the things to come,

Let the idolaters bring in their gods and tell what will happen, explaining what happened in the past ("the former things"), how it fits in the present, what it means for the future, or let them simply "declare . . . the things to come." Isaiah could make this challenge because Israel had seen his prophecies of Sennacherib's defeat fulfilled.

Because the pagans had a cyclical view of history (not recognizing a beginning or an end), they had no concept of the flow of history. The Bible's linear view of history, on the other hand, shows that the God who created in the beginning also works now, and has a plan for a future consummation.

> 23tell us what the future holds, so we may know
> that you are gods. Do something, whether
> good or bad, so that we will be dismayed and
> filled with fear.

The pagan gods are challenged to foretell the future. This would be a seal indicating they really "are gods"—but they cannot prophesy. They are then challenged to do something, anything—"good or bad"—that people may be afraid. The collective plural ("us," "we") implies that to be a legitimate show of power, all humankind must be able to observe it together (all at the same time).

> ²⁴But you are less than nothing and your works are utterly worthless; he who chooses you is detestable.

The LORD sums it up by saying the pagan gods "are less than nothing"; their works "are utterly worthless." Those who choose to worship pagan gods instead of the one true God are abominable to Him.

> ²⁵"I have stirred up one from the north, and he comes—one from the rising sun who calls on my name. He treads on rulers as if they were mortar, as if he were a potter treading the clay.

The "one from the north" that God "stirred up" is Cyrus. Because of the desert directly east of Israel and Judah, most invasions came down from the north. So although Cyrus will come from Persia in the east (v. 2), he will enter Israel "from the north." He will call on God's name, not because he would worship the LORD but because he would decree that the Jews return and rebuild the temple of the LORD. (This is quite different from Sennacherib's claim that the LORD had sent him, 36:10).[3] He will "tread on rulers," the provincial governors, and as mortar or clay cannot resist the worker or the potter, they will not be able to resist him.

> ²⁶Who told of this from the beginning, so we could know, or beforehand, so we could say, 'He was right'? No one told of this, no one foretold it, no one heard any words from you.

The LORD is the One who declared this "from the beginning" that his people may know, telling it beforehand so that his people may say, "Right!" The verdict is in God's favor because of prophecy fulfilled. But among the pagan gods—here, the Hebrew is emphatic—not even one tells anything; indeed, none proclaim anything, and no one at all hears their words.

---

[3]God is the one who calls Cyrus by name (see 45:4).

> ²⁷I was the first to tell Zion, 'Look, here they are!' I gave to Jerusalem a messenger of good tidings.

Only God truly foresees the future. The wording in the Hebrew shows excitement. In contrast to the pagan idols who cannot and do not speak, God was "the first" with prophetic words of deliverance. Without anyone else anticipating Him, God sent a messenger with good news (see 40:9–11; 52:7).

> ²⁸I look but there is no one—no one among them to give counsel, no one to give answer when I ask them.

In contrast, the pagan gods have "no one," no messenger, no counselor, that can answer with even a word. They cannot reveal anything. But God has a plan.

> ²⁹See, they are all false! Their deeds amount to nothing; their images are but wind and confusion.

All the pagan gods are "false," "nothing" (Heb. *'awen*), and their works are (lit.) "nothingness." Their molten images are wind[4] and emptiness, without reality. How utterly stupid to worship anything or anyone other than the one true God! He is the only one worth trusting. We can build our lives on His Word.

3. The Servant Of The Lord And His Mission 42:1–9

> ¹"Here is my servant, whom I uphold, my chosen one in whom I delight; I will put my Spirit on him and he will bring justice to the nations.

Now attention is directed away from the idols to the glory of the Servant of the LORD. That is, "my servant" here (in contradistinction to the "servant" of 41:8) is the Messiah making this the first of the Servant Songs in Isaiah.[5] Matthew 12:17–21 applies this passage to Jesus. We can see a parallel also when the

---
[4] The Heb. *ruach* also means "spirit," and some pagans claimed a spirit was in the images. Nevertheless, they had no spiritual power. Thus, the hollow images were only filled with air.

[5] Isa. 42:1–9; see also 49:1–7; 50:4–9; 52:13 to 53:12.

318 / Isaiah 42:2-4

Spirit descends on Jesus as a dove and the Father's voice from heaven declares: "'This is my Son, whom I love; with him I am well pleased'" (Matt. 3:17).

"Here is" (Heb. *hen,* "Behold") is a command to look at Him. God the Father firmly upholds Him, delights in Him from His soul (and heart), and puts His Holy Spirit upon Him. He will bring out compassionate "justice" (Heb. *mishpat*) to the nations.[6] This connects "my servant" with earlier messianic passages in Isaiah, 9:7 and 11:2 as well as 61:1. The term "servant" implies both obedience and delegated authority. It is parallel to Psalm 2:7,12, where the Father calls the Messiah His Son.

> ²He will not shout or cry out, or raise his voice in the streets.

He will not be like worldly conquerors, who shout out who they are and make great announcements of their exploits. He will be quiet and gentle. Unlike the Crusaders who thought they could do God's work by fighting and unlike the Muslims who think holy war (jihad) is God's will, the Messiah will not provoke bloodshed or hatred. In fact, He went to the cross, then sent the Holy Spirit, and now by that Spirit His work is to be done (cf. Zech. 4:6).

> ³A bruised reed he will not break, and a smoldering wick he will not snuff out. In faithfulness he will bring forth justice;

One breaks a "bruised reed" before discarding it. He will not throw anyone away as useless. A dimly burning wick is easy to "snuff out." But He will not put out the light of anyone's life. He will bring out justice "in faithfulness," that is, "according to the truth" (Heb. *le'emeth*).

> ⁴he will not falter or be discouraged till he establishes justice on earth. In his law the islands will put their hope."

The Messiah will not burn dimly or grow weak himself, nor will He be bruised or discouraged. That is, the things and the

---

[6]Cf. Ps. 82:3,8. His universal justice is another reason for accepting Him as the one true God.

people that cause others to be discouraged will not stop Him from giving light and being firm and strong. He will not give up until He establishes "justice on earth."⁷ The "islands" (that is, all the inhabited earth) will "put their hope" in (or "wait for," KJV, et al.) His "law" (Heb. *torah,* "instruction"). "Wait for" implies hope that endures. Those who accept the Messiah will put their hope in Him, look to Him for help and guidance, and will endure to the end (cf. Matt. 24:13).

> ⁵This is what God the LORD says—he who created the heavens and stretched them out, who spread out the earth and all that comes out of it, who gives breath to its people, and life to those who walk on it:

Again the one true God, the LORD *(Yahweh),* is identified as the Creator of "the heavens and . . . the earth" and "all" (people, animals and plants) created "out of it." He "stretched . . . out" the heavens as easily as one would a curtain. He is the one who "gives breath to . . . people" (as He did to Adam) and "life" to the human spirit (including the mind and disposition).

> ⁶"I, the LORD, have called you in righteousness; I will take hold of your hand. I will keep you and will make you to be a covenant for the people and a light for the Gentiles,

Like Cyrus (41:2), the Servant has been called by God the Father "in righteousness": that is, (as the Heb. indicates) to successfully bring justice (as a manifestation of His grace). God will hold Him by the hand, protecting and keeping Him. He will give Him "to be a covenant for the people"—the new covenant (cf. Mal. 3:1)—by which the Servant will bring people into right relationship with the LORD. The covenant will be in Him, through Him, and by Him. Furthermore, the covenant will not be limited to Israel, for the Servant will be "a light for the Gentiles" (i.e., nations). (See John 1:9; 8:12; 9:5; Heb. 8:6–13; 9:15.)

> ⁷to open eyes that are blind, to free captives from prison and to release from the dungeon those who sit in darkness.

---

⁷That is, "a just order." See F. Duane Lindsey, *The Servant Songs* (Chicago: Moody Press, 1985), 43–45.

He will not only "be . . . light" (v. 6), but He will also "open eyes that are blind" so they can see that light. The prisoners who "sit in [the] darkness" of the prison house of sin, He will bring out into the light (cf. 61:1; Rom. 5:21).

> ⁸"I am the Lord; that is my name! I will not give my glory to another or my praise to idols.

God declares His covenant-keeping Name, *Yahweh*,⁸ the Name that assured Israel He would be with them.⁹ He is not only the one true God, He is also a personal God. His "glory" includes His power, authority, and attributes. He will not give them to another, nor His "praise to idols." Because of His glory—because of who He is—He deserves all the praise. The idols are nothing and deserve none.

> ⁹See, the former things have taken place, and new things I declare; before they spring into being I announce them to you."

The "former things" are the events previously prophesied which are now fulfilled. (Isaiah is probably writing this in 700 B.C., after his prophecy of deliverance from the Assyrians was fulfilled.) The "new things" are prophecies not yet fulfilled but certain to be fulfilled, just as the former things were. God's prophetic word can be depended on.

4. A New Song 42:10–13

> ¹⁰Sing to the Lord a new song, his praise from the ends of the earth, you who go down to the sea, and all that is in it, you islands, and all who live in them.

The command to "sing to the Lord a new song" implies new revelation or new understanding of His word and of what He is about to do (cf. 43:18–19; 48:6). His praise should come from "the ends of the earth": from those who are on the sea and from all the inhabitants of the habitable world. This includes both

---

⁸See note on 1:2 for the meaning of Yahweh. The name indicates that He will continue to be the fulfiller of His plan—actively working among people.

⁹See Exod. 3:12 where "'I will be'" is the same word in Heb. *('ehyeh)* as the word translated "'I am'" in 3:14.

Gentiles and Israelites.

> ¹¹Let the desert and its towns raise their voices;
> let the settlements where Kedar lives rejoice.
> Let the people of Sela sing for joy; let them
> shout from the mountaintops.

"The desert and its towns" (where people then lived on a bare subsistence level), the Arabian Kedar tribe and its villages, and the residents of Sela (Petra) in Edom—former enemies of Israel—are to join with them in praising God.

> ¹²Let them give glory to the LORD and proclaim
> his praise in the islands.

Their shouts are to "give glory to the LORD" and announce His praise to the "islands" (the inhabited earth). His blessings are for everyone.

> ¹³The LORD will march out like a mighty man,
> like a warrior he will stir up his zeal; with a
> shout he will raise the battle cry and will triumph over his enemies.

The LORD himself will go out to battle as a hero. "Like a warrior he will stir up his zeal"—His fiery love that will not allow the enemy to destroy those who love Him. He will "shout." Indeed He will raise a war cry and "triumph over his enemies." In other words, He is a delivering God. (Cf. 27:4 and 63:1–6 for development of the theme of the LORD *[Yahweh]* as "Divine Warrior.")

5. GOD WILL JUDGE AND GUIDE 42:14–17

> ¹⁴"For a long time I have kept silent, I have
> been quiet and held myself back. But now, like
> a woman in childbirth, I cry out, I gasp and
> pant.

From eternity God has "held . . . back," postponed, this action of judgment and restoration. "But now" He speaks. He has become like a woman in labor and will not postpone it forever: When He does it, He will do it all at once.

> ¹⁵I will lay waste the mountains and hills and

dry up all their vegetation; I will turn rivers into islands and dry up the pools.

In contrast to the blessings that will come in the Millennium (41:18), God's judgment will dry up mountains, hills, and all their vegetation, as well as rivers and reed pools.

> ¹⁶I will lead the blind by ways they have not known, along unfamiliar paths I will guide them; I will turn the darkness into light before them and make the rough places smooth. These are the things I will do; I will not forsake them.

Now in contrast to His judgment He will "lead the blind" in new paths, turning "darkness into light" and smoothing the "rough places" as they follow Him. The "blind" are the spiritually blind who turn to Him. God will do this and emphatically "will not forsake them." This we can expect Him to continue to do.

> ¹⁷But those who trust in idols, who say to images, 'You are our gods,' will be turned back in utter shame.

In contrast to those who trust in God, the pagans who still "trust in idols," calling gold and silver images their gods, will shrink back and be totally put to shame.

6. Israel Blind And Deaf 42:18–25

> ¹⁸"Hear, you deaf; look, you blind, and see!
> ¹⁹Who is blind but my servant, and deaf like the messenger I send? Who is blind like the one committed to me, blind like the servant of the Lord?

The call is to the deaf and blind people of the world to listen and look. God and only God can cause them to hear and see. "My servant" in this passage refers to Israel. The world needs what God has given to and through Israel. But Israel is blind like the rest of the world, even though it is God's servant. That is, God intended Israel to give a message to the world, but its people had become too deaf to hear the message. Israel, who was rewarded by God, and who is still His servant, is now both blind and deaf.

> ²⁰You have seen many things, but have paid no attention; your ears are open, but you hear nothing."

Israel's blindness and deafness are not physical but spiritual. Its people (the words "you" and "your" refer to Israel) have seen miracles and fulfilled prophecies but they do not pay attention. Their ears are open but they "hear nothing." They are oblivious to what God wants them to see and hear.

> ²¹It pleased the LORD for the sake of his righteousness to make his law great and glorious.

The LORD was delighted for His righteousness' sake (in line with His righteous nature) to make His "law" (Heb. *torah*, "instruction," "teaching"; that is, the Scriptures) "great and glorious." It is all worth hearing and obeying; His Word would give then new opportunities for the blessings a loving God wanted to give them.

> ²²But this is a people plundered and looted, all of them trapped in pits or hidden away in prisons. They have become plunder, with no one to rescue them; they have been made loot, with no one to say, "Send them back."

The people who received this great and glorious instruction are plundered, pillaged, trapped (captured and chained) in pits, and kept hidden in prisons. This was not the case for the people taken to Babylon by Nebuchadnezzar (see Jer. 29:1–23). Archaeological remains show that most of them prospered during the seventy years of Babylonian exile,[10] so much so that most did not want to return to Jerusalem. The suffering described here was the actual result of Assyrian invasions of Israel and Judah in Isaiah's own day. The captives taken from the cities of Judah by Sennacherib had no one like Cyrus to "send them back."

---

[10] For example, archaeologists have discovered the remains of a Jewish banking and bonding house by the Chebar Canal east of Babylon.

> [23] Which of you will listen to this or pay close attention in time to come?

Isaiah asks who will listen. He is concerned about the "time to come" and wants the people to share that concern. The Old Testament as a whole has a forward look, recognizing that God will bring both judgment and restoration.

> [24] Who handed Jacob over to become loot, and Israel to the plunderers? Was it not the LORD, against whom we have sinned? For they would not follow his ways; they did not obey his law.

The LORD was behind what the Assyrians did to Israel and Judah. They had sinned against Him: They did not want to live according to His ways and would not listen to His teaching. They had become rebels whose lives expressed contempt for God. It seemed they would never learn.

> [25] So he poured out on them his burning anger, the violence of war. It enveloped them in flames, yet they did not understand; it consumed them, but they did not take it to heart.

They deserved God's anger and the judgment that He brought through the Assyrians (10:5–6). Even so, they did not perceive or acknowledge that the judgment came from the LORD; they did not "take it to heart." Neither did they pay attention to what the LORD was saying through the prophets nor recall Moses' warning that "the LORD your God is a consuming fire, a jealous God" (Deut. 4:24). God's mercy does not pamper sinners by allowing them to continue in pride and stubborn rebellion. His love seeks to challenge them "to repentance and obedience as the way back to the life-giving relationship with God."[11]

STUDY QUESTIONS

1. Who is God challenging in chapter 41 and why?
2. What indicates that the one "from the east" is Cyrus?
3. How does Isaiah contrast the idols to the true God in chapter 41?

---

[11] Paul D. Hanson, *Isaiah 40–66* (Louisville: John Knox Press, 1995), 57.

4. How does Matthew 12:17–21 confirm that the Lord's Servant in 42:1–7 is Jesus?
5. What does the "new song" praise the Lord for?
6. Who is the servant in 42:18–25 and what kind of blindness does this servant have?

C. A Redeemed Remnant Gathered 43:1–45:25

1. Israel's Loving Savior 43:1–7

¹But now, this is what the LORD says—he who created you, O Jacob, he who formed you, O Israel: "Fear not, for I have redeemed you; I have summoned you by name; you are mine.

In spite of Israel's lack of response to God's judgment, God has not changed His plan and purpose for His people. He created them. He formed the nation. He tells them to stop being afraid, for He has redeemed them. They should never give up their faith in him (cf. 43:5; 44:2; 54:4).

God gave them the name "Israel."[1] He claims them as His own just as He did when He brought them out of Egypt and brought them to himself (Exod. 19:4). As Moses wrote, He loved them because He loved them (Deut. 7:7–9; cf. 1 John 4:8).

²When you pass through the waters, I will be with you; and when you pass through the rivers, they will not sweep over you. When you walk through the fire, you will not be burned; the flames will not set you ablaze.

Because of God's judgment Israel would pass through waters, rivers, fire, and flames; but God would always be with them.[2] They could always put their complete trust in Him, and they

---

[1] See Gen. 32:22–32; 35:10; the name means "he struggles with God" or "God strives" or "God rules."

[2] "You" is singular. God promises to be with them individually and personally. He is Immanuel, the "with-us God."

would never be annihilated.

> ³For I am the LORD, your God, the Holy One of Israel, your Savior; I give Egypt for your ransom, Cush and Seba in your stead.

God is who He is: the LORD, *Yahweh,* the eternal, faithful, covenant-keeping God; He is Israel's God, the Holy One of Israel who revealed himself to Isaiah (chap. 6), Israel's Savior.

Because He is who He is, He could give a whole country, Egypt, as ransom. That is, He delivered the people of Israel from bondage at the cost of plagues on Egypt (Exod. 10:7) and the destruction of their army (Exod. 14:28,30–31; 15:1,3–10). Cush (the present Sudan) and Seba (northern Ethiopia including Meroe) were affected as well.

> ⁴Since you are precious and honored in my sight, and because I love you, I will give men in exchange for you, and people in exchange for your life.

Because Israel is valuable to God, honored by Him, and because He loves them, He will give other people instead of them. The repetition of this idea in different words shows emphasis. His purpose is to deliver Israel. God loved the world, but when the world turned away, He chose Israel to prepare the way for a Redeemer. But other nations would have to pay the cost of God's choice of Israel. This, however, put a great responsibility on them. Similarly, God's choice of the Church puts a great responsibility on believers. Because of the assurance of His love, however, this responsibility is not burdensome (cf. Matt. 11:28–30).

> ⁵Do not be afraid, for I am with you; I will bring your children from the east and gather you from the west. ⁶I will say to the north, 'Give them up!' and to the south, 'Do not hold them back.' Bring my sons from afar and my daughters from the ends of the earth—

Now God points them ahead to a time when Israel would be scattered in all directions. At the same time, He tells them to stop being afraid, for He is with them. He will bring their descendants who are alive at the end of the age in a new exodus from all directions, even "from the ends of the earth." (This does not refer to the return from Babylon in 538–536 B.C., for they came only from the east.)

> ⁷everyone who is called by my name, whom I created for my glory, whom I formed and made."

The primary reference here is back to 43:1, where God is talking about Israel. They are the ones called by His name, created for His glory, formed by His mighty hand—the nation He made. He will not give up on them.

2. Israel's Witness As God's Servant 43:8–13

> ⁸Lead out those who have eyes but are blind, who have ears but are deaf.

In another court scene, strangely enough the blind and deaf (see 42:18–20) are brought out as witnesses. But they are willfully blind and deaf, for they have eyes and ears. They are not acceptable witnesses in a court.

> ⁹All the nations gather together and the peoples assemble. Which of them foretold this and proclaimed to us the former things? Let them bring in their witnesses to prove they were right, so that others may hear and say, "It is true."

With all the nations assembled, they are challenged to produce from among themselves someone (some god or the prophet of some god) who can tell the future and show "former things." That is, let them show that they have prophesied and produced events like the Exodus from Egypt, the deliverance from Sennacherib, and other former things God has done in the history of Israel. They must do this to be justified, to have the verdict in their favor. Otherwise, let them hear what God has done and admit it is the truth.

> ¹⁰"You are my witnesses," declares the LORD, "and my servant whom I have chosen, so that you may know and believe me and understand

> that I am he. Before me no god was formed,
> nor will there be one after me.

God is speaking here to the godly remnant in Israel, especially those rescued from Sennacherib. They are His witnesses, His chosen servants. God has done great things in Israel so they might know, believe, and trust in Him and know that He alone is God (see 37:16).

Pagans believed that the gods they worshiped had been preceded by other gods. Pagans also believed in gods that had newly arisen or been born. But the one true God declares there was "no god . . . formed," or created, before Him and none would come after Him. He is the eternal God who always was, is, and will be (Exod. 3:14; Mal. 3:6; Heb. 13:8; Rev. 1:8, etc.).

> ¹¹I, even I, am the LORD, and apart from me there is no savior.

By saying "I am the LORD *[Yahweh],*" God is reminding them of the revelation of himself during the time of the Exodus (Exod. 3:12,14–15; 6:7; 7:17; 8:22; 15:1–2). He saved them then; He will save them now—because He is the Savior and there is no other.

> ¹²I have revealed and saved and proclaimed—I, and not some foreign god among you. You are my witnesses," declares the LORD, "that I am God.

God told Moses what He was going to do. He saved Israel and made himself heard among the Israelites at Mount Sinai. When the Israelites came to Sinai they had no idols among them.

The salvation and the voice of the LORD came only from Him, and, therefore, because Israel experienced this, the LORD says they are witnesses of who He is: God *('el).* The Hebrew word *'el* is the general word for God, which emphasizes that He alone is God. Even though Israel failed, God did not fail. They are witnesses to His faithfulness.

> ¹³Yes, and from ancient days I am he. No one can deliver out of my hand. When I act, who can reverse it?"

The Hebrew *miyom 'ani hu'*, "From day, I am He," may mean "Since time began, I am the one true God," or it may mean "Since I am the one true God today, none can rescue out of my hand." God will do His work, and no one can hinder or "reverse it."

3. A New Exodus From Babylon 43:14–21

> ¹⁴This is what the Lord says—your Redeemer, the Holy One of Israel: "For your sake I will send to Babylon and bring down as fugitives all the Babylonians, in the ships in which they took pride.

Now the Lord promises a new exodus, this time from Babylon. God who is doing this is the "Holy One of Israel" and is doing it for Israel's sake. Ships of the "Babylonians" (Heb. *kasdim*, "Chaldeans") bringing treasures on the Euphrates River caused shouts of joy when they arrived. But God will "bring down" the Chaldeans, and their ships will be used by fugitives seeking to escape.[3]

> ¹⁵I am the Lord, your Holy One, Israel's Creator, your King."

The judgment God brings on Babylon is related to what God will do for Israel. Again Isaiah emphasizes that He is Israel's "Holy One," "Creator," and "King."

> ¹⁶This is what the Lord says—he who made a way through the sea, a path through the mighty waters,

God provides "a way through the sea, a path through the mighty waters." He did that at the Exodus when He made a way through the Red (Reed) Sea. He is that kind of God.

> ¹⁷who drew out the chariots and horses, the army and reinforcements together, and they lay there, never to rise again, extinguished, snuffed out like a wick:

---

[3] Some suggest this verse refers to Sennacherib's driving out Merodach-Baladan in 700 B.C. Cf. W. A. Wordsworth, *En Roeh: The Prophecies of Isaiah the Seer* (Edinburgh, Scotland: T. & T. Clark, 1939), 315.

The victory over Pharaoh's crack chariot troops at the Red Sea is described dramatically (see Exod. 14:1–31). It was complete.

> **18"Forget the former things; do not dwell on the past.**

Nevertheless, the time comes when it is necessary to stop remembering and giving attention to the things of the past. God wants us to look ahead to new miracles that will overshadow the old. His loving purpose shows He is a good God.

> **19See, I am doing a new thing! Now it springs up; do you not perceive it? I am making a way in the desert and streams in the wasteland.**

God has a new deliverance for His people. It is ready to take place. They will know and experience it. God will make a road "in the desert" and rivers "in the wasteland" (wilderness). There was a return in Isaiah's day when Sennacherib destroyed Babylon in 689 B.C.[4]

His son Esarhaddon recorded the fact that captive people escaped at that time, for the Assyrians were concerned only with the Babylonians themselves.[5] However, Isaiah may be looking here to the return from the Babylonian exile that he prophesied in 39:6. There may be a further fulfillment at the end of the age.

> **20The wild animals honor me, the jackals and the owls, because I provide water in the desert and streams in the wasteland, to give drink to my people, my chosen, 21the people I formed for myself that they may proclaim my praise.**

"Wild animals," especially those living in desert areas, will honor God because of the rivers in the desert that God gives for the benefit of His returning people. He formed Israel for himself and He purposes for them to proclaim His praise. We too are brought to the Lord so that we may praise Him and call on others to praise Him.

---

[4]Oswald T. Allis, "Book of Isaiah," in *Wycliffe Bible Encyclopedia* (Chicago: Moody Press, 1975), 1:857.

[5]Benjamin R. Downer, "The Added Years of Hezekiah's Life," *Bibliotheca Sacra* 80, no. 319 (July 1923): 386; Daniel David Luckenbill, *Ancient Records of Assyria and Babylonia*, 2 vols. (Chicago: University of Chicago Press, 1926–27), 2:152.

4. Israel's Unfaithfulness 43:22–28

> ²²"Yet you have not called upon me, O Jacob,
> you have not wearied yourselves for me, O Israel.

God places the emphasis upon himself when He declares, "Not Me, you have called" (literal translation). These are the people of Isaiah's day whom God spoke of as "trampling my courts" (1:12). They were making many prayers (1:15). But they could not disguise their sin. They were not really seeking God. They were actually tired of Him; that is, they were tired of the Holy God that He is.

> ²³You have not brought me sheep for burnt offerings, nor honored me with your sacrifices.
> I have not burdened you with grain offerings nor wearied you with demands for incense.

They brought their "burnt offerings" and "sacrifices" but they were not really offering them to God. They were going through forms without faith in God and without honoring Him for who He is. They were multiplying sacrifices and incense offerings, but God had not asked for that (1:13).

> ²⁴You have not bought any fragrant calamus for me, or lavished on me the fat of your sacrifices.
> But you have burdened me with your sins and wearied me with your offenses.

Indeed, it was not the sweet calamus (or the oil from it) nor the fat of sacrifices that they "lavished" on God; instead they loaded Him down with their sins. The NIV translates the Hebrew verb as "lavished" here (but as "sated" in Lam. 3:15). And here it has a touch of irony. They neglected God, were stingy in their worship, and the only thing they "lavished" on God were sins that were bad enough to make one vomit (cf. 1:13). "Burdened me" (Heb. *he'evadtani*) can also mean "compelled me." That is, their sins compelled Him to do a work of judgment. Also their "offenses" (their guilt with its consequences) "wearied" Him. Repeated, unconfessed sins made judgment necessary.

> ²⁵"I, even I, am he who blots out your trans-

gressions, for my own sake, and remembers your sins no more.

At the same time, it is God alone who can blot out the sin resulting from willful rebellion—not because it is deserved, but for His own sake. When this is done, forgiveness is complete: The record is wiped clean. God will never remember their sins anymore. This is pure grace—flowing freely from God's inexhaustible mercy—which God is here offering to His people.

> 26Review the past for me, let us argue the matter together; state the case for your innocence.

Yet before there is divine forgiveness, before the record is cleansed, the sinner must go to trial. There must be confession, reminding God of the sins. It is very easy for us to block out things we do not want to remember, but we must not do that if we want God's forgiveness.

To "argue the matter together" means recognizing what the law requires and admitting that innocence cannot be proved. Only when the sinner admits his sin can there be justification that forgives and wipes the record clean.

> 27Your first father sinned; your spokesmen rebelled against me.

The "first father" is probably Adam. Some take it to be Abraham or Jacob. In any case, the first father also implies the first sin. And in Isaiah's own day, Israel's "spokesmen," that is, their priests (and probably their prophets), as intermediaries or mediators, had also rebelled against God.

> 28So I will disgrace the dignitaries of your temple, and I will consign Jacob to destruction and Israel to scorn.

Because of this rebellion God has disgraced the officers of the holy place (cf. 1 Chron. 24:5). He has given Jacob "to destruction" (Heb. *lacherem*, "to the ban")[6] as something God abhors. This also meant that he has given Israel over to be scorned and

---

[6]This was done to Jericho because its inhabitants were evil: All except Rahab totally rejected God even though they knew what He had done in delivering Israel and giving it victories (Josh. 6:17; see also Josh. 2:10).

reviled by the rest of the world (cf. Deut. 28:37). Their hearts were not open to His love.

5. God's Spirit To Be Outpoured 44:1–5

1"But now listen, O Jacob, my servant, Israel, whom I have chosen.

The prophesied destruction will not be total, however, and the scorn and revilings will not last forever. Nor will the sins of his people destroy God's purpose. God still calls the people of Jacob "my servant, Israel," His chosen, and wants them to listen.

2This is what the Lord says—he who made you, who formed you in the womb, and who will help you: Do not be afraid, O Jacob, my servant, Jeshurun, whom I have chosen.

God was their Maker, the One who formed them from their birth as a nation. He will keep on helping them. Again He tells them they must stop being afraid. Cowardly fear and faith do not mix (cf. 2 Tim. 1:7).

God calls Israel "Jeshurun," His "dear upright (righteous) one," because that is what He wants them to be (Deut. 32:15; 33:26–29). The repetition of "servant" and "chosen" from verse 1 indicates that God has not and will not change His mind about them (cf. Rom. 11:29). He will have a godly remnant from among them. God will not allow Israel's failure to cause Him to fail.

3For I will pour water on the thirsty land, and streams on the dry ground; I will pour out my Spirit on your offspring, and my blessing on your descendants.

God will bring about a change by pouring out His Spirit, becoming like water on a wasteland. The downpour will be so great that it will be like streams flooding dry ground. It will bring wonderful blessings from God. This outpouring, however, is in the future. It is not to be upon the people of Isaiah's day, but upon their descendants (cf. 32:15; 59:21; Jer. 31:33–34; Ezek. 36:26–27; 37:14; 39:29; Joel 2:25–29; Zech. 12:10 to 13:1).

The initial outpouring was on the Day of Pentecost (Acts

2:4,17–18). But there will be further fulfillment for Israel in the millennial restoration.

> ⁴They will spring up like grass in a meadow, like poplar trees by flowing streams.

The restoration will bring a fresh blessing. No longer will they continue to be in spiritually dry land.

> ⁵One will say, 'I belong to the LORD'; another will call himself by the name of Jacob; still another will write on his hand, 'The LORD's,' and will take the name Israel.

The work of the Spirit will cause every individual to testify, declaring their relationship to the LORD both in writing and in speaking. They will also take the "name" (character and nature) of Israel. That is, Jews who were not living for God will be transformed and become real Israelites, honoring God and enjoying the rights and privileges He gives them.

6. The Foolishness Of Idolatry 44:6–20

> ⁶"This is what the LORD says—Israel's King and Redeemer, the LORD Almighty: I am the first and I am the last; apart from me there is no God.

In another court scene, indicated by the questions and the call for witnesses in the verses that follow, the LORD now reassures Israel that He is indeed their King and Redeemer, the Almighty LORD of Hosts, having the armies of heaven at His disposal. By calling himself "the first and . . . the last," He is emphasizing that He alone is God. Whenever Israel forgot that and turned to other gods or other things, they blocked the flow of God's promise.

Again Isaiah emphasizes the contrast between the pagan concept of many gods and the existence of Israel's God: There was no god before Him, none will come after Him. He always was and always will be. Unlike the idols, He was not formed by anyone; He is not dependent on anyone. He is supreme. The New Testament applies this to Jesus (Rev. 1:17; 22:13): He is God manifest in the flesh (John 1:1,14).

> ⁷Who then is like me? Let him proclaim it. Let him declare and lay out before me what has

> happened since I established my ancient people, and what is yet to come—yes, let him foretell what will come.

God is the one who has directed the history of His eternal people (cf. 66:22; Jer. 31:35–37). He proclaimed it. He established it. He knows what is coming in the future as well. The challenge is to the pagans. Let them declare the future if their so-called gods are able to reveal it. Israel's God alone is omniscient. He can fulfill His promises.

> ⁸Do not tremble, do not be afraid. Did I not proclaim this and foretell it long ago? You are my witnesses. Is there any God besides me? No, there is no other Rock; I know not one."

God again reassures Israel, telling them to stop trembling in terror, to stop being afraid, that is, of their enemies (see 35:3–4; 41:10–13; 43:1–2). God has given prophecies that have been fulfilled, and they are His witnesses to this. God again stresses that there is no other God, "no other Rock," that is, a refuge, a strength, an assurance of power, permanence, and faithfulness. He is the only real God.

> ⁹All who make idols are nothing, and the things they treasure are worthless. Those who would speak up for them are blind; they are ignorant, to their own shame.

In contrast to the reality of the true God, the idol makers and their idols are "nothing" (Heb. *tohu,* "emptiness"), that is, they are meaningless. "All who make idols" and "those who would speak up for them" delight in what is worthless: without profit, without benefit. The idols are their own witnesses. They do not see or know, that is, they are not true witnesses, and consequently they will be put to shame (along with their worshipers).

> ¹⁰Who shapes a god and casts an idol, which can profit him nothing?

The question is brilliant sarcasm. The shaping of a god or the casting of an idol results only in an icon that is unable to help. Nothing is more stupid than thinking a human being can fashion something that can rise to the level of divinity and become capable of offering supernatural help.

> ¹¹He and his kind will be put to shame; craftsmen are nothing but men. Let them all come together and take their stand; they will be brought down to terror and infamy.

All those who join themselves to idols "will be put to shame." The workmen who made the idols are merely human. And they are the source of the ideas for the gods they make. In their weakness and sin, how can they make a real God? The time will come when they will "come together" (that is, before God's judgment bar). Then they will all be afraid and be "put to shame" at the same time.

> ¹²The blacksmith takes a tool and works with it in the coals; he shapes an idol with hammers, he forges it with the might of his arm. He gets hungry and loses his strength; he drinks no water and grows faint.

The following verses are full of tremendous satire showing the foolishness of idolatry. The example is an idol made of wood. The word "idol" is not in the Hebrew. The blacksmith is making the tool. Isaiah first reaches back and "reverses the procedures that we would have been inclined to follow."[7] Tools are necessary: There must be an ax to cut down the tree. So a "blacksmith" (Heb. *charash barzel,* "a craftsman of iron") makes it; he has a strong arm as he heats and shapes the ax. But he is only human and he gets hungry and thirsty. He hardly has the strength and endurance to finish making the ax. How different from the Lord who never grows tired or weary and who can indeed renew our strength (Isa. 40:28–31).[8]

> ¹³The carpenter measures with a line and makes an outline with a marker; he roughs it out with chisels and marks it with compasses. He shapes it in the form of man, of man in all

---

[7] H. C. Leupold, *Exposition of Isaiah* (Grand Rapids: Baker Book House, 1971), 2:105.
[8] The NIV and others interpret the verse of making a metal idol rather than an ax. However, the word "idol" is not in the Heb. and the irony seems to be of "clumsy tools and weak workmen" as "the source from which an idol springs." Leupold, *Exposition of Isaiah,* 2:106.

his glory, that it may dwell in a shrine.

The woodworker is just as foolish as the blacksmith. He takes a measuring line, spreads it out in the shape of a man, makes an outline with a "marker" (probably red chalk), shapes it with carving knives, makes an outline with a compass (for making circles), and makes it into "the form of a man." He does the best he can to make it like the beauty or glory of humankind, that is, like the most handsome of humankind—not to rule the universe but only to stay in a "shrine" (Heb. *bayith,* "house").[9] What a contrast to the true God who is everywhere present. As Solomon said of Him, "The heavens, even the highest heavens, cannot contain you. How much less this temple I have built" (2 Chron. 6:18).

> [14]He cut down cedars, or perhaps took a cypress or oak. He let it grow among the trees of the forest, or planted a pine, and the rain made it grow.

Isaiah looks with irony at the origin of the wood used to make the idol. The trees that are cut down are not cut down to be gods. The woodsman cuts them down for himself, unconcerned about what kinds of trees they are. Before that, he allows some to grow because they are in a forest. Or he may plant a pine tree nearby for himself, and the rain nourishes it.

> [15]It is man's fuel for burning; some of it he takes and warms himself, he kindles a fire and bakes bread. But he also fashions a god and worships it; he makes an idol and bows down to it.

The first reason for cutting down trees in those days was to provide fuel for warmth and for baking. But from the same log, a pagan makes a god, an idol, and "bows down to it."

> [16]Half of the wood he burns in the fire; over it he prepares his meal, he roasts his meat and eats his fill. He also warms himself and says, "Ah! I am warm; I see the fire." [17]From the rest

---

[9]A temple or shrine was often called the "house" of a god. But pagans also kept idols in their homes.

338 / Isaiah 44:17-20

> he makes a god, his idol; he bows down to it and worships. He prays to it and says, "Save me; you are my god."

He cuts the log in half. He uses half to cook with and warm himself, and "from the rest" (not a special part), he makes his idol. He sees the fire and exclaims over its warmth. Then he worships the part he has saved from the fire, prays to it, and asks it to save (or rescue) him, for it is his god, all the god the poor fellow has. What foolishness!

> ¹⁸They know nothing, they understand nothing; their eyes are plastered over so they cannot see, and their minds closed so they cannot understand.

The idol worshipers neither know nor discern the truth; God has smeared over their eyes and their hearts, so their eyes and their minds are stuck shut. They have become like their idols.

> ¹⁹No one stops to think, no one has the knowledge or understanding to say, "Half of it I used for fuel; I even baked bread over its coals, I roasted meat and I ate. Shall I make a detestable thing from what is left? Shall I bow down to a block of wood?"

The result is that none of the idol worshipers "stops to think" (Heb. *loʻ yashiv ʻel libbo*, "it does not return to his heart"). The contrast does not even occur to them, so they do not have enough knowledge or discernment to ask the right questions about their use of the same log for fire as well as for worship.

> ²⁰He feeds on ashes, a deluded heart misleads him; he cannot save himself, or say, "Is not this thing in my right hand a lie?"

Part of the log becomes ashes as the idolater cooks and warms himself. Part becomes an idol. So as he worships the idol, he is trying to nourish himself spiritually on little more than ashes.

He is deceived. He cannot rescue himself from the idol worship nor does he know enough to say the idol that is in his "right hand" (that he depends on) is false. His "deluded heart" (the Heb. includes the mind) leads him astray.

7. God Will Redeem And Restore Israel 44:21–45:25

a. Jerusalem To Be Inhabited 44:21–28

> ²¹"Remember these things, O Jacob, for you are my servant, O Israel. I have made you, you are my servant; O Israel, I will not forget you.

Israel did not form God; God formed Israel. He redeemed them from Egypt. He formed them from their very beginning, from their birth as a nation. God assures them that they are still His servants, and He will not forget them.

> ²²I have swept away your offenses like a cloud, your sins like the morning mist. Return to me, for I have redeemed you."

God assures Israel that He has wiped out their rebellion "like a cloud" and their sins "like the morning mist" (or "a mass of clouds"). God's call is for them to return to Him, for He has redeemed them. He has paid the price they could not pay. Even before they repent, the price is paid, and He is wooing them to himself.

> ²³Sing for joy, O heavens, for the LORD has done this; shout aloud, O earth beneath. Burst into song, you mountains, you forests and all your trees, for the LORD has redeemed Jacob, he displays his glory in Israel.

God had delivered Jerusalem from Sennacherib. But He promises a greater deliverance and restoration. The call is for the heavens to shout with joy and the "earth beneath" (the "lower parts of the earth," KJV; that is, on its surface, where the mountains and trees are[10]) to shout in triumph, because of what the Lord has done. Let the very mountains open up with a shout of joy and the forest with every individual tree as well, for the LORD has not only redeemed but will openly display His glory "in Israel."

---

[10] Heb. *tachtiyyoth 'erets*, "lower parts of the earth," a poetic phrase contrasting earth with heaven. Cf. Eph. 4:9 where Jesus descended to the lower parts of the earth to be born of a virgin.

The necessary fulfillment, of course, involved Christ openly manifesting the Father's glory during His life on the earth (John 1:14,18). But the glory will be manifest in and through national Israel when Jesus returns and establishes His millennial kingdom. This is the same concept which is expressed in Romans 8:22—creation involved in the restoration process. The glory also ties in with the "new heavens and new earth" motif (see Isa. 65:17).

> **24"This is what the LORD says—your Redeemer, who formed you in the womb: I am the LORD, who has made all things, who alone stretched out the heavens, who spread out the earth by myself,**

As a climax to this chapter God again declares who He is and what His purposes are. He is Israel's Kinsman-Redeemer. He not only formed the nation of Israel, He is the Maker of everything: stretching out the heavens, spreading out the earth. He alone made it. He, the eternal One, is both Redeemer and Creator.

> **25who foils the signs of false prophets and makes fools of diviners, who overthrows the learning of the wise and turns it into nonsense,**

He "foils the signs" of ignorant pagan prophets and diviners (braggarts who boast about the miracles they can perform). He "makes fools" of those who make predictions by casting lots. He "overthrows" the wise, making a mockery of their wisdom.

Archeologists have found thousands of messages from the wise men and diviners of Assyria and Babylonia telling their kings good things, promising victory, but not one foretelling the judgment that God caused to fall on them.

> **26who carries out the words of his servants and fulfills the predictions of his messengers, who says of Jerusalem, 'It shall be inhabited,' of the towns of Judah, 'They shall be built,' and of their ruins, 'I will restore them,'**

In contrast, God has confirmed and carried out the "words of his servants" (the prophets), and brought to completion the counsel of "his messengers." The prophecies foretell that Jerusalem will continue to be inhabited, the cities of Judah ruined by Sennacherib will be rebuilt, raised up. There was a further fulfillment in the return from Babylonian exile.

> ²⁷who says to the watery deep, 'Be dry, and I will dry up your streams,'

God dried up the "watery deep" for Israel to cross the Red Sea. He will dry up the rivers before Israel when this new exodus occurs (this imagery is part of the Exodus motif).

> ²⁸who says of Cyrus, 'He is my shepherd and will accomplish all that I please; he will say of Jerusalem, "Let it be rebuilt," and of the temple, "Let its foundations be laid."'

The God who delivered Israel from Egypt calls Cyrus[11] "my shepherd." He will fulfill all God's pleasure, and he will say the word for Jerusalem to be rebuilt and the foundation of the temple to be laid. This looks ahead to a distant future and was fulfilled exactly (2 Chron. 36:23; Ezra 1:2–3; 6:3–4). The Jewish historian Josephus said that this passage was shown to Cyrus and it encouraged him to make his decrees to send the Jews back to rebuild their temple.[12] This was soon after Cyrus conquered Babylon in 539 B.C. Jerusalem had, and still has, an important place in God's plan.

b. God Will Use Cyrus To Restore Israel 45:1–13

> ¹"This is what the LORD says to his anointed, to Cyrus, whose right hand I take hold of to subdue nations before him and to strip kings of their armor, to open doors before him so that gates will not be shut:

God addresses Cyrus, letting us know that all his great victories were really God's victories. Up to this time, God's "anointed" included priests, kings, prophets, and patriarchs (see Ps. 105:10–15). Now God calls a polytheististic pagan king His "anointed" (Heb. *mᵉshiach*, "messiah"). Although Cyrus did not

---

[11] Isaiah now specifically names Cyrus (cf. 41:2). See introduction, p. 23.
[12] Josephus *Antiquities* 11.1–2.

know it, God by His Holy Spirit had set him apart and would be directing him to bring deliverance and restoration to Israel. To enable Cyrus to do this, God would take hold of his "right hand . . . to subdue nations," opening doors and gates before him. God used the people of Babylon to throw open the gates to the army of Cyrus in 539 B.C. and give Cyrus a triumphal entry, complete with palm branches.[13]

"To strip kings of their armor" was an Assyrian custom. Sennacherib did this to Mushezibk-Marduk, the rebel king of Babylonia. Isaiah surely would have known about the custom and the history. It was a public demonstration signifying kings being stripped of their power.

> ²I will go before you and will level the mountains; I will break down gates of bronze and cut through bars of iron.

Because God would personally "go before" Cyrus, rough places and other barriers would become smooth and even metal doors and bars would not be able to hinder his progress. The ancient Greek historian Herodotus said the gates of Babylon were made of bronze.[14]

> ³I will give you the treasures of darkness, riches stored in secret places, so that you may know that I am the LORD, the God of Israel, who summons you by name.

The people Cyrus conquered would not be able to hide their treasures from Cyrus. God wanted Cyrus to know that He is "the LORD, the God of Israel," who called him "by name" in advance. Jewish tradition says Daniel took this prophecy and showed it to Cyrus, and this encouraged Cyrus to give the proclamations found in 2 Chronicles 36:22–23 and Ezra 1:2–4.

> ⁴For the sake of Jacob my servant, of Israel my

---

[13] John E. McKenna, "Isaiah: Background," in *Old Testament Survey,* ed. William S. LaSor, David A. Hubbard, and Frederic W. Bush, 2d. ed. (Grand Rapids: Wm. B. Eerdmans, 1996), 282–83, points out that some "thoroughgoing theists . . . believe that Cyrus' name indicates an exilic date for chs. 40ff." But he also says that "the argument for multiple authorship from the mention of Cyrus is not entirely compelling."

[14] Joseph A. Alexander, *Commentary on the Prophecies of Isaiah,* 2 vols. in 1 (1875; reprint, Grand Rapids: Zondervan Publishing House, 1975), 2:178.

chosen, I summon you by name and bestow on you a title of honor, though you do not acknowledge me.

As a polytheist, Cyrus told the Babylonians that their gods had chosen him to deliver them from the misrule of Nabonidus and Belshazzar.[15] He did not know the one true God before he entered Babylon. He actually gave the Babylonian god Marduk credit for his victories.[16] But God was the one who truly commissioned him. Because God chose Israel and made Israel His servant, He would personally call Cyrus and name him as His anointed one, chosen to fulfill His purpose for Israel.

> [5]I am the LORD, and there is no other; apart from me there is no God. I will strengthen you, though you have not acknowledged me, [6]so that from the rising of the sun to the place of its setting men may know there is none besides me. I am the LORD, and there is no other.

God's purpose in calling Cyrus and restoring Israel was to bring universal recognition that He alone is God, "there is no other." The east and the west still need to know this.

> [7]I form the light and create darkness, I bring prosperity and create disaster; I, the LORD, do all these things.

The contrast here is between "light" and "darkness" on the one hand and "prosperity" (Heb. *shalom,* including well-being, health, wholeness, harmony, blessing, fulfillment, and prosperity, especially spiritual prosperity) and "disaster" (Heb. *ra'*) on the other. The Hebrew word *ra'* is a general word including calamity and anything disagreeable or undesirable. It is some-

---

[15]James B. Pritchard, ed., *Ancient Near Eastern Texts Relating to the Old Testament,* 3d ed. (Princeton: Princeton University Press, 1969), 316.

[16]The records of Cyrus state: "Marduk . . . on account of (the fact that) the sanctuaries of all their settlements were in ruins and the inhabitants of Sumer and Akkad had become like (living) dead, turned back (his) countenance, 'his' an[ger] [abated] and he had mercy (upon them). He scanned and looked (through) all the countries, searching for a righteous ruler willing to lead him (i.e. Marduk) (in the annual procession). (Then) he pronounced the name of Cyrus, king of Anshan, declared him (lit.: pronounced [his] name) to be(come) the ruler of all the world." Pritchard, *Ancient Near Eastern Texts,* 315.

times used of moral evil, but God is never the creator of moral evil. As a holy God, He does bring judgment, however; the judgment He sends may be severe, even disastrous.

It should also be noted that in the sixth century B.C., at or shortly after the time of Cyrus, Zoroaster (Zarathustra) began teaching a dualistic religion. Zoroaster claimed a good god controlled good and spirit, while a bad god controlled evil and material elements—as well as created the physical universe while the good god was not looking. This verse leaves no room for any such dualism.

> 8"You heavens above, rain down righteousness; let the clouds shower it down. Let the earth open wide, let salvation spring up, let righteousness grow with it; I, the LORD, have created it.

What God wants is to bring not judgment but salvation. He calls for the heavens to "rain down righteousness" and for the earth to open up to receive it so that together they may cause salvation and righteousness to "spring up." God is determined to accomplish this in His own way, for He alone creates. This anticipates what Isaiah says about the new way of life that results from the work of the Suffering Servant, the Messiah.

> 9"Woe to him who quarrels with his Maker, to him who is but a potsherd among the potsherds on the ground. Does the clay say to the potter, 'What are you making?' Does your work say, 'He has no hands'?

The "woe" is directed to Israelites who questioned God's ways, challenging His right to do as He wills. This may refer specifically to their disapproval of God choosing to use a Gentile like Cyrus to deliver them. Broken pottery on the ground has no right to challenge the potter for what he has done. Neither does the clay have a right to challenge or question him concerning what he intends to make or whether he has the "hands" (i.e., the skill or ability) to make it.

> 10Woe to him who says to his father, 'What have you begotten?' or to his mother, 'What have you brought to birth?'

The same principle applies to anyone who would question a man or a woman about the children they intend to have. ("What have you begotten" could also be translated, "What right do you have to beget children?"[17]) Some questions are improper. To ask God such a question is certainly improper. Those who say this have no trust or faith in the Lord.

> [11]"This is what the LORD says—the Holy One of Israel, and its Maker: Concerning things to come, do you question me about my children, or give me orders about the work of my hands?

Now the LORD applies the above principle to Israel. God is Israel's "Maker," Israel's Potter. The invitations to ask and command (see KJV) are clearly ironic; thus they appear as questions rather than statements in many contemporary versions, including the NIV. They mean Israel has no right to question God's purposes with respect to the events to come, for they are sons (Exod. 4:22) and He is the Father. Nor do they have the right to command Him nor give orders to Him with respect to His work, for they are the clay and He is the divine Potter. This does not mean they need to be afraid, for He has already demonstrated that He is a loving Father and a skillful Potter. They are safe in his hands.

> [12]It is I who made the earth and created mankind upon it. My own hands stretched out the heavens; I marshaled their starry hosts.

God has, in fact, demonstrated His ability and skill by His work in the creation of the earth, humankind, and the heavens with all the host of stars that are there because of His command. The use of the word "created" here emphasizes the uniqueness of His creation of human beings. We owe allegiance to Him by right of His creation.

> [13]I will raise up Cyrus in my righteousness: I will make all his ways straight. He will rebuild my city and set my exiles free, but not for a price or reward, says the LORD Almighty."

---

[17] George A. F. Knight, *Servant Theology* (Grand Rapids: Wm. B. Eerdmans, 1984), 93.

This same mighty God will prove His power by raising up Cyrus in a right way and making his paths straight. God will be the one directing him so that he will become a builder of Jerusalem and will set the people of Israel free—free to go back to their own land. Because God will move upon Cyrus, no one will need to ransom them.

c. God Will Save Israel 45:14–25

> **14This is what the LORD says: "The products of Egypt and the merchandise of Cush, and those tall Sabeans—they will come over to you and will be yours; they will trudge behind you, coming over to you in chains. They will bow down before you and plead with you, saying, 'Surely God is with you, and there is no other; there is no other god.'"**

The remainder of this chapter continues to declare something far greater than deliverance from Babylon. As a result of God's work of restoration, the goods and the people of nations who were once enemies will come to Israel—recognizing God is among them and that "there is no other God." Ethiopia (Cush) is now what is called the Sudan. The Sabeans were the people of what is now Yemen. They were known as a great commercial people, even trading with India. The chains of these peoples are chains they put on themselves, indicating they come willingly, submitting themselves to the LORD, bringing their wealth with them.

> **15Truly you are a God who hides himself, O God and Savior of Israel.**

Those who come from the Gentile nations will recognize the God of Israel as the Savior, commenting that in the past He had been hidden from them. As the context indicates, He had hidden himself in Israel, so the Gentiles didn't know Him; at the same time, He was revealing himself to Israel, active in a relationship with them. Even so, His plans are still a mystery to those who do not let the Spirit reveal Himself to them through the written Word, the Bible (cf. Luke 10:21 where "Jesus, full of joy through the Holy Spirit, said, 'I praise you, Father, Lord of heaven and earth, because you have hidden these things from the wise and learned, and revealed them to little children. Yes, Father, for this was your good pleasure.' ").

> ¹⁶**All the makers of idols will be put to shame and disgraced; they will go off into disgrace together. ¹⁷But Israel will be saved by the Lord with an everlasting salvation; you will never be put to shame or disgraced, to ages everlasting.**

"The makers of idols will be put to shame and disgraced," indicating humiliation. (This fits the time of Isaiah, about 700 B.C., not the later times.) In contrast, the Lord has an "everlasting salvation" for Israel, and they[18] "will never be put to shame or disgraced" once they enter into that salvation.

> ¹⁸**For this is what the Lord says—he who created the heavens, he is God; he who fashioned and made the earth, he founded it; he did not create it to be empty, but formed it to be inhabited—he says: "I am the Lord, and there is no other.**

The guarantee of that "everlasting salvation" (v. 17) is the fact that God is the Creator of the heavens and earth. And He did not create it for emptiness, but "to be inhabited."[19] He has not changed His original purpose.[20] He does not intend to destroy all the people on earth. Nor will He allow wicked, ruthless men to do so. He will restore his creation and will always have a people who will love and serve Him. There is no one else worthy of worship, for He alone is God. That "there is no other" serves notice on the idolaters that ultimately they will be without a god when the Lord brings things to fulfillment.

> ¹⁹**I have not spoken in secret, from somewhere in a land of darkness; I have not said to Jacob's descendants, 'Seek me in vain.' I, the Lord, speak the truth; I declare what is right.**

---

[18]"You" (v. 17) is plural and refers to every individual Israelite who has been saved.
[19]Adam was the first man (1 Cor. 15:45). The earth was not inhabited before that time.
[20]Timothy Munyon, "The Creation of the Universe and Humankind," in *Systematic Theology*, ed. Stanley M. Horton, rev. ed. (Springfield, Mo.: Logion Press, 1995), 220–22.

God has openly confirmed His purpose. He never told Jacob's descendants to seek Him "in vain" (in emptiness or meaninglessness). He always conceived His word to be plain: In contrast to the pagan oracles, the false prophets, and the predictions of astrologers and other dabblers in the occult, what God says comes from His righteousness and is always right.

> **20"Gather together and come; assemble, you fugitives from the nations. Ignorant are those who carry about idols of wood, who pray to gods that cannot save.**

The call is for all the "fugitives [escapees, refugees] from the nations" to draw near to the LORD. Some consider the fugitives to be Israelites coming out of the nations; others take them to be Gentiles. Some apply this to nations that enter the Millennium: They have turned away from idols to seek the LORD and they recognize that Gentiles who carry images of wood are "ignorant" and do not know what they are doing. They realize that they have prayed to a god that by its very nature "cannot save." God's purpose was always for Israel to evangelize other nations, going forth in His name.

> **21Declare what is to be, present it—let them take counsel together. Who foretold this long ago, who declared it from the distant past? Was it not I, the LORD? And there is no God apart from me, a righteous God and a Savior; there is none but me.**

With irony, God again challenges the idol worshipers to "take counsel together" (see 41:21–22). They must admit that God alone has declared his eternal purposes of salvation "from the distant past." He is righteous and therefore He is to be trusted. He alone is a Savior. The world has no other hope.

> **22"Turn to me and be saved, all you ends of the earth; for I am God, and there is no other.**

Now God reveals that His salvation is not just for Israel, but for the "ends of the earth." He revealed His purpose to Abraham to bless all the families (nations) of the earth (Gen. 12:3; 18:18; cf. Pss. 22:27–28; 65:5). That has never changed.

Too many in the world are still looking in the wrong direction. Everyone needs to turn to the LORD and be saved.

> ²³By myself I have sworn, my mouth has uttered in all integrity a word that will not be revoked: Before me every knee will bow; by me every tongue will swear.

God made this same kind of oath to confirm his promise to Abraham (Gen. 22:16). That word is a righteous word from a truly righteous God, a faithful God, a God we can depend on. It will accomplish His purpose: "Every knee will bow" in submission and "every tongue . . . swear" allegiance to God. The New Testament makes it clear that the promise comes through Jesus and involves recognizing Him as Lord (Rom. 14:10– 11;[21] Phil. 2:10–11).

> ²⁴They will say of me, 'In the LORD alone are righteousness and strength.'" All who have raged against him will come to him and be put to shame.

Only in the LORD is true righteousness and the strength to live by it. He alone is our source. We can come into His presence, for He is accessible; we have a new and living (resurrected) Way, our Lord Jesus (Heb. 10:19–22). We stand in His righteousness, not our own (cf. Phil. 3:9). In contrast, all those who are angry with God (because they worship idols or want only material things) "will come to Him and be put to shame." This may mean they will repent or at least have opportunity to repent.

> ²⁵But in the LORD all the descendants of Israel will be found righteous and will exult.

But the "descendants of Israel" will not shrink back in shame. They will be justified, vindicated, treated as righteous, and will praise God and glory in the LORD, fulfilling their destiny (cf. Rom. 11:26).

---

[21] Paul quotes here from the Septuagint version.

STUDY QUESTIONS

1. What assurance does God give Israel and why?
2. In what sense does God make Israel His witnesses?
3. What will God do to bring about an exodus from Babylon?
4. What evidence is there for an exodus from Babylon in Isaiah's day?
5. Why was it necessary for God to judge Israel?
6. What shows God had not changed His plan for Israel in spite of their failures?
7. What will be the result of the outpouring of God's Spirit?
8. How does Isaiah contrast the true God with idols in chapter 44?
9. How will God display His glory in Israel?
10. How is God going to use Cyrus?
11. What is God going to do for Cyrus and why?
12. What does God say of himself in chapter 45?
13. Why did some Israelites question God, and what was His response to them?

D. Babylon's Fall 46:1–48:22

1. THE LORD SUPERIOR TO BABYLON'S DEITIES 46:1–13

> ¹Bel bows down, Nebo stoops low; their idols are borne by beasts of burden. The images that are carried about are burdensome, a burden for the weary.

Isaiah now returns to his own day, to the time when Sennacherib destroyed Babylon.[1] Cyrus is no longer in view. Cyrus honored and worshiped the gods of Babylon instead of carrying them off as Sennacherib did. Bel was the chief god of

---

[1] Oswald T. Allis, "Book of Isaiah," in *Wycliffe Bible Encyclopedia* (Chicago: Moody Press, 1975), 1:857.

Babylon. Nebo (or Nabu, Bel's son) was the god of writing, wisdom, learning, and astronomy. The state letters of Assyria mention Bel (usually equated with Marduk, also called Merodach) and Nebo (Nabu) more frequently than their own god, Ashur. Often Assyrian kings used such phrases as "with the help of Bel and Nebo" or "May Bel and Nebo bless my Lord" without any reference to any other god, just as if they were the chief gods of Assyria.[2]

Even so, Babylon's priests controlled the city and caused trouble for the Assyrians, especially Sennacherib. In 691 B.C., as payment for aid against him, they opened the treasury of the great Temple Esagila and sent Bel-Marduk's gold, silver, and jewels to Elam.[3] Elamites and others gave Sennacherib his first defeat.[4] This roused Sennacherib against the priests and he decided to get rid of the problem by destroying the city and its temples completely, as an inscription of Esarhaddon confirms.[5]

Sennacherib's opportunity came two years later, when the Elamite king was disabled by paralysis, and internal troubles kept his army at home. By the end of November the Assyrian siege engines broke through Babylon's defenses. Sennacherib's army mercilessly filled the public squares with corpses, and leveled the city.

Then, because he wanted to destroy the power of the Babylonian priesthood, he encouraged his soldiers to take gods from the temples and smash them. Only the images of the great gods of Babylon—Bel-Marduk and Nebo—escaped. These Sennacherib carried off to Assyria, where they remained until Esarhaddon came to the throne.

Babylon was too important, however, to be forgotten and left in its ruined condition. Esarhaddon's first great concern, after he had established himself on Assyria's throne, was to restore the prosperity of Babylonia. His records state: "He conciliated the population of that region by restoring to their former position

---

[2]Cf. Daniel David Luckenbill, *Ancient Records of Assyria and Babylonia*, 2 vols. (Chicago: University of Chicago Press, 1926–27), 2:99, 113, 200, 225, 233.

[3]Daniel David Luckenbill, *The Annals of Sennacherib* (Chicago: University of Chicago Press, 1924), 42.

[4]William Foxwell Albright, "The Biblical Period," in *The Jews*, ed. Louis Finkelstein (New York: Harper & Brothers, 1949), 1:43.

[5]Luckenbill, *Ancient Records,* 2:255.

the humiliated gods of Babylon. He lifted the royal city out of its wasteness and ruin, and made it the proud abode of Nebo and Marduk [Bel]."[6] According to Herodotus, the great image of Bel was not destroyed until the time of Xerxes.

Even at a later age Babylon was remembered as one of "the most renowned and strongest cities of Assyria."[7]

> [2]They stoop and bow down together; unable to rescue the burden, they themselves go off into captivity.

The great gods of Babylon "stoop," cringing before the Assyrians, unable to help themselves. They "bow down," or collapse; that is, they are taken down by the Assyrians. (Or, the meaning may be that the idols fall before the Assyrian conquerors the way worshipers fell before them—suggesting that the men who conquered Babylon were greater than Bel and Nebo.) The Assyrians then loaded the gods onto weary beasts of burden. Bel and Nebo could not rescue themselves or save themselves from captivity. Thus, Babylon's gods became a liability rather than saviors when their worshipers got in trouble.

> [3]"Listen to me, O house of Jacob, all you who remain of the house of Israel, you whom I have upheld since you were conceived, and have carried since your birth. [4]Even to your old age and gray hairs I am he, I am he who will sustain you. I have made you and I will carry you; I will sustain you and I will rescue you.

God commands Israel to listen as He draws a lesson from this for them—for the remnant. He as much as says, "You never had to carry me; in fact, I carried you—from the time you were born—and I will carry you as long as you live" (cf. Deut. 1:31; 32:11–12; Ps. 28:9; Isa. 40:31; 63:9). God will not only take up the load, carry them and sustain them, but He will also rescue them—something the idol gods could not do even for themselves.

---

[6]Ibid., 2:252; see also 2:203.

[7]Herodotus, *History*, trans. George Rawlinson, ed. Manuel Komroff (New York: Tudor Publishing Co., 1928), 66. Nabonidus spoke of Ashurbanipal as "my predecessor," recognizing Babylon as the successor of Nineveh. Charles Boutflower, *The Book of Isaiah (Chapters I–XXXIX) in the Light of the Assyrian Monuments* (London: Society for Promoting Christian Knowledge, 1930), 163.

> 5"To whom will you compare me or count me equal? To whom will you liken me that we may be compared?

Clearly, the LORD is not like any of the false gods in any way. He has nothing in common with them. How can the Creator of the universe be represented by a man-made image?[8]

> 6Some pour out gold from their bags and weigh out silver on the scales; they hire a goldsmith to make it into a god, and they bow down and worship it. 7They lift it to their shoulders and carry it; they set it up in its place, and there it stands. From that spot it cannot move. Though one cries out to it, it does not answer; it cannot save him from his troubles.

Again Isaiah describes with irony the manufacture of idols, this time great pagan gods such as Bel or Nebo. It is made of a lavish amount of gold and silver—"from their bags," weighed out, leaving some behind in the bag. A hired goldsmith (like the woodsman; see 44:16,17) will make a portion into a god and the portion left behind, which is no different, will be put to other uses. Thus the "god" is just so much metal. Although people fall down before it in worship, they also have to "lift it to their shoulders" to get it to its temple and stand it in its place. Then "it cannot move" from where it is set. And no matter how a person cries out to it, "it does not answer; it cannot save." How foolish is the worship of such an idol! It is a waste of gold and silver (cf. a similar rhetorical description in 44:14–21).

> 8"Remember this, fix it in mind, take it to heart, you rebels.

To apostate rebels in Israel God emphasizes what He has said about such idolatry as well as what He is about to say. Today we do not make gold and silver idols, but many of us may lavish our money on things that could become like gods to us.

> 9Remember the former things, those of long ago; I am God, and there is no other; I am God, and there is none like me.

---

[8]John R. Higgins, "God's Inspired Word," in *Systematic Theology,* ed. Stanley M. Horton, rev. ed. (Springfield, Mo.: Logion Press, 1995), 65.

The former events in Israel's history show the Lord alone is God and "no other" is like Him. He is still and always will be the "I Am" (Exod. 3:14).

> **10I make known the end from the beginning, from ancient times, what is still to come. I say: My purpose will stand, and I will do all that I please.**

From the beginning, God has declared "the end," the outcome, of His plan. His plan "will stand"; it will be carried out. He will do all He has purposed to do.

> **11From the east I summon a bird of prey; from a far-off land, a man to fulfill my purpose. What I have said, that will I bring about; what I have planned, that will I do.**

Most commentators suppose the "bird of prey" ("ravenous bird," KJV), picturing a ruthless conqueror, is Cyrus. However, Cyrus destroyed no Mesopotamian cities and he honored the gods of Babylon. The description suits better a conquering Assyrian[9] and likely refers to Sennacherib, who was ruthless and who did carry off the gods of Babylon in Isaiah's own day.[10] The Assyrians were God's "rod" (10:5).

> **12Listen to me, you stubborn-hearted, you who are far from righteousness.**

Those who are "stubborn" (strong or powerful) of heart, that is, stubborn in their minds, are "far from righteousness" (cf. Rom. 12:3); yet God wants them to listen. It takes a tender heart and a willing mind to receive God's righteousness.

> **13I am bringing my righteousness near, it is not far away; and my salvation will not be delayed. I will grant salvation to Zion, my splendor to Israel.**

God will make it easy for them. He will bring near his righteousness, so they do not need to be far from it. He promises to

---

[9]Armand Kaminka, *Le Prophète Isaïe* (Paris: Librairie Orientaliste, Paul Geuthner, 1925), 53.

[10]Luckenbill, *Ancient Records*, 2:203.

give "salvation to Zion" (Heb. *b*ᵉ*tsiyyon*, "in Zion"). God looks on Israel as His "splendor." He wants them restored to the beauty and glory of His image. This becomes a reality for us also as we "all reflect the Lord's glory, [and] are being transformed into his likeness with ever-increasing glory, which comes from the Lord, who is the Spirit" (2 Cor. 3:18).

2. No Hope For Babylon 47:1–15

1"Go down, sit in the dust, Virgin Daughter of Babylon; sit on the ground without a throne, Daughter of the Babylonians. No more will you be called tender or delicate.

Isaiah now comes back to his own day and gives another prophecy of the destruction of Babylon in 689 B.C. by Sennacherib.[11] It is chronologically before chapter 46. Babylon is called the "daughter of the Chaldeans" (KJV) not because Chaldeans founded the city but because they controlled it during much of Isaiah's life. There is a strong resemblance between 47:1–15 and 14:4–21.[12] There is also the same unexpectedness, suddenness, and completeness of doom that characterizes the description of Babylon's fall in chapter 13. Sitting "in the dust" speaks of dethronement and dispossession. Calling Babylon a "virgin" implies that it had not been destroyed and did not expect to be destroyed.[13] This could not have been said of Babylon in Cyrus's day, for ancient records show that Sennacherib's destruction of the city was not forgotten. The Babylonians, in fact, used that as an excuse for destroying Nineveh in 612 B.C.[14]

The Assyrians did not reduce Babylonia to a province at first, but recognized it as a subject kingdom. In 700 B.C., they were still treating the city of Babylon with respect, making it one of their capitals, and even sending some of their captured spoils to it. But no longer would it enjoy an easy life like a princess.

---

[11]Allis, "Book of Isaiah," 1:857.
[12]George L. Robinson, *The Book of Isaiah*, rev. ed. (Grand Rapids: Baker Book House, 1954), 137.
[13]In Heb., cities are feminine.
[14]James Frederick McCurdy, *History, Prophecy and the Monuments* (New York: Macmillan Co., 1911), 2:329.

> ²Take millstones and grind flour; take off your veil. Lift up your skirts, bare your legs, and wade through the streams.

Babylon's inhabitants would become like the lowest slaves, working hard turning heavy millstones, dressing poorly, and having to do such things as wading through the rivers or canals of Mesopotamia. Nothing like this happened when Cyrus took Babylon and made it one of his capitals.[15] Since the passage is a personification of Babylon itself, "wade through the streams" may refer to the fact that Sennacherib, in destroying it, made it a swamp, obliging anyone wanting to cross its site to wade (cf. 14:23; 21:1).

> ³Your nakedness will be exposed and your shame uncovered. I will take vengeance; I will spare no one."

God's vengeance is divine justice (cf. Deut. 32:35; Rom. 12:19). It will bring shame to the Babylonians. No one will be spared.

> ⁴Our Redeemer—the LORD Almighty is his name—is the Holy One of Israel.

Behind the judgment on Babylon is Israel's Kinsman-Redeemer. He hates sin but He loves his people. The threefold reference to the LORD ("Redeemer . . . Almighty . . . Holy One") emphasizes His power and His concern over Israel.

> ⁵"Sit in silence, go into darkness, Daughter of the Babylonians; no more will you be called queen of kingdoms.

Babylon, in Isaiah's day, was considered "queen of kingdoms," but its destruction by Sennacherib would leave it silent. Its glory would become darkness.

> ⁶I was angry with my people and desecrated my inheritance; I gave them into your hand, and you showed them no mercy. Even on the aged you laid a very heavy yoke.

God's anger with His people caused Him to use the Assyrians

---

[15]See James B. Pritchard, ed., *Ancient Near Eastern Texts Relating to the Old Testament*, 2d ed. (Princeton: Princeton University Press, 1955), 306, 316.

as His rod (cf. 10:5–6). Their lack of mercy on exiles, "even on the aged," reflects the conditions in Babylon shortly after 701 B.C., when Sennacherib drove out the Chaldean Merodach-Baladan. Then he brought in the 200,150 survivors of his campaign against Judah. The Assyrian hand under Sennacherib was heavier than what it would be under Nebuchadnezzar.[16] In Babylon itself Hezekiah's alliance with Merodach-Baladan might have made the lot of the Jewish captives even worse. The native Babylonians had no love for the Chaldeans or their friends. Sennacherib was in pursuit of Merodach-Baladan and he would not be likely to show kindness toward Jewish captives in Babylon. He would be more likely to treat them as allies of the enemy. In the later Babylonian exile under Nebuchadnezzar the Jews actually prospered.

> ⁷You said, 'I will continue forever—the eternal queen!' But you did not consider these things or reflect on what might happen.

In 700 B.C., Babylon in its pride supposed nothing could ever change its exalted state. It deified itself as the "eternal queen," a title Babylonians gave to a goddess. "I will continue" is the Hebrew *'ehyeh*, translated "I am" in Exodus 3:14. Babylon refused to consider the consequences of its immoral, corrupt conduct as well as its treatment of the captives. The Babylon world-city of the Book of Revelation will be like that (see Rev. 18:7).

> ⁸"Now then, listen, you wanton creature, lounging in your security and saying to yourself, 'I am, and there is none besides me. I will never be a widow or suffer the loss of children.' ⁹Both of these will overtake you in a moment, on a single day: loss of children and widowhood. They will come upon you in full measure, in spite of your many sorceries and all your potent spells.

Pleasure-loving Babylon exalted itself as if it were a god or goddess. Its unexpected fall is compared to a mother made a widow and robbed of her children. This was to happen "in a

---

[16]Muilenburg admits this. James Muilenburg, "The Book of Isaiah, Chapters 40–66," in *The Interpreter's Bible* (Nashville: Abingdon Press, 1956), 5:547.

moment" and cannot be applied to the takeover by Cyrus in any sense. He did not humiliate the city or shame it in any way.[17] Since the people threw open the gates and welcomed Cyrus, there must have been a strong anti-Nabonidus party in the city for some time. What happened in 539 B.C. was not completely unforeseen. Even so, Sennacherib's destruction of Babylon was a shock, both to Babylon and to the rest of the world. Isaiah said it would come in spite of the multitude of occultic practices they trusted in.

> [10]You have trusted in your wickedness and have said, 'No one sees me.' Your wisdom and knowledge mislead you when you say to yourself, 'I am, and there is none besides me.'

Isaiah calls Babylon's religion "wickedness." They were led astray because they had false "knowledge"[18] that perverted them and made them think it was wisdom to think of Babylon as a god. By saying "No one sees me," the Babylonians were denying there was any moral authority above them. Without realizing it they were saying their gods were without power.

> [11]Disaster will come upon you, and you will not know how to conjure it away. A calamity will fall upon you that you cannot ward off with a ransom; a catastrophe you cannot foresee will suddenly come upon you.

Disastrous judgment would come on Babylon and they would not be able to keep it away by their magic charms or by the payment of a ransom. Unexpected desolation would "suddenly come" on the city.

> [12]"Keep on, then, with your magic spells and with your many sorceries, which you have labored at since childhood. Perhaps you will succeed, perhaps you will cause terror. [13]All the counsel you have received has only worn you out! Let your astrologers come forward, those

---

[17]Pritchard, *Ancient Near Eastern Texts*, 306, 315.

[18]The Septuagint translates the Heb. *da'ath* ("knowledge") as the Gk. *porneia,* a general term for all kinds of habitual sexual sin. Compare this picture with that of the Babylon world system in Rev. 18.

stargazers who make predictions month by month, let them save you from what is coming upon you.

Babylon in Isaiah's day was the world's foremost center of pagan, astrological religion. They divided the sky into quarters to observe the movements of the stars in order to make their predictions. With irony Isaiah challenges them to "keep on" making magic spells and using all the supposed occultic powers of their professional religionists to try to save the city. But their religious practices do not help them. Rather, they tire them out. Today people are spending billions of dollars making new medicines and trying to bring a better world through science. The results are temporary and diseases thought to be conquered are coming back in a stronger form. People trusting in science are little better off than those who dabble in the occult.

> [14] Surely they are like stubble; the fire will burn them up. They cannot even save themselves from the power of the flame. Here are no coals to warm anyone; here is no fire to sit by.

They will all be cast into the fire, swallowed up in a holocaust. This accords well with 37:19 concerning the gods Sennacherib smashed and burned in 689 B.C.

> [15] That is all they can do for you—these you have labored with and trafficked with since childhood. Each of them goes on in his error; there is not one that can save you.

Those Babylon "trafficked with" are merchants who would go their way and leave the city to suffer its judgment. These merchants were nations such as Elam and Media, whom she had formerly hired to do her fighting for her. When Sennacherib destroyed Babylon, her former allies were scattered in all directions. That destruction may be taken as a type that points to the overthrow of the Babylonian world system in the end times (Rev. 17:1 to 19:3).

3. PROPHECIES WITNESS TO THE TRUE GOD 48:1–19

> [1] "Listen to this, O house of Jacob, you who are

> called by the name of Israel and come from the line of Judah, you who take oaths in the name of the LORD and invoke the God of Israel—but not in truth or righteousness—

Now Isaiah addresses Israel but the focus is on Judah. They call themselves "Israel," but they are still "Jacob"—"deceiver, supplanter." They make "oaths in the name of the LORD" and swear by the God of Israel, "but not in truth" (or faithfulness) and not in the righteousness that lines up with God's Word. They do not mean what they say. Their religion is only a form, an empty ritual. They are little better than the Babylonians who were deluded by their false gods.[19]

> ²you who call yourselves citizens of the holy city and rely on the God of Israel—the LORD Almighty is his name:

Now the focus is narrowed to the people of Jerusalem who call it a "holy city," trusting its privileges. They lean on the God of Israel for support, recognizing Him as the LORD of the armies of heaven. However, the people were not holy and they were taking their relationship to God for granted.

> ³I foretold the former things long ago, my mouth announced them and I made them known; then suddenly I acted, and they came to pass.

In former times, God gave prophecies and fulfilled them suddenly and decisively. This shows that the fulfillments did not come by mere chance, but were evidences of the power of God. Israel was without excuse for attributing them to an idol.

> ⁴For I knew how stubborn you were; the sinews of your neck were iron, your forehead was bronze. ⁵Therefore I told you these things long ago; before they happened I announced them to you so that you could not say, 'My idols

---

[19]Modern form critics try to split up this chap., supposing that a passage should not mix both salvation and judgment. However, Isaiah typically shows realistic awareness of both.

did them; my wooden image and metal god ordained them.'

God knew how obstinate, quarrelsome, and opinionated the people of Israel were (cf. Deut. 9:27; Isa. 30:1; 65:2; Ezek. 2:4; 3:7). Often they refused to humble themselves. This is one of the reasons God prophesied future events, to keep His people from giving credit to idols for causing them to happen. Fulfilled prophecy is an important evidence of the truth of God's Word and is a witness to the fact He alone is God.

> 6You have heard these things; look at them all. Will you not admit them? "From now on I will tell you of new things, of hidden things unknown to you.

The people had heard what God did in the past and needed to admit that what He said was true. But now God was showing them some "new things," prophecies previously unknown, prophecies no human being by their own reasoning could have foreseen. As we read on in Isaiah, these include truths about the Messiah and the new heavens and new earth (52:13 to 53:12; 65:17).

> 7They are created now, and not long ago; you have not heard of them before today. So you cannot say, 'Yes, I knew of them.'

The word "create" always has God as its subject in the Bible. He is promises new things that only He can do, lest they arrogantly say that they knew them before; that is, lest they fail to recognize them as supernatural. Again God is implying that they were without excuse in their rebellion.

> 8You have neither heard nor understood; from of old your ear has not been open. Well do I know how treacherous you are; you were called a rebel from birth.

The people of Israel "neither heard nor understood." They were not open to the truth God gave them. God knew how rebellious they were from the time He brought the nation into being (Deut. 31:27).

> ⁹For my own name's sake I delay my wrath; for the sake of my praise I hold it back from you, so as not to cut you off.

God had been patient for His own name's sake, that is, because of His own nature as a gracious, loving God. So that He might be praised He had not destroyed His people, even though death was the just reward for sin. This fits the context of 700 B.C. when, in fulfillment of Isaiah's prophecy, Sennacherib left Jerusalem without conquering it.

> ¹⁰See, I have refined you, though not as silver; I have tested you in the furnace of affliction.

God again calls attention to Israel's beginning as a nation. He had "refined" His people in a furnace, not of fire, as silver is refined, but "of affliction" (in the misery they suffered as slaves in Egypt). Egypt is regularly referred to as a "furnace" (Deut. 4:20; 1 Kings 8:51; Jer. 11:4), whereas Babylon is not. In fact, Babylonians resettled the exiles but did not enslave them (cf. Jer. 29:28). The exiles prospered in Babylon (see comment on Isa. 42:22).

> ¹¹For my own sake, for my own sake, I do this. How can I let myself be defamed? I will not yield my glory to another.

God does what He does (the new prophecies of verse 6) for His own sake. He does not intend to let His name (and character) "be defamed," nor will He give His glory to another (including Israel).

> ¹²"Listen to me, O Jacob, Israel, whom I have called: I am he; I am the first and I am the last. ¹³My own hand laid the foundations of the earth, and my right hand spread out the heavens; when I summon them, they all stand up together.

God challenges the "Jacob" people to be "Israel" as His chosen people and to listen to Him. He is the "I Am." He is the Eternal One who is "the first and . . . the last." He does not change. He was there at the beginning, and He will never come to an end. He founded the earth by His "own hand" (His power) and "spread out the heavens." He is greater than the earth and the heavens. They stand and continue their existence because of His word (cf. Col. 3:17).

> ¹⁴"Come together, all of you, and listen: Which of [the idols] has foretold these things? The LORD's chosen ally will carry out his purpose against Babylon; his arm will be against the Babylonians.

The call is still to Israel. Let them assemble and listen. No idol has prophesied what is going to happen to Babylon. Some apply what is prophesied here to Cyrus, but this is not necessary. What is meant is that the LORD loves Israel, and to show His love, He will execute His purpose in Babylon. The LORD's arm of power "will be against the Babylonians" (Chaldeans).

> ¹⁵I, even I, have spoken; yes, I have called him. I will bring him, and he will succeed in his mission.

"Him" refers to Israel.[20] God has called Israel, and will make their way prosper in order to accomplish His purpose of blessing and redemption.

> ¹⁶"Come near me and listen to this: "From the first announcement I have not spoken in secret; at the time it happens, I am there." And now the Sovereign LORD has sent me, with His Spirit.

The LORD again calls His people to "come near . . . and listen." God has made His prophecies publicly through a succession of prophets, for He has been present with His people. Then the Messiah speaks. The LORD has sent Him and has sent His Spirit. (Some commentators take this to refer to Isaiah rather than to the Messiah.)

> ¹⁷This is what the LORD says—your Redeemer, the Holy One of Israel: "I am the LORD your God, who teaches you what is best for you, who directs you in the way you should go.

---

[20]Joseph A. Alexander, *Commentary on the Prophecies of Isaiah* (Grand Rapids: Zondervan Publishing House, 1953), 2:217.

God again declares who He is to Israel. He is their Kinsman-Redeemer who will deliver them and set them free. Yet, He is the Holy One who must deal with their sin. He is also the covenant-keeping LORD, *Yahweh,* their God, the One who teaches them "what is best" for them, that is, how to be useful (or effective). He leads them in the right way. Christians whose lives are ineffective need to hear this message and follow Christ anew.

> **18If only you had paid attention to my commands, your peace would have been like a river, your righteousness like the waves of the sea. 19Your descendants would have been like the sand, your children like its numberless grains; their name would never be cut off nor destroyed from before me."**

God wants them to listen to His commands, for then their peace and well-being would be everflowing "like a river," their righteousness would be continuous and powerful "like the waves of the sea," and their descendants would be the fulfillment of the promise that they would be as numerous as the grains of sand (Gen. 22:17; 32:12; 41:49). Israel's name, that is, its character and nature as a nation, "would never be cut off nor destroyed." Israel will live on in the light of God's presence.

4. A Command To Flee From Babylon 48:20–21

> **20Leave Babylon, flee from the Babylonians! Announce this with shouts of joy and proclaim it. Send it out to the ends of the earth; say, "The LORD has redeemed his servant Jacob."**

The command to flee usually means to flee quickly, especially as fugitives escaping for their lives. It corresponds with 13:14, which indicates that foreigners who flee from Babylon would escape the fate of the Babylonians. There was no reason for Jews to flee from Babylonia on the eve of the entrance of Cyrus into the city.[21] There was, however, every reason for them to flee on the eve of its destruction by Sennacherib. For then Sennach-

---

[21]Cyrus was an enlightened ruler. Cf. William O. E. Oesterly, *A History of Israel* (Oxford, England: Clarendon Press, 1951), 2:64.

erib's anger was directed at the Babylonians. Esarhaddon's records state that people did flee at that time.²²

The command is plural, "You flee!" All the exiles are to leave with shouts of joy and declare the LORD's redemption of Jacob (Israel) as His servant prepares for what follows in chapters 49 to 57.

> ²¹They did not thirst when he led them through the deserts; he made water flow for them from the rock; he split the rock and water gushed out.

Their return is compared to the Exodus from Egypt, when Moses struck the rock with his rod and "water gushed out" (Num. 20:11; cf. Exod. 17:6). God will care for His people in a supernatural way.

5. No Peace For The Wicked 48:22

> ²²"There is no peace," says the LORD, "for the wicked."

Isaiah concludes this section of the Book with a warning from the LORD that coming back to Judah would not be enough. They must repent and come back to God. There is "no peace," no God-given well-being, for "the wicked," the unrepentant transgressor. Guilt still robs people of peace. People today need to do more than come back to church.

STUDY QUESTIONS

1. What lesson does God draw from Sennacherib's capture of the images of Bel and Nebo?
2. How is God contrasted to idols in chapter 46?
3. Who is the "bird of prey" from the east and how will God use him?
4. Why is Babylon called a "Virgin Daughter"?
5. What judgment does God prophesy on Babylon?
6. What has Babylon been trusting in?

---

²²Daniel David Luckenbill, *Ancient Records of Assyria and Babylonia*, 2 vols. (Chicago: University of Chicago Press, 1926–27), 2:245; see also 225, 244.

7. What will happen to the things Babylon trusts in?
8. For what reasons did God give prophecies to Israel?
9. Why did God delay His wrath and at the same time refine Israel?
10. How is God going to use Israel to help accomplish His purpose of blessing and redemption?
11. What evidence is there that people did flee from Babylon in Isaiah's day?

VII. REDEMPTION AND THE SUFFERING SERVANT 49:1–55:13

Isaiah now begins a new section where the Servant of the LORD, the Messiah, is exalted. He will bring a greater deliverance than the deliverance from Egypt and from Babylon. He will actually bring a deliverance from sin. Nothing more is said of Babylon or Cyrus or of the conflict with pagan gods and occult practices. He now continues to explain God's plan.

A. The Servant Brings Restoration 49:1–50:11

1. GOD'S CHOSEN SERVANT 49:1–7

¹Listen to me, you islands; hear this, you distant nations: Before I was born the LORD called me; from my birth he has made mention of my name.

In another court scene, the Servant-Messiah[1] calls on all the peoples of the world to pay attention. What He is about to announce is of extreme importance to the Gentiles. Isaiah views the Messiah here as the head or representative of ideal Israel. He is called from the womb (see Matt. 1:20–23; Luke 1:31–32). He is also God's Son. Naming Him before His birth indicates

---

[1] This is the second Servant Song; see 42:1.

God's love. It also calls attention to Him as the God-sent Messiah. *Yahweh* is the first word of the Hebrew sentence, which gives it emphasis: The Messiah's conception is God's work, not man's. He has not changed His eternal plan or His purpose to save and bless.

> ²He made my mouth like a sharpened sword, in the shadow of his hand he hid me; he made me into a polished arrow and concealed me in his quiver.

The LORD who called His Servant prepared Him as a weapon. His word will be as effective as "a sharpened sword" (cf. Eph. 6:17; Heb. 4:12; Rev. 19:15). Like "a polished arrow" He is held close in God's quiver, that is, in intimacy with the Father, and reserved for the future, when He will be effective and irresistible. In this way Jesus was quietly prepared during the first thirty years of His life.

> ³He said to me, "You are my servant, Israel, in whom I will display my splendor.

God names the Servant "Israel." The Servant personifies ideal Israel, summing up in himself the servanthood that God intended for Israel.² Thus, when natural Israel fails, the Servant becomes the antitype of Jacob (cf. 2:5; 27:6; 41:8) as He becomes God's Israel, God's Prince and Warrior. God's purpose in using Him is to bring glory to himself as the Servant displays the divine splendor of God. Consequently, as Jesus faced the cross He prayed, "'Father, the time has come. Glorify your Son, that your Son may glorify you'" (John 17:1).

> ⁴But I said, "I have labored to no purpose; I have spent my strength in vain and for nothing. Yet what is due me is in the LORD's hand, and my reward is with my God."

The Servant has spent His strength and the result has been emptiness, nothingness. He has had little results among His own nation. He cried out "'O unbelieving and perverse gener-

---

²F. Duane Lindsey, *The Servant Songs* (Chicago: Moody Press, 1985), 66. Note that "Israel" was the name of an individual (Jacob) before it became the name of the nation. National Israel cannot be meant here, for this Servant has a mission *to* Israel (see v. 5).

ation . . . how long shall I stay with you? How long shall I put up with you?' "(Matt. 17:17). And again, " 'O Jerusalem, Jerusalem, you who kill the prophets and stone those sent to you, how often I have longed to gather your children together, as a hen gathers her chicks under her wings, but you were not willing' " (Matt. 23:37). In the face of apparent failure the Messiah feels discouragement. Yet He believes the Father will provide due justice[3] and recompense for His work (cf. 53:10). This is the human side of the Servant, whose true humanity felt what we feel.

> [5]And now the LORD says—he who formed me in the womb to be his servant to bring Jacob back to him and gather Israel to himself, for I am honored in the eyes of the LORD and my God has been my strength—

Now the Messiah is clearly distinguished from Israel. God formed Him "in the womb" (specifically, Mary's). He is the Suffering Servant who will bring wandering Israel back to the LORD. God honors Him and is His strength. He will be effective. Jewish believers constituted the first Church; and a remnant will be restored as part of the Church in connection with our Lord's second coming.

> [6]he says: "It is too small a thing for you to be my servant to restore the tribes of Jacob and bring back those of Israel I have kept. I will also make you a light for the Gentiles, that you may bring my salvation to the ends of the earth."

The restoration involves conversion and salvation. But it is not enough "to restore" Israel from their degradation and estrangement. The Messiah is also appointed to be "a light for the Gentiles." He is "to *be*" (Heb. *lihyoth*), not merely "bring" (as NIV), God's salvation to the whole world (Luke 2:32; Acts 13:47; 26:23). Jesus gave the Great Commission for all believers—Jew and Gentile—to spread the good news that this salvation has arrived (Matt. 24:14; 28:19–20).

---

[3]The Heb. for "what is due me" is *mishpati:* "my justice," or "my cause" (RSV), or "my right" (NRSV), or "my case" (Jewish Publication Society).

> [7]This is what the LORD says—the Redeemer and Holy One of Israel—to him who was despised and abhorred by the nation, to the servant of rulers: "Kings will see you and rise up, princes will see and bow down, because of the LORD, who is faithful, the Holy One of Israel, who has chosen you."

God is still Israel's "Redeemer and Holy One." Even though Israel as a nation would despise the Messiah and even abhor Him, yet kings and princes will arise to acknowledge Him and "bow down" to worship the Lord, recognizing that the God of Israel chose the Messiah. He is the solution to their problems (cf. 1 Cor. 1:23–24).

2. RESTORATION BRINGS REJOICING 49:8–26

> [8]This is what the LORD says: "In the time of my favor I will answer you, and in the day of salvation I will help you; I will keep you and will make you to be a covenant for the people, to restore the land and to reassign its desolate inheritances,

Still addressing the Messiah, the verbs here are prophetic. The time of God's favor is the "day of salvation" when God will "answer," "help," and "keep" (cf. 2 Cor. 6:2 where Paul applies this to the times of the Messiah). The Messiah will embody the covenant of the people (Israel) to establish the land (or the earth, the Heb. may mean either) and restore the inheritance that had become desolate (cf. Acts 3:21, which applies to restoration from the ravages of sin). God's purpose for the earth is to reclaim it (cf. 42:6–7).

> [9]to say to the captives, 'Come out,' and to those in darkness, 'Be free!' "They will feed beside the roads and find pasture on every barren hill.

The Messiah will liberate those who are bound and bring into light those who are in darkness (cf. 61:1). They will be like a flock being provided for by the Lord in unexpected places, like (usually) barren roadsides and hillsides.

> [10]They will neither hunger nor thirst, nor will

> the desert heat or the sun beat upon them. He
> who has compassion on them will guide them
> and lead them beside springs of water.

God's provision will be complete. Conditions common in ancient Israel will be changed. For example, water has always been scarce, but no longer in the Millennium (cf. Rev. 7:16–17). His protection will not allow the parching heat of desert winds to strike them down (the meaning may refer to heated vapor causing a disappointing mirage), nor the sun to blind them. Like a shepherd, God will lead them, guiding them along springs of water (cf. Ps. 23:1,2), as in a new exodus.

> ¹¹I will turn all my mountains into roads, and
> my highways will be raised up.

Now the LORD speaks and promises that the whole earth will be changed. The mountains are God's mountains and they will no longer be a barrier. The highways are God's highways and He will use them to bring His people back.

> ¹²See, they will come from afar—some from
> the north, some from the west, some from the
> region of Aswan."

The future restoration will be from all directions, not just from Babylon in the east, but from the north, the west, and from "the region of Aswan" (Heb. *sinim*). This is the only place *sinim* is mentioned in the Bible. Some (as does the NIV) identify it with Aswan (ancient Syene) in upper Egypt.[4] Older commentators thought it was China.[5] The Jews did know of China early (wheat was imported) and there is some evidence of Jews in China before the time of Christ.

> ¹³Shout for joy, O heavens; rejoice, O earth;
> burst into song, O mountains! For the LORD

---

[4]R. N. Whybray, *Isaiah 40–66* (Grand Rapids: Wm. B. Eerdmans, 1981), 142. Although NIV, et al., changes the Heb. to *swenim* (mentioned in Ezek. 29:10; 30:6), there is no textual evidence for such a change here.

[5]Joseph A. Alexander, *Commentary on the Prophecies of Isaiah*, 2 vols. in 1 (1875; reprint, Grand Rapids: Zondervan Publishing House, 1975), 2:285. Francis Brown, S. R. Driver, and Charles A. Briggs, *A Hebrew and English Lexicon of the Old Testament* (Oxford, England: Clarendon Press, 1951), 696.

comforts his people and will have compassion on his afflicted ones.

The preceding truths bring rejoicing. With ringing shouts of praise to God and shouts of joy, the heavens and the whole earth, especially the mountains, will proclaim that the LORD has comforted and has had compassion on His afflicted people. Though Israel had rejected the Messiah, the light will finally penetrate the hearts and minds of the remnant.

> ¹⁴But Zion said, "The LORD has forsaken me, the LORD has forgotten me."

In response to this prophecy, Zion (personified, representing the people of Jerusalem in Isaiah's day) protests that the LORD (the covenant-keeping Yahweh) has forsaken her and that the LORD (the Sovereign Master) has forgotten her. They were implying that the LORD was not living up to His name and nature. They had forgotten and forsaken their calling to proclaim good news (40:9). They could not understand the gospel, the good news Isaiah was proclaiming.

> ¹⁵"Can a mother forget the baby at her breast and have no compassion on the child she has borne? Though she may forget, I will not forget you!

Zion had no reason for self-pity. God might abandon them "for a brief moment," but His "deep compassion" would always be there for them (54:7). He replies that though mothers might forget their babies, God will not forget Zion. His love is greater than mother love, greater than the foremost love on earth.

> ¹⁶See, I have engraved you on the palms of my hands; your walls are ever before me.

Zion is "engraved" on both of God's hands, meaning that it was always before His eyes and was under His protection. He would always see and care. The city's walls were still standing in Isaiah's day, and God would protect them also. The final fulfillment, however, will be in the New Jerusalem (cf. 62:6; Rev. 21:12–19).

> ¹⁷Your sons hasten back, and those who laid you waste depart from you.

Then "sons" who hurry back to Zion are contrasted with destroyers who will leave. The Dead Sea Scrolls read "builders" instead of "sons." (The Heb. words are almost the same.) As the NEB translates it, "Those who are to rebuild you make better speed than those who pulled you down."

> ¹⁸Lift up your eyes and look around; all your sons gather and come to you. As surely as I live," declares the LORD, "you will wear them all as ornaments; you will put them on, like a bride.

The LORD pledges His life that those who gather to Zion will be to her like ornaments that adorn a bride (cf. 52:1).

> ¹⁹"Though you were ruined and made desolate and your land laid waste, now you will be too small for your people, and those who devoured you will be far away.

The land will not be fully restored immediately and will therefore have waste places. Thus, there will not be enough room for its rightful inhabitants. But the Assyrians who plundered the land in 701 B.C. will be "far away." This was true when the remnant of those taken by Sennacherib returned from Babylon in 689 B.C.

> ²⁰The children born during your bereavement will yet say in your hearing, 'This place is too small for us; give us more space to live in.'

The returning exiles, who are numerous, will want to settle down and have plenty of room.

> ²¹Then you will say in your heart, 'Who bore me these? I was bereaved and barren; I was exiled and rejected. Who brought these up? I was left all alone, but these—where have they come from?'"

Jerusalem will be surprised by the returning exiles. It had been spared when Sennacherib destroyed the walled cities of Judah and carried off more than two hundred thousand captives. These captives were not expected to return. This is in contrast to the later return from Babylon. A later group would have the comfort of Jeremiah's prophecy (Jer. 29:10).

> ²²This is what the Sovereign LORD says: "See, I will beckon to the Gentiles, I will lift up my banner to the peoples; they will bring your sons in their arms and carry your daughters on their shoulders.

Now Isaiah looks into the future to a greater return. God, the Sovereign LORD, raises His hand, signaling the nations that He is about to act. The Messiah is His "banner," or ensign, "to the peoples" of the world. Because of Him, Zion's people will be restored (implying the conversion of Gentile nations). Nothing will be able to stop God from carrying out His plan.

> ²³Kings will be your foster fathers, and their queens your nursing mothers. They will bow down before you with their faces to the ground; they will lick the dust at your feet. Then you will know that I am the LORD; those who hope in me will not be disappointed."

God will use kings and queens to bring the restoration of Zion in the future millennial day. They will subject themselves to Zion, recognizing their spiritual indebtedness to Israel. By bowing down and licking the dust "at" (lit., "of") her feet[6] they will be recognizing Zion as the chosen bride of God (cf. v. 18) and will really be worshiping Him, submitting to Him and at the same time acknowledging that "'salvation is from the Jews'" (John 4:22). As Motyer comments, "The picture is of political subservience but the reality is the recognition of spiritual indebtedness."[7] Then the people of Zion will know in their experience that God is *Yahweh,* the covenant-keeping God. Because He is faithful, those who hope and trust in Him "will not be disappointed" or ashamed of having held that hope. His mercy and justice will triumph.

> ²⁴Can plunder be taken from warriors, or captives rescued from the fierce?

---

[6]In "your feet" *your* is feminine singular, referring to Zion.
[7]J. Alec Motyer, *The Prophecy of Isaiah* (Downers Grove, Ill.: InterVarsity Press, 1993), 395.

The answer to this rhetorical question is no. Who can take spoil from a mighty warrior? Or can the captive of the "fierce" (Heb. *tsaddiq*, "a righteous man" who has the right on his side[8]) get himself to safety?

> 25But this is what the LORD says: "Yes, captives will be taken from warriors, and plunder retrieved from the fierce; I will contend with those who contend with you, and your children I will save.

The LORD has a different answer. The captive of the mighty warrior will be taken away and the spoils of violent tyrants will be taken to safety. God will enter the battle on the side of His people. "I" is in the emphatic position in the sentence. Because God's power is greater than any human dictator, He will be victor and He will save.

> 26I will make your oppressors eat their own flesh; they will be drunk on their own blood, as with wine. Then all mankind will know that I, the LORD, am your Savior, your Redeemer, the Mighty One of Jacob."

God's victory will cause Israel's oppressors to destroy themselves, probably by fighting among themselves. Then "all mankind" (Heb. *kol basar*, "all flesh"), that is, all the people of the world, will know that the LORD is Israel's Savior, Kinsman-Redeemer, the powerful Father-God of Jacob (cf. Gen. 49:24–25). The same God who worked out His plan for Israel will continue to work it out for the whole world.

3. ISRAEL'S SIN AND LACK OF RESPONSE 50:1–3

> 1This is what the LORD says: "Where is your mother's certificate of divorce with which I sent her away? Or to which of my creditors did I sell you? Because of your sins you were sold; because of your transgressions your mother was sent away.

---

[8]The NIV prefers the translation "the fierce" because of the parallelism with v. 25 and because the Dead Sea Scrolls, the Vulgate, and the Syriac have "the fierce." NEB has "the ruthless." However, the Berkeley Version has "Shall lawfully held captives be rescued"; and Rotherham has "Can the captive of one in the right be delivered?"

Now Isaiah continues the thought of 49:14–16. The people have deceived themselves. The LORD has not divorced His people nor sold them to creditors. There are no divorce papers (such as the Law required, Deut. 24:1,3). Israel was to be punished for her sins. "You were sold" is a way of saying God allowed them to be conquered by their enemies (cf. Deut. 32:30; Judg. 2:14). But "God had not completely and finally dissolved the covenant relationship."[9] Redemption was still possible and God wanted reconciliation.

Creditors could sell a debtor's children into slavery (cf. 2 Kings 4:1). But the idea that God has creditors is ridiculous. Nevertheless, the sins of the people have put them in the position of being sold and put away. God did not want this. Their sins required it.

> ²When I came, why was there no one? When I called, why was there no one to answer? Was my arm too short to ransom you? Do I lack the strength to rescue you? By a mere rebuke I dry up the sea, I turn rivers into a desert; their fish rot for lack of water and die of thirst. ³I clothe the sky with darkness and make sackcloth its covering."

The problem is not that God is capricious or that He has forgotten His people. It is rather that no one responded to Him when He came wanting to restore their relationship with Him. No one answered when He called. The people acted as if God had no power to redeem or deliver.

But He never gives up. He is the Creator who can speak a word of rebuke and "dry up the sea" (cf. Exod. 14:21; Ps. 106:9), make rivers dry up, or darken the sky (see Exod. 10:21).

4. GOD'S OBEDIENT SERVANT: THE MESSIAH 50:4–9

> ⁴The Sovereign LORD has given me an instructed tongue, to know the word that sustains the

---

[9]Joe M. Sprinkle, "Old Testament Perspectives on Divorce and Remarriage," *Journal of the Evangelical Theological Society* 40, no. 4 (December 1997): 541. See also J. A. Motyer, *The Prophecy of Isaiah* (Downers Grove, Ill.: InterVarsity Press, 1993), 397.

weary. He wakens me morning by morning, wakens my ear to listen like one being taught.

In contrast to Israel's rebellion, the Suffering Servant of the LORD[10] is faithful. Now He speaks (see vv. 10–11).[11] The sovereign, covenant-keeping LORD has given Him the tongue of trained scholars. That is, by God's grace He speaks God's word as a Prophet and is recognized as a Teacher. His word is able to sustain the weak and the weary. He is awake and daily hears God's word. He is in constant communication with God the Father and is responsive to Him (cf. Mark 1:35; Luke 6:12). So He is able to communicate God's word to the weary.

> ⁵The Sovereign LORD has opened my ears, and I have not been rebellious; I have not drawn back.

The Servant emphasizes that the LORD is doing this. When the sovereign, covenant-keeping LORD tells the Messiah that the time of His suffering has come, He will not rebel or shrink back. He will be willing and obedient.

> ⁶I offered my back to those who beat me, my cheeks to those who pulled out my beard; I did not hide my face from mocking and spitting.

This describes what happened to Jesus prior to the cross (cf. Matt. 26:67; 27:26,30; Mark 15:16–20; Luke 18:32; John 18:22; 19:1). In spite of what His vicious enemies do to Him and in spite of their contempt He remains meek.

> ⁷Because the Sovereign LORD helps me, I will not be disgraced. Therefore have I set my face like flint, and I know I will not be put to shame.

In the midst of His suffering He can endure the pain because the LORD helps Him. His confidence in His Father made Him know that He would not be overcome by the mockery and mistreatment. Setting His face "like flint" pictures His determination to go to the cross, knowing His shameful death would not

---

[10] This is the third Servant Song; see 42:1.
[11] Some believe that Yahweh of v. 1 is still speaking here and the Servant is identified with Him.

end in hopelessness but in resurrection, ascension, and exaltation (cf. Luke 9:51).

> ⁸He who vindicates me is near. Who then will bring charges against me? Let us face each other! Who is my accuser? Let him confront me! ⁹It is the Sovereign LORD who helps me. Who is he that will condemn me? They will all wear out like a garment; the moths will eat them up.

The language is that of a court scene. God the Father is with the Messiah in a powerful way. Because God the Father justifies the Servant as having committed no sin, no one can condemn the Servant or successfully be His adversary. His accusers will be like a garment that falls apart with age or that is consumed by moths. They will have no lasting effect. The Messiah will triumph in spite of all they do.

5. THE CHOICE: RELY ON GOD OR LIE DOWN IN TORMENT 50:10–11

> ¹⁰Who among you fears the LORD and obeys the word of his servant? Let him who walks in the dark, who has no light, trust in the name of the LORD and rely on his God.

Isaiah[12] now exhorts the people to respond to the Servant and obey the One who supremely obeyed His heavenly Father.[13] To do so will be to come out of darkness and "trust in the name of the LORD" (cf. Rom. 8:32–39). The "name" indicates character—and "in him there is no darkness at all" (1 John 1:5). The one coming into His light will "rely on" (Heb. *yishsha'en*, "lean on") God, entering into a personal relationship with Him, for God will truly be "his God."

> ¹¹But now, all you who light fires and provide yourselves with flaming torches, go, walk in the light of your fires and of the torches you have

---

[12]Some take the speaker in vv. 10–11 to be Yahweh. F. Duane Lindsey, *The Servant Songs* (Chicago: Moody Press, 1985), 92.

[13]Stanley M. Horton, *The Ultimate Victory: An Exposition of the Book of Revelation* (Springfield, Mo.: Gospel Publishing House, 1991), 293, 295.

378 / Isaiah 50:11

set ablaze. This is what you shall receive from my hand: You will lie down in torment.

Isaiah now addresses the unbelieving world. Those who insist in lighting their own way by their own fires will suffer God's hand of judgment. They think they are people of enlightenment because of their humanistic philosophies (including New Age ideas today). But they will lie down in a place of torment because of their sins (cf. 66:24). It will be a fiery place, for fire is often a symbol of God's judgment in Isaiah (see 1:31; 5:24; 9:18; 10:16–17; 26:11; 29:6; 30:27,30; 47:14; 66:15–16; cf. 1 Cor. 3:13; Heb. 10:27; 12:29). They kindle a false light that becomes a fire to destroy them. They will end in the lake of fire—a very real contrast to their false fires (Rev. 20:14–15).

STUDY QUESTIONS

1. What evidence in chapter 49 shows that the Servant Israel is actually the Messiah?
2. What are the two most important aspects of the Servant's mission?
3. How does 49:8–13 apply to Jesus?
4. What assurance does God give that He will not forget the people of Zion?
5. How will God bring back the sons and daughters of Zion?
6. How does chapter 50 extend the thought of 40:14–16?
7. How does the obedient response of the Servant contrast with that of the people of Israel?
8. What is the Servant's attitude in the midst of His suffering?
9. What kind of responses will there be to the voice of God's Servant and what results will follow?

B. The Remnant Encouraged 51:1–52:12

1. Remember The Founder And Foundation 51:1–8

Three themes follow: God emphasizes His promises to the godly remnant of Israel; His salvation is available for all the peoples of the world; and nothing can stop Him from carrying out His purpose of salvation. It is imperative that we listen.

Isaiah first addresses the godly remnant who follow what is right in God's eyes and who seek Him. By looking to the past, the quarry, the rock they were cut from, they should be reminded of God's past blessings and grace.

> **1**"Listen to me, you who pursue righteousness and who seek the LORD: Look to the rock from which you were cut and to the quarry from which you were hewn; **2**look to Abraham, your father, and to Sarah, who gave you birth. When I called him he was but one, and I blessed him and made him many.

Usually Old Testament references to a "rock" are references to God. When Abraham put his faith in God, God made him rock-like. So the godly remnant is commanded to focus on Abraham and Sarah, not merely on them as individuals but on what God did for them. They should especially remember the promise of blessing that included numerous descendants (given when Sarah was barren and in the natural it seemed impossible). Then they should focus on the fulfillment (cf. Deut. 1:10; 10:22). The God who made a great nation out of such small beginnings is still able to do the same. He is a faithful God. All He has done for them is pure grace.

> **3**The LORD will surely comfort Zion and will look with compassion on all her ruins; he will make her deserts like Eden, her wastelands like the garden of the LORD. Joy and gladness will be found in her, thanksgiving and the sound of singing.

The LORD has determined to comfort Zion, implying also that He has already begun to do so. The parallel statements emphasize that He will make the waste places and the desert like the Garden of Eden. There will be no more sorrow or weeping, for it will be a place of undisturbed joy, with gladness, thanksgiving, and singing to the melody of musical instruments. This will have its great fulfillment in the Millennium.[1]

> 4"Listen to me, my people; hear me, my nation: The law will go out from me; my justice will become a light to the nations.

God now speaks. The godly remnant in Zion needs to listen, for He will send out instruction ("law," Heb. *torah*) about how to live in right relation to Him and to one another. He will also establish His "justice [as] a light," as a guide, and not just for Israel but for all the peoples of the world. "Justice" here includes the kind of life that pleases Him.

> 5My righteousness draws near speedily, my salvation is on the way, and my arm will bring justice to the nations. The islands will look to me and wait in hope for my arm.

God's "righteousness" and "salvation" are parallel in this sentence: a poetic way of saying they are intimately connected. His salvation will fulfill all the standards required by His righteousness. God's "arm" means His power, by which He will judge all nations, bring His justice, and carry out His decisions. The "islands" include all the continents of the earth, even the most distant parts. They "look to" (Heb. *yᵉqawwu*, "wait expectantly for") God; that is, they wait for Him to send the Messiah, hoping and trusting in His power to make His salvation available to all the world.

> 6Lift up your eyes to the heavens, look at the earth beneath; the heavens will vanish like smoke, the earth will wear out like a garment and its inhabitants die like flies. But my salva-

---

[1] J. Barton Payne, "The Unity of Isaiah," *Bulletin of the Evangelical Theological Society* 6, no. 2 (May 1963): 53–54.

tion will last forever, my righteousness will
never fail.

All creation, which was made by God, is still under His control. The present starry heavens are compared to a column of smoke that drifts away and vanishes. The earth will be like a garment that is old and simply falls to pieces (cf. Ps. 102:25–28). The people will also die. Like the NIV, many translations take the Hebrew to mean they will die "like flies" or gnats, rather than "in like manner" (KJV). In contrast, God's "salvation will last forever" and His righteousness will never be destroyed. The new heavens, the new earth, and the New Jerusalem will never end.

> ⁷"Hear me, you who know what is right, you people who have my law in your hearts: Do not fear the reproach of men or be terrified by their insults.

God again asks the godly remnant of Israel to listen. They experience righteousness and have God's instructions in their hearts. They must stop being afraid of human abuse or scorn. They must stop being thrown into shock by the revilings and hostile, insulting words of unbelievers. Why should mere human beings stop them from standing up for what is right?

> ⁸For the moth will eat them up like a garment;
> the worm will devour them like wool. But my righteousness will last forever, my salvation through all generations."

Those who abuse and insult God's people will be consumed, unable to withstand God's judgment any more than wool is able to withstand moth worms. But God's people have the assurance of His eternal righteousness and His never-ending salvation. They can count on this "through all generations," no matter what comes or goes.

2. GOD ASSURES A JOYFUL RETURN 51:9–16

> ⁹Awake, awake! Clothe yourself with strength, O arm of the LORD; awake, as in days gone by, as in generations of old. Was it not you who cut Rahab to pieces, who pierced that monster

> through? ¹⁰Was it not you who dried up the sea, the waters of the great deep, who made a road in the depths of the sea so that the redeemed might cross over?

The response of Isaiah and God's people expresses their longing for the salvation He promised. Asking God's arm to "awake" does not mean God has been asleep. Rather, it is a cry for God to go into powerful action, as He did in the Exodus from Egypt (here called "Rahab," the sea monster; cf. 30:7; Job 9:13; Pss. 87:4; 89:10). The Red Sea (Heb. *yam suph*, "sea of reeds") is compared to the "great deep" (Heb. *tᵉhom*, the primeval ocean of Gen. 1:2) because of the impossibility of Israel's crossing it by any natural means available to them.

> ¹¹The ransomed of the LORD will return. They will enter Zion with singing; everlasting joy will crown their heads. Gladness and joy will overtake them, and sorrow and sighing will flee away.

The Israelites sang after they crossed the Red Sea (Exod. 15:1–21). Those who are longing for God's salvation look forward to a greater exodus, where they will come "with singing" (Heb. *rinnah*, "ringing shouts of joy") into Zion. Because they follow the Lord, they will not need to seek gladness and joy. These emotions will pursue and "overtake them." With joy and gladness attained, all expressions of grief will have fled away (cf. 35:10). There was a partial fulfillment of this in 689 B.C. when captives returned from Babylon. There will be a greater fulfillment at the end of the age.

> ¹² "I, even I, am he who comforts you. Who are you that you fear mortal men, the sons of men, who are but grass, ¹³that you forget the LORD your Maker, who stretched out the heavens and laid the foundations of the earth, that you live in constant terror every day because of the wrath of the oppressor, who is bent on destruction? For where is the wrath of the oppressor?

God responds. The people of Israel need to recognize who

He is: the God who "comforts" or reassures them. They also need to realize their own relationship with God: God has made himself theirs. Why should they be afraid of any mortal (including powerful earthly oppressors and dictators), who will be like grass that soon withers (cf. 40:6–8)? When they are continually afraid of the wrath of the "oppressor" (or liquidator[2]) as though he is prepared to destroy, they are forgetting God, who—in contrast to the "grass"—"stretched out the heavens and laid the foundations of the earth."

> [14] The cowering prisoners will soon be set free; they will not die in their dungeon, nor will they lack bread.

Those who cower in prison or sprawl before the foe will soon be freed. "They will not die in their dungeon," as if doomed to go to the pit (hell); God will take care of their needs. This may be a general statement or may refer to the prisoners of Sennacherib who were taken to Babylon.

> [15] For I am the LORD your God, who churns up the sea so that its waves roar—the LORD Almighty is his name.

God does not need to be awakened or stirred to action (Ps. 121:4). He is "the LORD Almighty." Even the churning up of the sea's waves speaks of His continual power and control. The Hebrew is emphatic, reassuring His people.

> [16] I have put my words in your mouth and covered you with the shadow of my hand—I who set the heavens in place, who laid the foundations of the earth, and who say to Zion, 'You are my people.'"

God now speaks to the Servant, who speaks for God. God will cover Him until it is time for Him to be revealed. Through Him God will plant anew the heavens and the earth in a new creation, or a new order. God will still say to Zion that they are His people: God's choice has not and will not change; He still has a place for Israel in His plan and He always will.

---

[2] George A. F. Knight, *Servant Theology* (Grand Rapids: Wm. B. Eerdmans, 1984), 156.

3. The Cup Of God's Wrath Drained And Removed 51:17–23

> ¹⁷Awake, awake! Rise up, O Jerusalem, you who have drunk from the hand of the Lord the cup of his wrath, you who have drained to its dregs the goblet that makes men stagger.

The people had called on God to awake, to stir into action (51:9). But it is Jerusalem that really needs to do so, with vigor and resolve. Jerusalem has come under the fury of God's wrath and will receive it in its fullness. "The goblet that makes men stagger" indicates that God has given His verdict and the judgment will come.

> ¹⁸Of all the sons she bore there was none to guide her; of all the sons she reared there was none to take her by the hand.

Jerusalem, pictured as the mother of her people, should have had "sons [people] . . . to guide her" so that she could avoid God's wrath. But there were none; all the people were in the same sinful condition.

> ¹⁹These double calamities have come upon you—who can comfort you?—ruin and destruction, famine and sword—who can console you?

Their situation is desperate. The calamities are in doublets: "famine and sword" bring devastation and destruction. The prophet cannot comfort Jerusalem or even show sympathy. It is implied that only God can deal with it.

> ²⁰Your sons have fainted; they lie at the head of every street, like antelope caught in a net. They are filled with the wrath of the Lord and the rebuke of your God.

The people of Jerusalem are so under the wrath and rebuke of God that they have fainted and, "like antelope caught in a net," cannot escape.

> ²¹Therefore hear this, you afflicted one, made drunk, but not with wine.

God has a new word for His people who have been humbled and have received the cup of His wrath (cf. v. 17).

> ²²This is what your Sovereign LORD says, your God, who defends his people: "See, I have taken out of your hand the cup that made you stagger; from that cup, the goblet of my wrath, you will never drink again.

The Sovereign LORD, the covenant-keeping *Yahweh*, is still Israel's God and has a word of encouragement for them. He pleads their cause; He brings it to justice and defends them. Let the people see that God has taken the cup of wrath "out of [their] hand." The people of Isaiah's day would never have to drink it again (cf. vv. 17 and 21 above). What grace!

> ²³I will put it into the hands of your tormentors, who said to you, 'Fall prostrate that we may walk over you.' And you made your back like the ground, like a street to be walked over."

God would, in turn, show His justice by putting the cup of wrath "into the hands of [Israel's] tormentors," who had treated them literally like dirt (cf. 10:5–15), walking over their backs after they had been forced to prostrate themselves on the ground (cf. vv. 17,21–22 above). God's cup of wrath will again be poured out during the Great Tribulation (Rev. 6:16–17; 15:7; 16:1). Believers will not suffer that wrath, for Jesus took that cup for us (Matt. 26:42; John 18:11; 1 Thess. 5:9).

4. JERUSALEM TO BE REDEEMED 52:1–12

> ¹Awake, awake, O Zion, clothe yourself with strength. Put on your garments of splendor, O Jerusalem, the holy city. The uncircumcised and defiled will not enter you again.

The third call to awake (cf. 51:9; 51:17) comes to Zion because of the LORD's work of redemption. After drinking the cup of God's wrath, Jerusalem will again be "the holy city." The beautiful "garments of splendor" are priestly robes (cf. Exod. 28:2–5) provided by God. God's people will again fulfill the priestly function He intended (Exod. 19:6). Freedom from the "uncircumcised and defiled" (or unclean) indicates the people will have an inner holiness as well.

> ²Shake off your dust; rise up, sit enthroned, O Jerusalem. Free yourself from the chains on your neck, O captive Daughter of Zion.

Jerusalem will again become a royal city and its people king-priests (Exod. 19:6; cf. 1 Pet. 2:5,9). They must shake off the "dust" (representing sin), and put off the old "chains" that tyrannized them, the chains of sin.

> ³For this is what the LORD says: "You were sold for nothing, and without money you will be redeemed." ⁴For this is what the Sovereign LORD says: "At first my people went down to Egypt to live; lately, Assyria has oppressed them.

When the people were sold into bondage Assyria paid no price to God. So there was no need to pay a price to Assyria to redeem them from that bondage. So God would, "without money," redeem them freely by His grace.

The mention of Egypt as the first place of Israel's oppression and Assyria as oppressing them "lately"[3] (at this time of their history) indicates this passage is dealing with Isaiah's own day.[4]

> ⁵"And now what do I have here?" declares the LORD. "For my people have been taken away for nothing, and those who rule them mock," declares the LORD. "And all day long my name is constantly blasphemed.

The LORD has not gained anything by having His people taken away from Him. Their rulers "mock" (some take this to mean their oppressors "howl" [KJV, NASB]; others, that their own rulers lament [RSV, CEV]); God's name is reviled or blasphemed, probably because they are rejecting the fact that they deserve His judgment (cf. Rom. 2:24).

> ⁶Therefore my people will know my name; therefore in that day they will know that it is I who foretold it. Yes, it is I."

---

[3] Heb. *be'ephes;* this could also mean "in the end" (NEB) or "for nothing."
[4] F. Duane Lindsey, *The Servant Songs* (Chicago: Moody Press, 1985).

"Therefore" is repeated for emphasis. God is going to let the people "know [His] name" (including His nature and character) in their experience. The millennial day is coming when He will speak to them and they will see Him. Then they will know not only that God foretold the future, He is also the One who brought it to pass.

> ⁷How beautiful on the mountains are the feet of those who bring good news, who proclaim peace, who bring good tidings, who proclaim salvation, who say to Zion, "Your God reigns!"

Verses 7–12 are a hymn of praise. "The mountains" are God's mountains, the mountains of the whole world where the gospel of peace (God's goodness and salvation) is proclaimed (cf. 49:11). The "beautiful feet" may be bruised and bleeding, but they are beautiful because they bring a jubilant shout of "good news" that "God reigns": God is not dead. God is still the King of the universe, still sovereign, and still in control. The specific application here is to the good news being proclaimed on the mountains around Jerusalem. Romans 10:15 quotes from this verse and applies it to the New Testament gospel (cf. also Eph. 6:15).

> ⁸Listen! Your watchmen lift up their voices; together they shout for joy. When the LORD returns to Zion, they will see it with their own eyes.

Those who are watching, waiting expectantly, unite in a loud ringing shout of joy. For they will see clearly "when the LORD returns to Zion." He returns as the triumphant conqueror.

> ⁹Burst into songs of joy together, you ruins of Jerusalem, for the LORD has comforted his people, he has redeemed Jerusalem.

The city of Jerusalem is called "ruins," wasteland, because of the sins of its people as well as the siege of the Assyrians. But now, because of God's salvation, comfort, and redemption, even the wasteland breaks out in shouts and "songs of joy."

> ¹⁰The LORD will lay bare his holy arm in the sight of all the nations, and all the ends of the earth will see the salvation of our God.

For God to "lay bare his holy arm" means He will demonstrate His power and holy dedication of himself in His work of salvation. "All . . . the earth" will see it and recognize His greatness.

> ¹¹Depart, depart, go out from there! Touch no unclean thing! Come out from it and be pure, you who carry the vessels of the LORD. ¹²But you will not leave in haste or go in flight; for the LORD will go before you, the God of Israel will be your rear guard.

Isaiah is not in Babylon here, nor in exile. The call is a general one. The people are king-priests bearing holy "vessels [things, instruments] of the Lord." They must keep themselves ceremonially pure. Were they to touch an "unclean thing," they would not be able to continue bearing the holy vessels. Neither would they be allowed to enter the temple. The fact that they are "not [to] leave in haste" contrasts with the departure from Egypt (Exod. 12:33,39), and contrasts also with the earlier command to flee from Babylon (48:20). God will guard his king-priests, both in front of and behind them. There was only a partial fulfillment of this prophecy when Cyrus permitted the Jews to return from the later Babylonian exile (Ezra 1:7–10)

STUDY QUESTIONS

1. Why does the godly remnant need to look to Abraham and Sarah?
2. How is God's righteousness related to His salvation?
3. Why did the people cry out for God to awaken and what was His response?
4. Why does God cover the Servant?
5. Why do the people of Jerusalem need to awaken?
6. What does God want to do for them?
7. What must the people of Jerusalem do in response to this third call to awaken?
8. In what ways can we participate today in the hymn of praise (52:7–12)?

C. The Servant's Suffering And Atoning Death 52:13–53:12

1. THE WISE SERVANT WILL BE EXALTED 52:13

> ¹³See, my servant will act wisely; he will be raised and lifted up and highly exalted.

This verse is the beginning of the fourth Servant Song, which continues through chapter 53. Some critics are hesitant to apply it to Jesus, so they try to apply it to Israel, or to the godly remnant, or to some prophet, even to the writer himself.[1] But this passage "points beyond Israel as the servant of the Lord to the Messiah."[2] Isaiah pictures Israel as suffering for its own sins. The whole evidence is that this Servant is a sinless individual who suffers completely for others[3] "in total obedience to the Father."[4] It is a sublime, profound, and accurate picture of the Messiah. God's Servant will have the wisdom to accomplish successfully what God sends Him to do. This will result in a supreme exaltation, expressed by the threefold repetition (cf. 6:3): He will be "raised" (as God is exalted, cf. 2 Sam. 22:47), "lifted up," and "highly exalted" (cf. 6:1 where the same exaltation is applied to God). The verses following show he suffers as a man. Certainly, this prophecy of a God-Man fits no one but Jesus.

2. ASTONISHING SUFFERING 52:14–15

> ¹⁴Just as there were many who were appalled at him—his appearance was so disfigured beyond that of any man and his form marred beyond human likeness—

As Philippians 2:6–11 makes clear, the exaltation will come only after humbling and suffering. The "many" are the people

---

[1] Note discussion in Samuel J. Schultz, *The Old Testament Speaks*, 4th ed. (San Francisco: Harper, 1990), 317.

[2] Willem A. VanGemeren, *Interpreting the Prophetic Word* (Grand Rapids: Zondervan Publishing House, Academie Books, 1990), 280.

[3] Cf. Franz Delitzsch, *Biblical Commentary on the Prophecies of Isaiah*, trans. James Martin (Grand Rapids: Wm. B. Eerdmans, 1969), 2:303.

[4] VanGemeren, *Interpreting the Prophetic Word*, 280.

who look to Him hoping He will do God's work of redemption (cf. Luke 24:21). When they see Him they will be horrified, shocked at his disfigurement, for He no longer looks like a man.

> ¹⁵so will he sprinkle many nations, and kings will shut their mouths because of him. For what they were not told, they will see, and what they have not heard, they will understand.

"Sprinkle" is often used of sprinkling the blood of a sacrifice. (Some connect this with an Arabic root and translate it "startle";[5] however, this has problems. The Septuagint translates the phrase, "So will many nations marvel at Him.") In line with Isaiah's message of salvation available to all, the meaning seems to be that "many nations" will benefit from the Servant's sacrifice and the shedding of His blood.[6] "Kings will shut their mouths"; that is, they will be astonished and be respectfully silent, overwhelmed by the greatness of His salvation—something they, being Gentiles, had not understood or even considered before.

3. The Messiah Despised And Rejected 53:1–3

> ¹Who has believed our message and to whom has the arm of the Lord been revealed?

Israel, or rather, the godly remnant in Israel, speaks. Initially, not even they believed the "message," the report or good news they heard and must reveal (cf. Luke 24:25,41; John 12:38; Rom. 10:16). The "arm," that is, the power of the Lord, was revealed supernaturally. Jesus himself had to come to His disciples and explain the truth.

> ²He grew up before him like a tender shoot, and like a root out of dry ground. He had no beauty or majesty to attract us to him, nothing in his appearance that we should desire him.

The Servant grows up as a new, "tender shoot" before the Lord—in His presence and under His protection. But He

---

[5]Edward J. Young, *The Book of Isaiah*, 3 vols. (Grand Rapids: Wm. B. Eerdmans, 1969–72), 3:338–39; J. Alec Motyer, *The Prophecy of Isaiah* (Downers Grove, Ill.: InterVarsity Press, 1993), 426.

[6]H. C. Leupold, *Exposition of Isaiah* (Grand Rapids: Baker Book House, 1971), 2:225.

appears as in "dry ground," without any semblance of fertility that would make growth possible. The comparison to the "shoot" and the "root" ties the Servant to Isaiah's earlier messianic prophecies (see 11:1,10). But He is not described as coming like a King this time: There will be nothing wonderful or spectacular about Him, no outward evidence of royalty. Rather, there seems to be nothing especially appealing about the Servant "to attract us to him." Jesus did have a year of apparent success in Galilee (the second year of His ministry), but then He faced increasing opposition. The circumstances that surrounded the fulfillment of His mission seemed adverse.

> [3]**He was despised and rejected by men, a man of sorrows, and familiar with suffering. Like one from whom men hide their faces he was despised, and we esteemed him not.**

In the Servant's severe suffering He is characterized as "despised and rejected," or forsaken. He was a man of "sorrows" (Heb. *makh'ovoth*, "physical pains"), experiencing the same suffering that accompanies severe illness or sickness. People "despised" Him in a mocking way, or else they forsook Him (Matt. 26:56). Those who despised Him found His suffering so repulsive that they turned their faces away. How this must have hurt the One who loved them so!

4. Suffering For Others 53:4–6

> [4]**Surely he took up our infirmities and carried our sorrows, yet we considered him stricken by God, smitten by him, and afflicted.**

It was not for any sin of His own that He suffered. He boldly and willingly chose to take up and bear the heavy load of "our infirmities" (Heb. *chalayenu*, "our sicknesses") and "our sorrows" ("our pains," as in v. 3). Matthew 8:17 applies this to Jesus' healing ministry, where He took pain and sickness away. This He could do because He was going to die. The Hebrew words here, however, refer to His own physical suffering that He endured on the cross. Yet the nation as a whole thought He had become "stricken by God," the object of His judgment, struck down and humbled by Him to the point of death.

> ⁵But he was pierced for our transgressions, he was crushed for our iniquities; the punishment that brought us peace was upon him, and by his wounds we are healed.

The explanation is emphatic: He was wounded for "our [rebellious] transgressions" (against God and His Word) and crushed for "our iniquities," including our sinful guilt. (Both "pierced" and "crushed" are used of situations in which the person dies.) The punishment laid on Him was to secure our peace, including our eternal well-being, blessing, and joyful fellowship with the Lord. "By his wounds" (or "stripes," the marks left by blows) there is healing for us. This includes not only physical healing but restoration to fellowship with God (cf. Ps. 103:3–4; James 5:15; 1 Pet. 2:24–25).

> ⁶We all, like sheep, have gone astray, each of us has turned to his own way; and the Lord has laid on him the iniquity of us all.

Everyone needs the Redeemer, for "we all, like sheep," have wandered away from God and strayed into sin (cf. Ps. 119:176; Matt. 9:36). God caused all our sins (including both our guilt and the punishment we deserve) to fall on Him. His suffering was vicarious—completely for others; His sacrifice was substitutionary. We could not pay the penalty for our sins, so God "laid on him the iniquity of us all."

5. Dying For Others 53:7–9

> ⁷He was oppressed and afflicted, yet he did not open his mouth; he was led like a lamb to the slaughter, and as a sheep before her shearers is silent, so he did not open his mouth.

He was oppressed as one oppresses a debtor to exact payment, or as the slave driver whips the slave; yet He made no word of complaint, no attempt to defend himself. In His patience and silence, He was like a lamb "before her shearers" (cf. the Passover lamb of Exod. 12:3; John the Baptist calls Jesus "the Lamb of God" in John 1:29,35; cf. Rev. 5:6; 13:8).

> ⁸By oppression and judgment he was taken away. And who can speak of his descendants?

> For he was cut off from the land of the living;
> for the transgression of my people he was stricken.

"By oppression" means He was put under constraint (as Jesus was bound and placed under guard like a criminal). "Judgment" refers to the trial (though it was illegal) and the unjust sentence, after which He was led away to die. "And who can speak of [Heb. *y^esocheach*, "consider"[7]] his descendants [Heb. *doro*, "his generation," "his contemporaries"]?" As the Berkeley Version puts it, "And who of his contemporaries would consider." That is, no one at that time understood the meaning of all this (even His disciples did not understand He was suffering for them). He was "cut off" by violent suffering and death, a death deserved by His people, as well as all the people of the world.

> [9]He was assigned a grave with the wicked, and with the rich in his death,[8] though he had done no violence, nor was any deceit in his mouth.

It was intended that His grave be "with the wicked," that is, with the condemned criminals who were crucified with Him. Yet, when He actually died, He was buried with honor by a rich man (see Matt. 27:57–60).[9] This was God's assurance that the accusations that He was a violent man and a deceiver were false (cf. 1 Pet. 2:22). He was gentle with sinners, and His words were true.

6. An Acceptable Guilt Offering 53:10–12

> [10]Yet it was the LORD's will to crush him and cause him to suffer, and though the LORD makes his life a guilt offering, he will see his offspring and prolong his days, and the will of the LORD will prosper in his hand.

God not only allowed the Servant's death, it was His will (Heb. *chaphets*, "He delighted") "to crush him and cause him to

---

[7]As translated in Ps. 143:5.
[8]"Death" is a plural of emphasis in the Heb., indicating that it was real, violent, and supreme. See Motyer, *Prophecy of Isaiah*, 436.
[9]Young, *Book of Isaiah*, 3:355–56.

suffer." God did it out of pure grace and love (John 3:16) for us; we in no way deserved such a sacrifice on our behalf. God made the Servant's life, including His whole self, a "guilt offering" (ordinarily translated "trespass offering" in KJV; cf. 2 Cor. 5:21). By the shedding of His blood and the outpouring of His life, sufficient expiation was made for all our sin and guilt. But His death would not be the end. That He would "see his offspring" (lit., "view seed") means He would rise from the dead and see His spiritual children.[10] That He would "prolong his days" means He would live on after His resurrection. The "will of the LORD" includes the business of the LORD. It would be brought to a successful conclusion "in his hand," that is, by the power and administration of the Servant, the Messiah.

> [11]After the suffering of his soul, he will see the light [of life] and be satisfied; by his knowledge my righteous servant will justify many, and he will bear their iniquities.

He will see the outcome of His sufferings and "be satisfied." The NIV adds that "he will see the light [of life],"[11] which was indeed fulfilled in His resurrection. The Servant's "knowledge" means He knew the Father in a loving, personal way. He also knew what He was doing in His sacrifice of himself for us, and He knew who He was and is. Being a "righteous servant" means He was without sin and therefore could "justify [provide righteousness for] many"—not just one, but all who would come to Him (Rom. 1:17; 3:22; 1 Cor. 1:30; 2 Cor. 5:21; Phil. 3:9). He could do this because He would "bear their iniquities," including the consequences of their guilt.

> [12]Therefore I will give him a portion among the great, and he will divide the spoils with the strong, because he poured out his life unto death, and was numbered with the transgressors. For he bore the sin of many, and made intercession for the transgressors.

---

[10]Stanley M. Horton, *The Ultimate Victory: An Exposition of the Book of Revelation* (Springfield, Mo.: Gospel Publishing House, 1991), 314–21.

[11]The Septuagint has "to him light shows." The NIV here follows both the Septuagint and the Dead Sea Scrolls. Cf. NASB margin.

The Servant will triumph. God will richly reward Him. All the grandeur and power of His enemies will be among the spoils of His victory. All of this happens because He was willing to go down to death and let himself be identified with human beings, who were in a state of rebellion (see Mark 15:28). Though He let himself be "numbered with the transgressors," that is, treated as a rebel, He was freely making intercession for rebels and would continue to do so (cf. Luke 23:34; Rom. 8:34; Heb. 7:25; 1 John 2:1). It is clear from this He was not a victim of circumstances, not merely a martyr, not merely our example, not merely a teacher. He willingly and obediently carried the burden of the sins and guilt of all humankind, bearing it all away so we can be free to come into the presence of God and be in right relationship with Him. In this also He fulfilled the typology of the sin offering of the two goats on the Day of Atonement: One goat was sacrificed and the blood was sprinkled on the solid gold mercy seat that was the cover of the ark of the covenant. In that ark were the tablets of stone of the Law. The breaking of the Law demanded judgment. But when the blood was sprinkled, God no longer looked at the broken Law but at the life blood that covered it. The second goat was sent away into the wilderness to declare that the sins were not only covered, they were gone (cf. Isa. 43:25; Mic. 7:19).

STUDY QUESTIONS

1. What light does Philippians 2:7–11 shed on Isaiah 52:13–15?
2. What do the questions of 53:1 imply?
3. How is the mention of the shoot and root different from what is described in 11:1,10?
4. How are sufferings of the Servant related to the ministry of Jesus and to the Cross?
5. What is meant by calling His sufferings vicarious and substitutionary?
6. What lesson does the Bible want us to draw from His being buried in a rich man's tomb?
7. What in this passage indicates His resurrection?
8. What is the continuing ministry of the Servant?

D. The Messiah's Work Brings Growth And Blessing 54:1–55:13

1. Joyous Growth 54:1–3

¹"Sing, O barren woman, you who never bore a child; burst into song, shout for joy, you who were never in labor; because more are the children of the desolate woman than of her who has a husband," says the Lord.

This chapter calls for responses to the Servant's work. Two comparisons illustrate the future enlargement of Zion. First, the "barren woman" (Zion personified) is to sing and shout because the Servant's children (53:10) are made hers. Galatians 4:26–27 applies this to the spiritual children of the Jerusalem that is above (i.e., the New Jerusalem in heaven)—who are also (by faith) the spiritual children of Abraham. The emphasis here is on the supernatural nature of the relationship.

²"Enlarge the place of your tent, stretch your tent curtains wide, do not hold back; lengthen your cords, strengthen your stakes.

A second comparison calls for enlarging "the place of [the] tent." This indicates the need for making room for the great number of people who will come under blessings God has for His people because of the Servant's suffering, atoning death, and resurrection.

³For you will spread out to the right and to the left; your descendants will dispossess nations and settle in their desolate cities.

God's promise to Abraham was for numerous seed. In his seed, all the families of the earth would be blessed (Gen. 12:3). God promised Jacob that his seed would break out to the west, east, north, and south (Gen. 28:14). Now Isaiah sees a breaking out "to the right and to the left," with the seed possessing nations and populating their "desolate cities." This looks ahead to millennial times and Israel's glorious future.

2. The Compassionate Redeemer 54:4–8

⁴"Do not be afraid; you will not suffer shame. Do not fear disgrace; you will not be humiliat-

ed. You will forget the shame of your youth and remember no more the reproach of your widowhood.

Israel can stop being afraid for good reasons. Three synonyms—"disgrace," "humiliat[ion]," and "reproach"—emphasize that Israel will not "suffer shame." The shame of the past, from "youth" (probably in Egypt) to "widowhood" (later troubles), will all be forgotten. The Lord will bear it all away.

> 5For your Maker is your husband—the LORD Almighty is his name—the Holy One of Israel is your Redeemer; he is called the God of all the earth.

The reason Israel will not be put to shame is that her Maker is still her husband. He has not abandoned her forever (see v. 7). The imagery of God as Israel's "husband" is often employed (Jer. 3:14; Hos. 2:7, etc.). In the New Testament, a similar picture is found with Jesus being the Bridegroom of the Church. God is still the covenant-keeping *Yahweh* who controls the hosts of heaven. He is not only the Holy One of Israel, but Israel's Kinsman-Redeemer. He will also be recognized not only as the God of Israel but "the God of all the earth." No pagan god could claim that, for the pagans believed in many gods, each with limited power and often in competition with each other.

> 6The LORD will call you back as if you were a wife deserted and distressed in spirit—a wife who married young, only to be rejected," says your God.

The reason Israel can recognize that God is still her husband is because He has called her back, though she is like a wife abandoned and sorrowful, like a young wife who is "rejected," or cast off. But God is still her God. His Word gives her security.

> 7"For a brief moment I abandoned you, but with deep compassion I will bring you back. 8In a surge of anger I hid my face from you for a moment, but with everlasting kindness I will have compassion on you," says the LORD your Redeemer.

The time God left Israel was but "a brief moment." He did not divorce her (see 50:1). His anger was like a dam breaking, and He "hid [His] face" (removed His active presence) from them—but only for a very short time. His compassion is so great that He will gather Israel to himself. His eternal kindness (Heb. *chesed*, "covenant-keeping love") is behind His mercies. He was hurt by their sin and rebellion, but He remains and will always be Israel's Kinsman-Redeemer (cf. Hos. 11:8–9). Now the barren woman can indeed sing and shout for joy (54:1).

3. The Covenant Of Peace 54:9–10

> ⁹"To me this is like the days of Noah, when I swore that the waters of Noah would never again cover the earth. So now I have sworn not to be angry with you, never to rebuke you again.

Noah's flood was an act of judgment on the whole world. God's promise and covenant after the flood was "'Never again will I destroy all living creatures, as I have done'" (Gen. 8:21). Likewise, God's promise and oath to Israel is that His anger and rebuke are over. His new covenant will be as firm as the covenant made with Noah.

> ¹⁰Though the mountains be shaken and the hills be removed, yet my unfailing love for you will not be shaken nor my covenant of peace be removed," says the LORD, who has compassion on you.

Great changes came with the flood. New mountains and hills undoubtedly rose up. But though mountains and hills will come and go, God's "unfailing love," His covenant-keeping love, will never leave Israel nor will His "covenant of peace."

God's covenants were always put into effect by a sacrifice (cf. Heb. 9:15–18). In the background is the sacrifice of the Servant-Messiah. Thus, the "covenant of peace" must be the future new covenant, put into effect by the death of Jesus on the cross. VanGemeren suggests that it "incorporates all the promises of God."[1] Through His death, He left us His peace (John

---

[1] Willem A. VanGemeren, *Interpreting the Prophetic Word* (Grand Rapids: Zondervan Publishing House, Academie Books, 1990), 280.

14:27) and made peace between God and us (Rom. 5:1; Eph. 2:14–18). How wonderful to know He is the One who has compassion on each of us!

4. Jerusalem To Be Reestablished 54:11–15

> **11"O afflicted city, lashed by storms and not comforted, I will build you with stones of turquoise, your foundations with sapphires.**

God's compassion reaches out to the afflicted city of Jerusalem, battered by storms and given no comfort. God has a wonderful restoration in store for it, full of glory. He will build it with precious stones set in "turquoise" (Heb. *pukh,* "black antimony," not modern turquoise)[2] to make their beauty stand out. The foundation of that great city will be of sapphires (not modern sapphires but rich, azure-blue lapis lazuli). It will be firm and beautiful—no more instability.

> **12I will make your battlements of rubies, your gates of sparkling jewels, and all your walls of precious stones.**

The city's "battlements" will be made of rubies. Though some (like NIV and NASB) take it to be "battlements" or ("towers"), and others "pinnacles" (ASV) or "windows" (KJV) that reflect sunlight, the Hebrew *shimshoth* (lit., "suns") probably means sun-shaped shields. The gates will be of beryl of various colors, and the walls or borders of the buildings will be precious stones. The New Jerusalem will be beautiful in a similar way (Rev. 21:10,18–21).

> **13All your sons will be taught by the LORD, and great will be your children's peace.**

The "sons" (children) are the inhabitants of the city who will be disciples of the LORD, continually taught by Him.[3] They will enjoy great peace and well-being, including the full blessings of the salvation God has in store. God will fulfill His purpose for Israel.

---

[2]Some take it to be black lead sulfide. The same word is used of black eye-paint in 2 Kings 9:30.

[3]Some take "sons" to mean "builders" since the Heb. consonants are the same.

> **¹⁴In righteousness you will be established: Tyranny will be far from you; you will have nothing to fear. Terror will be far removed; it will not come near you.**

The city will be founded and established on God's righteousness (including His love and compassion). It will be far from any oppression or social evil and, therefore, from fear and terror.

> **¹⁵If anyone does attack you, it will not be my doing; whoever attacks you will surrender to you.**

Should there be any attack against the city, it will fail. There may be unprovoked attacks, but God will not cause war against it as He did when the Assyrians and Babylonians brought His judgment.

5. God's Servants To Be Vindicated 54:16–17

> **¹⁶"See, it is I who created the blacksmith who fans the coals into flame and forges a weapon fit for its work. And it is I who have created the destroyer to work havoc;**

"I" is in the emphatic position in the sentence. The Hebrew word translated "created" is used only of God and here emphasizes His sovereign control over human workers, weapons, destroyers (warriors), and the destruction they bring. (Cf. 45:7 and see also 10:5–19 for the application of this to the Assyrians.)

> **¹⁷no weapon forged against you will prevail, and you will refute every tongue that accuses you. This is the heritage of the servants of the Lord, and this is their vindication from me," declares the Lord.**

"No weapon" will be able to take away from Zion what God will provide. Neither will any "tongue that accuses" in court be able to stand against God's people and take away the "heritage," the rights and blessings He has given them. This is God's declared word.

They will have a heritage that is indeed theirs; these true

believers are all "servants of the LORD." They will have a righteousness that is from the LORD, provided by Him. As 53:11 makes clear, it is provided through the death and resurrection of the Suffering Servant, the Messiah. (See Rom. 4:20–25; Phil. 3:9).

6. A UNIVERSAL INVITATION 55:1–2

> ¹"Come, all you who are thirsty, come to the waters; and you who have no money, come, buy and eat! Come, buy wine and milk without money and without cost.

Now God reveals His purpose in a wonderful way. In the light of the salvation provided through the Servant of chapter 53 a door is thrown wide open to all. The LORD calls all to come—regardless or race, color, or social condition. The invitation has only one condition: thirst. There is plenty of water for everyone who thirsts if they will come. "Wine and milk" imply provision for every need. It all speaks of a rich, full and free salvation (cf. Matt. 5:6). Those "who have no money" can come because the Servant-Messiah has already paid the full price: He died for the whole world—including the inner cities, the third world countries, those who have no money and nothing to offer in exchange.

> ²Why spend money on what is not bread, and your labor on what does not satisfy? Listen, listen to me, and eat what is good, and your soul will delight in the richest of fare.

Poverty-stricken pagans were spending their wealth and labor on temples and gods that could not satisfy (46:6–7). What they had received was nothing but an illusion. The call is to listen diligently and solely to the LORD. Then they could eat real food and find not only satisfaction but also joy and delight in the richness of what God provides (cf. the parables of the wedding feast in Matt. 22; Luke 14).

Too many today are spending their money and labor on the empty things of the world. They are in a mad rush after power or pleasure. Their selfish desires blind them to biblical values and they fail to seek the blessings of God.

7. An Everlasting Covenant 55:3–5

> ³Give ear and come to me; hear me, that your soul may live. I will make an everlasting covenant with you, my faithful love promised to David.

The commands are plural and amplify the thought of verse 1: Let all who are thirsty listen, come to the LORD, obey, and "your soul" (your whole self) will be revived. God will "make [Heb. *'ekhrᵉthah*, "cut" by a sacrifice] an everlasting covenant" with all who come. It is the new covenant put into effect by the sacrificial death of Jesus, the Suffering Servant of chapter 53. This new covenant will bring the fulfillment of the covenant love "promised to David." That is, these promises assured him that there would always be a man from his descendants for the throne (2 Sam. 7:14–16; Ps. 89:3–4,28–37). They will be fulfilled when Jesus comes again and makes the throne of David eternal as He reigns in Jerusalem in the Millennium and on into the New Jerusalem. The resurrection of Jesus identifies Him with this prophecy (cf. Acts 13:34).

> ⁴See, I have made him a witness to the peoples,
> a leader and commander of the peoples.

The Person God gives as "a witness to the peoples" of the world is the Messiah, who fulfills God's promise to David. He will be a witness to the truth (cf. John 18:37). He will also be God's appointed leader or sovereign prince. By His nature, He will be a "commander of the peoples," that is, all the peoples of the world.[4] As Jesus said, "'All authority in heaven and on earth has been given to me'" (Matt. 28:18; cf. Num. 24:17–19; Isa. 9:6–7; Rev. 2:26–27; 12:5; 19:15).

> ⁵Surely you will summon nations you know not, and nations that do not know you will hasten to you, because of the LORD your God, the Holy One of Israel, for he has endowed you with splendor."

---

[4] Joseph A. Alexander, *Commentary on the Prophecies of Isaiah*, 2 vols. in 1 (1875; reprint, Grand Rapids: Zondervan Publishing House, 1975), 2:326.

Jesus, as the Davidic King, "will summon nations" (Gentiles) that He did not know or come in contact with during His earthly ministry. Nations that did not know Him will run to Him because of His relation to God the Father and because the Holy One of Israel has glorified and exalted Him (cf. Hag. 2:7; Zech. 8:20–23; Mal. 1:5; Phil. 2:9, etc.).

8. GOD WILL FREELY PARDON THE REPENTANT 55:6–9

> ⁶Seek the LORD while he may be found; call on him while he is near.

In view of God's love and the provision of mercy and of the Messiah's leadership, the command given is to "seek the LORD" intensely with a desire to worship. He will be found by those who seek; He is near to those who call on Him. But the opportunity will not last forever (cf. Isa. 49:8; 2 Cor. 6:1–2). Some suggest that the Hebrew may be translated "Seek the LORD *where* he may be found." This might indicate joining people who are worshiping Him. As Jesus said, " 'Where two or three come together in my name, there am I with them' " (Matt. 18:20).

> ⁷Let the wicked forsake his way and the evil man his thoughts. Let him turn to the LORD, and he will have mercy on him, and to our God, for he will freely pardon.

For guilty wrongdoers to seek the LORD, they must first "forsake [their] way," that is, change their lifestyle. People full of misdeeds and who cause injustice must forsake their "thoughts" (including their plans and intentions). Then they can "turn" (Heb. *yashov*, "return") to the LORD to freely receive mercy and abundant pardon and forgiveness.

> ⁸"For my thoughts are not your thoughts, neither are your ways my ways," declares the LORD. ⁹"As the heavens are higher than the earth, so are my ways higher than your ways and my thoughts than your thoughts.

Furthermore, the wicked must forsake their thoughts

because God's thoughts, plans, intentions, and ways are not only different from ours, they are infinitely higher. We can all apply this to ourselves, "for all have sinned and fall short of the glory of God" (Rom. 3:23). God, however, has bridged the gap between us and Him through a new and living (resurrected) Way: Jesus who is "the way" (John 14:6; see Heb. 10:19–20).

9. God's Word Will Bring Joy 55:10–13

> **10As the rain and the snow come down from heaven, and do not return to it without watering the earth and making it bud and flourish, so that it yields seed for the sower and bread for the eater, 11so is my word that goes out from my mouth: It will not return to me empty, but will accomplish what I desire and achieve the purpose for which I sent it.**

God's provision of rain and snow does not simply come down and go back up. Rather, it comes down to have an important effect, making possible plant growth that supplies human need. God does not speak his word to have it simply echo back to Him. It will hit the target. It will do what God desires and will succeed, having the effect He intends (cf. 45:23; 53:10). Therefore, we should seek God because of the great blessing that will result.

> **12You will go out in joy and be led forth in peace; the mountains and hills will burst into song before you, and all the trees of the field will clap their hands.**

The ultimate promise of God's Word (the Bible) is that repentant sinners (cf. vv. 7–10) will go out of the bondage of sin "with joy" and be led by the LORD "in peace" and well-being. It will be the kind of joy and peace Jesus gives—a peace different from anything the world gives (John 14:27). It makes all nature seem to sing and rejoice. The transformation looks ahead to the Millennium when all nature will be transformed as well (Rom. 8:21).

> **13Instead of the thornbush will grow the pine tree, and instead of briers the myrtle will grow. This will be for the LORD's renown, for an everlasting sign, which will not be destroyed."**

Adam's fall brought a curse on the ground so that it produced thorns and thistles (Gen. 3:17–18). That curse will be removed, and evergreen trees will take their place. This transformation of people and nature will be for God's "renown" (Heb. *shem,* "name," that is, an expression of God's name—of His nature and character). It will be an eternal, supernatural sign proving the effectiveness of God's word. This sign will never be eliminated. It will forever give glory to God and inspire praise, for He is worthy.

STUDY QUESTIONS

1. What is Zion expected to do because of the Servant's work?
2. How does this relate the promises given to Abraham and Jacob?
3. What are God's promises to the people of Israel as their "husband"?
4. To whom does the invitation of 55:1 come and why?
5. What is implied by calling God Israel's husband as well as the God of all the earth?
6. What do you learn about God's thoughts and God's Word in chapter 55?
7. What assurance does God give to repentant sinners in chapter 55?

VIII. GLORY FOR GOD'S PEOPLE; JUDGMENT ON OTHERS 56:1–66:24

A. BLESSING AND JUDGMENT 56:1–58:14

1. Blessing Includes Eunuchs And Foreigners 56:1–8

¹This is what the Lord says: "Maintain justice

and do what is right, for my salvation is close at hand and my righteousness will soon be revealed.

Some take this chapter as beginning a new section.[1] However, this section is closely connected to the preceding prophecy and concludes it. The LORD's complete and free salvation, offered to everyone who thirsts, is near, but it brings responsibilities as well as blessings. The "wine and milk" were "without money and without cost" (55:1). Although the promised salvation is not by works but by grace, people need to be reminded that God expected good works (cf. 51:1,7; Gal. 6:9–10). His command was to put into practice justice and righteousness, anticipating His salvation and the revelation of His righteousness.

> ²**Blessed is the man who does this, the man who holds it fast, who keeps the Sabbath without desecrating it, and keeps his hand from doing any evil."**

A blessing is pronounced on people who continue doing this consistently and faithfully. The "man" (Heb. *ben 'adham,* "the son of humankind") who "holds it fast" means every individual human being who takes hold of it and keeps hold of it. In Isaiah's day, this meant coming under the old covenant. Because the Sabbath was the heart as well as the symbol of the old covenant and because it was central to the expression of their relationship to the LORD, keeping the Sabbath was important (cf. Jer. 17:19–27; but compare Heb. 4:9–11, where the new covenant Sabbath-rest is every day ceasing from our own works in order to do God's will in obedience to Him). Their relationship to other human beings was also important, so the command was to avoid "doing [any kind of] evil."

> ³**Let no foreigner who has bound himself to the LORD say, "The LORD will surely exclude me from his people." And let not any eunuch complain, "I am only a dry tree."**

---

[1] Many liberals who deny the supernatural take chaps. 56 to 66 as a "Third Isaiah," most assuming that the chaps. were written by multiple authors. Form, content, and theology, however, are consistent with the unity of the whole book.

The Law forbade two classes of people to come into the sacred assembly of God's people as they worshiped. "No one who has been emasculated by crushing or cutting may enter the assembly of the LORD.... No Ammonite or Moabite or any of his descendants may enter the assembly of the LORD, even down to the tenth generation" (Deut. 23:1,3). The implication is that the foreigners among them have been and continue to be involved in pagan rites and ceremonies. However, the door was always open for foreigners to give their allegiance to the LORD and to join Israel to receive the blessings God promised to His people. Moses said to his brother-in-law, Hobab, who was a Gentile, "'Come with us and we will treat you well, for the LORD has promised good things to Israel'" (Num. 10:29; cf. Exod. 12:48–49). Hobab refused; but many others did say as Ruth did, "'Your people will be my people and your God my God'" (Ruth 1:16). They joined themselves not just to Israel but to the LORD, and were generally welcomed. Yet, because many of the promises were given specifically to Israel (and possibly because of prejudice that might have been shown by some of the Israelites), some foreigners expressed a fear that God eventually would separate them from His people. God told them not to say this—implying that they should continue trusting God and He would take care of them. He would never treat them as second-class citizens.

Also, because the increase of offspring of faithful Israelites was often a sign of blessing, eunuchs expressed disappointment about not being able to have children to carry on their family line. God told them not to say they were a "dry tree," unable to produce fruit. People might look on them that way, but God does not. Each person is valuable to Him.

> **4For this is what the LORD says: "To the eunuchs who keep my Sabbaths, who choose what pleases me and hold fast to my covenant— 5to them I will give within my temple and its walls a memorial and a name better than sons and daughters; I will give them an everlasting name that will not be cut off.**

God had a wonderful promise for eunuchs, who were considered defiled and not permitted to enter the assembly of the

LORD (Deut. 23:1). He expects them to keep not only the weekly Sabbath, but also the other Sabbaths of Leviticus 23. They must also choose, and keep choosing, not their own ways but the things that please the LORD.[2] This included strongly supporting God's covenant. Then God would give the eunuchs a "memorial," that is, He would give them a portion or possession "within [His] temple and its walls," in His presence, and a continuation of the family name better than through sons or daughters. The name God will give will be an "everlasting name," one that will never be "cut off," removed or wiped out. They will have a choice place in the resurrection and will live forever with the LORD.

> [6]And foreigners who bind themselves to the LORD to serve him, to love the name of the LORD, and to worship him, all who keep the Sabbath without desecrating it and who hold fast to my covenant— [7]these I will bring to my holy mountain and give them joy in my house of prayer. Their burnt offerings and sacrifices will be accepted on my altar; for my house will be called a house of prayer for all nations."

God expects the foreigners who join themselves to Him to worship Him, to love His name (His nature and character), to be His trusted servants, to keep the Sabbath,[3] and to strongly uphold His covenant. Then God will not only permit them to ascend His holy hill (cf. Ps. 24:3–5), but He will also bring them to it and make them rejoice in the temple, His house of prayer. Their burnt offerings (wholly burnt to indicate complete dedication of the worshiper and complete exaltation of the LORD) and their sacrifices (offered to seek and experience communion with God) will be well pleasing to Him. In this they will be fulfilling God's purpose. He always wanted His temple to be "a house of prayer for all nations," as Solomon recognized (1 Kings 8:41–43; 2 Chron. 6:32) and as Jesus proclaimed (Matt. 21:13). Note that the temple was still in existence when

---

[2]The words "choose" and "hold fast" in the Heb. indicate continual, persistent action.

[3]Foreigners, whether Canaanites, Egyptians, Assyrians, or Babylonians, never had the idea of ceasing (as "sabbath" means) work for one day in seven. See G. A. F. Knight, *Isaiah 56–66* (Grand Rapids: Wm. B. Eerdmans, 1985), 4–5.

Isaiah wrote this. He recognized its chief function as prayer (cf. 1 Kings 8:29–30,35–36,42–43,52).

> ⁸The Sovereign LORD declares—he who gathers the exiles of Israel: "I will gather still others to them besides those already gathered."

The "exiles of Israel" that are scattered are the ones who have turned away from the LORD. He will gather them to himself. They would probably include those of the northern kingdom of Israel, which came to an end when Shalmaneser destroyed Samaria in 722 B.C. The ten tribes were not lost, as some false teachers claim. Many of the ten tribes came down and joined the people of Judah. Others joined in the synagogues that arose after the later Babylonian exile. By New Testament times Jews of all twelve tribes met together in the synagogues, both in Palestine and everywhere Jews were found in the known world (Luke 2:36 shows Anna was of the northern tribe of Asher; Paul spoke of "our twelve tribes" as present in his day, Acts 26:7).

In addition, God promised to gather "still others." Jesus also promised this: "'I have other sheep that are not of this sheep pen. I must bring them also. They too will listen to my voice, and there shall be one flock and one shepherd'" (John 10:16; cf. Eph. 2:11–22). God's purpose is that all believers become one gathered people.

2. GODLESS RULERS AND IDOLATERS DESERVE JUDGMENT 56:9–57:13

a. Stupid, Greedy Leaders 56:9–12

> ⁹Come, all you beasts of the field, come and devour, all you beasts of the forest!

Isaiah now moves to the time after the fifteen years that God had added to Hezekiah's life. His son Manasseh turned away from the LORD and neglected the temple. It became a time for God to bring judgment.[4] The "beasts of the field," wild animals of the open country, and "beasts of the forest" may represent enemies God will again use to judge Israel (cf. 7:18; 9:12).

---

[4] J. Barton Payne, *An Outline of Hebrew History* (Grand Rapids: Baker Book House, 1954), 143–44. Payne recognized that Isaiah rebuked the sins of Manasseh's time.

> ¹⁰Israel's watchmen are blind, they all lack knowledge; they are all mute dogs, they cannot bark; they lie around and dream, they love to sleep.

Israel's leaders have forgotten the lessons learned in Hezekiah's day. They ought to be watchmen, guarding God's people and keeping them in the path of righteousness, but they are blind to the truth, without knowledge of God and His ways. They are like "mute dogs," unable to warn the people of danger. All that these lazy, unfaithful leaders do is sleep and dream. They do not care about the work the LORD has given them to do.

> ¹¹They are dogs with mighty appetites; they never have enough. They are shepherds who lack understanding; they all turn to their own way, each seeks his own gain.

These leaders are not only stupid (spiritually asleep); they are also greedy, never satisfied with what they have. As shepherds they should guide the people, but they have no "understanding," or discernment. They have turned from God's way to their own. They use whatever segment of the government is under their control to get gain for themselves, whether by violence or by intrigue (cf. Ezek. 34:8 where the leaders fell into similar patterns after Josiah's revival).

> ¹²"Come," each one cries, "let me get wine! Let us drink our fill of beer! And tomorrow will be like today, or even far better."

They invite each other to drunken feasts and suppose that their prosperity and their partying will only continue and increase. Revelry and intemperance were the order of the day.

b. Worse Judgment Will Come 57:1–2

> ¹The righteous perish, and no one ponders it in his heart; devout men are taken away, and no one understands that the righteous are taken away to be spared from evil.

In Manasseh's day the nation as a whole was stupid. While the leaders were indulging in luxury and a lascivious lifestyle, in sharp contrast "the righteous" (the godly remnant) were perishing and no one seemed to care or notice.

"Devout men" (Heb. *'anshe-chesed,* "people of covenant love," those who retained faithful, covenant love and who continued to express the same faith that praised God for past deliverances) were taken away in death. See 2 Kings 21:16 where Manasseh "shed so much innocent blood that he filled Jerusalem from end to end." But no one seemed to understand that those killed were escaping future calamity. It is implied that future disasters would bring suffering worse than death. (Cf. Rev. 14:9–13 where the prospect of suffering in the lake of fire is contrasted with the blessedness of those who die in the Lord.)

> ²Those who walk uprightly enter into peace;
> they find rest as they lie in death.

When the righteous die they enter into peace—God-given peace and well-being in His presence. As the psalmist Asaph wrote, "You guide me with your counsel," that is, during this life, "and afterward you will take me into glory," that is, into God's presence in heaven (Ps. 73:24; cf. Pss.16:9,11; 17:15).[5] Death was no defeat for them. The bodies of those who lived in a way that pleased God rest "as they lie in death" (Heb. *'al-mishk^evotham* "on their beds," that is, in tombs or graves).

c. Apostates Warned Of Judgment 57:3–6

> ³"But you—come here, you sons of a sorceress,
> you offspring of adulterers and prostitutes!

Isaiah, with biting force, condemns the wicked who have caused the death of the righteous. In Manasseh's time, sorcery (including the conjuring up of spirits and black magic), adultery, and prostitution (connected with idolatry) became common. "Offspring" means those who habitually and devotedly took part in these sins. God calls them to draw near to listen to His warning.

> ⁴Whom are you mocking? At whom do you
> sneer and stick out your tongue? Are you not a

---

[5]See Stanley M. Horton, *Our Destiny: Biblical Teachings on the Last Things* (Springfield, Mo.: Logion Press, 1996), 49.

brood of rebels, the offspring of liars?

Mocking ("jesting," "making merry over"), sneering ("opening the mouth wide"), and sticking out the tongue indicate a scornful, careless rebellion against the LORD and perhaps also despising and making fun of the godly. They have become offspring of "liars" (Heb. *shaqer*, "deception," including idolatry), instead of being children of God.

> ⁵You burn with lust among the oaks and under every spreading tree; you sacrifice your children in the ravines and under the overhanging crags.

Idolatry is so widespread there is no part of the land where it is not found. The lustful prostitution among luxuriant green trees was part of the Canaanite fertility cult—intended to encourage Baal to give fertility to their animals and to the land. Abominable slaughtering of children as sacrifices in the dry "ravines" ("wadis" [NASB margin]—streambeds or torrent valleys: dry in the summer, a torrent after a rainstorm⁶) in Judah and under overhanging rock cliffs was part of the worship of Molech (cf. Lev. 18:21; 20:2–4; 2 Kings 23:10; Jer. 7:31; 32:35). This was common during the reign of Manasseh, who even sacrificed one of his own sons (2 Kings 21:3,6). Appeasing Molech was supposed to avert bad luck or even death.

> ⁶[The idols] among the smooth stones of the ravines are your portion; they, they are your lot. Yes, to them you have poured out drink offerings and offered grain offerings. In the light of these things, should I relent?

The Hebrew from here through verse 13 switches from the plural to the second feminine singular. Probably the nation is being addressed as if it were a prostitute. The smooth, slippery stones of the streambed are characteristic of the "portion," or "lot," of these idolaters. The repetition of "they" gives emphasis to the fact that their relationship to the idols of Baal and Molech is not on firm ground; trusting in false gods offers no

---

⁶There were none of these wadis in Babylonia.

permanent or reliable foundation. To them they have poured out drink offerings and brought grain offerings. God asks if He should "relent," or change His attitude, in light of their evil practices. The answer is obvious: He should not and will not. That would be contrary to His nature. Sin demands judgment.

d. Persistent Idolatry 57:7–10

> ⁷You have made your bed on a high and lofty hill; there you went up to offer your sacrifices.

The people also practice their prostitution openly and shamelessly on the heights, where they offer pagan sacrifices. High places in the Old Testament were generally chosen as sites for cultic emplacements for fertility worship. The people supposed higher ground literally put them closer to the god, and the hill was as well a symbol of the female breast. The entire endeavor was an attempt to manipulate the gods so they would give their fertility to crops, flocks, and women.

> ⁸Behind your doors and your doorposts you have put your pagan symbols. Forsaking me, you uncovered your bed, you climbed into it and opened it wide; you made a pact with those whose beds you love, and you looked on their nakedness.

The reminders they put behind the doors and doorposts were possibly phallic symbols.[7] This may mean that while some practiced pagan religious prostitution openly (v. 7), others merely pretended to serve the LORD; secretly they were involved in the same religious prostitution as those who made their bed on the "high and lofty hill" and also had made a covenant with heathen idols. Looking on nakedness was what brought a curse on Canaan, the son of Ham (Gen. 9:22,25).

> ⁹You went to Molech with olive oil and increased your perfumes. You sent your ambassadors far away; you descended to the grave itself!

---

[7]Motyer believes they were "the Lord's words on the doorposts (Dt. 6:9)" put out of sight. J. Alec Motyer, *The Prophecy of Isaiah* (Downers Grove, Ill.: InterVarsity Press, 1993), 473.

Going "to Molech" (Heb. *lammelek,* "to the king") here refers to making foreign alliances, as Ahaz did when making a treaty with Tiglath-Pileser (2 Kings 16:7–10). The NIV and others take the literal reference to "the king" (see KJV, NASB) to mean the god Molech. However, the reference to ambassadors implies making treaties with actual kings. Instead of trusting the LORD, Israel committed spiritual prostitution.

Their having "descended to the grave" (rather, "sending down to Sheol" or "debasing to Sheol") means they had sinned to the point that they deserved death and Sheol (hell[8]).

> **10You were wearied by all your ways, but you would not say, 'It is hopeless.' You found renewal of your strength, and so you did not faint.**

Exerting themselves over a great number of journeys gave them new life so that they did not become weak. That is, they found resources to keep going on their way to hell. This may be an ironic parallel or echo of 40:28–31, where God who is never weary gives renewed strength to those who wait for Him.

e. Idolatry Brings No Benefit 57:11–13

> **11"Whom have you so dreaded and feared that you have been false to me, and have neither remembered me nor pondered this in your hearts? Is it not because I have long been silent that you do not fear me?**

The LORD asks whom they really dread and fear so that they cheat Him and do not remember or consider Him (lit., "You did not put [me] on your heart"). That is, they do not even think about the LORD ("did not remember Me, / Nor give Me a thought," NASB). Because God delayed sending judgment a long time the people no longer feared Him. Thus, most Jews in Manasseh's time became apostate.[9]

> **12I will expose your righteousness and your works, and they will not benefit you.**

---

[8]See Horton, *Our Destiny,* 44–49.

[9]This was worst during the years before Esarhaddon took Manasseh to Babylon in chains in 679 B.C. (2 Chron. 33:11).

God will "expose," that is, He will denounce, their righteousness —which was obviously unlike God's (more irony)—and He will denounce their works. Neither will help or profit them.

> ¹³When you cry out for help, let your collection [of idols] save you! The wind will carry all of them off, a mere breath will blow them away. But the man who makes me his refuge will inherit the land and possess my holy mountain."

When they cry out, calling to God for help, He tells them to let their collection of gods rescue them. But they can't even rescue themselves; a bit of wind or even "a mere breath will blow them away." (Likewise, all human activity that does not depend on God's Spirit is in vain [cf. Zech. 4:6].) Only the person who takes refuge in the LORD will possess the land as an inheritance from Him and take possession of (or inherit) His holy mountain in Jerusalem (see 27:13; 56:7). God is the only refuge, the only security.

3. RESTORATION AND BLESSING FOR THE CONTRITE 57:14–21

a. *Prepare The Way 57:14–15*

> ¹⁴And it will be said: "Build up, build up, prepare the road! Remove the obstacles out of the way of my people."

Preparing the road, building it up, and taking away the obstacles from the road of God's people reminds us of 40:3–4, where God is coming back to His people. Now the way is to be prepared for God's people to come and claim the inheritance of the land and of God's "holy mountain" (v. 13).

> ¹⁵For this is what the high and lofty One says— he who lives forever, whose name is holy: "I live in a high and holy place, but also with him who is contrite and lowly in spirit, to revive the spirit of the lowly and to revive the heart of the contrite.

God now speaks as the One exalted and lifted high over all,

the One who fills the eternity of time and space and whose name (character and nature) is holy. His holy dwelling place is in heaven. Yet He also dwells with the person who is "contrite" (Heb. *dakka'*, "crushed" by life's burdens, troubles, and sorrows). He lives with the "lowly in spirit" (Heb. *shephal-ruach*, "the humble of spirit").

This is not a temporary visit. Though God is transcendent, He is also immanent. He continues to live within to give life to the spirit of the humble and to the heart of the crushed. What a wonderful revelation of God this is!

b. Comfort And Peace For Mourners 57:16–19

16 I will not accuse forever, nor will I always be angry, for then the spirit of man would grow faint before me—the breath of man that I have created.

God will come to dwell with the humble and the crushed because He will not conduct a lawsuit against ("accuse") Israel forever, nor will His anger continue. Though the time of His anger may be long, He knows the limits of the people He has created (cf. Ps. 103:14) and He knows their spirits would grow weak before Him, that is, in the presence of His anger. He does not intend to destroy them all.

17 I was enraged by his sinful greed; I punished him, and hid my face in anger, yet he kept on in his willful ways.

Because the people were guilty of greedily seeking profit in ways contrary to the Law, God's anger was stirred and He struck him (Israel) down. He "hid [His] face," that is, removed His active presence and blessing. Yet this did not cause the people to repent. They continued in their "willful ways," faithless, rebellious, following whatever pleased them and going wherever their own hearts and minds wished to go.

18 I have seen his ways, but I will heal him; I will guide him and restore comfort to him,

In spite of Israel's rebellion, God has looked on their ways and will "heal" (save and restore) them and lead them. He will also "restore comfort" (or consolation) to them, even those among them who mourn. God takes the initiative because of who He is, not because their ways have changed.

> ¹⁹creating praise on the lips of the mourners in Israel. Peace, peace, to those far and near," says the LORD. "And I will heal them."

For the mourners, God will do what He alone can do. He will "[create] praise on the lips of the mourners": He will make it possible for them to praise Him and announce peace, peace to "those far and near," for He will heal them (cf. Mal. 4:2, which shows He will heal through Jesus). Ephesians 2:11–18 applies this to the Gentiles who are far off but made near by the blood of Christ. Ephesians 2:17–18 says, "He [Jesus] came and preached peace to you who were far away [the Gentiles] and peace to those who were near [the Jews]. For through him we both [Jews and Gentiles] have access to the Father by one Spirit."

c. No Peace For The Wicked 57:20–21

> ²⁰But the wicked are like the tossing sea, which cannot rest, whose waves cast up mire and mud. ²¹"There is no peace," says my God, "for the wicked."

Sinners are in contrast to those whom God heals and restores. The guilty who continue in their wrongdoing are like a "tossing sea"—never peaceful, but continually stirring up or tossing up "mire [slime or seaweed] and mud." God's word is that there is no peace for them; they cannot expect the blessings of God or the joy of His presence.

4. HYPOCRITICAL WORSHIP 58:1–2

> ¹"Shout it aloud, do not hold back. Raise your voice like a trumpet. Declare to my people their rebellion and to the house of Jacob their sins.

"Shout it aloud" (Heb. *qara' b*ᵉ*garon*, "proclaim with a throat") and using the "voice like a trumpet" indicates every means should be taken to be sure the people hear. The people need to hear God's declaration of their rebellion and be convicted of their sins.

> ²For day after day they seek me out; they seem eager to know my ways, as if they were a nation that does what is right and has not forsaken the commands of its God. They ask me for just decisions and seem eager for God to come near them.

The religious practices of the people seem commendable. Every day they seem to seek the LORD and seem to delight in the knowledge of His ways. They act "as if they were a nation that does what is right and has not forsaken the commands of its God." They ask God for right decisions and seem to delight in the nearness of God, probably meaning they offer the sacrifices which are intended to bring them near to God and which show they want God to come near to them. They want everyone to see how pious they are.

5. Hypocritical Fasting 58:3–5

> ³'Why have we fasted,' they say, 'and you have not seen it? Why have we humbled ourselves, and you have not noticed?' "Yet on the day of your fasting, you do as you please and exploit all your workers.

All their worship is merely outward form, without reality, without power (cf. 2 Tim. 3:5). While they are doing these religious acts they are complaining, especially about fasting without getting results from God. The only fast God commanded in the Law was on the Day of Atonement (one day of fasting each year). The fasts they had been observing were additional fasts, by which they were trying to coerce God to give them what they wanted. While they were fasting, they were acting like slave drivers, exploiting people who were working hard for them.

> ⁴Your fasting ends in quarreling and strife, and in striking each other with wicked fists. You cannot fast as you do today and expect your voice to be heard on high.

Fasting which "ends in quarreling and strife" and "striking each other with wicked fists" means that all they want is to get their own way, even when they are wrong. Thus, their fasting ends in quarreling and fighting and they never get through to God. Because of their strife He does not answer their prayers.

> ⁵Is this the kind of fast I have chosen, only a day for a man to humble himself? Is it only for bowing one's head like a reed and for lying on sackcloth and ashes? Is that what you call a fast, a day acceptable to the LORD?

The conventional forms the people were going through in the day of their fast did not please God. The Law did not ask them to bow their heads very properly. The Law never commanded sackcloth and ashes. These things were ways they tried to express humility before the LORD, but they had degenerated into mere show.

6. GOD WANTS FASTING FROM SIN 58:6–10

> ⁶"Is not this the kind of fasting I have chosen: to loose the chains of injustice and untie the cords of the yoke, to set the oppressed free and break every yoke?

What God wanted was not a fast (abstaining) from food, but a fast from sin and from oppression of the poor, the workers, and the slaves. God wanted justice and freedom for His people. He loves the poor and the oppressed and hated their being selfishly and ruthlessly exploited.

> ⁷Is it not to share your food with the hungry and to provide the poor wanderer with shelter—when you see the naked, to clothe him, and not to turn away from your own flesh and blood?

Instead of fasting to get something for themselves God wanted them to feed the hungry, shelter the poor, and clothe those who had insufficient clothing. They were especially to care for their "own flesh and blood" (cf. 1 Tim. 5:8). God still wants this. Jesus put it plainly in Matthew 25:31–46.

Galatians 6:10 also exhorts us, "Therefore, as we have opportunity, let us do good to all people, especially to those who belong to the family of believers."

> **8Then your light will break forth like the dawn, and your healing will quickly appear; then your righteousness will go before you, and the glory of the Lord will be your rear guard.**

Those who fast from sin and greed and who feed the hungry and give shelter and clothes to the poor will see wonderful results. Their glorious light will burst in upon them "like the dawn," for it will be a new day for them. New flesh will quickly spring up in the healing of their wounds, for the defeats in the battle of life will be forgotten. They will march ahead triumphantly with their God-given righteousness going before them and God's glory as their "rear guard."

> Is this a fast, to keep
> The larder lean?
> And clean
> From fat of veals, and sheep?
> Is it to quit the dish
> Of flesh, yet still
> To fill
> The platter high with fish?
> Is it to fast an hour,
> Or ragged to go,
> Or show
> A downcast look, and sour?
> No: 'tis a fast, to dole
> Thy sheaf of wheat
> And meat,
> Unto the hungry soul.
> It is to fast from strife,
> From old debate,
> And hate;
> To circumcise thy life.
> To show a heart grief-rent;
> To starve thy sin,
> Not bin;
> And that's to keep a fast.
> —Robert Herrick
> (1591–1674)

> **9Then you will call, and the LORD will answer; you will cry for help, and he will say: Here am I. "If you do away with the yoke of oppression, with the pointing finger and malicious talk,**

Whenever they call, God will answer. Whenever they cry for help, God will be there.

Now Isaiah proceeds to amplify what should be expected, not only on a fast day, but also in the fast from sin and greed that should be kept by every individual every day. Negatively, it means getting rid of the yoke of oppression, the extended finger (of mischief), and of speaking falsely and maliciously to cause harm or trouble.

> ¹⁰and if you spend yourselves in behalf of the hungry and satisfy the needs of the oppressed, then your light will rise in the darkness, and your night will become like the noonday.

Positively, it means spending (granting) yourselves (your souls, that is, your desires), that is, what you want for yourselves, for the hungry. It means satisfying the "oppressed" (or, humbled, unfortunate). Then the darkness and obscurity of life's problems will be replaced by full, brilliant light.

7. God Will Guide 58:11–12

> ¹¹The Lord will guide you always; he will satisfy your needs in a sun-scorched land and will strengthen your frame. You will be like a well-watered garden, like a spring whose waters never fail.

God's guidance will be continual. He will satisfy their needs (their "soul" [KJV], their desires, and their "bones" [KJV], their needs), even in an arid land. Strong bones would mean inner strength, stability and stamina. "A well-watered garden" and "a spring whose waters never fail" indicate provision for every need, both natural and spiritual.

> ¹²Your people will rebuild the ancient ruins and will raise up the age-old foundations; you will be called Repairer of Broken Walls, Restorer of Streets with Dwellings.

Future generations who respond to God's order of justice, mercy, and loving compassion will build up the ancient ruins. Those of verses 9–10 will raise the foundations of many earlier generations and be named "Repairer of Broken Walls" and "Restorer of Streets with Dwellings." The people of Isaiah's day needed to do this, as 1:7–9 indicates. If we are to rebuild our nation today, we must build "upon a foundation that is both consistently moral and deeply spiritual" or the calamities of the past will be repeated.[10]

---

[10]Paul D. Hanson, *Isaiah 40–66* (Louisville: John Knox Press, 1995), 207.

8. THE SABBATH BRINGS BLESSING 58:13–14

> ¹³"If you keep your feet from breaking the Sabbath and from doing as you please on my holy day, if you call the Sabbath a delight and the LORD's holy day honorable, and if you honor it by not going your own way and not doing as you please or speaking idle words,

Now Isaiah returns not to a fast day but to a feast day, the Sabbath, an important covenant sign under the Law. The Sabbath day was to be "to the LORD" (Lev. 23:3). They were abusing it by using it as a day to do what they pleased. God wanted it to be holy, separated from other days, so that they could worship the LORD and express their love to Him with their whole heart, soul, mind, and strength, delighting themselves in Him. It was to be an honored day and they must honor it by not doing their own business, finding their own pleasure, or "speaking idle words," that is, talking about things that have nothing to do with honoring the LORD. The Sabbath was an opportunity for them to express delight in the service of God. It was also a time for a holy convocation, where the local community was to come together for worship and teaching.

> ¹⁴then you will find your joy in the LORD, and I will cause you to ride on the heights of the land and to feast on the inheritance of your father Jacob." The mouth of the LORD has spoken.

Then, with the Sabbath a great delight, they will take great delight in the LORD every day. Riding "on the heights of the land" and feasting "on the inheritance of . . . Jacob" indicate might and victory while enjoying the covenant blessings given to Israel.

STUDY QUESTIONS

1. What is the relation between good works and salvation?
2. On what grounds are foreigners and eunuchs included in the promised blessing?
3. Why was the Sabbath so important in Old Testament times?

4. Why did the leaders in Manasseh's day deserve judgment?
5. What happened to the godly in Manasseh's day and why?
6. What was the attitude of idolaters in Manasseh's day and how did they show it?
7. Who will not be restored and why not?
8. Who will be restored and why?
9. What was wrong with the people's worship?
10. Why did God not accept their fasts?
11. What kind of fast did God really want?
12. What blessings are promised to those who fast from sin and oppression?
13. What was God looking for during the Sabbath?
14. How does finding our joy in the Lord relate to the Sabbath-rest that God expects us to seek every day? (See Heb. 4:9–11.)

B. Zion's Confession, Redemption, And Glory 59:1–60:22

1. SIN SEPARATES FROM THE SAVIOR 59:1–3

¹Surely the arm of the LORD is not too short to save, nor his ear too dull to hear.

After briefly speaking of future restoration, Isaiah returns to the situation in Manasseh's day. As in 49:14–15, the problem is not with God but with the people. God's ability "to save" and "to hear" the prayers of His people is not limited in any way. He is ready and waiting.

²But your iniquities have separated you from your God; your sins have hidden his face from you, so that he will not hear.

Actually, willful sins were separating the people from their God. All sins are really against God, who created and loves everyone. Their sins were like a wall that hid God's face (separated them from His presence) and kept Him from listening and heeding their requests.

> ³For your hands are stained with blood, your fingers with guilt. Your lips have spoken lies, and your tongue mutters wicked things.

Isaiah now depicts Israel's exceeding sinfulness. "Hands . . . stained with blood" (i.e., defiled with vengeful bloodshed) and "fingers [stained] with guilt" indicate the people were unclean and not fit to enter the presence of God. Violence, rebellion, lies, and the proclaiming of perverse wickedness were part of those sins that separated them from God. This was not the case with Jews in the later Babylonian exile but with those in Judah in Isaiah's day, especially in the time of Manasseh.[1]

2. No Justice And No Peace 59:4–8

> ⁴No one calls for justice; no one pleads his case with integrity. They rely on empty arguments and speak lies; they conceive trouble and give birth to evil.

No one proclaims what is right or true. Those who seek their claim in court do not seek it honestly or conscientiously. They try to make their claim look legal when it is really wrong. There is no integrity. Because of this corruption they cannot trust the LORD, so they trust in emptiness, which usually means idols but may mean "empty arguments" (as in the NIV et al.). They speak not just lies but worthless, false, deceitful words. Then Israel is pictured as a pregnant woman with her womb full of "trouble," so she gives birth to "evil" (Heb. *'awen*, "harm," "misdeeds," "injustice"). The idolatry in Manasseh's day was leading to social disintegration and all kinds of injustice.

> ⁵They hatch the eggs of vipers and spin a spider's web. Whoever eats their eggs will die, and when one is broken, an adder is hatched.

Their sins are compared to a viper's eggs and their plans to weaving spider webs. Eating a viper's eggs, that is, partaking of

---

[1] Oswald T. Allis, "Book of Isaiah," in *Wycliffe Bible Encyclopedia* (Chicago: Moody Press, 1975), 1:857.

those sins, brings death. When such an egg "is broken," perhaps opposing the sins, "an adder is hatched," that is, makes things worse.

> ⁶Their cobwebs are useless for clothing; they cannot cover themselves with what they make. Their deeds are evil deeds, and acts of violence are in their hands.

Their plans will prove to be as insufficient for their needs as a covering made of spider webs. Specifically, "their deeds are evil deeds and acts of violence are in their hands."

> ⁷Their feet rush into sin; they are swift to shed innocent blood. Their thoughts are evil thoughts; ruin and destruction mark their ways.

Every part of the bodies of these sinners is involved: from their hands (v. 6) to their feet to their thoughts. Their feet rush to do evil and kill innocent people. They think and plan trouble, harm, and injustice. Their lives are a highway for destructive violence and the breakdown and collapse of society.

> ⁸The way of peace they do not know; there is no justice in their paths. They have turned them into crooked roads; no one who walks in them will know peace.

"The way [the lifestyle] of peace" with God that brings His blessing they do not know or experience. Their lifestyle shows "no justice" and is crooked. Those who follow them and their ways get entangled in the same mess and cannot "know [or experience] peace" (blessing and well-being that God gives) either.

3. Isaiah Confesses The People's Sins 59:9–15

a. Walking In Darkness 59:9–11

> ⁹So justice is far from us, and righteousness does not reach us. We look for light, but all is darkness; for brightness, but we walk in deep shadows.

Isaiah changes to the first person plural here, identifying himself with his people, lamenting over and confessing their situation. Because of their sins, the people are under God's judgment and there is no justice (because they do not let God rule) or righteousness (because they reject God's righteous purposes). The result is "darkness," and they walk around aimlessly in "deep shadows." There is not even a gleam of light or brightness that would show God's mercy to them.

> **10Like the blind we grope along the wall, feeling our way like men without eyes. At midday we stumble as if it were twilight; among the strong, we are like the dead.**

The constant groping shows the depth of their spiritual blindness. Stumbling in darkness and obscurity "at midday" shows the degree of their insensitivity to the light of spiritual truth. In contrast to those who are "strong," healthy and vigorous, the ones that stumble and grope are "like the dead"—without any spiritual life.

> **11We all growl like bears; we moan mournfully like doves. We look for justice, but find none; for deliverance, but it is far away.**

Growling like bears indicates anger because of sin and its results in their lives and in human society. Moaning like doves indicates frustration because of the lack of justice and the absence of deliverance (including salvation, God's help, and the blessing and prosperity He had formerly given to Israel).

b. Sins Acknowledged 59:12–15

> **12For our offenses are many in your sight, and our sins testify against us. Our offenses are ever with us, and we acknowledge our iniquities:**

Isaiah pictures God as the Judge; and the people's sins individually testify against them. The people recognize that rebellious sins are with them and they know they are guilty.

> **13rebellion and treachery against the LORD, turning our backs on our God, fomenting oppression and revolt, uttering lies our hearts have conceived.**

There is, however, no repentance on the part of the people. They are indeed rebelling and treacherously denying or disowning the Lord. They turn away from the true God in disloyalty. Their words are full of oppression and revolt that include spiritual apostasy. Their hearts and minds are the source of muttered expressions of falsehood and deception.

> **14So justice is driven back, and righteousness stands at a distance; truth has stumbled in the streets, honesty cannot enter.**

The reason there is no repentance is that any attempt at justice is "driven back." Righteousness is pictured as standing "at a distance," unable to do anything about the situation. Truth (including security and reliability) falters and stumbles "in the streets" (open squares or marketplaces), and what is honest (including straight and right) cannot come within. There is complete moral collapse in the cities.

> **15Truth is nowhere to be found, and whoever shuns evil becomes a prey. The Lord looked and was displeased that there was no justice.**

Truth, security, integrity, and reliability are lacking. Most pitiful of all, the person who avoids evil "becomes a prey," stripped of everything as if he were a prisoner of war.

The Lord responded to Israel's confession (cf. v. 9) with displeasure because there was "no justice," no defense of the godly remnant among His people. Truly, sin had separated the people as a whole from God.

4. The Lord Himself Will Save 59:16–21

> **16He saw that there was no one, he was appalled that there was no one to intervene; so his own arm worked salvation for him, and his own righteousness sustained him.**

The Lord himself is driven to astonishment and indignation that there was no intercessor, "no one to intervene," no one to stand against all the sin and evil, no one to defend the godly in Israel, no one to make Israel a light to the nations.

Because God had promised salvation, by His own power and

might He brought salvation, but in a way that His righteousness could uphold. Thus, His salvation was and is pure grace.

> **17He put on righteousness as his breastplate, and the helmet of salvation on his head; he put on the garments of vengeance and wrapped himself in zeal as in a cloak.**

God's righteous nature and character are like a "breastplate" or coat of mail, armor made of overlapping pieces of metal. Sin that He opposes cannot affect Him. His salvation is like a "helmet," so nothing could change His mind or purpose to save. Then, because of His holiness, His purpose of "vengeance" (recompense and requital) was like clothing and His "zeal," or passion to save and help, is like an outer robe or cloak. In Ephesians 6:14 Paul uses this metaphor of spiritual protection and applies it to the Christian.

> **18According to what they have done, so will he repay wrath to his enemies and retribution to his foes; he will repay the islands their due.**

God's judgment is always according to people's works, their deeds. He will "repay wrath to his enemies," and repay or give reprisal to the "islands" (or "coastlands," that is, to all nations in all parts of the world, not merely people of Asia Minor). They will all get what they deserve.

> **19From the west, men will fear the name of the LORD, and from the rising of the sun, they will revere his glory. For he will come like a pent-up flood that the breath of the LORD drives along.**

The whole world, from east to west, will reverence the LORD and His glory. The latter half of this verse can be translated in two ways, each with a different nuance in meaning. First, the NIV has "He will come like a pent-up flood that the breath of the LORD drives along." A slight variation on the NIV is: "He will come like the river is narrow, the wind of the LORD driving onward in it" (cf. NIV). "He" would refer back to the LORD in His glory. The river usually refers to the Euphrates. A great wind driving the water of the river between high banks where the river is narrow would sweep everything away before it. This pictures the irresistibility of God when He comes.

The word translated "narrow" also means "adversary," or "enemy." "Wind" also means "breath" or "Spirit." "Driving onward" can also mean "raise a banner." So an alternate translation takes an adversary as the subject: "An adversary will come like the river [or "like a river, a great overflowing stream," according to the Septuagint]; the Spirit of the LORD raises a banner against him." That is, the Spirit defeats the adversary (along with all the evil in the world) and causes the whole world to reverence the LORD and His glory. Either translation shows that the LORD is victorious and all opposition will be swept away, defeated.

> 20"The Redeemer will come to Zion, to those in Jacob who repent of their sins," declares the LORD.

As a result, the Kinsman-Redeemer will come to Zion (cf. Rom. 11:26), and specifically to Israelites who turn back from rebellion and repent of their sins. They are called "Jacob" ("deceiver") because they are not living up to the name "Israel" ("God's fighter and prince"). This is an utterance from the LORD, an assurance that He will fulfill His word.

> 21"As for me, this is my covenant with them," says the LORD. "My Spirit, who is on you, and my words that I have put in your mouth will not depart from your mouth, or from the mouths of your children, or from the mouths of their descendants from this time on and forever," says the LORD.

"As for me" emphasizes God's commitment to carrying out His promise. His covenant is "with them," that is, with the people who turn back from rebellion and repent. God then addresses the Redeemer. His Spirit is upon the Redeemer. He is the Anointed One, the Messiah, the Christ. God the Father puts His words in the Redeemer's mouth (see John 14:10,24).

His words will continue to be in the Redeemer's mouth and in "the mouths of [His] children" (Heb. *zarakha*, "your seed") and "the mouths of their descendants." The term "seed" refers back to 53:10, which affirms that the Redeemer will "see his seed" (KJV). His spiritual seed, all true believers, will become proclaimers of the same word (implying that they do so by the same Spirit).

5. Light And Glory Come To Zion 60:1–3

> **1"Arise, shine, for your light has come, and the glory of the LORD rises upon you.**

After prophesying of the coming of the Redeemer and the abiding Spirit (59:20–21), Isaiah now addresses the coming Zion.[2] Zion's light will have come and filled and transformed Zion. Thus, Zion can respond to the command "Arise, shine," or give off the light of God's glory to others.

> **2See, darkness covers the earth and thick darkness is over the peoples, but the LORD rises upon you and his glory appears over you.**

The world and the peoples in it need the light, for "darkness covers the earth" and gloom envelops the peoples of the world. The LORD will counteract that darkness by shining upon Zion so all will see His glory (cf. 9:2; 42:16).

> **3Nations will come to your light, and kings to the brightness of your dawn.**

God's light becomes Zion's light and His light shines through them. Nations and their kings or rulers from all the world will come "to the brightness of [their] dawn," to the gleam of the shining out of its light. The light will attract all of them out of their darkness. This was anticipated by the call given to everyone in 55:1–5. It involves the spread of the gospel. It will find its greatest fulfillment at the beginning of the Millennium. See Amos 9:11–12 which "refers to the restoration of David's twelve-tribe kingdom under the Messiah, with His rule over converted nations or peoples who are blessed by Israel and now bear God's name. The remnant of Edom [that Amos mentions] is representative of those who are left of the former enemies of Israel, or of all the peoples of the world who are left after the tribulation and who come to be possessed by or belong to Israel."[3]

---

[2]The Septuagint has "Shine, shine, Jerusalem, for your light has come."
[3]Stanley M. Horton, *Our Destiny: Biblical Teachings on the Last Things* (Springfield, Mo.: Logion Press, 1996), 207.

6. Worship Restored 60:4–22

a. Gentiles Restore And Serve Zion 60:4–7

> ⁴"Lift up your eyes and look about you: All assemble and come to you; your sons come from afar, and your daughters are carried on the arm.

As the people of Zion look in all directions they will see the nations coming, but not alone. They will be bringing Zion's scattered sons and daughters with them.

> ⁵Then you will look and be radiant, your heart will throb and swell with joy; the wealth on the seas will be brought to you, to you the riches of the nations will come.

When the people of Zion see this, they will be radiant. Their hearts will "throb and swell with joy," because they will be relieved of all fear and doubt. Another reason for the great joy will be the abundance brought by way of the sea, the "riches of the nations." Foreigners will be bringing many precious gifts as they come to Zion (cf. Hag. 2:7–8).

> ⁶Herds of camels will cover your land, young camels of Midian and Ephah. And all from Sheba will come, bearing gold and incense and proclaiming the praise of the LORD.

The mass of camels covering Zion—including young bull camels of Midian (southeast of Israel) and Ephah (a subtribe of the Midianites), along with "all from Sheba" (Yemen)—pictures the wealth of the nations being brought overland to Zion. Camel caravans would do that in Isaiah's day. Along with gold and frankincense (from South Yemen and Somalia, as they are known today), they will bring news of the glory of the LORD, indicating that God's glory and His praise will be spreading over the earth.

> ⁷All Kedar's flocks will be gathered to you, the rams of Nebaioth will serve you; they will be accepted as offerings on my altar, and I will adorn my glorious temple.

Flocks of the Ishmaelite tribes of Kedar and Nebaioth will be part of the wealth of the nations brought to Zion in the service of God. The livestock will go up as burnt offerings with God's favor on His altar.[4] By this, God will keep glorifying and beautifying His splendid house (i.e., the temple in Jerusalem). (See Hag. 2:9.)

b. Sons From Afar Honor God 60:8–9

> [8]"Who are these that fly along like clouds, like doves to their nests? [9]Surely the islands look to me; in the lead are the ships of Tarshish, bringing your sons from afar, with their silver and gold, to the honor of the LORD your God, the Holy One of Israel, for he has endowed you with splendor.

Ships with billowing sails look like clouds against the distant sky or like doves flying home. "The islands [coastlands, inhabited parts of the earth] look to [wait expectantly for]" the LORD. Their great Tarshish ships give first importance to bringing Zion's sons along with silver and gold to honor the name, the person, of Zion's God, who is the Holy One of Israel. They do this because God has "endowed" (glorified, exalted) Zion with splendor.

c. Foreigners Rebuild And Honor Zion 60:10–14

> [10]"Foreigners will rebuild your walls, and their kings will serve you. Though in anger I struck you, in favor I will show you compassion.

The "foreigners" who come to Zion will become citizens and will enlarge and beautify the city, for God's wrath will be replaced by His grace and mercy. Some apply the building of the walls to Nehemiah's time. However, the people of Jerusalem

---

[4]Most premillennialists feel that these sacrifices are memorials, just as the Lord's Supper is a memorial, not a substitute for the finished work of Christ. "Others, on the basis that the Book of Hebrews treats the Old Testament law and ritual as types and shadows, say that . . . the personal presence of Jesus, who is himself the fulfillment of the entire sacrificial system," fulfills these prophecies (see Heb. 8:13; 9:9–18; 10:1,18). Horton, *Our Destiny*, 204.

built the wall then. This passage has such sweeping assurances that it must apply to millennial times.

The people will become fellow citizens with God's people, just as Gentile believers do when they accept Christ in this age (Eph. 2:19). Thus, in the light of New Testament revelation, the foreigners who come to Zion must have also come to Christ.

> ¹¹Your gates will always stand open, they will never be shut, day or night, so that men may bring you the wealth of the nations—their kings led in triumphal procession.

Gates that "will never be shut" indicate peace and safety as well as freedom of access. This will also be the case in the New Jerusalem (Rev. 21:25). Through Zion's gates, however, people will bring the "wealth of the nations," their kings made subject as Zion triumphs. (See Hag. 2:6–8; Zech. 8:20–23; 14:14.)

> ¹²For the nation or kingdom that will not serve you will perish; it will be utterly ruined.

In fact, no nation will continue to exist unless it becomes subject to Zion because its people are drawn by the LORD's light, holy character, and love (Zech. 14:17–19).

> ¹³"The glory of Lebanon will come to you, the pine, the fir and the cypress together, to adorn the place of my sanctuary; and I will glorify the place of my feet.

The best of wood from the best of trees, including the cedars of Lebanon, will beautify the LORD's holy millennial temple in Jerusalem. God will glorify the "place of [His] feet." The place where God manifests his presence fully and continually is in heaven. In Old Testament times the temple in Jerusalem, especially the ark of the covenant, was called the place of His feet, or His footstool (1 Chron. 28:2; Pss. 99:5; 132:7; Lam. 2:1). However, God also calls the earth His footstool (66:1; Matt. 5:35; Acts 7:49). Jeremiah also makes it clear that the ark would no longer be needed, missed, or even remembered (Jer. 3:16). The millennial kingdom will be operating under the new covenant of Calvary, thus the place of God's feet in millennial times will not be the ark of the old covenant but the whole earth.

> ¹⁴The sons of your oppressors will come bowing before you; all who despise you will bow down at your feet and will call you the City of the LORD, Zion of the Holy One of Israel.

The descendants of Zion's former oppressors will humble themselves, showing the deepest respect, and they will recognize that Jerusalem is truly the LORD's city, belonging to "the Holy One of Israel" (Isaiah's favorite name for God). Now His holiness attracts them.

d. God's Purpose to Transform Zion 60:15–18

> ¹⁵"Although you have been forsaken and hated, with no one traveling through, I will make you the everlasting pride and the joy of all generations.

The Jerusalem of the Millennium will be in sharp contrast to the Jerusalem of the past. God will make it the "everlasting pride [Heb. $g^e\text{'}on$, "loftiness," "majesty"] and the joy of all generations" to come.

> ¹⁶You will drink the milk of nations and be nursed at royal breasts. Then you will know that I, the LORD, am your Savior, your Redeemer, the Mighty One of Jacob.

Isaiah uses the figure of "the milk of nations" and of kings to mean they will all nourish Zion with loving, personal care. Then the people of Zion will know that God is their Savior and Kinsman-Redeemer—not only the Holy One of Israel but also "the mighty One of Jacob."

> ¹⁷Instead of bronze I will bring you gold, and silver in place of iron. Instead of wood I will bring you bronze, and iron in place of stones. I will make peace your governor and righteousness your ruler.

That God will turn things around is shown by replacing bronze with gold, iron with silver, wood with bronze, and stones with iron. In contrast to the former sin and corruption, the government will be changed to peace and righteousness. This will be brought about by the rule of the King-Messiah (9:7)

> ¹⁸No longer will violence be heard in your land, nor ruin or destruction within your borders, but you will call your walls Salvation and your gates Praise.

Instead of violence, ruin, and destruction, the walls of the city will be named "Salvation" (*Yeshu'ah*, simply another form of the Heb. word for the name of Jesus) and the gates, "Praise" (*t^ehillah*, singular of the Heb. name for the Book of Psalms). Thus, the city will be full of the blessings of salvation and the people will be full of praise to the LORD for those blessings.

e. God's People Will Display His Splendor 60:19–22

> ¹⁹The sun will no more be your light by day, nor will the brightness of the moon shine on you, for the LORD will be your everlasting light, and your God will be your glory. ²⁰Your sun will never set again, and your moon will wane no more; the LORD will be your everlasting light, and your days of sorrow will end.

The transformation will be complete. The city will no longer have the sun and moon for light. Instead, the LORD's glory will give it a supernatural, "everlasting light," for He will manifest His presence there in a new way. With the LORD as their sun and moon, that is, as the source and manifestation of their light, there will be constant light. With the fact there will be no more darkness comes the assurance that their "days of sorrow will end," no more sorrow, crying, or mourning.

> ²¹Then will all your people be righteous and they will possess the land forever. They are the shoot I have planted, the work of my hands, for the display of my splendor.

The sin that causes sorrow will be no more, for all the people, not only of Jerusalem but of the whole land, will be righteous (Zech. 14:20–21; Rev. 21:27).[5] Never again will God need to use enemies to bring judgment because of His people's sins (cf. 10:5–6). The people will be a "shoot," or branch (Heb. *netser,* the same word used of the Messiah in 11:1), planted by the LORD, "the work of [His] hands" (His power being manifest), so that His glory and splendor will be clearly displayed for all to see.

> [22]The least of you will become a thousand, the smallest a mighty nation. I am the LORD; in its time I will do this swiftly."

What God has planted will grow. The little shoot that God has planted will "become a thousand," the smallest will become a vast nation: No one will be insignificant or unimportant. God guarantees that it will be done swiftly "in its time"—when He sees fit. It is also possible to translate "do . . . swiftly" by a word spelled the same but meaning "to enjoy." Truly, God will enjoy what He sees and does during the Millennium.

STUDY QUESTIONS

1. What was keeping God from saving—from even listening to the cries of—His people?
2. What do the comparisons used teach us about the nature of sin?
3. How did God respond when he saw there was no intercessor?
4. Why will people revere God's glory?
5. What is included in God's covenant with the repentant?
6. When Zion arises and shines, how will the nations of the world respond?
7. Who will the nations bring with them to Zion and how will the people of Israel respond?
8. What will the foreigners who come to Zion do?
9. What contrasts will there be between the Jerusalem of the Millennium and the Jerusalem of Isaiah's day?

---

[5]Allis, "Book of Isaiah," 1:857.

C. The Messiah Announces His Mission 61:1–63:6

1. Anointed To Preach Good News 61:1–2

> ¹The Spirit of the Sovereign LORD is on me, because the LORD has anointed me to preach good news to the poor. He has sent me to bind up the brokenhearted, to proclaim freedom for the captives and release from darkness for the prisoners,

Now the Messiah announces His mission. Jesus expressly applied this passage to himself at the beginning of His Galilean ministry in Nazareth (Luke 4:16–22). The Lord's Spirit being on the Person who speaks here identifies Him as the anointed Servant of the LORD of 42:1 and the anointed messianic King of 11:2.

Here He speaks as the anointed Prophet preaching "good news to the poor," those who humble themselves before God, gently taking a low place and acknowledging their need. (The New Testament understands them as poor in the world's eyes and needing God's help; see Matt. 5:3; Luke 4:18; 1 Cor. 1:26.) He is sent with loving, personal attention: (1) to "bind up" the wounds of those whose hearts are broken, distressed, or afflicted for any reason; (2) to "proclaim freedom . . . and release" to those taken captive and release to those held in sin's darkness (including the opening of eyes).

> ²to proclaim the year of the LORD's favor and the day of vengeance of our God, to comfort all who mourn,

"The year of the LORD's favor" may allude to those Israelites who had sold themselves being set free in the Year of Jubilee (Lev. 25:39–43; cf. Ezek. 46:17). It may also be identified with the time of God's favor: the day of salvation (49:8) and the year of God's redemption (63:4). Parallel, "day" and "year" are in apposition, therefore used synonymously to refer to an indefinite point in time. When Jesus applied this to His own ministry, He was not intending to limit His ministry to a day or a year. From John's gospel it is clear that He ministered at least three and one-half years before the cross. His proclamation was a proclamation of liberty to those bound by sin.

Jesus did not go on to quote "the day of vengeance of our God." In His first coming, He did not come to condemn the world (John 3:17); rather, He came to be a ransom for sin (Heb. 9:28; Mark 10:45). The "vengeance," or righteous judgment, of God will come at the end of the age (Revelation 6 to 19), which culminates in the Battle of Armageddon, when Jesus comes and triumphs over the Antichrist. Then, too, He will comfort those who mourn, for all tears will be wiped away.

2. Priests Of The Lord 61:3

> ³and provide for those who grieve in Zion—to bestow on them a crown of beauty instead of ashes, the oil of gladness instead of mourning, and a garment of praise instead of a spirit of despair. They will be called oaks of righteousness, a planting of the Lord for the display of his splendor.

Zion is in the foreground, for the Messiah's comfort will be especially "for those who grieve"[1] there. Ashes on the head were a sign of mourning. The Messiah will instead give them "a crown of beauty" (Heb. $p^{e'}er$, turban or headdress such as priests and those celebrating a feast wore). "The oil of gladness" is the anointing oil that symbolized the Holy Spirit. Oaks with their deep roots and spreading branches symbolized permanence and stability. In their God-given righteousness "those who grieve in Zion" will be recognized as the "planting of the Lord," for they will display His glory and splendor.

3. Happy Results 61:4–6

> ⁴They will rebuild the ancient ruins and restore the places long devastated; they will renew the ruined cities that have been devastated for generations.

The land and the cities of Israel will be restored after many generations of devastation. This verse does not say who will do

---

[1] The same word is translated "mourn" in v. 2.

the work, but the next verse suggests that God will use Gentiles.

> ⁵Aliens will shepherd your flocks; foreigners will work your fields and vineyards. ⁶And you will be called priests of the LORD, you will be named ministers of our God. You will feed on the wealth of nations, and in their riches you will boast.

Instead of foreign oppressors ruling in Zion, they will be working in Zion—for its people, who will be priests and ministers of God, ministering His blessings to all. The people of Zion will "feed on the wealth of the nations" and boast in, or inherit, "their riches" (Heb. *kᵉvodam*, "their glory"). (See Isa. 60:5–7,9,11,16.)

4. REJOICING IN THEIR INHERITANCE 61:7–9

> ⁷Instead of their shame my people will receive a double portion, and instead of disgrace they will rejoice in their inheritance; and so they will inherit a double portion in their land, and everlasting joy will be theirs.

The world has heaped shame on the people of Zion. Dictators and tyrants have persecuted Jews, using them to draw attention away from their own problems. Hitler is an example. Anti-Semitism is still rampant in many parts of the world, but Israel will have the "double portion" that belongs to the heir. Gone will be the former dishonor as they "rejoice in their inheritance." That double portion of the heir, a rich inheritance, will be "in their [own] land," which will be restored to them, and this will bring them "everlasting joy."

> ⁸"For I, the LORD, love justice; I hate robbery and iniquity. In my faithfulness I will reward them and make an everlasting covenant with them.

God's love for justice assures this inheritance, as does His hatred for "robbery and iniquity," better translated "robbery offered in burnt offerings" (Heb. *'olah;* cf. NASB). The burnt offering was completely burnt and its smoke went up wholly before the Lord, indicating complete exaltation of the Lord and complete dedication of oneself to Him. There could be no partial dedication. That would be robbery of what belongs to God. Some translators change "in burnt offerings" to "with perverse wickedness" or "crime" (Goodspeed), but that misses the point.

Because God is faithful, He will "reward them and make an everlasting covenant with them." This future covenant is the new and better covenant sealed by the blood of Jesus at Calvary (Heb. 9:15–18). There is no other new covenant.

> ⁹Their descendants will be known among the nations and their offspring among the peoples. All who see them will acknowledge that they are a people the Lord has blessed."

The descendants of Israel will be recognized and loved among the nations. Because of their receiving the inheritance in the land, all "will acknowledge that they are a people the Lord has blessed," a people who are chosen of Him. Many other Old Testament passages show that God will make them a blessing to all (e.g. Zech. 8:13).

5. The Messiah's Joy 61:10–11

> ¹⁰I delight greatly in the Lord; my soul rejoices in my God. For he has clothed me with garments of salvation and arrayed me in a robe of righteousness, as a bridegroom adorns his head like a priest, and as a bride adorns herself with her jewels.

Now the Speaker of verses 1–3 tells of His joy in the Lord (cf. Heb. 12:2).² Being "clothed" with salvation and righteousness indicates His nature. He is Salvation and Righteousness as well as the Bearer of salvation. On Him salvation and righteousness are like the priestly turban worn by a bridegroom and like the jewels a bride adorns herself with.

> ¹¹For as the soil makes the sprout come up and

---

²Since the Messiah is to give joy and righteousness, most of the older commentators take the speaker here to be Zion.

a garden causes seeds to grow, so the Sovereign LORD will make righteousness and praise spring up before all nations.

In the spring, it is a beautiful sight to see the seeds that were planted in a field or garden spring up. So the LORD will do something beautiful as He causes "righteousness and praise" to "spring up before all nations." The parallel with verse 10 shows that the praise is because of the salvation the LORD gives through His suffering and resurrected Servant. This is a reason for His joy.

6. THE MESSIAH'S CONTINUING CONCERN FOR ZION 62:1–63:6

a. Zion's Future Glory 62:1–5

¹For Zion's sake I will not keep silent, for Jerusalem's sake I will not remain quiet, till her righteousness shines out like the dawn, her salvation like a blazing torch.

The Anointed One's concern over Zion will cause Him to keep speaking and acting until Zion's "righteousness shines out" with brightness and her salvation becomes like "a blazing torch," giving light to the world and setting the hearts of believers on fire. The Messiah will be victorious over all the powers of evil.

²The nations will see your righteousness, and all kings your glory; you will be called by a new name that the mouth of the LORD will bestow.

Nations and kings will see and be attracted to Zion's righteousness and glory. The "new name" indicates a new nature and character given by the LORD (cf. Ezek. 48:35; Rev. 2:17; 3:12).

³You will be a crown of splendor in the LORD's hand, a royal diadem in the hand of your God.

The "crown of splendor" and the "royal diadem in the hand of your God" indicate the new royal character and nature of God's people being upheld and protected by Him. They do not wear the crown, however. They *are* the LORD's crown, and they are witnesses and evidence that He is King of the universe.

> ⁴No longer will they call you Deserted, or name your land Desolate. But you will be called Hephzibah, and your land Beulah; for the Lord will take delight in you, and your land will be married.

The name, or character, of Zion in the past was "Deserted" and "Desolate." These old names recalled past suffering and defeat. Its new name and nature will be "Hephzibah," meaning "my delight is in her," and "Beulah," meaning "married." The Lord will change their relationship and their situation. The country and people of Israel will be together again in a way that shows God's love.

> ⁵As a young man marries a maiden, so will your sons marry you; as a bridegroom rejoices over his bride, so will your God rejoice over you.

God's delight is compared to a marriage and a honeymoon's joy and love. The "sons" marrying Zion means the people will inhabit and cherish the city. However, the parallel with "so will your God rejoice over you" causes some to translate "your sons" as "your Builder,"³ which involves only a slight vowel change because the consonants are the same. This corresponds to Psalm 147:2 where God is the Builder.

b. The Lord Proves His Favor 62:6–9

> ⁶I have posted watchmen on your walls, O Jerusalem; they will never be silent day or night. You who call on the Lord, give yourselves no rest, ⁷and give him no rest till he establishes Jerusalem and makes her the praise of the earth.

As a proof of his favor the Lord sets "watchmen" on the walls. Ancient cities had walls for their protection. Watchmen were on towers ready to warn the people of any danger. In this context, the watchmen are prophets (cf. 21:11–12, where the

---

³See NIV note. It could also be translated "He who rebuilds you." See *The Prophets* (Philadelphia: Jewish Publication Society of America, 1978), 497 n.

watchman is Isaiah himself). They are the ones who continue to "call on the LORD." (The Hebrew *mazkirim* can also mean that the prophets keep "putting God in remembrance." When God "remembers," it does not mean He has forgotten. It is a way of saying He goes into action and does something about the situation.) These watchmen-prophets will not stop calling on God to act until He fulfills His promise to make Jerusalem "the praise of the earth." It will be the capital of the world in the Millennium.

> **8The LORD has sworn by his right hand and by his mighty arm: "Never again will I give your grain as food for your enemies, and never again will foreigners drink the new wine for which you have toiled; 9but those who harvest it will eat it and praise the LORD, and those who gather the grapes will drink it in the courts of my sanctuary."**

As another proof of His favor, God has "sworn," made an oath, guaranteed by His own power and strength, concerning Israel's restoration. "Never again" will He use foreign enemies to bring His judgment so that they rob the people of their food (grain for bread) and drink (sweet grape juice). The people will eat what they have worked for and drink the unfermented grape juice in festive worship in the courts of God's holy temple.

c. Zion's Savior Will Come 62:10–63:6

> **10Pass through, pass through the gates! Prepare the way for the people. Build up, build up the highway! Remove the stones. Raise a banner for the nations.**

In summary, the people are commanded to go through open gates and prepare the road, removing the stones, raising up the highway, and lifting up a flag over the peoples (including those who have come to Zion from afar). All hindrances are to be removed for God to come to His people (v. 11).

> **11The LORD has made proclamation to the ends of the earth: "Say to the Daughter of Zion, 'See, your Savior comes! See, his reward is with him, and his recompense accompanies him.'"**

What God proclaims is for the whole world. To the "Daughter of Zion" (the people of Jerusalem) the watchmen-prophets are to say "Your Savior [Heb. *yish'ekh,* "your salvation"] comes." "Savior," rather than "salvation" (KJV), is correct: "Salvation" is personified here, for He brings His reward with Him and His work is before Him (cf. 40:10). Jesus applies this to His second coming (Rev. 22:12). Matthew 21:5 combines Isaiah 62:11 with Zechariah 9:9, which also states that the lowly King comes, literally "being salvation." Thus, Matthew shows that both prophecies are fulfilled in Jesus.

> ¹²They will be called the Holy People, the Redeemed of the Lord; and you will be called Sought After, the City No Longer Deserted.

The new name, or character, is further described. The "Holy People, the Redeemed of the Lord" includes the peoples (Gentiles) from all directions who come to Zion's light. Zion will thus be a place of glory and prominence, called "Sought After," a city no longer deserted or forsaken (and never to be forsaken again).

> ¹Who is this coming from Edom, from Bozrah, with his garments stained crimson? Who is this, robed in splendor, striding forward in the greatness of his strength? "It is I, speaking in righteousness, mighty to save."

The land of Edom ("red") and the city of Bozrah ("vintage") represent the world that is against God and opposes His people. The watchmen-prophets (62:6) are expecting Salvation to come as a King. They are surprised, perhaps shocked, as they ask who this Person is who is "robed in splendor"—dressed in vivid colors—yet "stained crimson" (with the blood of His enemies, v. 2), walking vigorously with abundant strength. His response shows He is the Anointed One, "speaking in righteousness, mighty to save." Because He is righteous, there is no limit to His ability to save. But before He saves, He judges those represented by Edom and Bozrah.

> ²Why are your garments red, like those of one treading the winepress? ³"I have trodden the winepress alone; from the nations no one was

> with me. I trampled them in my anger and trod them down in my wrath; their blood spattered my garments, and I stained all my clothing.

When asked why His clothes are the color of blood, spattered like those who trample the grapes in the upper vat of the winepress, He declares that He alone trampled the winepress. But "winepress" is figurative, representing people—specifically, the enemies of both God and His people—not grapes. They suffered the wrath of the Lamb (Rev. 6:16). His clothes were spattered and stained with their blood (cf. the One coming at the battle of Armageddon; Rev. 19:13,15).[4]

> [4]For the day of vengeance was in my heart, and the year of my redemption has come.

The "day of vengeance" indicates just judgment done quickly, to be followed by the "year of [the Messiah's] redemption." The ones He redeemed are already redeemed before the judgment.[5] The "year" indicates a longer period of time. Many believe the judgment will be the seven years of the Tribulation.[6] The Tribulation will then be followed by the Millennium, the one thousand years of Christ's reign on earth.[7]

> [5]I looked, but there was no one to help, I was appalled that no one gave support; so my own arm worked salvation for me, and my own wrath sustained me. [6]I trampled the nations in my anger; in my wrath I made them drunk and poured their blood on the ground."

Again the Messiah recognizes that none can help Him. He alone can bring salvation. He alone is without sin and worthy to be the Judge of the nations bringing divine vengeance.[8] By His own strength, He brings salvation and tramples the sinful

---

[4]Stanley M. Horton, *The Ultimate Victory: An Exposition of the Book of Revelation* (Springfield, Mo.: Gospel Publishing House, 1991), 213, 283–84.

[5]They are redeemed because of the work done in Isa. 53.

[6]Stanley M. Horton, *Our Destiny: Biblical Teachings on the Last Things* (Springfield, Mo.: Logion Press, 1996), 91–102, 117–18.

[7]Ibid., 199–214.

[8]The Heb. *go'el* means both "the kinsman-redeemer" and "the avenger of blood." Jesus fulfills both functions by redeeming and judging.

peoples of the world, making them drunk on His wrath, which is still the wrath of the Lamb (Rev. 6:16), the wrath of the One who died to bring them salvation. They rejected His blood that was poured out for them. Now their blood is poured out on the earth, because they have chosen to pay the penalty for sin themselves. Many passages show that the millennial kingdom and its peace must be brought in through judgment (e.g., Dan. 2:44–45).

STUDY QUESTIONS

1. How do we know that the Spirit-inspired mission in chapter 61 refers to the Messiah?
2. Why did Jesus stop His quotation in the middle of verse 2?
3. What comfort will the Messiah give to mourners in Zion?
4. What will be involved in the restoration of Israel to be priests of the Lord?
5. How is the everlasting covenant (61:8) related to the new covenant that has been put into effect by the death of Jesus?
6. What does 61:10–11 show us about the nature of the Messiah?
7. Who will cause Zion to give light to the world and how will this be accomplished?
8. What is the significance of the new names and the comparison to a marriage?
9. Who are the watchmen and what is their work?
10. What is necessary for God to come to His people?
11. Who are included in the redeemed of the Lord and what is their relation to Zion?
12. Who is the One who comes with clothing stained crimson and why is it so stained?
13. Why is the Messiah there alone?

D. Isaiah Prays For Mercy And Pardon 63:7–64:12

1. Praise For God's Kindnesses 63:7–15

⁷I will tell of the kindnesses of the LORD, the deeds for which he is to be praised, according to all the LORD has done for us—yes, the many good things he has done for the house of Israel, according to his compassion and many kindnesses. ⁸He said, "Surely they are my people, sons who will not be false to me"; and so he became their Savior.

Isaiah as a watchman-prophet (62:6) now begins a prayer for mercy and pardon that continues through chapter 64. He begins by telling that he is mindful of the acts of God's "kindnesses" (Heb. *chasde*, "steadfast, unfailing, covenant love"), His great gifts and goodness toward the household of Israel, acts worthy of praise. God has treated them as His family, bestowing many mercies in these frequent acts of covenant love. He expected them as His people and as His children not to be "false," or faithless, toward Him. "So he became their Savior" (implying that He saved and repeatedly rescued them in several situations).

⁹In all their distress he too was distressed, and the angel of his presence saved them. In his love and mercy he redeemed them; he lifted them up and carried them all the days of old.

God was personally present with them in every distressing situation (such as the slavery in Egypt and the oppression during the time of the judges), and "he too was distressed." The "angel [or messenger] of his presence" is no ordinary angel. God is personally present in Him, and He is the divine Mediator between God and humankind, the Messiah, the Anointed One, who accomplishes the Father's work. In His love and compassion, He redeemed them as a Kinsman-Redeemer. He protected and cared for His people during their history, "all the days of old."

¹⁰Yet they rebelled and grieved his Holy Spirit. So he turned and became their enemy and he himself fought against them.

Now Isaiah confesses the people's sins: "they rebelled and grieved his Holy Spirit"—not once but again and again.[1] Ephesians 4:30–31 lists some of the actions that grieve the Holy Spirit of God: bitterness, rage, anger, brawling, slander, and malice of all kinds. God could not allow them to continue in presumptuous ingratitude and indifference to His love. He "became their enemy." He used human armies to bring judgment in the times of the judges and the Assyrians, as well as later. It was in that sense that He "fought against them."

> ¹¹Then his people recalled the days of old, the days of Moses and his people—where is he who brought them through the sea, with the shepherd of his flock? Where is he who set his Holy Spirit among them,

These judgments caused the godly remnant among His people to remember the time of Moses and his leadership, and to ask about the One who brought them all through the Red Sea. He put His Holy Spirit not only on Moses and the seventy elders (Num. 11:17) but others as well, such as Bezalel and Oholiab (Exod. 31:2–3,6; 35:30–35). Now the people ask where is God now? Where is the work of His Holy Spirit?

> ¹²who sent his glorious arm of power to be at Moses' right hand, who divided the waters before them, to gain for himself everlasting renown,

Moses experienced the power of the LORD. Israel saw it when the waters of the Red (Heb. *Suph*, "Reed") Sea were divided (Exod. 14:16). Israel continued to look back at the deliverance from Egypt through the Red Sea as a prime evidence of the power and greatness of the LORD, an eternal reminder of His name and character as Savior of His people.

> ¹³who led them through the depths? Like a horse in open country, they did not stumble;

The LORD led them through the watery depths of the Red

---

[1] The fact that the Holy Spirit can be grieved shows He is a distinct Person. See Stanley M. Horton, *What the Bible Says About the Holy Spirit* (Springfield, Mo.: Gospel Publishing House, 1976), 10, 65.

Sea. While "open country" (Heb. *midhbar*, "wilderness") does not always refer to level ground, here it probably does mean level, uncultivated, open country where a horse can run without stumbling. No obstacle was in Israel's way as God enabled them. How different this was in the days of Manasseh, when they were stumbling at midday (59:10).

> [14] like cattle that go down to the plain, they were given rest by the Spirit of the Lord. This is how you guided your people to make for yourself a glorious name.

The Israelites coming out of the wilderness were like cattle coming down from barren hills into the lush green pastures of the Promised Land. Through the Holy Spirit and Spirit-filled leaders such as Joshua (Num. 27:18), they "were given rest" again and again,[2] as God promised (Josh. 23:1). God's guidance thus brought glory to His name.

> [15] Look down from heaven and see from your lofty throne, holy and glorious. Where are your zeal and your might? Your tenderness and compassion are withheld from us.

After remembering what God did in the beginnings of the nation, Isaiah cries out to God in prayer, asking Him to "look down from heaven," where His holiness and glory are constantly in evidence. By asking where His zeal (His zealous love for His people and His zeal to uphold His honor) and His mighty acts are, Isaiah expresses his desire to see again the power and glory which were manifested in the days of Moses and Joshua. However, at this time God's "tenderness and compassion are withheld" because of Israel's sins.

2. God Is Still Our Father 63:16

> [16] But you are our Father, though Abraham does not know us or Israel acknowledge us; you, O Lord, are our Father, our Redeemer from of old is your name.

---

[2] The Heb. *t^enichennu* is frequentative.

Isaiah makes an appeal on the basis of the important fact that God is the Father of His people. They cannot call on Abraham (their earthly father) to help, nor on his grandson, Israel (Jacob), for they know nothing about the present suffering of the people. But God is still Father to His people and their Kinsman-Redeemer. He will never cast them off. His name and character are "from of old" (Heb. *me'olam*, "from antiquity" or "from eternity"). He is the same and He always will be.

3. Hardened Hearts 63:17–19

> ¹⁷Why, O LORD, do you make us wander from your ways and harden our hearts so we do not revere you? Return for the sake of your servants, the tribes that are your inheritance.

Isaiah is not blaming God for the people's wandering from His ways and the hardening of their hearts so that they do not fear or reverence Him. As Isaiah 6:10 indicates, when the people's hearts are hardened by sin, God's message only makes them harder.

But Isaiah turns this into a cry for God to "return," that is, to manifest His presence, power, and grace in the midst of His people. After all, they are the "tribes that are [His] inheritance," chosen by Him.

> ¹⁸For a little while your people possessed your holy place, but now our enemies have trampled down your sanctuary.

Israel as a holy people, set apart for the worship and service of the LORD, possessed their inheritance in the Promised Land for only a short time. Then adversaries and oppressors "trampled," or desecrated, God's holy place, which may mean God's holy land. Isaiah may be expressing the conditions in Manasseh's time, or he may be prophesying what would happen when the Babylonians came, as he foresaw in 39:5–7.

> ¹⁹We are yours from of old; but you have not ruled over them, they have not been called by your name.

Isaiah laments that though the people of Israel were God's

people from a long time ago, yet God had not "ruled over them" (His people in the past) and did not call His name over them, that is, name them by His name and thus declare that they belonged to Him. Leupold suggests, "The space of time where the Lord effectively upheld his people was comparatively so short that it hardly seemed worth considering. It is as though he 'had never ruled' over his people."[3] The sins of Israel had cut them off from the blessing and privileges God gave them. They had broken the covenant.

4. Isaiah Cries Out For God To Act 64:1–9

> ¹Oh, that you would rend the heavens and come down, that the mountains would tremble before you!

Isaiah passionately laments over the past.[4] "Oh, that" (Heb. *lu'*) introduces a condition contrary to fact here. He means, if only God had come down, then the mountains would have quaked as at Sinai. Circumstances would have been different. Yet he implies he still wants God to act decisively.

> ²As when fire sets twigs ablaze and causes water to boil, come down to make your name known to your enemies and cause the nations to quake before you!

If God had come down in power "as when fire sets twigs ablaze and causes water to boil," then His name would have been "known to [His] enemies" and the nations would have trembled at His presence and God's people would have responded by repentance! Isaiah is concerned about God's name, that is, about God's honor.

> ³For when you did awesome things that we did not expect, you came down, and the mountains trembled before you.

Isaiah reflects on the past, when God did unexpected, awe-inspiring acts. For God "came down" at Sinai and the "moun-

---

[3] H. C. Leupold, *Exposition of Isaiah* (Grand Rapids: Baker Book House, 1971), 2:148.
[4] J. Alec Motyer, *The Prophecy of Isaiah* (Downers Grove, Ill.: InterVarsity Press, 1993), 518.

tains trembled" at His presence. Now, during Manasseh's evil reign, Isaiah feels that God is doing nothing.

> ⁴Since ancient times no one has heard, no ear has perceived, no eye has seen any God besides you, who acts on behalf of those who wait for him.

Isaiah has not forgotten that God acts on behalf of "those who wait" in expectant faith for Him. He is the only God who responds. No one in the past or present has heard or seen (by revelation) any other God except Him. (See the application of this verse to those who love the Lord in 1 Cor. 2:9.) The fact that He alone is God implies His sovereignty.

> ⁵You come to the help of those who gladly do right, who remember your ways. But when we continued to sin against them, you were angry. How then can we be saved?

God comes "to the help of" (Heb. *paga'ta*, "meets," "acts to bless") those who rejoice as they "gladly do right" (act in righteousness). They not only find joy in righteousness, they remember God in His ways. That is, they have a personal relationship with Him as they follow in His ways, the ways revealed in His Word, ways made clear to them as they pray.

However, Isaiah identifies himself with the people and confesses that they "continued to sin" against those ways even though they knew it would anger God. It did not seem that this long-continued rebellion would ever meet with salvation.

> ⁶All of us have become like one who is unclean, and all our righteous acts are like filthy rags; we all shrivel up like a leaf, and like the wind our sins sweep us away.

The confession continues: "All . . . have become . . . unclean" in God's eyes. All their righteous acts, done to fulfill the requirements or forms of their religion, are like "filthy rags" (lit., like a garment bloodied from a woman's menstrual period, which was ceremonially unclean under the Law and kept a person from entering the temple). The result is divine judgment: They fade and "shrivel up like a leaf." Then their guilty sins carry them away like the wind carries away dead leaves.

> **7No one calls on your name or strives to lay hold of you; for you have hidden your face from us and made us waste away because of our sins.**

In the midst of God's judgment (probably in Manasseh's time), no one was calling on God's name for mercy and none stirred themselves to lay hold on God (as Jacob did when he wrestled with the Angel, Gen. 32:24–28; Hos. 12:4). God had "hidden [His] face" (removed His manifest presence and blessing) and caused their guilty sins to make them "waste away" (Heb. *t^emugenu*, "melt us down"), that is, bring discouragement and death. This fits Manasseh's time rather than the later Babylonian exile.[5]

> **8Yet, O LORD, you are our Father. We are the clay, you are the potter; we are all the work of your hand.**

Now Isaiah cries out again to God, recognizing that God has not changed: He is still Israel's Father, the One who called the nation into being. He is also the divine Potter who shapes the clay, making it "the work of [His] hand." Surely He is concerned over the people who are the work of His hand. (The beautiful imagery of the LORD as the Potter and as Father is often attested—Deut. 32:6; Pss. 68:5; 89:26; 103:13; Isa. 29:16; 63:16; Jer. 18:6; Mal. 2:10; Matt. 6:6–8; Rom. 9:21; Gal. 1:3; Col. 1:12.) God is able to change them in spite of what they have done in the past.

> **9Do not be angry beyond measure, O LORD; do not remember our sins forever. Oh, look upon us, we pray, for we are all your people.**

Isaiah pleads that God will not let the full weight of His anger fall on them and that He will not remember forever the sins that caused the anger. Asking God to "look" is a call for His grace and mercy: Let Him see and recognize that they are still His people.

---

[5]Oswald T. Allis, "Book of Isaiah," in *Wycliffe Bible Encyclopedia* (Chicago: Moody Press, 1975), 1:857.

5. Jerusalem Ruined 64:10–12

> ¹⁰Your sacred cities have become a desert;
> even Zion is a desert, Jerusalem a desolation.

Some take this to be what the exiles said when they came back from Babylon. But the exiles would not have said what we read in verse 12. In view of what Isaiah knows will happen (39:5–7), he sees in a vision that the "sacred cities" (cities of God's holiness; that is, the whole land of Israel), including Zion, will be a wilderness, for Jerusalem will be "a desolation" that will show the awesomeness of God's judgment.

> ¹¹Our holy and glorious temple, where our
> fathers praised you, has been burned with fire,
> and all that we treasured lies in ruins.

As a climax to their sufferings, Israel's house of holiness and splendid beauty where the fathers of the nation praised God will be burned and "all that [they] treasured," the temple's precious items, will become a pile of rubble. This will be the climax of the trampling, or desecration, of the temple that took place in Manasseh's day.⁶

> ¹²After all this, O LORD, will you hold yourself
> back? Will you keep silent and punish us
> beyond measure?

Isaiah's response to this vision is to ask God if in light of it He will continue to restrain himself (especially after the prayer of v. 9), remaining silent and punishing (humbling and afflicting) Israel more. (The exiles returning from Babylon did not have to say this.)

STUDY QUESTIONS

1. What does Isaiah emphasize in his prayer?
2. What lessons should Israel have learned from the Exodus?

---

⁶Many critics use vv. 10–11 to argue that an unknown author wrote this after Jerusalem was destroyed in 586 B.C. But as Bultema says, "This shows how little these men have penetrated the spirit of this prophecy." Harry Bultema, *Commentary on Isaiah*, trans. Cornelius Lambregtse (Grand Rapids: Kregel Publications, 1981), 612.

3. What is Isaiah's appeal in 63:16–18 and on what basis does he make it?
4. What do God's actions in the past cause Isaiah to expect?
5. What is significant about Isaiah's prayer of confession?
6. Why does Isaiah refer to God as both Father and Potter?
7. What was the condition of Jerusalem and the temple in the latter part of Manasseh's reign?

E. Mercy, Blessing, Joy, And Judgment 65:1–66:24

1. God's Gracious Answer 65:1–7

¹"I revealed myself to those who did not ask for me; I was found by those who did not seek me. To a nation that did not call on my name, I said, 'Here am I, here am I.'

God then responds to the confession and prayer of chapter 64 by saying He revealed himself (or, let himself be sought), even though they (Israel in its beginnings) did not ask for Him; He let himself be found, even though they did not seek Him. He repeatedly made friendly overtures, saying, "Here am I" (Heb. *hinneni*, "Behold me") to an Israel that "did not call on my name."

That is, God takes the initiative and makes it possible for people to seek and find Him, and Paul points out that some do. (See Rom. 10:20–21, where Paul applies 65:1 to the Gentiles[1] and 65:2 to Israel.) However, Israel was too self-centered and too concerned about their own plans and desires to respond.

²All day long I have held out my hands to an obstinate people, who walk in ways not good, pursuing their own imaginations—

In contrast, God's constant, loving, urgent, "all day long"

---

[1] "Nation" is Heb. *goi*, a term usually referring to Gentiles, though the initial reference here is to Israel acting as if they were not God's people.

appeal to Israel found them stubborn in their rebellion, for they continued to walk in ways that God saw were not good, following their "own imaginations," thoughts, and plans. They were responsible for the condition they were in. (Cf. Rom. 10:21.)

> ³a people who continually provoke me to my very face, offering sacrifices in gardens and burning incense on altars of brick;

In God's very presence, "to [His] very face," they constantly provoke Him, actually defying Him. (This continued in Ezekiel's day; see Ezek. chap. 8.) Sacrificing "in gardens and burning incense on altars of brick" was contrary to the Law and showed that the people of Israel were following pagan rituals.

> ⁴who sit among the graves and spend their nights keeping secret vigil; who eat the flesh of pigs, and whose pots hold broth of unclean meat;

To "sit among the graves," the tombs, indicates spiritist attempts to contact the dead. Spending the night in "secret vigil," guarded places (some suggest "among rock cliffs"; the Septuagint says "in caves where they lie for the sake of dreams"), indicates occult practices. All of these activities were an abomination to the LORD.

They also ate pork and made soup of "unclean meat," again contrary to the Law (Lev. 11:7) and in imitation of pagan practices. This also points to Manasseh's time.

> ⁵who say, 'Keep away; don't come near me, for I am too sacred for you!' Such people are smoke in my nostrils, a fire that keeps burning all day.

They also followed pagan ideas of holiness or separation (what we would call "taboos" today). Probably they so identified with false spirits or false gods that they thought anyone who touched them would be in trouble. Such people are a "smoke in [God's] nostrils," a continual fire. In the Hebrew, the idea of the nasal area being heated often indicates anger, as does fire (cf. TEV). Thus, these people are objects of God's wrath.

> ⁶"See, it stands written before me: I will not

> keep silent but will pay back in full; I will pay it back into their laps—

These sins stand written in a book (like a debit on an account). God, in due time, will end His silence and long-suffering and will "pay [them] back in full" measure. The "lap" here refers to the fold of the garment above the belt where an object could be put (cf. Neh. 5:13; Ps. 79:12; Luke 6:38).

> ⁷both your sins and the sins of your fathers," says the LORD. "Because they burned sacrifices on the mountains and defied me on the hills, I will measure into their laps the full payment for their former deeds."

Because they continued in "the sins of [their] fathers," they would now reap judgment for both their sins and their fathers' sins (cf. Exod. 20:5). Burning sacrifices "on the mountains and . . . hills" (high places; cf. 15:2) was in defiance of God and deserved full punishment. It would be the first form of punishment the LORD would do in His agenda of judgment. That is, it must begin among the people of God (cf. 1 Pet. 4:17). This too fits Manasseh's time. There were no mountains in Babylonia.

2. THE REMNANT WILL POSSESS THE LAND 65:8–10

> ⁸This is what the LORD says: "As when juice is still found in a cluster of grapes and men say, 'Don't destroy it, there is yet some good in it,' so will I do in behalf of my servants; I will not destroy them all.

Now the LORD gives a further response. He still has true servants in Israel. They are like a cluster of grapes with juice still in it, so Israel has "some good" (Heb. *berakhah*, a "blessing") in it. Because of this remnant of servants who are a blessing, God "will not destroy them all."

> ⁹I will bring forth descendants from Jacob, and from Judah those who will possess my mountains; my chosen people will inherit them, and there will my servants live.

God will bring forth descendants from the remnant of Jacob and Judah and they will possess the land of Israel (which God refers to as "my mountains") as their inheritance and live there. This looks forward to millennial times.

> ¹⁰Sharon will become a pasture for flocks, and the Valley of Achor a resting place for herds, for my people who seek me.

The once fertile plain of Sharon, on the seacoast south of Mount Carmel, which became like the dry Arabah south of Beersheba, will be restored to green pastures. The Valley of Achor, by Jericho, once a place of judgment (Josh. 7:24–26), will be transformed into "a resting place for herds." Characteristically, Isaiah refers to representative examples. Thus, he means that from west to east the whole land will be restored for the remnant, "my people who seek me."

3. GOD WILL JUDGE THOSE WHO FORSAKE HIM 65:11–16

> ¹¹"But as for you who forsake the LORD and forget my holy mountain, who spread a table for Fortune and fill bowls of mixed wine for Destiny,

Those "who forsake the LORD and forget [His] holy mountain," turning away from worshiping Him in the temple, will have a different reward. They have turned to pagan worship, preparing a table of food offerings for the goddess Fortune[2] and filling up a cup of wine mixed with spices and drugs to pour out as a drink offering to the god Destiny (or Fate).

> ¹²I will destine you for the sword, and you will all bend down for the slaughter; for I called but you did not answer, I spoke but you did not listen. You did evil in my sight and chose what displeases me."

The god Destiny will not determine the Israelites' future; the LORD will "destine" them, for the sword. They are bowing down

---

[2]Some take "Fortune" (Heb. *gad*) to be a Syrian god. J. Alec Motyer, *The Prophecy of Isaiah* (Downers Grove, Ill.: InterVarsity Press, 1993), 527.

to the god Fortune, but they are really bowing down to slaughter. Death will become their fortune. God was patient. He called them to himself. He spoke, warning them. But they "did not answer," they did not even listen. Instead, they persisted in doing and choosing what was displeasing to God.

> **13Therefore this is what the Sovereign LORD says: "My servants will eat, but you will go hungry; my servants will drink, but you will go thirsty; my servants will rejoice, but you will be put to shame.**

Five contrasts in verses 13–15 show the LORD's blessings will be on His servants: First, they will (1) eat, (2) drink, and (3) rejoice, while those who chose to do what was displeasing to Him will be hungry, thirsty, and ashamed (thus, frustrated, disillusioned, and disappointed).

> **14My servants will sing out of the joy of their hearts, but you will cry out from anguish of heart and wail in brokenness of spirit.**

God's servants will also (4) sing (Heb. *yaronnu*, "shout for joy") from happy hearts because of the blessings He sends (v.13). But the unfaithful will "cry out" from hearts filled with anguish and pain, and "wail" from crushed, depressed spirits.

> **15You will leave your name to my chosen ones as a curse; the Sovereign LORD will put you to death, but to his servants he will give another name.**

Finally, (5) the name of the unfaithful will be used in an oath-curse, such as, "May you be cursed like [the name of the person]" (cf. Ps. 102:8). The plural "you" changes to the singular when the curse leads to death as God's judgment, indicating it will be on an individual basis. Then God will call His servants by "another name," a new name (see 62:2; cf. Rev. 2:17; 3:12).

> **16Whoever invokes a blessing in the land will do so by the God of truth; he who takes an oath in the land will swear by the God of truth. For the past troubles will be forgotten and hidden from my eyes.**

Those seeking a blessing or making a promise confirmed by an oath will do it by the God of "truth" (Heb. *'amen*). *Amen*, usually meaning "surely" or "truly," is a great word of response and acceptance.

When used of God, *Amen* means He is the God who is faithful to His promises. For believers today this is made real through Christ (2 Cor. 1:20–22; Rev. 3:14). God's response as the *Amen* is freely given because He has forgotten "the past troubles" and has hidden them from His eyes. This means the troubles, along with the forgiven sins, are out of existence as far as God is concerned.

4. A New Creation 65:17–25

> ¹⁷"Behold, I will create new heavens and a new earth. The former things will not be remembered, nor will they come to mind.

The reason the former troubles will be hidden from God's eyes is because He will create brand new heavens and a brand new earth. All the "former things" will be obliterated from memory; they will never "come to mind" (cf. Rev. 21 and 22). (But God is not yet through with the present earth and the present Jerusalem.)

> ¹⁸But be glad and rejoice forever in what I will create, for I will create Jerusalem to be a delight and its people a joy.

"But" (Heb. *ki-'im*, "nevertheless") is an emphatic, strong contrastive.³ There will be new heavens and a new earth; "nevertheless," Israel is to be glad and rejoice, for the present Jerusalem will also experience restoration. Nothing can stop God from fulfilling His promises and His righteous purpose.

"Create" is used only of God's supernatural activity. His creative activity will make Jerusalem "a delight [Heb. *gilah*, an object causing ecstatic rejoicing or shouts of joy] and its people a joy." This must refer to the restoration in the Millennium, for the description that follows in the rest of this chapter fits millennial times, not the new heaven and the new earth or the New

---

³Ibid., 529.

Jerusalem that John saw in Revelation 21 and 22.

> ¹⁹I will rejoice over Jerusalem and take delight in my people; the sound of weeping and of crying will be heard in it no more.

God will "rejoice over Jerusalem" and in His people. That there will be "no more" weeping or crying means there will be no more sorrow or pain (cf. Rev. 7:17; 21:4).

It also implies that the unfaithful of 65:14 will not be there. Most of the people will be God's servants in the truest sense.

> ²⁰"Never again will there be in it an infant who lives but a few days, or an old man who does not live out his years; he who dies at a hundred will be thought a mere youth; he who fails to reach a hundred will be considered accursed.

Throughout much of the world's history, half of the babies born died within the first year of life. Modern medicine and sanitation has helped to change that to a great degree. But in the Millennium no babies will die and old people will not die prematurely. (The armies of the Antichrist will be destroyed when Jesus returns in glory, but there will still be people who survive the Tribulation. "The fact that Satan is bound, . . . 'to keep him from deceiving the nations anymore until the thousand years' are ended [Rev. 20:2–3], clearly indicates that there will be those of the nations of the world still left on earth who could be subject to his temptations if he were present."[4])

A person dying at one hundred years of age will be like a baby dying today. There will still be habitual sinners, however. God will be patient, but by the time they reach the age of one hundred they "will be considered accursed." This means death; as Psalm 37:22 says, "Those he curses will be cut off." Resurrected and raptured believers, however, will have new bodies that are immortal and will never decay (1 Cor. 15:52–53).

> ²¹They will build houses and dwell in them; they will plant vineyards and eat their fruit.

---

[4]Stanley M. Horton, *Our Destiny: Biblical Teachings on the Last Things* (Springfield, Mo.: Logion Press, 1996), 212.

> ²²No longer will they build houses and others live in them, or plant and others eat. For as the days of a tree, so will be the days of my people; my chosen ones will long enjoy the works of their hands.

The average life expectancy in Isaiah's day was about thirty-one to thirty-five years. It was disappointing for people to build houses and plant vineyards and die without having enjoyed them. But in the Millennium, the life expectancy will be like that of a tree, that is, they will continue to enjoy life through the whole time. As God's chosen people, they will "long [or fully] enjoy" (Heb. *yᵉvallu*, "use daily and completely")⁵ the work⁶ of their hands.

> ²³They will not toil in vain or bear children doomed to misfortune; for they will be a people blessed by the LORD, they and their descendants with them.

Their work will not be worthless or meaningless, nor will their children be "doomed to misfortune" (Heb. *behalah*, "terror," as when raiding tribes would come in to steal and destroy). They will enjoy the fullness of the blessing the Lord promised to the seed of Abraham (Gen. 12:3; 17:7) and the seed of the Suffering Servant (53:10). They will live long and their offspring, their descendants, will be with them, enjoying the same millennial blessings.

> ²⁴Before they call I will answer; while they are still speaking I will hear.

Their relationship with God will be so close that He will anticipate their requests and have the answer for them even before they call, and when they do speak, God will hear before they finish.

> ²⁵The wolf and the lamb will feed together, and the lion will eat straw like the ox, but dust will be the serpent's food. They will neither harm nor destroy on all my holy mountain," says the LORD.

---

⁵The word also means to use until worn out (cf. NASB).
⁶The Heb. is singular but used collectively.

In the Millennium the whole sphere of life will be restored to something better than the Garden of Eden. The promise of the Messiah's work in transforming nature (see commentary on 11:6–9) will be fulfilled. No longer will anything or anyone cause hurt or destruction in God's "holy mountain," that is, in the whole earth where God dwells with His people in millennial blessing and fellowship.

5. THE EARTHLY TEMPLE AND ITS WORSHIP ARE INSUFFICIENT 66:1–6

> ¹This is what the LORD says: "Heaven is my throne, and the earth is my footstool. Where is the house you will build for me? Where will my resting place be?

After prophesying the new heavens and the new earth and the blessings of the Millennium, Isaiah returns to the needs of his own day. The worship was still empty ritual that honored the temple but not the true greatness of God.

Solomon recognized that the heavens, even the highest heaven, cannot contain the LORD, and how much less the temple he built. Yet he recognized God did manifest His presence on earth in the temple, the place where God said, "My name shall be there" (1 Kings 8:27–29).

Now God says through Isaiah, "Heaven is my throne," the place He manifests his presence in full power and glory, and "The earth is my footstool" (see Matt. 5:34–35), the place where His sovereign will is to be carried out. He does not ignore the temple in Isaiah's day. Yet He asks where it is; that is, the temple is not the center of His attention. Isaiah saw that in chapter 6.

This does not fit the return from Babylonian exile. They came back specifically to rebuild the temple.

> ²Has not my hand made all these things, and so they came into being?" declares the LORD. "This is the one I esteem: he who is humble and contrite in spirit, and trembles at my word.

God made the heavens and the earth and everything in them. But His special concern is the person who is humble (taking a low place before God), with a "contrite" (Heb. *nᵉkeh,* "broken") spirit (crying for help [cf. Job 30:24] and wanting to please God), who "trembles at" (is frightened because of) God's word (wanting to obey it but not knowing how). God wants to come and help such a person (see 57:15; cf. Ps. 51:17). Such a person can enter into the kind of relationship with God that He wants (cf. Mic. 6:8).

> ³But whoever sacrifices a bull is like one who kills a man, and whoever offers a lamb, like one who breaks a dog's neck; whoever makes a grain offering is like one who presents pig's blood, and whoever burns memorial incense, like one who worships an idol. They have chosen their own ways, and their souls delight in their abominations;

Isaiah 1:10–20 spoke of God's hatred of worship and sacrifices that were offered in the wrong spirit. Now, at the conclusion of the book, God again condemns those who offer the right sacrifices but continue in sinful living. They are like murderers and those who offer pagan sacrifices of dogs and pigs. They are no different from those who praise an idol. (See Ps. 50, which points out that God does not need the sacrifices. They were given for the people's benefit, not His. Nor does He want the religious forms of the wicked who recite God's laws and go out and do and say evil things.) Since the people have "chosen their own ways" and "delight in . . . abominations," it is also possible to take this verse to refer to people who offer sacrifices to the LORD and also offer pagan sacrifices. The mixing of religions (syncretism) was always an abomination to the LORD. Liberals, New Age groups, and cults like Baha'i are mixing religions today. God hates it.

We should note also that Hebrews 10:4 points out that "it is impossible for the blood of bulls and goats to take away sins." The Old Testament sacrifices were temporary and God could accept them only because they were symbols that pointed ahead to the death of Christ. His blood is the only thing that can really take away sins (cf. Heb. 9:10,13–14; 10:10,14).

> ⁴so I also will choose harsh treatment for them and will bring upon them what they dread. For

> when I called, no one answered, when I spoke, no one listened. They did evil in my sight and chose what displeases me."

They chose their own ways, but God "will choose [their] harsh treatment," that is, their judgment, bringing their fears upon them. Choosing their own ways included refusing to answer (and obey) when God spoke and doing what was evil in God's eyes, deeds in which God had no delight. They set up their own standards of living and ignored God's standards. They had no regard for the position and nature of God. The same attitude causes much delusion today. All the way through his book Isaiah emphasizes the importance of true worship, worship that honors and obeys God in humility and in brokenness of the human spirit.

> ⁵Hear the word of the LORD, you who tremble at his word: "Your brothers who hate you, and exclude you because of my name, have said, 'Let the LORD be glorified, that we may see your joy!' Yet they will be put to shame.

People tremble at God's word because of an intense desire to obey it. The brothers who hate those "who tremble at his word" and cast them out "because of [God's] name" are the religious leaders who are concerned with their place in the religious hierarchy and the forms of religion. They mock those who really want to obey God's word and who expect to rejoice in Him. This took place in Manasseh's time. The leaders in Jerusalem could also have said this to Isaiah when he was warning them not to make an alliance with Egypt and when he was condemning their formal religion. But God says they are the ones who will be "put to shame."

> ⁶Hear that uproar from the city, hear that noise from the temple! It is the sound of the LORD repaying his enemies all they deserve.

When they are put to shame, there will be "uproar from the city," for the voice of the LORD from the temple (which is still standing at this time) will proclaim that He is "repaying his enemies" in full.

6. Sudden Enlargement Of Zion 66:7–14

⁷"Before she goes into labor, she gives birth; before the pains come upon her, she delivers a son.

Pain in childbirth has been experienced ever since the judgment given at the Fall (Gen. 3:16). But after the judgments of the Great Tribulation, the Millennium will see the curse removed from the earth and from humankind. However, the prophecy here is explained in the next verse.

⁸Who has ever heard of such a thing? Who has ever seen such things? Can a country be born in a day or a nation be brought forth in a moment? Yet no sooner is Zion in labor than she gives birth to her children.

Such a miraculous event has never been heard or seen in this age. However, something even more unusual will take place. A nation will be "born in a day." Zion will bring forth children—that is, an entire nation that calls Zion "Mother."

⁹Do I bring to the moment of birth and not give delivery?" says the LORD. "Do I close up the womb when I bring to delivery?" says your God.

God is the giver of life. He will not shut Zion's womb. He will restore the nation of Israel.

¹⁰"Rejoice with Jerusalem and be glad for her, all you who love her; rejoice greatly with her, all you who mourn over her.

Those who love Jerusalem are commanded to "rejoice . . . with her" and shout for joy in her. So are all those "who mourn over her." Ezekiel 9:4 speaks of "a mark" (Heb. *tau*, which in old Heb. had the shape of a cross) put on the foreheads of those who sigh and cry over the abominations done in Jerusalem. Those who mourn because of the past sins will mourn no longer.

¹¹For you will nurse and be satisfied at her comforting breasts; you will drink deeply and

delight in her overflowing abundance."

Jerusalem is again pictured as a mother. She will bring satisfaction, consolation for past sufferings, and delight because of her full, "comforting breasts" (lit., "the nipple of her glory"). That is, there will be no limit to the supply of glory and blessing God provides through her (see similar imagery of abundance in 60:16).

> ¹²For this is what the LORD says: "I will extend peace to her like a river, and the wealth of nations like a flooding stream; you will nurse and be carried on her arm and dandled on her knees.

"Peace [including health, prosperity, and well-being] . . . like a river" and the "wealth [Heb. *kᵉvod,* "glory"] of nations" like an overflowing stream again indicate a limitless supply. Returning to the figure of a mother, the limitless supply is for the people of Jerusalem to nurse or be nourished by. Being "carried on her arm [Heb. *tsad,* "side" or "hip"] and dandled on her knees" indicates the fond care, caress, and delight of a mother that God will offer to His people in the Millennium.

> ¹³As a mother comforts her child, so will I comfort you; and you will be comforted over Jerusalem."

Extending the maternal metaphor, God's loving comfort of the people of Jerusalem is compared to the comfort a loving mother gives to her child. "Over Jerusalem" implies that restoration will bring comfort for the past troubles and destructions of Jerusalem. It can also be translated "*in* Jerusalem" (KJV, NASB, RSV, Knox, Fenton): Jerusalem will be a center from which God will manifest His presence and His never-ending comfort, love, and mercy.

> ¹⁴When you see this, your heart will rejoice and you will flourish like grass; the hand of the LORD will be made known to his servants, but his fury will be shown to his foes.

The people who see and experience this comfort "will rejoice and . . . flourish." To "your heart" the Hebrew adds "and your bones," representing the whole person (see Ezek. 37). "The hand of the LORD," that is, His power, will be a part of the experience of His servants. But the warning to the people of Isaiah's day is still that God will pass a sentence of judgment on all of His enemies.

7. FIERY JUDGMENT 66:15–17

> ¹⁵See, the LORD is coming with fire, and his chariots are like a whirlwind; he will bring down his anger with fury, and his rebuke with flames of fire.

The warning to God's enemies continues. He will come "with [or "in"] fire," His chariots (armies) like a tornado. They have disregarded His anger and rejected His rebukes. He will pay them back with fierceness and "flames of fire." The judgment will be severe.

> ¹⁶For with fire and with his sword the LORD will execute judgment upon all men, and many will be those slain by the LORD.

Not only His fire but also "his sword" will bring judgment. The "many" judged includes all sinners of all the world.

> ¹⁷"Those who consecrate and purify themselves to go into the gardens, following the one in the midst of those who eat the flesh of pigs and rats and other abominable things—they will meet their end together," declares the LORD.

The sinners Isaiah has especially in view are those in Manasseh's day already mentioned in 65:2–5. They observe pagan rites of purification in order to "go into the gardens," where fertility cults carried on lewd practices as part of their worship. They followed a leader among them, eating pork (unclean under the Law), something detestable (cf. Lev. 11:41 where this is applied to creeping things), and even rats. Such gross idolatry was not practiced after the Babylonian exile. That they shall "meet their end together" means none of them will be left after God's judgment falls on them (cf. Ps. 73:19).

8. God's Glory Seen 66:18–24

¹⁸"And I, because of their actions and their imaginations, am about to come and gather all nations and tongues, and they will come and see my glory.

The Hebrew is difficult in the first part of the verse. It is literally, "And I their deeds and their thoughts coming [Heb. *ba'ah*, a feminine singular participle] to harvest all the nations [Heb. *haggoyim*, "nations," "Gentiles"] and the tongues." It may refer to God's coming in judgment. Then, after the judgment, God will gather all the peoples and languages (that are left) so that they may come and see His glory.[7]

¹⁹"I will set a sign among them, and I will send some of those who survive to the nations—to Tarshish, to the Libyans and Lydians (famous as archers), to Tubal and Greece, and to the distant islands that have not heard of my fame or seen my glory. They will proclaim my glory among the nations.

Many take the (supernatural) "sign among them," that is, the people, to be the cross or else Jesus himself, as in Matthew 24:30. God will send to the nations those who "survive" His judgment (possibly because they repented, cf. Rev. 11:13; see also commentary on 65:20). The mention of Tarshish (probably Tartessus in Spain, cf. 2:16), Libya in North Africa, Lydia in western Asia Minor, Tubal in central Asia Minor, and the distant coastlands shows they will be sent in all directions to nations around the world. Special attention will be given to those who have not heard God's fame or seen His glory. Isaiah foresees a worldwide missionary endeavor.

²⁰And they will bring all your brothers, from all the nations, to my holy mountain in Jerusalem as an offering to the LORD—on horses, in chariots and wagons, and on mules and camels," says the LORD. "They will bring them, as the

---

[7]Some take God's judgment itself to be a manifestation of His glory. H. C. Leupold, *Exposition of Isaiah* (Grand Rapids: Baker Book House, 1971), 2:377.

Israelites bring their grain offerings, to the temple of the LORD in ceremonially clean vessels.

The brothers "from all the nations" are distinguished here from the Israelites.[8] They have heard God's fame, seen His glory, and have become brothers to the people of God (cf. John 11:51–52; Eph. 2:19). The missionaries will bring them as an "offering" (Heb. *hamminchah,* "the gift-offering") to the LORD. Isaiah mentions every means of transportation known in his day to emphasize the variety of means that will be used to bring them to the restored Temple in Jerusalem. Each one will bring the gift-offering in a "clean vessel," that is, one acceptable to God. These Gentiles are thus cleansed and in right relationship with the LORD as they come to the millennial Jerusalem.

> [21]And I will select some of them also to be priests and Levites," says the LORD.

God will also take some of these converted Gentiles "to be priests and Levites." The restored millennial worship will not be limited by restrictions given under the old covenant of the Law.

> [22]"As the new heavens and the new earth that I make will endure before me," declares the LORD, "so will your name and descendants endure.

In the last three verses, Isaiah moves from the millennial age to the new creation. The present heavens and earth will pass away,[9] but "the new heavens and the new earth" that God makes "will endure" before Him. That is, they will not come to an end. So the "descendants" ("seed," KJV [the family]) and "name" (the new, redeemed character) of God's people will also "endure," never coming to an end.

> [23]From one New Moon to another and from one Sabbath to another, all mankind will come and bow down before me," says the LORD.

Isaiah sees a regularity of worship, from month to month and

---

[8]J. Alec Motyer, *The Prophecy of Isaiah* (Downers Grove, Ill.: InterVarsity Press, 1993), 542.

[9]Stanley M. Horton, *The Ultimate Victory: An Exposition of the Book of Revelation* (Springfield, Mo.: Gospel Publishing House, 1991), 307–8.

from Sabbath to Sabbath. The "descendants" (v. 22), or family, now includes "all mankind"—all human beings who remain. Isaiah must be looking ahead here to the new heavens and the new earth.

> 24"And they will go out and look upon the dead bodies of those who rebelled against me; their worm will not die, nor will their fire be quenched, and they will be loathsome to all mankind."

The final verse reminds us of the seriousness of rejecting the salvation offered by our God. He sent His Son to die in our place so that we might share in His resurrection life through eternity in the new creation. The alternative is eternal death. Outside the new creation will be the corpses of "those who rebelled" against God (cf. Zech. 14:12–13,17–19; Rev. 22:15). Worms in the rubbish heap gave the Hebrew a picture of decay and fire a picture of destruction (cf. Mark 9:48 where Jesus used "worm" and "fire" to refer to the fires of hell). Those who worship God in the new earth will go out and look on them, doubtless to remind themselves of the holiness of God, the results of rebellion, the triumph of God's justice, and the judgment they have been delivered from.

That judgment will continue, for their worm will not die and their fire will never be quenched (cf. Matt. 3:12; Mark 9:44 where Gehenna represents the lake of fire of Rev. 20:10,15). They will be a loathsome abhorrence to all humankind because of their rebellion against God. This also indicates that all of humankind on the new earth will not only worship the LORD, they will never again rebel against Him.

STUDY QUESTIONS

1. How does God respond to the preceding prayer?
2. How does Paul apply this to the Gentiles?
3. What pagan practices were the people involved in and what similarities do you see in today's world?
4. What did God promise to do for His true servants that remain?

5. How is the description of Jerusalem in 65:18–25 like that described in chapters 9 and 11 and how is it different from the description of the New Jerusalem the Book of Revelation?
6. Why was the earthly temple insufficient for God's dwelling?
7. What was wrong with the sacrifices the people were making in Isaiah's day?
8. Why and how will the people be put to shame?
9. When will the sudden enlargement of Zion take place?
10. What lessons can be drawn from the figure of a mother used in chapter 66?
11. What will God do before the people of the world can come and see His glory?
12. What indicates that the millennial restoration will be under the new covenant?

Appendix A:

Great Themes In The Book Of Isaiah

The New Testament refers to the Book of Isaiah in sixty-six passages.[1] Its great theological and prophetical themes are in the background of much more. Jesus not only quoted from Isaiah, He used Isaiah 61:1–2 to introduce himself and declare His ministry (Luke 4:18–19). Books were expensive. When the Ethiopian eunuch wanted a portion of Scripture to take home with him, he considered the Book of Isaiah to be one of great benefit. Philip began where the eunuch was reading and preached the gospel to him (see Acts 8:26–39). We can be sure that many others followed Philip's example and used Isaiah in a similar fashion. There is so much gospel in the Book of Isaiah that some have called it "The Gospel according to Isaiah." Its great themes reveal much about the nature of God and about His plan. We begin with a most important key theme.

1. God, The Holy One Of Israel

The Bible is first of all a revelation of God. The prophets knew God in a personal way and their vision, or revelation, of God is always the basis and ground of their message. Isaiah's vision of God as the supremely Holy One in chapter 6 changed his life and became the background for all he prophesied.

Isaiah refers to God twenty-five times as "the Holy One of Israel,"[2] once as the Holy One of Jacob who is the God of Israel

---

[1] Gleason L. Archer and Gregory Chirichigno, *Old Testament Quotations in the New Testament* (Chicago: Moody Press, 1983), 92–135.

[2] Isa. 1:4; 5:19,24; 10:20; 12:6; 17:7; 29:19; 30:11,12,15; 31:1; 37:23; 41:14,16,20; 43:3,14; 45:11; 47:4; 48:17; 49:7; 54:5; 55:5; 60:9,14.

(29:23), and once as the Light of Israel who is their Holy One (10:17). Elsewhere in the Bible only three psalms (71:22; 78:41; 89:18) and two passages in Jeremiah (50:29; 51:5) refer to God as the Holy One of Israel.

Isaiah uses the phrase six times in contexts of God's judgment, ten times in contexts of trust and rejoicing, and nine times in contexts of redemption and restoration. As the Holy One, He is Israel's great God among them (12:6), the Giver of salvation through repentance and rest, and the Giver of strength through quietness and trust (30:15). He is their Maker (45:11) and Redeemer who will help, teach, direct, and endow them with splendor (41:14; 43:14; 47:4; 48:17; 54:5; 55:5). He will honor them, restore them, and make Zion the City of the LORD (60:14)

The seraphs declared that the whole earth is full of His glory (6:3). He is the Creator, the God of the whole earth (54:5). From all that Isaiah says about Him it is clear that He alone is God; He is holy in all that He is and does. Thus there is no room for other gods, and though God can and will forgive sin and restore sinners who repent, He cannot tolerate persistent, rebellious sin. "Holy" (Heb. *qadosh*) comes from a root term meaning "to separate." God is separate from all sin and evil, and He must judge it.

But "holy" as used in the Bible emphasizes not separation *from* but separation *to*. Under the Law, holy vessels could not be put to ordinary use, for example, in the kitchen. But that is not what made such vessels holy. They became holy when they were used in the worship and service of the tabernacle and later the temple. So God wants a holy people (4:3; 62:12), but He is not pleased if our holiness is merely a matter of " 'Do not handle! Do not taste! Do not touch!' " (Col. 2:21). Pagans can achieve that with their taboos. God wants a positive holiness, a holiness that is consecrated and dedicated to His worship and service. He has dedicated himself to the carrying out of His plan to bring redemption, restoration, and glory, a glory that all believers will share through Jesus Christ when He comes again, a glory that Isaiah saw as eternal in the new heavens and the new earth (66:22).

2. God, The Mighty One Of Israel

Very early Isaiah gives a threefold emphasis to God's power and authority, calling Him "the Lord, the LORD Almighty, the Mighty One of Israel" (1:24). "The Lord" (Heb. *'adon*) means He is Lord and Master. He is over all. No one controls Him. "The LORD Almighty" (Heb. *YHWH tseva'oth*, "Yahweh of armies") means He is the Covenant Keeper who has the armies of heaven at His disposal. "The Mighty One" (Heb. *'avir*) describes Him as strong and powerful. He comes with His power, bringing judgment on sinners. He punishes "with His sword, his fierce, great and powerful sword" (27:1). He marches out "like a mighty man, like a warrior he will stir up his zeal; with a shout he will raise the battle cry and will triumph over his enemies" (42:13). All He has to do is speak a word. With "a mere rebuke" He can "dry up the sea [and] . . . turn rivers into a desert" (50:2). The very heavens remind us of "his great power and mighty strength" (40:26).

God's people, however, do not have to cower before Him. Isaiah cried out, "Surely God is my salvation; I will trust and not be afraid. The LORD, the LORD, is my strength and my song; he has become my salvation" (12:2). He looked back and remembered how God "sent his glorious arm of power to be at Moses' right hand" (63:12). In Isaiah's day God was still "a source of strength" (28:6), giving strength to the weary and increasing the power of the weak (40:29). His promise was that "those who hope in [and wait for] the LORD will renew their strength. They will soar on wings like eagles; they will run and not grow weary, they will walk and not faint" (40:31). He is the all-powerful One who is also gentle. "He tends his flock like a shepherd: He gathers the lambs in his arms and carries them close to his heart; he gently leads those who have young" (40:11). His mighty power is under perfect control. What a wonderful Lord He is!

3. God, The Omniscient One

Isaiah recognized that God has all knowledge and understanding. He needed no one to teach Him (40:14). He knows the past, present, and future. Because some of Isaiah's prophecies with regard to Assyria and Jerusalem were fulfilled in his own day, Isaiah could challenge the false gods of Israel's pagan neighbors: "Bring in [your idols] to tell us what is going to happen. Tell us what the former things were, so that we may consider them and know their final outcome. Or declare to us the things to come, tell us what the future holds, so we may know that you are gods. Do something, whether good or bad, so that we will be dismayed and filled with fear" (41:22–23). But to Israel he said, "Do not tremble, do not be afraid. Did I not proclaim this and foretell it long ago?" (44:8).

God sees and knows what individuals are doing, whether they realize it or not. He pronounced a woe on "those who go to great depths to hide their plans from the LORD, who do their work in darkness and think, 'Who sees us? Who will know?'" (29:15; see also 29:16; 47:10). But to those who turn to Him in repentance, He says, as He did to Hezekiah, "I have heard your prayer and seen your tears." (38:5). He is the high and lofty One, who lives forever (inhabiting the eternity of time and space), living in a high and holy place, yet also living with him who is contrite and lowly in spirit (57:15). He sees and knows us in a close, personal relationship, so we can trust Him to guide and help us (57:18).

4. GOD, THE CREATOR OF ALL

God demonstrated His power and wisdom in a special way in all His acts of creation. The term "create" (Heb. *baraʻ*) always has God as its subject. The Bible never uses it of what human beings can do or imagine. It is used of God's special unique acts, even in what He does in judgment (45:7).[3] Again and again Isaiah reminds us that God created the heavens, the earth, and humankind (17:7; 27:11; 37:16; 40:26,28; 42:5; 44:24; 45:9,12,18; 51:13,16; 57:16; 66:1–2). He will also create a new heavens and a new earth (65:17). God's purpose in reminding Israel of this was to encourage them to believe He created them as well (43:15) and that He has the power to create circumstances that will help them (44:2). He does not need to wait

---

[3] Cf. Num. 16:30 where "'brings about something totally new'" is *bᵉriʼah yivraʼ*, lit., "creates a creation."

until the occasion seems right. As the Creator He is so powerful that He can use and direct pagan nations such as Assyria and pagan kings such as Cyrus. He will work out His plan for His people Israel, for as their Maker He is their husband (54:5), a picture of His covenant-keeping love. He will also create Jerusalem in the Millennium to be a delight and its people a joy (65:18).

He says He created Israel for His glory (43:7) and made them His witnesses (43:10), formed for himself to proclaim His praise (43:1,21). They were to let the world know that because He created all things He alone is God and He alone has the power to save and ultimately to make everything new (Rev. 21:5). In His omnipotence and control, He is thus the Lord of history.

5. GOD, THE REDEEMER AND SAVIOR

Isaiah's name (Heb. *Y^esha'yahu*), "the LORD saves," draws attention to an important part of his message. The verb *y^esha'* means "to help, save, rescue, or come to the aid of someone in trouble." It implies victory, liberation, and divine favor. God has saved Israel (43:12; 63:9). He is Israel's Savior (17:10; 43:3; 45:15,21; 49:26; 60:16; 62:11; 63:8), "mighty to save" (63:1). He will save Israel (25:9; 33:22; 35:4; 45:17; 49:25). Apart from Him there is no Savior (43:11).

Coupled with the term "Savior" is the word "Redeemer" (49:26; 60:16). "Redeemer" (Heb. *go'el*) is the "kinsman-redeemer" who buys freedom for a close relative who has fallen into slavery, who makes payment for a wrong, or who, like Boaz, delivers a childless widow from childlessness by marriage. When God redeems, He takes care of the penalty and does it by grace. "For this is what the LORD says: 'You were sold for nothing, and without money you will be redeemed'" (52:3). God's future restoration is for the redeemed (35:9). He has also promised to redeem Jerusalem (52:9) along with its people.

Another word for "redeem" is *padah* (1:27; 29:22), which may also be translated "ransom" (as in Jer. 31:11). The corresponding noun, *paduth*, can be translated "ransom" or "redemption." Again, God pays the price for redemption and deliverance.

As Israel's Redeemer God is the Holy One of Israel (41:14; 43:14; 48:17; 49:7; 54:5), Israel's King (44:6), and Creator (44:24). He redeems those who repent of their sins (59:20). He redeems with justice and righteousness (1:27) but also with love and mercy (63:9) and with everlasting kindness and compassion (54:8). He teaches what is best for His people and directs them in the way they should go (48:17). Even when they offend Him, He sweeps away their offenses like a cloud, their sins like the morning mist, and calls for them to return to him, for He has redeemed them (44:22) and they belong to Him (43:1).

6. God, The Restorer Of Israel And Jerusalem

Isaiah gives many promises of restoration to Israel and Jerusalem. However, the restoration of the people applies only to a remnant who will "truly rely on the LORD, the Holy One of Israel" (10:20–22). God's first concern is the remnant that will return to the "Mighty God" (Heb. *'el gibbor;* 10:21), a name of the Messiah-King (9:6). God will use the Messiah—not as King but as the Suffering Servant—to bring Israel back to himself as well as to take His salvation to the ends of the earth (49:6).

God's purpose also is to bring the remnant of Israel back to Jerusalem and the Promised Land. There will be a new exodus, from all the lands Israel has been scattered to (see commentary on 11:10–16). This exodus looks ahead to the millennial day, when the Lord himself will be a victor's crown for the remnant of His people (28:5). Jerusalem will be called "the City of Righteousness, the Faithful City" (1:26). With a song of praise it will be transformed into a city of peace. God will fulfill His redemptive purpose (26:1).

There was a return in Isaiah's day of a remnant of the 200,150 people Sennacherib took captive to Babylonia. Then Cyrus, by his decree, fulfilled prophecy and encouraged a remnant to return from Babylonia in 538 B.C. Isaiah also sees a country born in a day, a nation brought forth in a moment, and an entire nation that will call Zion mother (66:8). A partial fulfillment took place in 1948. But none of these returns were the final fulfillment of Isaiah's prophecies. God has yet to "say to the north, 'Give them up!' and to the south, 'Do not hold them back.' Bring my sons from afar and my daughters from the ends of the earth" (43:6). The time will come when foreigners will aid Israel in this return and in the restoration of Jerusalem (60:10; 61:4–6). God will then cause the desert to rejoice and blossom (35:1), as He pours water on the thirsty land and, most importantly, His Spirit on Israel's offspring and His blessing on their descendants (44:3). Then they will be called holy (4:3). For in the coming millennial day the LORD will once again choose Israel, settle them in their own land, and as Ezekiel 47:22 also prophesies, aliens will join them and unite with them, sharing their inheritance (14:1).

In that millennial day the prophecies of the Messianic King and His reign will be fulfilled (9:6–7; 11:1–16; 32:1; 33:17; 61:3–7). Then the present Jerusalem will receive its fulfillment (65:17–25). What a wonderful day that will be, for "They will neither harm nor destroy on all my holy mountain, for the earth will be full of the knowledge of the LORD as the waters cover the sea" (11:9).

7. GOD, THE SAVIOR OF THE GENTILES

After saying "Israel will be saved by the LORD with an everlasting salvation" (45:17), God goes on to say, "Turn to me and be saved, all you ends of the earth; for I am God, and there is no other" (45:22). He did send the Messiah first to the people of Israel (49:5), which Jesus recognized (Matt. 15:24), but He also promised to make the Messiah a light for the Gentiles to bring salvation to the ends of the earth (49:6). He "will stand as a banner for the peoples; the nations will rally to him" (11:10).

Isaiah had to recognize—like Daniel (Dan. 2), Jesus (Matt. 24), and John (Rev. 19)—that the kingdom would have to be brought in through judgment. Isaiah proclaimed that because of sin and rebellion, God is angry with all nations and will totally destroy their armies (34:2; Rev. 19:15,21). But, just as God promised restoration for Israel, He has restoration for the Gentiles. Early in his ministry Isaiah saw that "in the last days [i.e., in the Millennium] the mountain of the LORD's temple will be established . . . and all nations will stream to it. Many peoples will come and say, 'Come, let us go up the mountain of the LORD. . . . He will teach us his ways.' . . . Nation will not take up sword against nation, nor will they train for war anymore" (2:2–4).

8. THE SERVANT OF GOD

The Hebrew *'eved* originally meant a slave but came to mean a trusted servant, especially one depended on to do a work for a king, a ruler, or God. Accordingly, kings and prophets are called servants of the LORD (2 Sam. 3:18; Ezek 34:23–24; Amos 3:7). Isaiah himself is the first one in the Book of Isaiah whom the LORD calls "my servant." Isaiah serves as he goes stripped and barefoot like a captive slave, God's warning and sign concerning Egypt and Cush (20:3). Other individuals included Eliakim, who was to replace Shebna as the manager of the royal household of Hezekiah (22:20), and David, for whose sake God would defend and save Jerusalem from the Assyrian king Sennacherib (37:35).

The latter part of Isaiah records four "Servant Songs," telling of the work of the LORD (42:1–4; 49:1–6; 50:4–9; and 52:13 to 53:12). Other passages that refer to or deal with the servant of the LORD include 41:8–16; 42:18–21; 43:10–13; 44:1–5, 21–23; 48:14–16,20; 49:7–13; 50:10–11; 51:9–16; 61:1–3; 65:9,14; 66:14. The use of the phrase "the servant of the LORD" can be pictured as three concentric circles: the outer circle is the nation of Israel as a whole, for it was called to do a work for the LORD; the middle circle is the godly remnant of Israel who were faithful to the LORD but who could not do the great work that needed to be done, the work of redemption and restoration; and the innermost circle is the Messiah himself, the One who accomplishes that work through His death and resurrection.

Israel as God's servant is called and chosen (41:8–9; 43:10,20; 44:1–2; 45:4; 65:9). They are His witnesses (43:10; 44:8). God formed them for himself that they may proclaim His praise (43:21) and rejoice in Him (41:16). They are not to do His work in their own strength, for they are small and there are many obstacles and enemies to cause them to fear (41:14). God is their Helper (41:13–14; 44:2) and Redeemer.

In the four Servant Songs mentioned above, an individual is

in view.⁴ He does a work for the benefit of Israel and the nations. The climax is in 52:13 to 53:12. Though the term "servant" is not used in 61:1–3, it contains terminology that connects it with the Servant Songs. Jews in New Testament times applied these passages to the Messiah, though they avoided attributing the sufferings to Him. It took Jesus himself to identify the Messiah as the Suffering Servant who would shed His blood and die as a ransom for sinners and rise again. Some today have tried to identify the Suffering Servant as the nation of Israel, "Jeremiah, Ezekiel, or some unknown martyr . . . who could take all these words in their entirety."⁵ See the commentary notes on these passages.

9. THE HOLY SPIRIT OF GOD

As we have already noted, Isaiah saw a most important ministry of the Spirit of God as the Spirit rested on and worked in and through the Messiah (11:1–5; 42:1; 48:16; 61:1–4). Isaiah also refers to the work of the Spirit in the past, present, and future.

He reminds the people of the good things God did for Israel in the past and how "He said, 'Surely they are my people, sons who will not be false to me'; and so he became their Savior. In all their distress he too was distressed, and the angel of his presence saved them. In his love and mercy he redeemed them; he lifted them up and carried them all the days of old. Yet they rebelled and grieved his Holy Spirit. So he turned and became their enemy and he himself fought against them. Then his people recalled the days of old, the days of Moses and his people—where is he who brought them through the sea, with the shepherd of his flock? Where is he who set his Holy Spirit among them, who sent his glorious arm of power to be at Moses' right hand, who divided the waters before them, to gain for himself everlasting renown?" (63:8–12).

Here we see the Holy Spirit treated as a Person who can be grieved (cf. Eph. 4:30). The Holy Spirit was also in Moses

---

⁴Christopher R. North, *The Suffering Servant*, 2d ed. (London: Oxford University Press, 1969), 6.

⁵F. B. Meyer, *Christ in Isaiah* (London: Marshall, Morgan & Scott, 1950), 125.

(63:11). Some suppose that the meaning here is that because the Holy Spirit was in Miriam, the seventy elders, and Joshua, as well as Moses, He was in the midst of the congregation of Israel. Therefore, when the Israelites complained rebelliously, they grieved the Holy Spirit who was among them. However, since 63:12 emphasizes the leadership of Moses, we can see that the Spirit was specifically in Moses. Thus, Isaiah in 63:14 compares the Spirit's leading Israel into the rest (of Canaan) to a good shepherd leading a flock into a valley (where they would enjoy tender green grass and still waters). Spirit-filled leaders brought Israel into victory and blessing. Yet the true leader and guide was always the Spirit of God.

In Isaiah's own day his prophecies of judgment were mocked by drunken people and priests, saying that they were not babies (28:9). To them, Isaiah's prophecies were like the ABC's or baby talk. (Isa. 28:10 in Heb. reads something like *"tsau latsau tsau latsau kow lakow kow lakow,"* as if he were repeating letters of the alphabet or talking gibberish.)

Isaiah replied, "With foreign lips and strange tongues God will speak to this people, to whom he said, 'This is the resting place, let the weary rest'; and, 'This is the place of repose'—but they would not listen. So then, the word of the LORD to them will become: Do and do, do and do, rule on rule, rule on rule; a little here, a little there *[tsau latsau tsau latsau kow lakow kow lakow]*—so that they will go and fall backward, be injured and snared and captured" (28:11–13). God used Sennacherib to fulfill this prophecy when he took all the cities of Judah except Jerusalem (36:1) and, according to his records, sent 200,150 people of Judah into exile, probably to Babylon to replace the 208,000 Babylonians he had just deported.

When Isaiah deals with the present he most often contrasts it with the future. We see this in his first mention of the Spirit. "Those who are left in Zion, who remain in Jerusalem, will be called holy ["dedicated," "consecrated to the worship and service of the one true God"], all who are recorded among the living in Jerusalem. The LORD will wash away the filth of the women of Zion; he will cleanse the bloodstains from Jerusalem by *a spirit of judgment and a spirit of fire"*—and this will prepare for the Messianic glory to come in the future (4:3–5). Some take the "spirit" here to be just a burning, cleansing wind. However, this is a work of God. His Spirit brings the fire of divine judgment to end this evil age and introduce the millennial reign of the Messiah.

We see this contrast between Isaiah's day and the future in several other passages. A rebellious people and unscrupulous leaders reject the guidance, power, and purity of the Holy Spirit (30:1). But a future outpouring of the Spirit from heaven will make the desert a fruitful field, like the gardenlands of Carmel (33:9; 35:2). The Spirit will transform both land and people and bring new enjoyment to the whole world (32:16–18).

The word of the LORD and His Spirit together assure us that the Creator-God will keep His promises, for He has made provision for His entire creation (34:16; see Ps. 33:6,9,11). But He is just as certain to judge. The Spirit of God comes in judgment like a drying wind that withers grass and flowers. This will be true because the word of God stands forever (40:7–8).

Isaiah 40:13 recognizes God's Spirit[6] as sovereign, active in the work of creation (see 40:12), needing no one to instruct or counsel Him. Here He seems almost unapproachable. Yet in 44:3 there is a parallel between God's pouring water on a thirsty land and pouring out His Spirit on the offspring of His chosen people. This is then linked to their salvation and spiritual renewal (44:5–6).

Still another contrast is found in Isaiah 59:19–21. Verse 19 speaks of the mighty power of God sweeping everything before it. The meaning is similar to the usual translation, but the Hebrew is better taken to read, "And they shall fear the name of the LORD from the west and His glory from the rising of the sun, for he [God] shall come like the river [the Euphrates] narrowed, the Spirit of the LORD driving it on."

"The preceding passage has to do with God's judgment on His enemies. When He moves against them, no enemy will be able to stand before Him. Just as the Euphrates River coming to a narrow place between high banks redoubles its speed and sweeps everything before it, so the Spirit of God is the driving force against God's enemies and will sweep them all away."[7]

---

[6]The NIV has "mind" but recognizes in the margin that the Heb. means "Spirit."

[7]Stanley M. Horton, *What the Bible Says About the Holy Spirit* (Springfield, Mo.: Gospel Publishing House, 1976), 64–65.

The same power is available to the people, for "He will be a spirit of justice to him who sits in judgment, a source of strength [courageous strength like the Messiah's in 11:2] to those who turn back the battle at the gate" (28:6).

"In contrast to this, the Redeemer (Kinsman-Redeemer who restores the inheritance) will come to Zion, even to those in Jacob (the Jews) who turn back to God from their transgression (rebellion). To them, God's covenant is that His Spirit which is upon them (and has been upon them since they were restored to God) and His words which the Spirit puts in their mouth will not depart (be removed) forever (59:21)."[8]

Isaiah's attention is primarily on the Spirit being on the Messiah and on Israel, though he does see hope for the Gentiles who turn to God. As Joel 2:28 promised, the Spirit will be poured out on all flesh, on all people, a promise whose fulfillment began on the Day of Pentecost, continues today, and will continue in the Millennium (Isa. 32:15).

10. God Deserves Pure Worship

Isaiah's vision of the LORD on a throne "high and exalted" made it easy for him to understand the foolishness of occult practices and idol worship, idols of wood, stone, and metal fashioned by human hands (see 1:29; 8:19; 40:18–26; 41:5–7; 45:20–21). It made him realize the greatness of the one true God (40:10,12,16). His vision also must have influenced others, including King Hezekiah (37:15–20).

His vision humbled him and made him realize his sinfulness and his need of cleansing. The cleansing was provided (6:7). Then he was able to experience what the high, holy, eternal God says: "I live in a high and holy place, but also with him who is contrite and lowly in spirit, to revive the spirit of the lowly and to revive the heart of the contrite" (57:15).

Humble worship then leads to joyous worship, with shouts and songs of praise and with musical instruments (12:1–6; 30:29; 58:13–14). This worship from the heart honors God and also spreads the good news to others. The command is to "Give thanks to the LORD, call on his name; make known

---

[8]Ibid., 65.

among the nations what he has done, and proclaim that his name is exalted. Sing to the LORD, for he has done glorious things; let this be known to all the world" (12:4–5; see also 42:10–12; 56:7; 63:7).

God's purpose was that the temple would be "'a house of prayer for all nations'" (56:7). That did not happen in Old Testament times, but God promised that the time would come when all nations would worship Him. In Isaiah's day the two great world powers were Assyria to the north and Egypt to the south. To Isaiah they represented the idolatrous nations of the world. Both of them opposed the LORD. But the day will come when both will worship the LORD together with Israel (19:21–24). Isaiah sees beyond them also to the islands of the sea (24:15), so the whole world will enjoy God's blessings (25:6–8).

The true worshiper says, "Your name and renown are the desire of our hearts" (26:8); and, "My soul yearns for you in the night; in the morning my spirit longs for you" (26:9). On the other hand, God hates meaningless worship (1:12–15), worship that is not backed up by a life consecrated to God and dedicated to doing what is right in His eyes (1:16–17; 55:7; 58:1–11). Yet He loves His people and is patient and long-suffering, holding out his hands all day long "to an obstinate people, who walk in ways not good, pursuing their own imaginations" (65:2). He calls on them to seek Him, offering them salvation, but warns them of judgment if they refuse and rebel (1:18–20; 55:6–7). Let us then remember that "the arm of the LORD is not too short to save, nor his ear too dull to hear" (59:1); and let us "delight greatly in the LORD" (61:10); "tell of the kindnesses of the LORD" (63:7); and "find our joy in the LORD" (58:14). He deserves pure, wholehearted, humble worship that gives glory to His name.

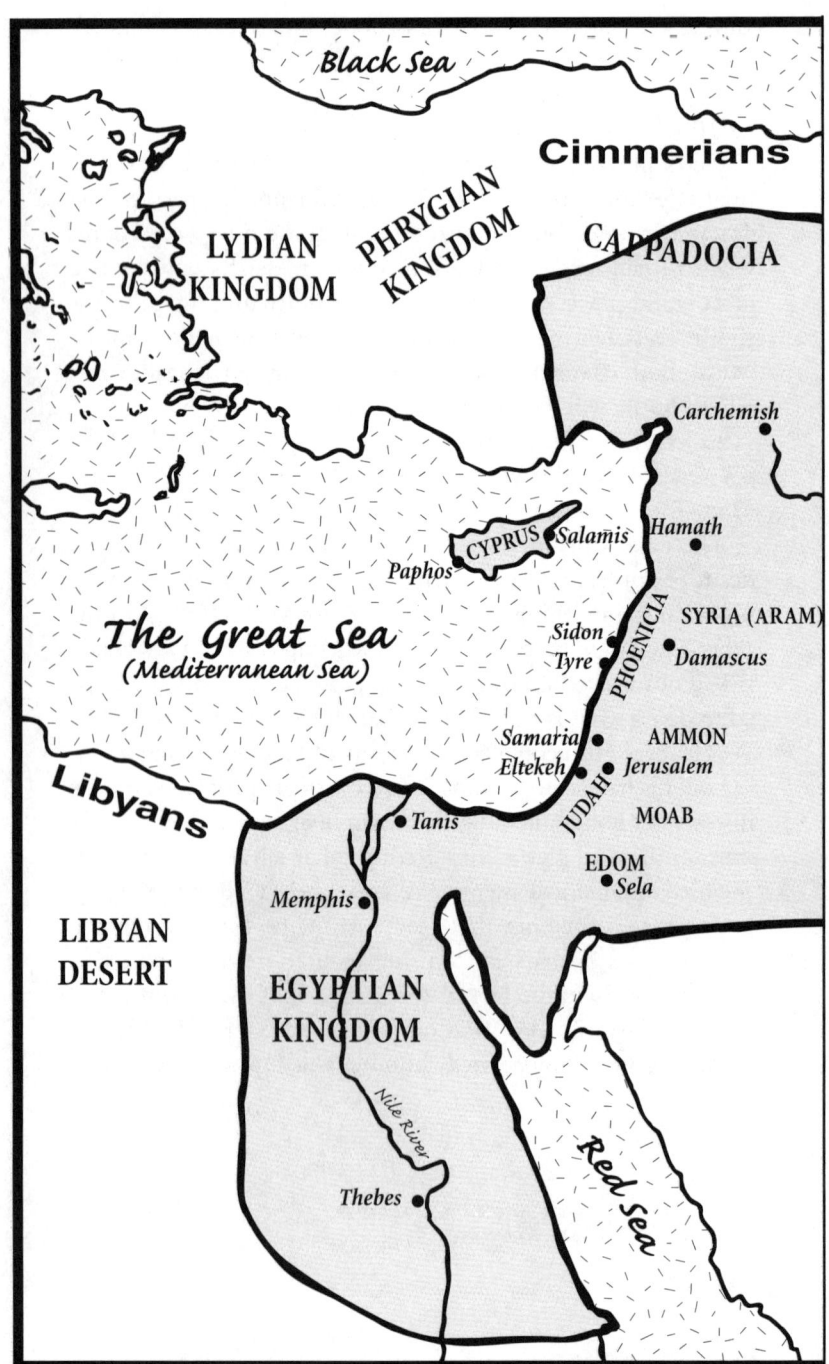

Appendix B / 487

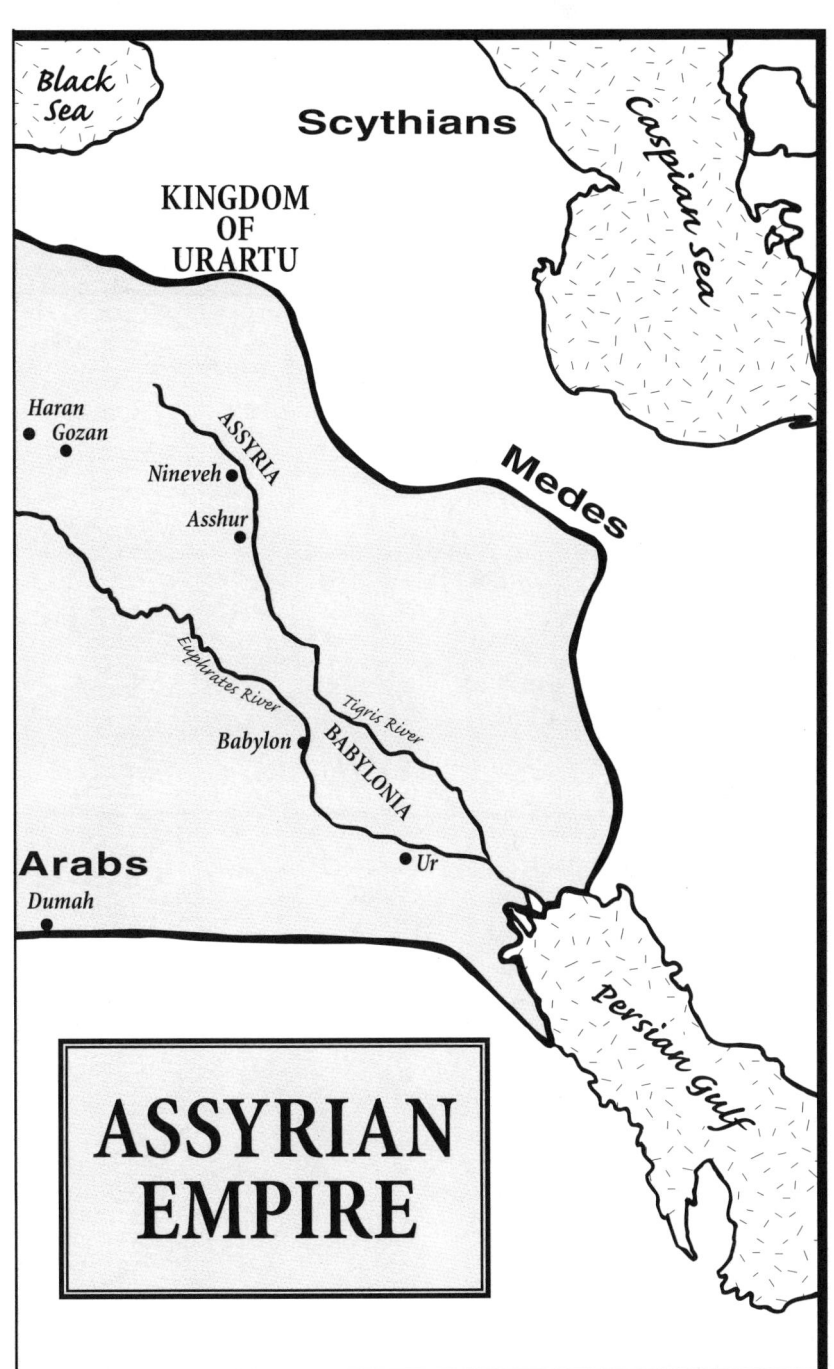

SELECTED BIBLIOGRAPHY

Alexander, Joseph A. *Commentary on the Prophecies of Isaiah.* 2 vols. in 1. 1875. Reprint, Grand Rapids: Zondervan Publishing House, 1975.

Allis, Oswald T. "Book of Isaiah." In *Wycliffe Bible Encyclopedia.* Chicago: Moody Press, 1975.

Freeman, Hobart E. *An Introduction to the Old Testament Prophets.* Chicago: Moody Press, 1969.

Herodotus, *History.* Trans. George Rawlinson, ed. Manuel Komroff. New York: Tudor Publishing Co., 1928.

Horton, Stanley M. "A Defense on Historical Grounds of the Isaian Authorship of the Passages in Isaiah Referring to Babylon." Th.D. diss., Central Baptist Theological Seminary, 1959.

———. *Our Destiny: Biblical Teachings on the Last Things.* Springfield, Mo.: Logion Press, 1996.

———. *The Ultimate Victory: An Exposition of the Book of Revelation.* Springfield, Mo.: Gospel Publishing House, 1991.

Knight, George A. F. *Servant Theology.* Grand Rapids: Wm. B. Eerdmans, 1984.

Leupold, H. C. *Exposition of Isaiah.* Grand Rapids: Baker Book House, 1971.

Luckenbill, Daniel David. *Ancient Records of Assyria and Babylonia.* 2 vols. Chicago: University of Chicago Press, 1926–27.

———. *The Annals of Sennacherib.* Chicago: University of Chicago Press, 1924.

McKenna, David L. *Isaiah 1–39.* In *The Communicator's Commentary.* Dallas: Word Books, 1993.

Motyer, J. Alec. *The Prophecy of Isaiah.* Downers Grove, Ill.: InterVarsity Press, 1993.

Oswalt, John N. *The Book of Isaiah: Chapters 1–39.* Grand Rapids: Wm. B. Eerdmans, 1986.

Pritchard, James B., ed. *Ancient Near Eastern Texts Relating to the Old Testament.* 2d ed. Princeton: Princeton University Press, 1955.

Schultz, Samuel J. *The Old Testament Speaks.* 4th ed. San Francisco: Harper, 1990.

VanGemeren, Willem A. *Interpreting the Prophetic Word.* Grand Rapids: Zondervan Publishing House, Academie Books, 1990.

Wolf, Herbert M. *Interpreting Isaiah.* Grand Rapids: Zondervan Publishing House, Academie Books, 1985.

Young, Edward J. *The Book Of Isaiah.* 3 vols. Grand Rapids: Wm. B. Eerdmans, 1969.

SCRIPTURE INDEX

OLD TESTAMENT

Genesis

1:1	67
1:2	199, 263, 382
2:7	301
3:16	466
3:17–18	405
6:6	162
7:11	202
8:2	202
8:21	398
9:1–16	198
9:22,25	413
11:1–4	150
12:3	63, 95, 176, 216, 233, 348, 396, 462
14:18–20,22	150
17:7	462
18	158
18:18	348
19:21–22	158
19:36–37	156
22:16	349
22:17	364
22:18	63
24:43	101
25:26	64
27:36	64–65
28:14	396
32:12	364
32:22–32	325n
32:24–28	215, 453
32:28	65, 307

Genesis (cont.)

35:10	65, 325n
41:41–44	190
41:49	364
49:11	80n
49:24	223
49:24–25	374

Exodus

1:8–10	124
2:8	101
3:12	320n
3:12,14–15	328
3:14	320n, 328, 354, 357
4:22	51, 155, 345
10:7	326
10:21	375
12:3	392
12:12,23	213
12:33,39	388
12:48–49	407
14:1–31	330
14:14	125
14:16	448
14:16,19–22	125
14:21	132, 375
14:28,30–31	326
15:1,3–10	326
15:1–21	382
15:2	133
15:11	113
15:13	51
15:20	106
17:6	314, 365

Exodus (cont.)

17:15	130
19:4	131, 325
19:5–6	312
19:6	385, 386
20:3–4	306
20:5	457
20:20	100
21:10–11	77
23:4	266
23:14–17	258
24:9–10	203
28:2–5	385
31:2–3,6	448
32:33	78n
34:13	165
35:30–35	448

Leviticus

2:1	295
3:9–11, 14–16	261–62
10:9–10	221
11:7	456
11:41	468
18:21	412
19:31	110
20:2–4	412
20:6	110
23	56, 227
23:1–44	56
23:3	422
23:32	65
25:13–34	82
25:39–43	437

Scripture Index

Leviticus (cont.)
25:48–49	313
26:8	238

Numbers
10:35	253
11:1	233
11:17	448
11:24–25,29	221
16:30	476n
20:11	314, 365
20:14–21	261
21:15	156
24:4	49
24:6	61
24:17–19	402
24:18	51
27:18	449
32:3	158
35:19–27	313

Deuteronomy
1:10	379
1:31	352
4:20	362
4:24	324
6:5	5
6:16	99
7:7–9	325
7:8	59
8:15	314
9:27	361
10:22	379
12:2	61
12:2–14	272
12:5	149
14:29	119
16:21	165
18:10,14	65
18:11	110
23:1	408
23:1,3	407
24:1,3	375
28:37	333
28:64	17
30:19	51
31:27	361
31:28	51
32:1	51
32:6	453

Deuteronomy (cont.)
32:11–12	352
32:15	333
32:30	238, 375
32:35	356
33:26–29	333
34:6	158

Joshua
2:10	332n
6:17	260, 332n
7:21	136
7:24–26	458
10:10–14	225
12:2	163
13:25	163
13:27	158
21:39	157, 161
23:1	449

Judges
2:14	375
7:2–25	113
13:18	113

Ruth
1:16	407
2:1	313
3:2,9–13	313
4:1–11	313

1 Samuel
3:1	49
22:1	66
25:11,25	248
28:3	70n
30:28	163

2 Samuel
3:18	480
5:17–23	225
7	287
7:4–17	97
7:12–13	114
7:14–16	402
22:47	389

1 Kings
1:39	107
5:1–12,18	191
7:2–5	186
8:27–29	463
8:29–30, 35–36, 42–43,52	409
8:41–43	408
8:51	362
9:26	68
9:28	141
10:11	141
10:22	68, 141, 259
14:23	61
14:29	195
16:31–33	191
18:19	191
19:2	191

2 Kings
3:4	159
4:1	375
4:39	213
8:12	12
9:30	399n
13:20	206
13:25	12
14:7	12
14:8	12
14:19	12
14:21	50
14:22,25	12
14:25	12
15:5	14
15:19	17
15:19–20	17
15:25	107
15:29	112
16:2	102n
16:2–4	96
16:5	65, 96
16:7	269
16:7–9	100
16:7–10	414
16:10–11	106
16:10–16	15
17:3–6	14
17:4	234
17:24	17, 282

Scripture Index / 493

2 Kings (cont.)	
18:1–4	272
18:2	102n
18:3	290
18:4	217
18:7	269
18:8	269
18:9	109
18:10	269
18:12	302
18:13	15, 18, 95, 109, 249
18:13 to 20:21	268
18:14–16	185, 255, 270
18:21	234
19:3–4	253
19:8	19n
19:9	19n
19:9–14	19
19:35	19, 167, 246
19:36	19
19:37	21
20:6	257
20:7–11	294
20:20	187
21:3,6	412
21:16	22, 51, 411
22:14	106
23:10	243n, 412
24:14	71

1 Chronicles

14:11–16	225
15:20	101

2 Chronicles

6:18	337
6:32	408
20:7	312
21:16–17	261
24:5	332
26:9,11–15	12
26:10–20	14
26:16	66
26:16–18,20	9
26:16–20	29
26:21	50
27:2	9, 29

2 Chronicles (cont.)	
27:3	14
27:3–5	14
27:6	66
28:1–3	96
28:1–27	9, 29
28:2	433
28:2–3	15
28:2–4	66
28:4	15
28:5	65
28:5–8	13, 15, 96
28:16,21	15
28:17–18	15
28:22–25	15
29:1,13	106
29:3	269
29:3 to 30:27	156
29:6–9	9, 29
29:36	290
30:1 to 31:1	290
32:3–8	187
32:5	187
32:22–23	200
32:23	21, 170, 291, 295
32:30	187
32:31	295n
33:11	19, 414n
34:22	106
36:22–23	310, 342
36:23	341

Ezra

1:1–2,7–8	310
1:2–3	341
1:2–4	342
1:7–10	388
4	280
4:2	98
4:9–10	17
5:13	310
6:3	310
6:3–4	341

Nehemiah

5:13	457

Esther

6:1	195

Job

9:13	382
13:4	66
19:26	213
25:6	313
26:6	84n
30:24	464
41:1	214
42:10	228n

Psalms

1	61
2:7,12	318
14:7	228n
16:9,11	411
16:10	213
17:15	411
19:1	306
19:5	79
22:6	313
22:26–29	205
22:27–28	348
23:6	213
24:3–4	248
24:3–5	408
24:4	92
27:14	308
28:9	352
30:3	84n
33:6,9,11	483
37:7,34	308
37:22	461
42:4	293
45:1–7	257
46	101
46:4–5	258
48:1–2	149
49:13–15	84n
50	464
51:17	464
55:15	84n
65:5	348
68:1	253
68:5	453
68:25	101
69:28	78n
71:22	474
73:19	468
73:24	213, 411
77:15	51

494 / Scripture Index

Psalms (cont.)

78:41	474
79:12	457
82:3,8	318n
85:8–13	57
87:4	382
88:11–12	84n
89:3–4,28–37	402
89:10	382
89:18	474
89:26	453
90:5–6	301
91:1–2	234
99:5	433
102:25–28	381
103:3–4	392
103:13	453
103:14	416
104:26	214
105:10–15	341
106:9	375
111:10	128
118:22	223
119:176	392
120 to 134	291
121:4	383
126	228, 291
126:1	228n
130:5–6	308
131:2	292
132:7	433
137	142n
143:5	393n
147:2	442
147:4	307

Proverbs

1:7	128
5:5	84n
7:27	84n
8	128
9:18	84n
15:10–11	84n
25:1	291
27:20	84n
30:19	101

Ecclesiastes

4:1	299

Song of Solomon

1:3	101
6:8	101

Isaiah

1	10, 30
1:2	320n
1:2,18	309
1:4	473n
1:7–9	421
1:8	81n, 202
1:10–20	464
1:11–12	261
1:12	331
1:12–15	485
1:13	331
1:15	58, 331
1:16–17	485
1:18–20	485
1:22	101n
1:24	122, 475
1:26	478
1:27	477, 478
1:29	484
1:31	378
1 to 39	23, 25, 26
2:2–3	78, 218
2:2–4	62, 205, 480
2:8,20	283
2:9,17	84
2:12–18	240
2:13	147
2:16	469
2:19,21	67
3:13	309
3:16–26	248
4:1	76
4:3	196, 474, 479
4:3–5	482
5	215
5:7	74
5:11–17	219
5:14	150n
5:19,24	473n
5:21	128
5:24	111, 378
5:30	141
6	10, 27, 30, 52, 133, 326, 463, 473

Isaiah (cont.)

6:1	154, 389
6:3	10, 30, 301, 389, 474
6:5	201
6:7	328, 484
6:9–10	229
6:10	28, 450
7	154
7:1–2	65
7:3	29, 124
7:5–6	164
7:10–17	10
7:14	31, 106, 108, 112n, 113
7:14–16	103n
7:17	328
7:18	409
7 to 11	103n
7 to 12	135
8:1,3	120
8:7	223
8:8	10, 31, 102, 112n
8:10	102
8:11–22	103n
8:14	223
8:19	484
8:22	112, 141, 328
9	102, 108, 216, 246
9:1–7	10, 31
9:2	430
9:6	106, 478
9:6–7	402, 479
9:7	127, 318, 435
9:10	68
9:12	409
9:14–15	155
9:18	378
10:4	116
10:5	139, 223, 242, 273, 354
10:5–6	84, 324, 357, 436
10:5–11	285
10:5–15	385
10:5–19	400
10:7–12	139
10:12	147, 212, 242, 306

Scripture Index / 495

Isaiah (cont.)		Isaiah (cont.)		Isaiah (cont.)	
10:13	126	17:12	168	29:16	453, 476
10:16–17	378	18:2	170	29:19	473n
10:17	474	19:1–17	171	29:22	477
10:20	473n	19:18–22	171	29:23	474
10:20–22	478	19:21–24	485	30:1	361, 483
10:21	114, 478	19:23	266, 300	30:1,10–14	86
10:34	147	20:1	185, 270	30:7	214, 382
11	102, 108, 133, 216, 246	20:1–5	18	30:11,12,15	473n
		20:3	480	30:15	308, 474
11:1	95, 436	21:1	356	30:27,30	378
11:1–5	481	21:2	182	30:29	484
11:1,10	391	21:11–12	442	31:1	473n
11:1–10	10, 31	22:1–2	198	31:7	283
11:1–16	479	22:4	201	32:1	257, 479
11:2	254, 318, 437, 484	22:11	189	32:1–5	10, 31
		22:20	480	32:12	214
11:4	130	23:1	193, 195	32:15	333, 484
11:6–9	463	24:4	255	32:15–18	10, 31
11:9	64, 479	24:15	485	32:16–18	483
11:10	479	24:23	241	33:1	182
11:10–16	478	25:2	217	33:9	147, 483
11:12–13	103n	25:6–8	485	33:13	260
11:16	300	25:9	477	33:17	479
12:1–6	484	26:1	478	33:22	477
12:2	475	26:2	213	34:1	264
12:4–5	485	26:5	212	34:2	282, 479
12:6	473n, 474	26:6–8	485	34:5–15	183
13	355	26:8	485	34:10	241
13:10	241	26:9	485	34:16	483
13:14	132n, 364	26:11	378	34:36–37	154
14:1	479	27:1	475	35:1	479
14:4–21	355	27:4	321	35:2	483
14:9	149	27:11	476	35:3–4	335
14:17–20	146	27:13	415	35:4	477
14:18–20	146	28:5	478	35:8	300
14:23	356	28:6	475, 484	35:9	477
14:31	241	28:7	229	35:10	382
15	162, 206	28:9	482	36	54, 107
15:1	161	28:9–15	86	36:1	20, 482
15:1–2	328	28:10	482	36:3	189
15:2	159, 457	28:11	258	36:3,22	255
15:5,8	161	28:11–13	482	36:6	21, 234
15:9	162	28:12	238	36:10	316
16	206	28:14	225	36:15,18,21	223
16:5	10, 31	28:16	10, 31	36:18–20	150, 304
16:7	162	28:17	263, 264	36:19	282
16:14	184	29:6	378	36:20	303
17:6	200	29:9	247	36:21	25, 298
17:7	473n, 476	29:14–16	244	36 and 37	156
17:10	208, 223, 477	29:15	476	36 to 39	268

Isaiah (cont.)

37	54, 107
37:1–2	21
37:5–7	284
37:8	280
37:8 and 9	19n
37:9	280
37:9–20	20
37:10	20
37:11	182
37:15–20	223, 484
37:16	328, 476
37:18	151
37:19	182, 359
37:23	473n
37:24	147
37:33	21
37:35	480
37:36	123, 246
37:36–38	278
37:37–38	125
37:38	3
38	275
38:1	270
38:5	476
38:5–6	270
38:5–6,21	124
38:6	276, 281
38:18	84n
39	25, 274n
39:5–7	450, 454
39:6	330
39:6–7	180
40	10, 22, 25, 30, 63, 276
40:1	21, 25, 133
40:3–4	415
40:6–8	383
40:7–8	483
40:8	10, 30
40:9	371
40:9–11	317
40:10	444
40:10,12,16	484
40:11	475
40:12	483
40:13	483
40:14	475
40:15	193
40:18–26	484
40:26	475

Isaiah (cont.)

40:26,28	476
40:28–31	336, 414
40:29	475
40:31	309, 352, 475
40 to 55	27
40 to 66	23, 24, 25, 26, 27n, 95
41:2	319, 341n
41:5–7	484
41:8	317
41:8–9	480
41:8–16	480
41:10–13	335
41:13–14	480
41:14	474, 478, 480
41:14,16,20	306n, 473n
41:16	480
41:18	322
41:21–22	348
41:22–23	476
41:22–24,26–27	183
41:25	310n
42:1	366n, 376n, 437, 481
42:1–4	480
42:1–9	317n
42:1–12	10, 31
42:5	476
42:6	112
42:6–7	369
42:10–12	485
42:13	475
42:16	430
42:18–20	327
42:18–21	480
42:22	362
43:1	478
43:1–2	335
43:1,21	477
43:3	477
43:3,14	306n, 473n
43:5	325
43:6	479
43:7	477
43:10	477, 480
43:10–13	480

Isaiah (cont.)

43:10,20	480
43:11	477
43:12	477
43:14	474, 478
43:15	476
43:18–19	320
43:19	300
43:21	480
43:25	395
44:1–2	480
44:1–5,21–23	480
44:2	325, 476, 480
44:3	479, 483
44:5–6	483
44:6	478
44:8	475, 480
44:14–21	353
44:22	267, 478
44:24	307n, 476, 478
44:28	22, 310
45	63
45:1	310
45:1,13	22
45:2	300
45:4	316n, 480
45:7	400, 476
45:9,12,18	476
45:11	473n, 474
45:15,21	477
45:17	477, 479
45:20–21	484
45:22	10, 30, 479
45:23	404
46	182, 355
46:1–2	19
46:6–7	401
47:1–15	355
47:4	306n, 473n, 474
47:10	476
47:14	378
47:22	479
48	36
48:6	320
48:14–16,20	480
48:16	481
48:17	306n, 473n, 474, 477, 478
48:20	132n, 388

Scripture Index / 497

Isaiah (cont.)	
49	10, 30
49:1–6	31, 480
49:1–7	317n
49:1–13	10
49:5	479
49:6	112, 478, 479
49:7	306n, 473n, 478
49:7–13	480
49:8	403, 437
49:11	387
49:14–15	423
49:14–16	375
49:25	477
49:26	477
49 to 57	365
50	10, 30
50:1	398
50:2	475
50:4–9	317n, 480
50:4–11	10, 31
50:10–11	480
51:1,7	406
51:9	384
51:9–16	480
51:13,16	476
52:1	372
52:3	477
52:7	317
52:9	477
52:13 to 53:12	10, 31, 317n, 361, 480, 481
53	10, 30, 401, 402
53:1	28
53:2	95
53:10	368, 396, 404, 429, 462
53:11	201, 401
54	10, 31
54:1	398
54:4	325
54:5	306n, 473n, 474, 477, 478
54:7	371
54:8	478
55	10, 30, 31
55:1	406
55:1–5	430

Isaiah (cont.)	
55:5	306n, 473n, 474
55:6–7	10, 30, 485
55:7	485
56:7	26, 415, 485
56 to 66	23, 406n
57:5	26, 61n
57:15	464, 476, 484
57:16	476
57:18	476
58:1–11	485
58:13–14	484
58:14	485
59:1	485
59:2	10, 30
59:10	449
59:19–21	483
59:20	478
59:20–21	430
59:21	333, 484
60:5–7,9,11,16	439
60:5–9	196
60:7	26
60:9,14	473n
60:10	479
60:14	474
60:16	467, 477
60:19–20	241
61:1	318, 320, 369
61:1–2	473
61:1–3	480, 481
61:1–4	481
61:1–11	10, 31
61:3–7	479
61:4–6	479
61:6–7	196
61:10	485
62:2	459
62:6	371, 444, 447
62:6,9	26
62:10	300
62:11	444, 477
62:12	474
63:1	477
63:1–6	321
63:4	437
63:7	485
63:8	477

Isaiah (cont.)	
63:8–12	481
63:9	352, 477, 478
63:11	482
63:12	475, 482
63:14	482
63:16	453
64	455
65:2	361, 485
65:2–5	468
65:3	61n
65:9	480
65:9,14	480
65:11	26
65:17	202, 340, 361, 476
65:17–25	479
65:18	477
65:20	469
65:25	130
66:1	433
66:1–2	476
66:6	26
66:8	478
66:14	480
66:15–16	378
66:17,24	61n
66:22	335, 474
66:24	378

Jeremiah	
2:13	134
2:21	80n
3:6,13	61n
3:14	397
3:16	433
3:17	63
7:31	243n, 412
9:4	65
11	61
11:4	362
12:10	74
17:11	248
17:19–27	406
18:6	453
19:11–14	243n
23:5–6	77
23:16	49
29:1–23	323

498 / Scripture Index

Jeremiah (cont.)

29:10	373
29:28	362
31:11	477
31:33–34	333
31:35–37	335
32:9	105
32:35	412
33:15–16	77
48:11–12	205
48:36	162
50:29	474
51:5	474

Lamentations

2:1	433
3:15	331

Ezekiel

2:4	361
7:13,26	49
8	456
9:4	466
14:3	53
27:20	183
29:10	370n
30:6	370n
31:3–9	68
33:31–32	230
34:8	410
34:23–24	480
36:26–27	333
36 and 37	213
37	468
37:14	333
38:13	183
39:29	333
40:2	63
43:15–16	227n
46:17	437
47:1–5	258
48:1–29	132
48:35	441

Daniel

1:3	297
1:17	49
2	130, 479
2:44–45	446

Daniel (cont.)

4:17,24–25	150
12:1	78n
12:2	213

Hosea

2:7	397
3:1	161
4:1–2	59n
10:1	74
10:8	69
11:8–9	398
12:4	453
12:10	49
14	61

Joel

2:16	79
2:23	239
2:25–29	333
2:28	250, 484
2:30	241
2:31	241
3:2,12	185
3:10	64

Amos

1:1	87, 202
2:1–3	156
3:7	480
3:15	13, 83
4:1	220, 248, 249
4:1–3	75
4:2	11
5:11	214
5:18	141
5:18–19	202
5:24	57
6:1	248
6:1,6	220
6:4	13
7:7–8	263, 264
8:9	241
9:11–12	430
9:12	63

Obadiah

1	49
10	262

Obadiah (cont.)

15–16	261

Micah

2:2	82
3:6	49, 241
4:1–4	62
4:10	297
6:6–8	57
6:8	464
7:19	395

Nahum

1:1	49
1:8–9	204
1:15	147
3:8	169

Habakkuk

2:2–3	49
3:11	241

Haggai

2:6–7	63
2:6–8	433
2:7	403
2:7–8	431
2:9	432

Zechariah

1:11	147
3:8	77
4:6	234, 318, 415
5:3–4	198
6:12	77
8:13	440
8:20–22	63
8:20–23	403, 433
9:9	444
11:17	66
12:10 to 13:1	333
14:5	87
14:12–13, 17–19	471
14:14	433
14:16–17	63
14:17–19	433

Scripture Index / 499

Zechariah (cont.)		Malachi		2:10	453
14:20–21	436			3:1	319
		1:3–5	204	3:6	328
		1:5	403	4:2	241, 417
		1:6	52		

NEW TESTAMENT

Matthew		Matthew (cont.)		Luke (cont.)	
1:20–23	366	25:31–46	419	15	218
1:23	102	26:42	385	15:11–32	58
2:23	128	26:52	252	18:32	376
3:3	28, 300	26:56	391	21:25	241
3:12	471	26:67	376	24:21	390
3:17	127, 318	27:26,30	376	24:25,41	390
5:3	437	27:57–60	393		
5:6	401	28:18	402	**John**	
5:34–35	463	28:19–20	368		
5:35	433	28:20	102	1:1,14	334
6:6	213			1:3	114, 307
6:6–8	453	**Mark**		1:9	319
6:7	230			1:14,18	340
7:21–23	129	1:35	376	1:18	90
8:17	391	7:6–15	230	1:29,35	392
9:36	392	9:44	471	2:25	129
10:30–31	307	9:48	471	3:16	58, 394
11:4–5	265	10:45	438	3:17	438
11:28–30	146, 326	13:32–33	175	3:19	94
12:17–18	28	15:16–20	376	3:34	128
12:17–21	317	15:28	395	4:10,14	134
12:20	241			4:22	373
15:8–9	230	**Luke**		4:24	90
15:18	92			5:28–29	213
15:24	479	1:31–32	366	6:44	63
17:17	368	1:32–33	114	7:38	134
18:20	403	2:32	368	8:12	319
21:5	444	3:4	28	8:46	81
21:13	408	4:16–21	10	9:5	319
21:33–44	80	4:16–22	437	10:16	409
21:42	223	4:17–21	37	11:51–52	470
22	401	4:18	437	12:32	63
23	73	4:18–19	473	12:38	390
23:37	368	6:12	376	12:38–41	28
24	479	6:38	457	12:41	91
24:13	319	7:22	265	14:2	213
24:14	368	9:51	377	14:6	404
24:29	141, 203, 241	10:18	149	14:10	49
		10:21	346	14:10,24	429
		10:30–37	266	14:16	113
24:30	469	13:34	161	14:27	114, 398–99, 404
24:35	10, 301	14	401		

John (cont.)

15:3	266
16:8–11	63–64
17:1	367
18:11	385
18:22	376
18:37	402
19:1	376

Acts

1:7	175
1:8	250
2:4	250
2:4,17–18	334
2:5	131
2:20	241
3:19	267, 267n
3:21	369
4:11	223
7:49	433
8:26–39	473
8:28	28
9:15	63
13:34	402
13:47	368
17:22	173
21:3–6	192
21:9	106
26:7	409
26:23	368

Romans

1:17	394
2:24	386
3:22	394
3:23	93, 94, 404
4:20–25	401
5:1	399
5:21	320
8:17	176
8:18–25	10
8:21	130, 404
8:22	340
8:32–39	377
8:34	395
9:21	453
9:33	223
10:11	223
10:15	387
10:16	390

Romans (cont.)

10:16,20	28
10:20–21	455
10:21	456
11:25–27	232
11:26	349, 429
11:29	333
12:3	354
12:19	356
14:10–11	349

1 Corinthians

1:7	206
1:20–25	230
1:23–24	369
1:26	437
1:30	394
2:9	452
3:11	223
3:13	378
11:5	106
14:21–22	222n
15:32	188
15:45	347n
15:50–53	213
15:52–53	461
15:54	206

2 Corinthians

1:20–22	460
3:18	355
5:21	394
6:1–2	403
6:2	369
12:10	308

Galatians

1:3	453
4:26–27	396
6:7	198
6:7–8	73
6:9–10	406
6:10	420

Ephesians

2:11–18	417
2:11–22	409
2:14–18	399

Ephesians (cont.)

2:17–18	417
2:19	433, 470
2:20	223
4:9	339n
4:30	481
4:30–31	448
5:15	293
5:18	221
6:11–12	202
6:14	428
6:15	387
6:17	129n, 367

Philippians

2:6–11	389
2:9	403
2:10–11	349
3:9	349, 394, 401
3:21	213

Colossians

1:12	453
1:16–17	307
2:21	474
3:17	363

1 Thessalonians

1:9–10	206
4:16–17	213
5:1–2	175
5:1–3,9	197
5:2	67
5:9	213, 385

2 Thessalonians

2:4	150
2:9–12	198

1 Timothy

6:10	86

2 Timothy

1:7	333
3:5	418

Scripture Index / 501

2 Timothy (cont.)
4:3–4	236
4:6	51
4:8	206

Titus
2:13	206

Hebrews
1:2	114, 307
2:13	110
4:9–11	406
4:12	367
7:25	395
8:6–13	319
8:13	432n
9:9–18	432n
9:10,13–14	464
9:15	319
9:15–18	398, 440
9:28	438
10:1,18	432n
10:4	464
10:10,14	464
10:19–20	404
10:19–22	349
10:27	378
11:37	51
11:37	16, 22
12:2	440
12:29	378
13:5	313
13:8	328

James
1:1	131
1:6	208
1:27	57
2:23	312
5:15	392

1 Peter
1:1	131
2:4–8	223
2:5,9	386
2:22	393
2:24–25	392
4:17	457

2 Peter
1:20–21	49
3:9–10	85
3:10	67

1 John
1:5	377
1:6	229
1:7,9	93
2:1	395
3:1,14–15	59
3:3	64
3:19	231
4:8	325
4:19	312

Jude
6	202

Revelation
1:8	328
1:17	334
2:17	441, 459
2:26–27	402
3:7	190
3:12	441, 459
3:14	460
4:4	203
4:5	128
5:6	392
6:12	241
6:12–13	141
6:12–14	260
6:15	66
6:16	445, 446
6:16–17	385
6 to 19	438
7:9	205
7:16	241
7:16–17	370
7:17	461
8	197
8:12	241
9	197
9:2	241
9:17–18	241
11:13	469
12:5	402

Revelation (cont.)
12:7–9	202
13:8	392
14:8	182
14:9–13	411
15	197
15:4	210
15:7	385
16:1	385
16:16	240
16:19	217
17 to 18	138
17:1 to 19:3	359
18	197, 358n
18:2	182
18:7	357
18:9,18	241
18:20	200
19	197, 479
19:3	241
19:11–21	198, 240
19:13,15	445
19:15	129, 253, 367, 402
19:15,21	479
19:19–20	254
19:20	243
19:21	260
20:1–3,11–15	202
20:2–3	461
20:7–10	114
20:10,15	471
20:11	261
20:12	78n
20:14–15	62, 378
21	460, 461
21:1	202, 261
21:4	206, 461
21:5	477
21:10,18–21	399
21:12–19	371
21:23	241
21:25	433
21:27	436
22	460, 461
22:5	241
22:6	244
22:12	444
22:13	334
22:15	471

SUBJECT INDEX

ABC's, 221–22
Abraham
  call of, 312
  promise of, 216
  seed of, 216, 396
  as a source of blessing, 63, 348–49
Abundance, 213, 240–41, 265, 431
Adad-Nirari III, 12
Adam, 332
Ahab, 191
Ahaz
  accession of, 14–15, 50
  apostasy of, 96, 99–100
  penalty for the sins of, 105
  prophecy concerning, 31
  reign of, 96
  warnings to, 97–98
Alexander the Great, 192, 274
Alliances, foreign, 166
Amaziah, 12
Amman, 161
Amos, prophecies of, 11, 13, 115–16, 156
Angel of the LORD, 287
Angels, 447
Animals, wild, 263, 330

Anointed One, 441, 444
Antichrist, 150, 253–55, 438
Apostasy, 245, 414, 427
Ar, 156
Arabia, destruction of, 183–84
Arabs, 264
Aramaic language, 17, 274
Ariel, 226–27, 229
Armageddon, Battle of, 129, 240, 438
Armor, 428
Arnon River, 156–57, 159
Aroer, 163
Arrogance, 67
Asherah, 165, 217
Ashur, 351
Asshur, 11
Assyria
  arrogance of, 121–22, 258
  as conquerors, 11, 32
  conquests of, 18, 32, 54, 120, 143
  defeated by God, 242–43
  destruction of, 245–46
  destruction of, prophesied, 153–54

Assyria *(cont.)*
  devastation of the armies of, 108, 126, 170
  expansion of, 17
  as the foe of Rezin, 116
  as God's people, 176–77
  as an instrument of judgment, 120, 122, 139, 219, 227, 324, 356–57
  judgment of, prophesied, 124–25
  policy of deportation, 146, 275
  prophecy against, 119–20
  as a razor, 104
  ruthlessness of, 16, 142–43
  terror of, 224
Astrology, 348
Atonement, 259, 401
Azariah, 12

Babel, tower of, 138, 150
Babylon
  Assyrian conquest of, 18–19
  as an Assyrian possession, 136–38

Babylon *(cont.)*
  as a center for religion, 359
  destruction of, 26, 36, 137–45, 152, 180–82, 195, 280–81, 350–51, 358
  greatness of, 136
  importance of, 296
  judgment of, 139
  leaders of, 138
  prominence of, 26
  prophecies against, 32–33, 137–45
  as queen of kingdoms, 356
  rebuilding of, 145, 351–52
  as a symbol of evil, 182
  as a virgin, 355
Babylonian exile, 25–26, 298
Banner, 87–88
Bar Kochba, 131
Bashan, oaks of, 68
Bel, 136–37, 182, 273, 350–51
Belshazzar, 143, 343
Beth Shemesh, 12
Beulah, 442
Bitterness, 293
Blacksmith, 336, 400
Blasphemy, 277–78, 386
Blessing
  of Abraham, 63, 118, 348, 379, 396, 462
  cannot be taken away, 400
  of the covenant, 51
  for the faithful, 205, 239
  follows judgment, 251, 264

Blessing *(cont.)*
  through keeping the Sabbath, 406, 422
  through the Messiah's death and resurrection, 36, 396
  in the Millennium, 38, 264, 462
  for others besides Israel, 37, 63, 64, 95, 134, 176, 348, 396
  repentance brings, 58
Blindness, 230–32, 320, 322–23, 426
Blood, 261–62
Boaz, 267
Bribery, 59, 86
Bridegroom, 397, 440
Briers, 105, 215, 249
Bulls, 262

Calvin, 149
Canaanites, 166, 412–13
Celebration, 134–35, 185
Chaff, 310, 314
Chaldeans, 329, 355
Chaos, 72, 118
Chemosh, 157
Chiasm, 305–6
Children, lack of, 384
China, 370
Christ
  burial of, 393
  death of, 393–94
  as a foundation stone, 223
  fulfilling prophecy, 340
  second coming of, 368
Church Age, 64
Civil war, 118

Comfort, 206, 335
  Book of, 298
Compassion, 399
Confession, 334
Coregency, 50
Corruption, 118–19
Court setting, 74–75, 327, 334
Covenant, 198, 223–24, 451
Crown, 441
Curse, 198, 405
Cush, 168–70
Cyrus, 192, 311
  conquests of, 342
  as a deliverer, 143
  as God's anointed, 35, 316, 341–42
  as God's shepherd, 341

Damascus, 98, 106–7, 163
Daniel, 297
David, 57, 190–91, 216, 287
Day of Atonement, 395, 418
Day of the LORD, 76, 103, 123, 165, 202–3
  imminence of, 139–40
  judgment during, 217–18, 261
  phenomena surrounding, 241
  restoration during, 206
Deafness, spiritual, 231, 322–23
Death, fear of, 291–92
Deliverance, 216, 228, 278, 287
Desolation, 53–54, 199, 249–50
Deutero-Isaiah, 23

Subject Index / 505

Dew, as symbol of blessing, 213
Dibon, 157, 159
Discipline, 216–17
Dove, 318
Dross, 59–60
Drunkenness, 83, 219–21, 410

Earth, redemption of, 369
Earthquake, 87, 202
Edom, 12, 204, 444
  desolation of, 263
  geography of, 183
  judgment of, 261
Egypt, 11
  civil war in, 171
  defeated by Assyria, 88, 104, 235
  as God's people, 176–77
  as an unreliable help, 233–37
  Judean alliance with, 234
  judged by God, 174
  reconciled to God, 175–76
  restoration of, 174–75
  ruled by a Cushite king, 171–72
  as a trading partner of Tyre, 193
Elam, 359
Eliakim, 190–91
Enemies, 60, 63, 321
Ephraim, judgment of, 116
Esarhaddon, 19
Eternity, 308, 450
Euphrates River, 11, 214
  destruction of, 132
  as a symbol of power, 107–8

Euphrates River *(cont.)*
  as a trade route, 329
Exile
  causes of, 72
  results of, 76–77
  return from, 330, 341, 372–73, 382, 388
Exodus
  from Egypt, 78
  from exile, 132, 327, 341, 365
Extortion, 118–19

Faith, 223, 276
  in God, 313, 377
  in human strength, 238, 311
  of Jerusalem, 298
False prophets, 117
Fasting, 419–21
Favor of God, 437
Feast of Tabernacles, 134
Feasts. *See* Festivals
Fellowship, restoration of, 232
Fertility cults, 61
Festivals, 56, 227, 258
Fire
  destruction of, 256
  as judgment, 61, 359, 362, 378
  lake of, 243, 411
  as punishment, 210, 454
  purification by, 61–62, 92–93
Flies, 103, 381
Flood, 428
Foolishness, 247–48
Forgiveness, 293, 332
Foundation, 223
Future, foretelling of, 387

Galilee, 112
Garden of Eden, 130, 380, 463
Gehenna, 243
Gentiles. *See* Nations
Gibeon, Valley of, 225
Gihon spring, 107
Glory, 430, 435
God
  arm of, 253, 302, 380, 388
  attributes of, 60, 242, 256, 324, 326, 334, 373, 385, 416
  as a builder, 442
  as the Creator, 303, 307, 319, 329, 333, 345, 347, 375, 476
  discipline of, 212
  faithfulness of, 284, 293, 311
  as the Father, 345, 377, 450
  as a foundation stone, 223
  glory of, 300–301
  grieving over Moab, 157–58
  hand of, 206, 315
  His word fulfilled, 198
  holiness of, 85, 91–92, 109
  as Israel's Redeemer, 369
  as the Judge, 426
  judgment of, 69, 111, 255
  as a king, 329
  kingdom of, 146
  laws of, 209
  majesty of, 210
  manifestation of, 78–79

506 / Subject Index

God *(cont.)*
  name of, exalted, 134
  neglected in Hezekiah's crisis, 187–88
  offices of, 259
  omniscience of, 214, 335, 475
  people of, 209
  permanence of, 301
  power of, 283, 304–5, 475, 483
  presence of, 110, 246, 463
  as a refuge, 109, 204, 215, 415
  reputation of, 451
  righteousness of, 354–55, 400, 420
  as a rock, 166, 208–9
  salvation of, 328
  as the Savior, 477
  self-revelation of, 328
  as a shepherd, 370
  as the source of strength, 308–309
  sovereignty of, 122, 452
  strength of, 220
  strong hand of, 108
  as the true leader, 211
  upraised hand of, 116–18
  as a warrior, 138–39, 238, 321
  word of, 209, 317
  wrath of, 87, 445
  zeal of, 286
  See also Titles of God
God's Word, 209, 236, 317, 404

Gomorrah, 54–55, 144, 262
Gospel
  choice demanded by, 58
  as the good news, 371
  of peace, 387
  present in Book of Isaiah, 473
  spread through Zion, 430
Grace, 406, 428
Grain, 182
Great Commission, 368
Great Tribulation, 64, 182, 197, 210, 214, 264, 385, 430, 445, 461
Guidance
  for all peoples, 380
  continual, 421
  failure to seek, 234
  false, 73–74, 117, 223, 240, 410
  from God, 35, 51–52, 213
  from the Holy Spirit, 482, 483
  from the Messiah, 130, 319
  for the spiritually blind, 322
Gulf of Aqaba, 68

Hades, 84
Hamath, 12
Hanes, 234–35
Harvest, 217–18
Healing, 265–66, 320, 417
Heavens, 306
Hell, 84, 383
Herodotus, 184, 281, 342, 352

Heshbon, 161
Hezekiah, 15, 18, 21
  alliances of, 243–44, 255, 269
  coregency with Ahaz, 50, 109, 269
  faith of, 282–83
  gifts for, 295–296
  healing of, 124, 200, 257, 270, 289–90
  humility of, 293
  illness of, 289
  mocked, 272–75
  paying tribute to Assyria, 185–86
  religious reforms of, 217, 269
High places, 156, 413
Highway, 266, 300, 370, 415, 443
Hinnom, Valley of, 243
History, 311
  biblical view of, 67–68, 315
  controlled by God, 335
  cyclical view of, 315
  God's purposes in, 325
  of Israel, 386
Holiness, of God, 254, 474
Holy Spirit, 448
  activity of, 481
  conviction of, 63–64
  guidance of, 240
  inspiration of, 264
  outpouring of, 35, 250, 333–34, 483
  power of, 257
  presence of, 128
  protection of, 234

Subject Index / 507

Hosea, 74, 115–16
Humanity, weakness of, 244
Humiliation, 104, 178, 312–13, 434
  as a judgment, 84
  of idol worshipers, 336, 347
  removed by God, 397
Hussein, Saddam, 145n
Hypocrisy, 230, 418

Idolatry, 15
  delusion of, 338
  futility of, 66, 121, 283, 305, 311–12, 335–38, 353
  punishment for, 166
  rejected, 165, 245
  ridiculed by Isaiah, 305–6
  supplanted by the Lord, 68–69
  trusting in, 70
Ignorance, 84, 217, 324, 410
Immanuel
  birth of, 100–102
  identity of, 100–102
  as the Messiah, 79, 107–8, 113
  See also Messiah
Indifference, 231
Inheritance, 400–401, 450
Irony, 331, 335, 337, 348, 353, 359, 415
Isaiah, Book of
  authorship of, 22–28
  stylistic variations in, 26–27, 298–99

Isaiah, Book of *(cont.)*
  themes of, 473
  unity of, 24–28
  as a vision, 49
Isaiah, the prophet
  biography of, 29–30
  calling of, 9, 30–31, 90–95
  emotions of, 201
  as God's servant, 178
  ignored by the people, 188
  message of, 64
  meaning of the name of, 49
  mocked, 482
  sinfulness of, 92
  sons of, 30–32, 97, 106–7, 110
  in a state of mourning, 177–78
  wife of, 106
  worshiping the Lord, 203–4
Islands, 311, 380, 432
Israel
  allied with Damascus, 164
  Assyrian conquest of, 13–14
  as a blessing, 95
  enemies of, 216
  as Ephraim, 96–97
  as evangelists, 348
  exile of, 17, 112
  as God's firstborn, 155
  as God's nation, 65, 327
  as God's servant, 322–23, 333
  history of, 216
  holiness of, 450
  idolatry of, 66

Israel *(cont.)*
  as Jeshurun, 333
  loved by the nations, 440
  meaning of the name of, 65
  permanence of, 364
  prosperity of, 65–66
  purification of, 233
  redemption of, 339
  repentance of, 233
  restoration of, 145, 264–68
  righteousness of, 349
  scattering of, 326
  as a vineyard, 80–82
  See also Babylonian exile

Jacob
  descendants of, 233
  meaning of the name of, 64–65, 429
  name changed to Israel, 64–65, 215
  wrestling with an angel, 453
Jehoash, 12
Jericho, Joshua's conquest of, 136
Jeroboam II, 12
Jerusalem
  Assyrian invasion of, 126
  deliverance of, 339
  desolation of, 454
  as God's capital, 49
  as a mother, 467
  prophecies against, 184
  purification of, 78
  redemption of, 208
  restoration of, 60

Jerusalem *(cont.)*
  as a virgin, 284
Jesse, root of, 127, 130–31
Jesus, 128, 259, 307
Jezebel, 191
Jihad, 318
Jonah, 12
Josephus, 341
Joshua, victories of, 225
Jotham, 14, 50
Joy, 267–68, 339, 387, 459
Judah
  Babylonian conquest of, 127
  conquered by Assyria, 186–88
  destruction of, 15, 107–8, 109
  exile of, 36, 111, 216
  as Immanuel's land, 102
  restoration of, 33
Judges, 60, 86
Judgment, 212
  of Assyria, 228
  God's, inescapable, 202
  God's, righteousness of, 200
  of Judah, 228
  of the nations, 141
  of pagans, 62
  severity of, 237
  for sin, 413, 457, 465
  sudden, 117
Justice
  definition of, 57
  divine, 356
  of God, 380, 385
  of the Messiah, 318
  perversion of, 248
  restoration of, 250

Justice *(cont.)*
  spirit of, 220

Kingdom, 52, 103, 301
Kinsman-Redeemer, 267, 313, 340, 356, 374, 429, 450, 477
Knowledge, 128, 247

Lachish, 11–12, 54, 279
Lamb of God, 392
Lamentation, 167
Land, 197, 372, 438–39
Law
  of God, 55, 319, 323
  scope of, 63–64
  sealed up, 109–10
Leaders
  corruption of, 117
  culpability of, 74–75
  deportation of, 70–71
  indifference of, 229–30
  insignificance of, 306
  sins of, 37, 86
  weakness of, in Israel, 74
Lebanon
  cedars of, 68, 147, 255, 284, 433
  geography of, 231
Leviathan, 214
Lions, 244–45, 292
Love, 398, 447
Lucifer, 149
Luther, 149

Manasseh, 16, 19
  coregency with Hezekiah, 50–51

Manasseh *(cont.)*
  sins of, 21–22, 51, 409, 423–24
Manure, 206–7
Marduk, 137, 343, 351–53
Medes. *See* Media
Media, 143, 359
Medical treatment, 294
Mediterranean Sea, 192–93
Mediums, forbidden, 110–11
Memphis, 173
Mercy, 238–39, 332
Merism, 117, 155
Merodach-Baladan, 18, 295–96, 357
Mesopotamia, 11, 282, 356
Messiah
  as the Anointed One, 125
  as a banner, 131
  as the Branch, 77–78, 127–28, 151
  divinity of, 114, 367
  as God's servant, 317–18
  as God's Son, 318, 368
  justice of, 319
  as the Lamb, 445–46
  ministry of, 447
  mission of, 437
  names of, 124, 132
  peace of, 258
  preaching of, 37
  rejection of, 371, 390
  reign of, 113, 133, 160, 246–47, 254, 257, 430
  resurrection of, 441

Messiah *(cont.)*
 righteousness of, 129
 as the ruler of
  Israel, 366–67
 salvation of, 35, 380
 suffering of, 27, 30,
  391–92
 as the Suffering
  Servant, 344, 366,
  376–77, 478
 as a tender shoot,
  390–91
 virgin birth of, 31
 See also Suffering
  Servant
Micah, 62, 115–16
Millennium, 38, 60,
 177, 445
 blessings of, 322,
  462
 characteristics of,
  64, 254
 restoration during,
  146, 314
 restoration of tribes
  during, 132
 rule of Christ during, 211–12
Moab
 alliance with Assyria,
  207
 defeat of, 206
 extinction of
  Moabites, 163
 geography of,
  157–59, 161–62
 historical events surrounding, 157
 prophecies against,
  156–63
 ruled by the
  Messiah, 160
Molech, 243, 412–14
Mountain, holy, 130
Mountains, of God,
 387
Mourning, 157, 277

Muslims, 318

Nabonidus, 143, 343,
 358
Nabu. *See* Nebo
Naphtali, geography
 of, 112
Nations
 blessed by God,
  176–77
 conversion of, 63,
  346, 373, 403, 407
 destruction of, by
  God, 167
 insignificance of, 304
 as instruments of
  judgment, 87–88
 judgment of, 135,
  154, 259–64
 repentance of, 204,
  309
 salvation of, 208,
  379, 444, 479–80
Nebo, 136, 157, 182,
 273, 351–53
Nebuchadnezzar,
 invasions of, 297
Neo-Assyrian Empire,
 90
New covenant,
 398–99, 433–34
New creation, 460
New Jerusalem, 114,
 371, 381, 399, 433
Nile River, 11, 169,
 172, 285
Nimrud Tablet, 137
Nineveh, 11, 123,
 204, 252
Noah, 198, 202, 398
Northern Kingdom,
 219

Obstinancy
 despite God's
  appeal, 455–56,
  485

Obstinancy *(cont.)*
 of Israel, 360–61
 and pride, 116
 in rejecting the
  LORD, 233–34
 of sinners, 85
Occult, 348, 456
Offerings. *See* sacrifices
Olives, Mount of,
 126, 185
Ophir, 141
Orphans, 118–19
Osorkon IV, 234
Oxen, 52, 240, 262

Paganism, 121, 322
 in Babylon, 359
 beliefs of, 61, 328,
  468
 rejection of, 111
Palestine, geography
 of, 68
Pantheism, 91
Passover, 213, 290
Peace, 113, 176–77,
 208, 251, 310, 392,
 411, 467
Pekah, 31, 96–99,
 107, 109
Pentecost, Day of,
 250, 333–34, 484
Petra, 159, 264, 321
Philistines, 154–55,
 178–79
Phoenicia, 194
Plumb line, 224
Politicians, sins of, 86
Polytheism, 334
Poor, the, 13, 75, 204,
 232, 419
Potter, 231, 316, 344,
 453
Praise, 201, 293–94,
 435
Prayer, 278, 283
 answers to, 476

Prayer *(cont.)*
  offered in vain, 57
  protected by God, 204
Premillennialism, 432n
Presence of God, 325–26
Proclamation, 302, 387, 417–18
Promised Land, 131, 225, 45
Promises of God, 307–8
Prophecy
  false, 236
  fulfillment of, 179–83, 316, 479
  partial fulfillment of, 95
Prophetess, 106
Prophets, 442–43
Prosperity, during exile, 323, 357, 362
Prostitution, 195–96, 412–13
Psalms of Ascent, 291
Pul. *See* Tiglath-Pileser III
Pulu. *See* Tiglath-Pileser III
Pyramid, Great, 175

Rahab, 214, 235–36
Ransom, 267, 326, 438
Rebellion
  brings judgment, 95, 485
  despite God's provision, 51–52
  and grieving the Spirit, 38, 448, 481–82
  hardening in, 94
  and idolatry, 61, 353

Rebellion *(cont.)*
  leads to corruption, 58–59
  not tolerated by God, 324
  and rejection of God's Word, 236
  results in death, 58, 471
  of rulers, 59, 74
  stubbornness in, 456
  turning from, 429
  wiped clean by God, 339
  in words and deeds, 72
Red Sea, 125
  compared to the deep, 382
  deliverance at, 329–30, 448–49
  trade by way of, 12–13
Redeemer, God as, 326
Redemption, 375, 385
Reincarnation, 67
Relationship, with God, 324, 377
Religion
  empty forms of, 331, 360, 463–64
  false, 237
  perverted, 358
Remnant, 35, 95
  confessions of, 211
  deliverance of, 286
  God's concern for, 127
  joy of, 200
  of Edom, 430
  of Israel, 381
  poverty of, 104
  prayer for, 278
  purification of, 239

Remnant *(cont.)*
  returning from exile, 123–24, 458
  smallness of, 141, 164–65, 200
  sustained by God, 352
  as witnesses, 328
Repentance, 58, 94, 188, 403
Rephaim, Valley of, 164
Restoration
  after judgment, 209, 268, 421
  during the Millennium, 206, 334, 460
  of Israel, 250–51
Resurrection, 212–13, 394, 408
Revelation of God, 455, 469, 473
Rezin, 13, 15, 31, 96–98
  conspiracy of, 109
  death of, 107
Rich, the, 13, 83
Righteous, the, 73, 209
Righteousness, 435
Rulers. *See* Leaders
Rye, 226

Sabbath
  observance of, 408, 422
  observed in vain, 56
Sacrifices, 295–96, 304, 331, 390, 439–40, 470
  offered in vain, 55–56
  substitutionary, 392
Salvation
  available for all, 379, 380, 390, 478

Subject Index / 511

Salvation *(cont.)*
  through Christ, 10, 27, 114, 441, 444, 445–46
  day of, 369, 437
  for each individual, 218
  everlasting, 36, 381
  fulness of, in Christ, 254
  garments of, 440
  of Gentiles, 112, 348, 368, 479–80
  God as source of, 29, 32, 37, 133, 211, 427–28, 474
  and God's righteousness, 380
  helmet of, 428
  seriousness of rejecting, 471, 485
  way of, always open, 215
  of Zion, prophesied, 37–38, 354–55, 441
Samaria
  besieged by Shalmaneser, 220
  conquest of, 124
  destruction of, 98, 409
  exile of, 156
  judgment of, 116
  plundering of, 106–7
Sarah, 379
Sarcasm, 162, 189
Sargon II, 14, 17–18, 33, 177
Satan, 114, 149–50
Scepter, 122, 147
Seed, 396, 462
Seleucids, 152
Self-deception, 247
Sennacherib
  arrogance of, 182

Sennacherib *(cont.)*
  assassination of, 21, 288
  boasting of, 276
  blasphemy of, 281
  campaigns of, 280–81
  chronology of Judean invasion of, 20–21
  as conqueror of Babylon, 18–19, 139–40
  as conqueror of Judah, 11, 33–34, 54, 109
  death of, 51, 278
  defeat of, 200
  destruction of the army of, 123, 287–88
  as king of Arabia, 184
  ruthlessness of, 354
Servant of God, 480–81
Servant Songs, 317, 367n , 389
Shalmaneser V, 13–14, 17, 98, 156
Shamelessness, 73
Shebna, 188–90
Sheol, 84, 148, 211, 213, 223, 291, 293, 414
Shepherd, 302–3
Shiloah, 107
Sidon, 12, 192–93
Siege, deprivations of, 239
Sign, 286, 290–91
Siloam
  Pool of, 134, 187
  tunnel, 187, 189
Sin
  consequences of, 256, 423

Sin *(cont.)*
  forgiveness of, 332
  normalization of, 86
  original, 150
  punishment for, 392
Sinai, 451
Skilled workers, 71
Slavery, 131, 299, 375
So, 234
Sodom, 54–55, 73, 144, 262
Solomon, 107, 141, 186, 218
Sorcery, 411
Spiritists, 110–11
Stars, 260–61
Stone of stumbling, 109
Suffering Servant, 30, 36–37, 201, 389
  See also Messiah
Sword, 214, 261
Synagogue, 409
Syncretism, 464
Syro-Ephraimite War, 118

Tarshish, 68, 191–94
Temple
  cleansing of, 156
  desecration of, 90
  as God's dwelling place, 169
  location of, 110
  as a place of prayer, 408
  purpose of, 485
Temple hill, 63
Testimony, 206, 210
Thanksgiving, 134, 293–94
That day. *See* Day of the LORD
Theophany, 241–42
Thirst, 314
Threshing, 226, 313–14

Threshing *(cont.)*
  floor, 182
Tiglath-Pileser III
  arrogance of, 148
  brutality of, 16
  conqueror of Damascus, 15
  expanding empire of, 17
  humiliation of, 151
  military exploits of, 90
  as Pulu, 17
  as ruler of Assyria, 13–14, 32
  ruthlessness of, 147
Tigris River, 11, 214
Tinder, 61–62
Tirhakah, 281
Titles of God
  the first and the last, 362
  the Holy One of Israel, 165, 313
  the Holy One of Jacob, 233
  the LORD is my Banner, 130
  the LORD of Hosts, 164
  the LORD, the LORD, 133–34, 208
  the Lord, the LORD Almighty, 70
  our Mighty One, 258
  the Most High, 150
  Redeemer, 313
  the Righteous One, 201
  the Sovereign LORD, 363
  the upright One, 209
  Yahweh, 320, 328
Topheth, 243

Torah. *See* Law
Travels, 235, 267
Treason, 109
Tribute, 258, 279
Trial, legal, 393
Trinity, 91, 93
Trito-Isaiah, 23, 406n
Trumpet, 218
Truth, 390
Typology, 395
Tyre, 12, 191–96

Uncleanness, 452–53
Understanding, 128
Uzziah, 12, 14, 30–31, 50, 90
  See also Azariah

Vengeance, 262
Vineyard, 81–82, 161–62
Violence, 410, 424
Viper, 424–25
Virgin birth, 100–102
Vision, 49
  Valley of, 184
Voice of God, 239–40
Vulgate, 149

War, 88, 187, 216, 374
War party, 221, 245, 277
Weaver, 292
Wick, 318
Wicked, the, 73, 212–13, 365, 381
Widows, oppression of, 118–19
Wine, 59, 198–99, 214–15, 401
Wisdom
  definition of, 128, 247
  of God, 244, 303
  practical, 226
Witness, Messiah as, 402

Women, 75, 248–49
Wood, 337–38
Wordplay, 82, 139–40, 159, 162, 170
Works, good, 406
Worship, 484–85
Wrath, 384–85
Wreath, 219–20

Xerxes, 352

Yahweh, the name, 51n
Year of Jubilee, 437

Zeal, 449
Zebulun, geography of, 112
Zechariah, king of Israel, 13
Zerubbabel, 264
Zion, 196
  corruption of, 58–59
  enlargement of, 396
  fighting against God, 245
  filled with justice, 254
  as God's bride, 373
  as a mother, 466
  as the place of God's presence, 149
  prosperity of, 125
  redemption of, 60, 484
  restoration of, 77–79
Zoan, 173, 234–35
Zoroaster, 344